Educating for Unemployment

European Perspectives:
A Series of the Columbia University Press

Marzio Barbagli

EDUCATING FOR UNEMPLOYMENT

Politics, Labor Markets, and the School System — Italy, 1859-1973

TRANSLATED BY ROBERT H. ROSS

New York Columbia University Press *1982*

First published in Italian as *Disoccupazione intellettuale e sistema scolastico in Italia,*

Printed in the United States of America

Library of Congress Cataloging in Publication Data

Barbagli, Marzio, 1938–
Educating for unemployment.

(European perspectives)
Translation of: Disoccupazione intellettuale e sistema scolastico in Italia (1859–1973)
Bibliography: p.
Includes index.
1. Education—Italy—History. 2. Industry and education—Italy—History. I. Title.
II. Series.
LA791.B3213 370'.945 82-4190
ISBN 0-231-05284-7 AACR2

Columbia University Press
New York Guilford, Surrey

Clothbound editions of Columbia University Press books are Smyth-sewn and printed on permanent and durable acid-free paper.

To Donatella

Contents

Translator's Introduction

Since its publication in 1974, Marzio Barbagli's work on intellectual unemployment and the educational system in Italy has been widely acclaimed among European sociologists and social historians. It is a fundamental contribution to a literature by now ample, but sometimes spotty and often narrowly contemporary, on the complex interrelations between schooling and society. What became an acute problem for many of the Western industrialized societies in the 1970s – the concurrent oversupply and un(der)employment of persons with post-compulsory educational qualifications – is shown by Professor Barbagli to have been chronic in Italy since the 1880s.

Historical research comes naturally to the Italian sociologist of whatever theoretical or ideological persuasion, however much the pragmatic empiricism and more present-bound functionalism of Anglo-Saxon sociology may have been imported by the Italians in recent years. Something like the reverse appears to be the case among American sociologists, especially for whom the historical dimension has recently reemerged and regained legitimacy after a long winter's guild-like division of labor between the sociologist's "research" and the historian's "scholarship."[1] The present translation is offered, therefore, not only out of a conviction regarding the intrinsic value of cultural and intellectual exchange but also, more didactically, to exemplify and in fact recommend one particularly artful and rigorous marriage of sociological problematic and historical inquiry.

From the outset it is clear that Barbagli's work aims to considerably revise, at least with reference to the Italian case, the received social scientific wisdom of the 1950s and 1960s concerning the relationship between educational and societal development: a knowledge-qua-creed created and transmitted by a host of university, government, and foundation supported economists and sociologists according to which, in the author's words, "all that was required for man's ills to be ended, tyrannies crushed, poverty, unemployment, and underdevelopment extinguished, was for education to be planted, take root, and grow healthy and robust."[2] The social upheavals of the 1960s and early 1970s, during which "the university" and "the school" were often the leading institutional subjects and objects of contention, as well as the disillusionment and realism with which the "decade of development" and the "war on poverty" ended, respectively, for the developing countries and for America's poor, managed to stagger even the most zealous proponents of the "educational cure." And in the aftermath, phrases once connoting undisputed relationships, such as "education, manpower, and economic growth,"[3] gave way among both the "higher circles" of policy planning and the population at large to new expressions such as "the great training robbery," "overeducation," "diploma disease," "mismatch" and "noncorrespondence" between education and employment, and the "credential society."[4]

Crisis and even breakdown of social institutions may tend to roll back the taken-for-granted and reveal the limits of social scientific knowledge and related policy. Yet, as Barbagli notes, critique falls short of theory, and so if the old conceptual structures have collapsed in the face of reality, new ones have yet to be constructed. In short, we lack a theory that might comprehend the considerable historical and contemporary evidence which suggests that in many of the industralized societies, and over more or less extensive periods of their nation-building and industrialization, it may not have been so much the demand for qualified labor which has provoked an increase in supply, but rather the contrary: an increasing supply has itself acted to provoke an "artificial" demand. Hence the importance of the leading supplier, the secondary school and the university. No doubt significant national, and indeed subnational, differences exist in the way educational and occupational structures interact as related moments in the process by which populations are instructed and employed. Indicative in this regard is the difference between Italy and England to which Barbagli points in chapter 1. And certainly an adequate explanation of historical continuity or change in the structure and functioning of both educational and occupational systems must consider the effects of both sides of the market for qualified labor. At issue, however, is the relative importance that the actual course of historical events has assigned to the dynamics of both supply and demand in determining the market for educational qualifications in a particular national setting. Given the not insignificant costs – economic, social, and individual – of "mismatch" between educational supply and economic demand, the direction of causality would appear to be neither a trivial nor an "academic" question.[5]

If the absence, then, of a fully adequate theory, there is at least an important shift of emphasis contained in the following proposition, whose plausibility over a century of Italian national development constitutes Barbagli's central thesis:

> If... we consider the school in capitalist society as an institution that confers status and privilege, then it is legitimate to think that the growth and the stagnation of education may have been due not only and not so much to the rise and fall of demand for technical qualifications provided by the economy – as functionalist theory argues – but rather to the power relations among various social groups and to the struggles that these have conducted in order to maintain or improve their own position in the system of social stratification.

As the reader will soon note, Barbagli's is not an attempt to labor a favored "approach," an economic, political, cultural, or organizational sociology, for example, but rather a detailed assertion, in effect, that a range of interacting factors coalesce over time to determine the structure and functioning of an educational system. Hence the importance of rooting explanation in the historical subject matter.

If there is a more fundamental level of analysis, the ground on which the peculiarly Italian scarcity of occupational channels of upward mobility rests, it is certainly economic: industrialization was late in coming to Italy, and since the first "great leap" at the turn of the last century it has been concentrated disproportionately in the North, thereby leaving the South chronically underdeveloped and the Center weighed down by the ponderous and unproductive machinery of the state bureaucracy in Rome. However, in the "funnel of causality"[6] leading to observable variation in the arrangement and workings of the educational system, analysis is focused more on the consequences than on the causes of such late and geographically unbalanced economic development. Thus it is the conflict – economically conditioned yet possessing its own relatively autonomous political and organizational dynamic[7] – between external social groups over the internal structure of the school that receives the most immediate attention; conflict, that is, over the very institutional means by which titles to an always limited number of "dignified" occupations might be sought and acquired.

Two important qualifications attend this situated emphasis on social conflict and the balance of political power among external actors as these have fought to structure the educational system according to their own needs. The first is that the system itself, under the weight of its own internal constituents, has always mounted considerable resistance to change whatever forces were arrayed.[8] The second is that the term "social groups" cannot be restricted to the major social classes, to the bourgeoisie and the proletariat, for:

> If these were, in fact, the protagonists that moved on the national stage, the collective subjects whose action has formed and transformed the educational system, it is also true that other actors have recited parts not irrelevant to the script: the *ceti sociali* and among these, in particular the intellectual strata that have arisen from the educational system and by means of it both earned and legitimated a living.

Thus the problem of the professional middle strata in a late-industrializing and highly state-organized society such as Italy runs throughout Barbagli's text:[9] the fragility of their employment prospects in the face of the vicissitudes of the "intellectual" labor market; the related instability of their (rightward or left-ward) political identification; their individual and corporate access to the corridors of political power, and thus their strategic importance for the political cast and social impact (whether conservative or progressive) of reform measures such as those affecting the educational system.[10] The reader must judge for himself the acuity of the author's ideas on the relationship between the chronic occupational insecurity of Italian professionals, their political radicalization, and their mobilization to modify market conditions either to restrict supply among their ranks or to increase demand for their services. In any case, whether as producer of professional qualifications or as employer of a significant proportion of them, the school, particularly the secondary school and the university, is at center stage.

Professor Barbagli's single-nation study,[11] precisely because of its exemplary integration of sociological problematic and historical inquiry, would appear to invite an equally rigorous cross-national research endeavor in the field of educational development.[12] It is no secret that a truly scientific sociology that employs the classical method of comparing historical cases not for merely descriptive purposes but in order to ascertain the validity and the range of competing explanations of stability and change in particular social institutions requires, in the effort to control variation, a considerable groundwork of prior classification, description, and measurement of historical data.[13] This type of painstaking comparative research has, after all, distinguished many of the fundamental and enduring contributions in the field of sociology.[14] More to the point, such research would provide the only basis on which the geographical and temporal limits for the type of general hypothesis that informs the present study – that is, of a tendentially *inverse* relationship between economic development and expansion of post-compulsory education – could ever be fully established.

In the absence of such a research endeavor, many interesting questions of the following type cannot be answered: To what extent would Italy figure among such late-industrializing European nations as France, Spain, Portugal, Greece, even Yugoslavia, as a unique case, or instead only as an extreme one, of a persistent incapacity to provide for its professional strata so as to secure the continuity of careers-in-course and simultaneously to absorb new cohorts of secondary and university graduates into suitably qualified employment? Similarly, to what extent are the labor market – hence educational, political, and economic – determinants of radicalization among Italian professionals (and thus of their mobilization to affect or block periodic attempts at institutional reforms) "peculiar" to the Italian case or common to a type of social organization, prevalent among the southern European nations, that has been termed "neo-corporatist?"[15] Finally, might the same questions be posed with respect to a comparison between the Italian and Iberian cases, for example, and those of certain of the more industrialized Latin American countries, such as Mexico, Brazil, and Argentina, that have inherited the statist and corporatist traditions of their southern European mother countries? While one should harbor no illusions about the difficulties of such cross-national research, the work at hand on the century-old relationship between intellectual unemployment and the educational system in Italy provides a worthy example, conceptually and methodologically, of how to proceed.

In concluding, let me draw the reader's attention to the glossary and three appendices that I have added at the end of the book as well as to the fact that the footnotes to the text are my own whereas the backnotes are those of the author. Then too, I wish to gratefully acknowledge the support and assistance of the following persons over the period since the spring of 1979 during which I prepared the present manuscript: Professor Juan J. Linz, Pelatiah Perit Professor of Political and Social Science at Yale University, who recommended the work in the first place; Betsy Frey Wenger, Ph.D. candidate in Religious Studies, Yale University, who typed all but two chapters of the manuscript; Lucia Re, Ph.D. candidate in Comparative Literature, Yale University, who proofread the better part of the manuscript; Janice Delbert, secretary to the Bologna Center of the Johns Hopkins School of Advanced International Studies, who typed the remainder of the manuscript; and Anne Derse, masters degree candidate in International Relations, Johns Hopkins University, who proofread the remaining chapters. And finally, the author himself, Marzio Barbagli, who contributed long hours of preparation.

Author's Acknowledgments

This study arose within the activity of the Instituto C. Cattaneo. In particular it is at the Instituto Cattaneo that I have conducted the many statistical elaborations the results of which, in a certain sense, constitute the framework of this volume. Thanks are due, for having assisted me in these elaborations, to Raffaella Rago and Marina Turchetti. Many colleagues and friends have read the manuscript and have helped me, with their criticisms and suggestions, to improve it. They are: Mario Caciagli, Valerio Castronovo, Furio Cerutti, Francesco Ciafaloni, Piergiorgio Corbetta, Marcello Dei, Giorgio Galli, Pierpaolo Giglioli, Enrico Luzzati, Roberto Moscati, Guido D. Neri, Anna Oppo, Fiorella Padoa Schioppa, Umberto Paniccia, Arturo Parisi, Gianfranco Poggi. Naturally, the errors which the reader may find in this book are my responsibility.

It is said that the universities are factories of misfits and that it is necessary to uncrowd them. But pray, where do you intend the young people to go? They don't go to the universities for convenience or ambition, but rather from necessity: business, industry, agriculture and related institutions require neither workmen nor minds, or at least they take what they require and reject the surplus; if outlets were opened for the subsistence of the many young people who issue forth from the Italic fertility, many would abandon higher studies and would go where a living proved more easily obtained. Nor do I say to the rulers: open these outlets. I am convinced that society must open them, certainly not the state. Whenever society has opened one, we have seen a throng at the door and immediately a plethora of applicants.

—G. Arangio-Ruiz in *L'Università italiana,* August 10, 1902.

CHAPTER ONE

Hypotheses on Italian Education

To reconstruct and to explain the characteristics and the development of education in Italy in the last one hundred years is certainly not an easy thing to do. To the difficulties that a research undertaking of this sort normally involves must be added others of more recent origin that are even more serious. It almost seems that the more education spreads, embracing everyone, becoming a substantial and material reality, the more difficult it becomes to grasp, to penetrate, and to understand. Our conceptual castles, constructed with years of toil, are revealed as fragile constructions of sand, our schemes and our interpretive hypotheses as rusty scrap iron. But above all our basic attitude toward education has changed and the limitless faith that we once had in it has entered into crisis.

Never, perhaps, was confidence in education so strong and undisputed as at the end of the 1950s. A new priesthood of sociologists and economists, supported and financed by goverments and foundations, then preached its virtues and invested their best energies in the fascinating enterprise. They dusted off old concepts or fashioned new ones. They gathered, elaborated, and scrutinized data. They filled the pages of their books and articles with austere mathematical formulae which guaranteed the scientific validity of their commentaries. But they also sought to be understood, and so they lectured widely and wrote brief popular works. From these most people developed a sense of the virtues of education. They learned that all that was required for man's ills to be ended, tyrannies crushed, poverty, unemployment, and underdevelopment extinguished, was for education to be planted, take root, and grow healthy and robust.

The rapid diffusion of this modern myth was abruptly interrupted by the struggles of the students. It is not necessary to recall here the accusations which "the men of '68" brought against the school and society. It suffices to say that the crisis which they opened was so severe that it quickly staggered even the priests of the new religion. One who at the beginning of the 1960s viewed with confidence the prospects of educational expansion and considered intellectual unemployment* "a loose phrase" would announce some time later, "signs precursory to a storm," noting that "a part of the credits and outlays intended to serve instruction serve instead to produce groups of demonstrators and unemployed."[1] One who in 1961 thought that Italy was facing a shortage of qualified personnel writes today that "the serious danger that weighs upon every country, and on our country in particular, [is that] of an excess of *diplomati and laureati*[†] relative to the possibility of employment offered to persons of a high level of learning."[2]

Nevertheless, while the old conceptual structures have collapsed, new ones have not yet been constructed, or else they have been drawn up hastily and already show the first cracks. The assertion in 1969 that "we are still little more than blind kittens in confronting the great problems of education" retains most of its validity today.[3] We lack a theory. To which hypotheses may we refer, then, in order to interpret the course of Italian education in the last one hundred years?

The following passage, written by an authoritative scholar for an authoritative work of social science, is useful for our purposes:

> As a society undergoes industrialization and modernization, its instruction of the young becomes extensively differentiated, internally complex, and elaborately connected with other features of society. Education becomes more necessary for the economy and linked closely to it as a major mediator between manpower demand and labor supply. Occupational competence, general and specific, is increasingly certified by schooling, and achievement is thereby prefigured, as labor shifts from manual to mental and from low to high degree of skill. In the aggregate, those who leave school early are designated for unskilled work, and those who remain on the educational escalator are carried to the jobs for which their general education and specialized vocational training have earmarked them. Higher education is also deeply involved in technological advance, as a location for scientific

*The term "intellectual" is used throughout the text to refer to persons possessing a certificate that indicates completion of requisite instruction or training and is granted by a state or state-recognized post-compulsory educational institution.

† *Diplomati*: graduates (holders of the *diploma*) of the schools that constitute the upper-secondary level of the Italian educational system. *Laureati*: graduates (holders of the *laurea*) of the university.

> work and as the enterprise that trains the modern researcher and technologist. Thus, education becomes a way of investing in human capital across many levels of skill.[4]

This passage is a good example of the position most commonly taken to explain the development of education in its relationship with the labor market and the system of social stratification: that designated as "functionalist theory" or the model of "functional differentiation" by its supporters, and as the "technocratic conception of education" by its adversaries.[5] According to this explanatory model, the expansion of education is a consequence of modernization and of increasing institutional differentiation, an effect of society's tendency to become more complex, to articulate itself into a multiplicity of institutions and roles, some of which require "strategic human capital."[6]

More analytically, this interpretive model, which is itself a particular application to the problems of education of the more general functionalist theory of social stratification, may be articulated in the following propositions:[7]

1. The level of qualification required by the occupations of industrial society increases constantly through two different processes. There is, in the first place, a tendency for the percentage of positions in the labor force that require a high level of qualification to increase, and a parallel tendency toward the reduction of those that require a low level. In the second place, there is a tendency for the *same* positions in the labor force to require ever higher levels of qualification.

2. It is the instruction furnished by educational institutions that provides the level of qualification required. This means, first, that education renders the labor force more productive and, second, that it is furnished not by many institutions but by a single specialized one, the school.

3. It follows that, as the level of qualification required by occupations in industrial society rises, and the percentage of the population which must pass through eductional institutions increases, so too the duration of the period which must be spent in these institutions increases for those enrolled.[8]

Can this model assist us in explaining the course of education in Italy over the last one hundred years? Only in part. It is undeniable that the increased power over nature, the changes realized in the organization of labor, the increasing application of science to the economy, with the consequent heightening of the level of qualification required for a certain number of functions, have contributed to the growth of education. Nevertheless, a number of recent studies conducted on different countries and historical periods indicate that the functionalist model is not sufficient to explain the phenomena which concern us. For example, it has been shown that, especially in countries beyond a certain threshold in the level of industrialization, only part of the rise in the level of education can be attributed to an increase in the percentage of highly qualified positions; that sometimes it was not the demand for qualified labor which produced an increase in the supply but, on the contrary, the former which increased only to cope with the latter; that in many capitalist countries there is a strong tendency to underutilization of the general training and specialized knowledge of large segments of the population; that education does not always increase the productivity of the labor force, but can produce opposite effects as well; that in certain cases the only form of valid instruction is that imparted not by the school but by other institutions not specialized to this end (as in the case of on-the-job training).[9] As far as Italy is concerned, even without anticipating here the results of the analysis conducted throughout this volume, one can say that it would certainly be impossible to give an adequate interpretation of the course of education over the last one hundred years employing the functionalist model alone.

If, distancing ourselves from this perspective for a moment, we consider the school in capitalist society as an institution that confers status and privilege, then it is legitimate to think that the growth and the stagnation of education may have been due not only and not so much to the rise and fall of the demand for technical qualification provided by the economy – as functionalist theory argues – but rather to the power relations among various social groups and to the struggles that these have conducted in order to maintain or improve their own position in the system of social stratification. However, in examining more analytically this interpretive hypothesis, to which this study principally refers, it is necessary to introduce two qualifications. The first is that a fundamental intervening variable, necessary in order to explain the course of education, is the internal structure of the educational system itself. The second is that the term "social groups" does not here refer only to social classes – to the bourgeoisie and to the proletariat. If these were, in fact, the protagonists that moved on the national stage, the collective subjects whose action has formed and transformed the educational system, it is also true that other actors have recited parts not irrelevant to the script: the *ceti sociali*,* and, among these,

**Ceti sociali*: social strata or classes, usually with reference to the *ceti medi* or "middle strata" in contrast to the bourgeoisie and the proletariat. As a subdivision of the *ceti sociali* or *medi*, the *ceti intellettuali* would be those groups whose employment depends particularly on the possession of post-secondary educational qualifications.

particularly the intellectual strata that have arisen from the educational system and by means of it both earned and legitimated their living.

Among the many mechanisms by which the educational institution filters and sifts the population, selects and contains the demand for education which it originates, the most important is certainly constituted by its internal structure. In the course of this study we will examine this structure at two different levels: the lower- and upper-secondary.

At the lower-secondary level the internal structure of the Italian educational system varies, in the historical period considered, in its degree of openness. By "openness" and "closure" I mean the degree of specialization and internal differentiation. More precisely, I consider "closed" an educational system that presents, besides a preparatory school for upper-secondary and university studies, also one or more "blind-alley" or dead-end schools that do not allow passage to higher levels. I consider "open" a system without these blind-alley schools. To give some examples, the most open system yet known in Italy has been that instituted at the end of 1962. But the one created by Casati Law* was also relatively open. On the other hand, the system begun by the Gentile Reform† was closed, and still more closed, if possible, was that which Bottai with his Carta della Scuola‡ and Gonella§ with his bill of law of 1951 sought in vain to realize.

At the upper-secondary level, the internal structure of the educational system varies, during the historical period considered, in its degree of "professionalization." I consider professionalized an educational system that, together with secondary schools preparatory for higher studies (for example, the *liceo*),‖ has other schools that do not allow access to the university and that have in view the training of intermediate cadres (for example: *diplomati tecnici and magistrali*).#

*Prepared by Count Gabrio Casati and promulgated by Vittorio Emanuele II on November 13, 1859, the Casati Law, which reflected the more advanced educational and social conditions of the northern regions of Piedmont and Lombardy, was to serve as the foundation of the Italian educational system until the Gentile Reform of 1923. See chapter 3.

†Series of reforms initiated by Minister of Public Education Giovanni Gentile in 1923 upon delegation of governmental powers to Mussolini. The Gentile Reform was to be termed "the most fascist of reforms" by Mussolini. See chapter 5.

‡"Charter for the School," subtitled "Principles, Purposes, and Methods of the Fascist School." It was presented to the fascist Grand Council on January 19, 1939 by Minister of National Education Giuseppe Bottai. See chapter 7.

§Guido Gonella, Minister of Public Education, January 1947 to July 1951. See chapter 10.

‖*Liceo*: upper-secondary school preparing for university studies. Since the Gentile Reform, it has had two branches: the *classico* and the *scientifico*.

#*Diplomati tecnici, diplomati magistrali*: graduates of the upper-secondary *istituti* in, respectively, technical and pedagogical subjects.

I consider de-professionalized a system in which these latter secondary schools give access to the university* and lose most of their original function of training intermediate cadres. To give some examples, the most de-professionalized system yet known in Italy is that begun at the end of 1969. But, as we will see, there have been other processes of de-professionalization, such as in 1870 – 75 and in 1930 – 35. The most professionalized system, on the other hand, was that created by the Gentile Reform.

The actions and struggles of classes and social groups have affected in various ways the degree of openness and professionalization of the Italian educational system. It is clear, first of all, that as the school institutionalizes itself, and its function of distributing qualifications comes to be socially recognized, it creates a demand for education on the part of families, and provokes movements within the various social classes either to preserve or improve, by means of these qualifications, their own positions in the system of stratification. In particular, the social classes excluded from the higher levels of education mobilize themselves and, organized for the most part by a political party but sometimes spontaneously, work to crush the barriers within the educational system and to render it more open; or else, when it is already somewhat open, they array themselves in its defense against any threat from the dominant classes or from the other social groups. Thus the most profound transformation of the educational system in the second postwar period – the institution of the *scuola media unica*† in 1962 – was produced by the demand from the proletariat for education and for change, and by the capacity of the workers' parties, after years of uncertainty, oscillations, and mistakes, to accept and to articulate this demand. Thus also, if after having been alert enough at the beginning of the century to realize that the educational system of Casati was no longer suited to the new situation, the bourgeoisie took some two decades to change it, to render it more closed and selective, this was at least partly due to the pressure and the resistance of the workers' movement. And so too, the partial failure of the Gentile Reform, which compelled Gentile himself, the philosopher of fascism, as well as his successors to revise a law which had been

*Given a tradition of state bureaucratic centralization, derived from the Naploeonic university from which in part it drew inspiration, the Italian university has always been a single national entity, juridically and practically, with separate municipal sites. As a university system per se, it is referred to, therefore, in the singular. See Burton Clark, *Academic Power in Italy: Bureaucracy and Oligarchy in a National University System* (Chicago and London: University of Chicago Press, 1977), passim.

†*Scuola media unica*: unified lower-secondary school established in 1962. See chapter 10.

elaborated with so much care, plainly arose from a form of passive and spontaneous resistance on the part of the social classes that it sought to exclude definitively from the higher levels of education (namely, the lower strata of the middle class and the higher strata of the proletariat).

All these struggles, defensive or offensive, organized or spontaneous, have had in common the characteristic of never questioning the first principle on which the functioning of the school in capitalist society is based, and have thus carried within themselves "unresolved since the start and rarely conscious, the ambiguity between the 'egalitarian' thrust, that is, the right of all to knowledge, on the one hand, and on the other, the acceptance of the concept of 'self-promotion' that takes for granted not only the technical but also the social division of labor."[11] And yet, they have been no less tough and bitter for this ambiguity and have produced over time (because it is an obvious yet forgotten fact that the consequences of changes in the educational system are felt only after many years) profound effects on the functioning of the labor market, strong changes in patterns of social stratification, and cracks and creaks in the entire social structure.

It must not be thought, however, on the basis of what has so far been said, that the dominant classes have always and only opposed the growth of education and have done everything possible to make or to keep the educational system closed. While this has been the prevalent tendency, there have been exceptions. In fact, the bourgeoisie has also at times needed to expand the educational system, and for two kinds of reasons that could be loosely termed economic and political. Among the economic reasons, it has been more or less due to instruction furnished by the school that the bourgeoisie has had at its disposal the personnel at high and middle levels of qualification required by industrialization and economic development. Among the political reasons, the school has always had the function, from the primary schools up to the university, of transmitting not only knowledge but also values, of furnishing not only technical qualification but also ideological training, of influencing not only the cognitive but also the affective aspects of the personality.[12] In Italy the dominant classes at various times and in very different situations have shown an awareness of the role performed by the school in the political socialization of the younger generations – certainly in 1959 – 60, when they looked with less hostility upon the opening and democratization of the educational system, not only in anticipation of a strong increase in the demand for diplomati and laureati but also because they were convinced of the necessity to furnish, through the school, ideological training suitable for a labor force that was shifting from the primary to the secondary sector of the economy.

But the awareness of the importance of the school as an ideological apparatus of the state goes back much further, directly to the formation of the nation-state. At that time, within the dominant classes two different conceptions collided: one that saw the most effective form of social control in keeping the majority of the population illiterate and ignorant (according to the eighteenth-century saying: "Should a Horse know as much as a Man I should not like to be his Rider");[13] and another that perceived it, instead, in the diffusion of education. If the educational system which then arose–that of Casati–had a relatively open internal structure, it was because within the dominant classes the second conception temporarily prevailed of the groups convinced that for the new state to put down roots and to strengthen its authority, it was necessary to extend primary education and, above all, to develop the secondary and higher schools, which were the only ones capable of providing a body of competent and ideologically trustworthy functionaries.

On the other hand, the dominant classes at times found themselves facing what we could call the selection-socialization dilemma. In fact, in order to function effectively as an instrument of social control, an educational system must be structured in such a way as to develop these two functions in a balanced manner. It must not, that is, give too much weight to one at the expense of the other. If it gives too much weight to selection, and consequently has a closed internal structure, it runs the risk of not letting through a sufficiently large number of youth for a sufficient number of years, that is, of not performing adequately the function of political socialization. If, on the other hand, it gives too much importance to the function of socialization and thus provides an open internal structure, it runs the risk of not developing adequately the function of selection and therefore of producing a surplus of qualified personnel. This explains, at least in part, how, when the Italian bourgeoisie sought to confront the phenomenon of the intellectual unemployment (both in the facist period and in the second postwar period) by increasing the selective function of the school, it never quite lost sight of the socializing function. It also explains how it did not limit itself then to attempting the pure and simple expulsion of "surplus" students from the secondary schools, but tried instead to channel them into blind-alley schools, capable of detaining them for a certain number of years and of furnishing them with an adequate ideological training without, however, allowing them to continue their studies.

As for the intellectual strata, their influence on the internal structure of the Italian educational system was undoubtedly very important. The surplus supply of laureati and diplomati – which, as we shall see, has been an endemic characteristic of Italian society from 1880 to the present – has often put the intellectuals in a situation of status imbalance, of incongruence between the educational qualification achieved and the occupation, level of income, and prestige that the *social norms prevailing at that moment* have considered fitting for that qualification.[14] Like other groups that have found themselves in this situation, intellectuals too have sought to escape it, to reequilibrate their status, to occupy positions comparable on all the hierarchies. This has led them to act collectively, through their professional organizations, to modify market conditions, and thus to apply pressure in two different directions: toward an increase in demand and toward a decrease in supply of qualified labor. Not always have the various intellectual categories and organizations found themselves in agreement on a course of action. Thus the efforts of the secondary school teachers to produce an increase in the demand for their labor (and therefore an expansion of the school population) have at times collided with those of physicians and engineers to effect a reduction of the supply (and therefore a contraction of the school population). So, too, the pressures of university students and of laureati to reduce the flow of supply by introducing rigid regulatory mechanisms on entrance into the universities (the *numero chiuso*)* have often collided with the counterpressures of diplomati for expanding access to higher education. The latter have been at times, in the presence, naturally, of other conditions, the initiators of processes of de-professionalization in the secondary schools. One can say, nevertheless, that the tendency to support a Malthusian line in educational policy has nearly always prevailed among the intellectual strata.

More generally, the situation of status imbalance has produced a strong political radicalization of the intellectual strata. It is difficult to say whether in Italy this political radicalization has had the characteristics of the right or of the left, whether it has made of the intellectuals – as Wilhelm Riehl said in the last century, "the true *ecclesia militans* of the fourth estate"[15] – or on the other hand has led them to support fascist movements.[16] In the past, this has varied according to a multiplicity of factors and conditions, for example, on whether their condition was one of partially blocked upward mobility or of partial downward mobility.[17] The first situation has obtained in periods of stagnation or

**Numero chiuso*: "fixed number" or quota.

moderate economic growth, during which the demand for qualified labor increased at a slower pace than supply, and has led the intellectuals (above all new laureati and new diplomati) to positions on the left. The second has obtained in periods of economic crisis, characterized by the collapse of demand for qualified personnel, and has pushed the intellectuals (especially those already established) to positions on the right. In either case, the political radicalization of intellectuals has always been reason for concern for the dominant classes and has led them to embrace a Malthusian line of educational policy.

The hypothesis advanced at the outset of the preceding section is not, however, sufficient. It must be further elaborated. Besides examining the struggles conducted by various social groups to modify or preserve the educational system, to increase or reduce the level of education of the population, it is also necessary to determine on which economic stage these actors have moved. For, although recognition of the school as the institution authorized to distribute status and privilege automatically produces movements by the excluded social classes to acquire education and opposing movements by the dominant classes and privileged strata to prevent this from happening or to recreate the situation of exclusion at a higher level, the strength and the intensity of these pressures vary according to the situation and to the course of the economy.

If, however, we attempt to go beyond this general "economic" proposition, things become remarkably complicated. That the course of the economy affects private demand for education (namely, the demand by youth and their families) is undeniable. But in what way? What type of relationship is there between the first and second variables? Unfortunately, the great majority of studies conducted on the relationship between the course of the economy and the demand for education have considered not the former but the latter as the independent variable. In cases where the demand for education has been considered as a dependent variable, the conclusion is reached that between these two variables there is always a positive relationship.* Yet however plausible or even obvious this proposition might appear, it cannot, in fact, explain the course of education in Italy in the period under consideration without the introduction of some important qualifications.

*That is, in the statistical sense of co-variation of the same sign.

In this period in Italy the relationship between economy and education differs according to the level of the educational system. If we examine compulsory schooling (limited for a long period of time to the elementary schools),* we see that there is always a positive relationship between economy and education. This relationship is sometimes disturbed by the interference of other variables – it may be reduced, and may even become very weak. But it always exists. The situation is rather different in the case of the secondary schools and the university, where analysis of the relationship between these two variables becomes very difficult and requires the greatest caution. For certain periods we lack any information on some economic indicators which are vital to widening the discussion, and the comparable data on education are full of gaps. It is difficult, moreover, and in certain cases practically impossible, to control other variables and to determine, for example, whether the growth or the stagnation of education was due to the course of the economy or rather to intervening changes within the internal structure of the educational system itself. But even the most cautious analysis reveals many elements, as we shall see, which suggest that over the entire period considered there is either no relationship or, in fact, an inverse one between the economy and secondary as well as higher education.

How can this be interpreted? In an important essay Joseph Ben-David has sought to explain how some European countries, such as Germany or France, have had a much higher number of students in the twentieth century than Great Britain, Belgium, or Switzerland (so many as to produce an excessive number of graduates in certain periods), taking as the independent variable "the presence or absence of channels of mobility other than that of higher education." According to Ben-David, in England and in Switzerland "there usually existed a strong and articulate middle class prior to the rise of the modern universities in the nineteenth century. . . . Thus professional people did not become a separate class, and were far from being alienated. Rather they became an integral part of a prosperous and educated middle class. . . . Higher education. . . never became the only, nor even the main channel of mobility through which one could rise from the 'masses.'"[18]

This interpretation applies to the Italian case as well. The absence in Italy, in the period under consideration, of any relationship between the course of the

*The Gentile Reform of 1923 extended compulsory schooling to 14 years of age, that is, to include the lower-secondary school. The obligation was still not enforced, however, well into the period following the Second World War.

economy and the course of secondary and higher education, or the presence even of an inverse relationship, indicates that, besides that offered by the school, there were no alternative channels of social mobility, or that these existed to a lesser extent than in other countries. Thus the strong demand for education, the rapid expansion of enrollments in the secondary schools and the university, the unemployment of laureati and of diplomati – all of which have characterized long periods of the post-unification history of Italy, and which have been moralistically attributed to an obscure psychological tendency of the average citizen to "chase titles" – are also explained, apart from the variables recorded in the preceding pages, by the particular characteristics of Italian economic development: the slowness with which it began, its dualistic nature, its lulls and delays. These, then, are the particularly Italian economic characteristics which, together with the resulting lack of alternative channels of social mobility, have rendered stronger among us, more insistent, and at times even desperate, that demand for self-promotion by means of education which the school, by the principles which regulate it and by the nature of the system of stratification in which it operates, tends to provoke in all capitalist societies.

CHAPTER TWO

Intellectual Unemployment and Illiteracy

Analyzing national statistics of the preceding twenty years, Ernesto Nathan wrote in 1906: "In relation to our social position, we are both overeducated and too ignorant – afflicted on the one hand by illiteracy and on the other by academic literacy."[1] That Italy was "afflicted" at that time by illiteracy is a well-known fact. Starting with an illiteracy rate of 74 percent at the time of national unification [1859 – 60], even by the beginning of the present century nearly half the population could neither read nor write. There were, in addition, serious imbalances among geographic areas (in 1901, 32 percent were illiterate in the North, 52 percent in the Center, and 70 percent in the South). Much less known is the fact that Italy was also afflicted by "academic literacy" and that there was already in the last years of the preceding century widespread unemployment of intellectuals. This chapter will be devoted to the reconstruction and analysis of this contradictory phenomenon during the period from 1880 to the outbreak of the First World War.

It seems difficult to believe, at first glance, that a country notoriously characterized by such high rates of illiteracy might also produce a surplus of laureati. Nor, certainly, do these difficulties diminish if we analyze the data of that period from a current viewpoint. In the last two decades of the nineteenth century, university enrollments fluctuated between fifteen and twenty thousand persons. On the basis of these enrollments, the educational system managed to produce a few thousand laureati per year, increasing from 2,600 in 1880 – 81 to nearly 4,500 in 1895 – 96 (table 2.1). These numbers seem quite modest today, especially considering that the country's population was then about thirty million. And yet, the social and the economic structure of the Italy of that day was such that demand for intellectual labor was much lower than supply.

Table 2.1. Number of Lauree Granted, 1882 to 1896

Year	*University*	*Higher Institutes*	*Total*
1881–82	2,210	415	2,625
1882–83	2,272	374	2,646
1883–84	2,339	395	2,734
1884–85	2,565	315	2,880
1885–86	2,679	418	3,097
1886–87	2,804	427	3,231
1887–88	2,992	484	3,476
1888–89	2,966	446	3,412
1889–90	3,208	430	3,638
1890–91	3,405	418	3,823
1891–92	3,544	483	4,027
1893–94	3,757	546	4,303
1894–95	3,880	547	4,427
1895–96	3,976	584	4,560

SOURCE: Elaboration of data taken from F. S. Nitti, *La ricchezza dell'Italia*.

If, for a moment, we contrast the level of development of both the Italian economy and the educational system with that of other European countries, our first impression of these data is shown to be mistaken, and the difficulty in believing that widespread intellectual unemployment existed over the period in question is overcome. At the end of the last century Italy still had the highest rate of illiteracy among the countries considered in table 2.2. Completely conquered in Germany, France, and Holland, illiteracy was in the process of being overcome in Belgium and in Austria. The one country in which it constituted a dramatic problem, therefore, was Italy. On the other hand, Italy was also the country, among these, with the lowest level of socioeconomic development. If the percentage of the population employed in agriculture is taken as a rough indicator of the level of development (table 2.3), one easily recognizes the backwardness of Italian economic and social structures at the close of the last century.

The image of Italy that emerges from these two tables is the well-known one of an educationally and economically backward country. But it is an image that captures only one aspect of the social reality of that time. As may be seen from the data of table 2.4, in the last two decades of the previous century, Italy had a higher number of university students in relation to its population than did Germany, France, or Holland, and a number nearly equal to that of Austria. It

Table 2.2. Percentages of Illiteracy among Recruits

Year	*Germany*	*Austria*	*Italy*	*France*	*Belgium*	*Holland*
1880	1.50	39.0	48.88	13.84	21.66	11.50
1881–85	1.38	—	47.27	11.99	18.70	11.10
1886–90	0.69	—	43.10	9.02	16.42	7.80
1891–95	0.29	22.0	39.37	6.01	15.07	5.60
1896–1900	0.08	—	35.53	4.73	12.78	3.50
1901	0.05	—	32.61	4.38	12.38	2.30

SOURCES: F. Corridore, *L'istruzione in Italia (dal 1871 in poi):* part 1, *L'analfabetismo* (Turin: Paravia, 1908); for Austria: C. M. Cipolla, *Literacy and Development in the West* (Turin: UTET, 1971).

Table 2.3. Distribution of the Employed Male Population by Economic Sector

Countries	*Agriculture*	*Industry*	*Commerce and Transport*	*Other Occupations*	*Total*
Germany (1895)	35.7	43.6	11.4	9.3	100
Austria (1891)	56.6	29.3	8.1	6.0	100
Italy (1901)	58.9	23.8	9.3	8.0	100
France (1896)	48.4	33.0	12.1	6.5	100
Belgium (1901)	23.3	46.0	13.1	17.6	100

SOURCE: Data taken from Ministry of Agriculture, Industry, and Commerce, *Censimento della Popolazione del Regno d'Italia al 10 Febbraio 1901. Relazione sul metodo di esecuzione e sui risultati del censimento, raffrontati con quelli dei censimenti italiani precedenti e dei censimenti esteri* (Rome, 1904), 5:110.

was lower only than that of Belgium. The Italian educational system, therefore, produced a relative quantity of intellectual labor higher than or equal to that of the other European countries. Considering that Italy also had the lowest level of socioeconomic development, and consequently presented, in all likelihood, the lowest demand for this type of labor, it is not hard to imagine how difficult it was for graduates of the Italian university to find work. Thus the backwardness of the educational situation was only one side of the problem at the end of the century. In fact, among the many other contradictions of the time, Italy had simultaneously the highest rate of both illiteracy and intellectual unemployment in Europe.

There is no doubt that intellectual unemployment in Italy was already in evidence by the last decades of the nineteenth century. In a study published in 1878, one of the most attentive observers of the vicissitudes of the Italian

Table 2.4. University Students per 100,000 Inhabitants

Year	*Germany*	*Austria*	*Italy*	*France*	*Belgium*	*Holland*
1831–32–36	28.1	—	—	—	24.7	—
1861–62–66	24.8	26.0	—	—	36.6	—
1871–72–76	31.9	33.5	39.9	25.4	40.6	—
1876–77–81	37.8	37.8	35.5	26.9	57.4	31.7
1881–82–86	45.5	46.4	47.6	36.5	77.6	37.7
1886–1891	48.0	55.9	51.3	42.6	82.3	45.4

SOURCE: J. Conrad, "Die Frequenzenverhältnisse der Universitäten der hauptsächlichsten Kulturländern auf dem europäischen Kontinent," *Jahrbücher der Nationalökonomie* (1891).

school, Aristide Gabelli, commenting on the statistics of the preceding years, observed that the number of university students was in excess of the social needs of the country. "But it must be added," he said, "that the situation used to be much worse, when the number of those who attended the *ginnasio* nearly equaled the number of those who went on to the university and exceeded by far the requirements of the higher professions and therefore increased the number of misfits and malcontents."* Thanks to the growth of "material activity" and to the advent "of the lesser professions by means of technical instruction," there was "reestablished little by little a certain equilibrium between university instruction and the social conditions of the country."[2] Nevertheless, returning to this question ten years later, Gabelli offered a rather different analysis of the situation. He argued that the expansion of secondary education, brought about by the "democratic surge" and by "certain string-pulling in the examinations for yearly promotion and final certification at the secondary level," itself due to the weakness of the government in confronting this surge, produced "an abundance of doctors without patients, lawyers without cases, engineers without bridges and buildings to construct. The unemployment and disillusionment of so many people, forced to descend from a level achieved with considerable difficulty, only prepares the way for a perennial source of morbid anxiety and discontent."[3] "The laurea – what a wondrous thing it is!" wrote Ettore Ciccotti a year later. "But one who has only the laurea finds himself often enough in the happy position of a person who has set the table for a banquet without paying heed whether he will have anything to eat."[4]

Among the contradictions of the Italian educational system, it was intellec-

**Ginnasio*: lower-secondary school with humanistic curriculum and instruction in Latin for children intending to go on to the liceo and hence to the university.

tual unemployment which most struck Bolton King and Thomas Okey, two English scholars who published a book on Italy in 1902 that received wide attention. "Men, who in England would go into business," they wrote, "and be trained for it, here swell the ranks of the educated unemployed. . . . Every successful tradesman hopes to see his son a lawyer or doctor or civil servant and spends L. 300 to L. 500 in educating him for a useless life. It is impossible for many men to make a living in the overcrowded professions; and the majority, who can earn little or nothing, turn for bread to the one calling open to them and clamour for Government appointments. They and their parents put remorseless pressure on the Deputies, and a Ministry knows it can hold so many constituencies, if it creates a sufficient number of unnecessary posts. Even then there is a large residuum, who cannot find employment."[5]

The indicator of intellectual unemployment to which contemporary observers usually referred was the strong imbalance registered at all *concorsi** between the number of applications and of positions offered. In the article cited earlier, Aristide Gabelli observed that "the unemployed are so numerous that when the Ministry of Education opened a concorso recently for eighteen inspectors at L 1,500, and required university studies for a third of these, there were 840 competitors."[6] With much greater force he wrote in *La riforma universitaria*: "The spectacle of misfits is, unfortunately, continually before us: laureati who are employed as copyists at a fraction of a lira per page and as town clerks at L 800 a year. . . . Once a concorso is opened for, say, twenty available positions at a salary of L 1,000, we have seen a crowd raised, with all their academic qualifications, of up to 1,700 of society's parched fruit, 1,700 starving graduates in white gloves, 1,700 misfits."[7]

The two English scholars wrote that at a concorso for positions in the postal administration there had been 3,400 competitors, "including several laureati," for 150 positions.[8] Finally, Luigi Lucchini, testifying in 1901 during debate on the budget for the Ministry of Public Education in the Chamber of Deputies, suggested that for the culling of census data, rather than employing "certain American machines that render a much more exact, prompt, and safe product," it was preferable to utilize the "human machine," "considering the many people who were out of work." Thus a concorso was opened to hire personnel for a period of fifteen months and the applications for admission, which reached

**Concorso*: public examination held to fill civil service positions, including, therefore, all official teaching and administrative positions in the school and university systems.

3,000, "were then reduced to 1,279 by imposing the severest conditions: the majority of competitors held the diploma from the liceo when all that was required was that from the ginnasio. Among the remainder were counted hundreds of lawyers, architects, and doctors."[9]

A Comparison with Germany

A rather different contemporary analysis of the situation was made by one of the most diligent and documented scholars of Italian society and politics, Robert Michels. It is worthwhile to consider this analysis for a moment (and to disprove it), not only because of the indisputable influence of Michels, but also because it will allow us to expand the preceding discussion. Michels considered the "intellectual proletariat" not as an Italian but as a "universal" phenomenon, or rather as "a concomitant and spontaneous phenomenon of capitalist society."[10] And in fact, in the years in which Michels wrote, the existence of an "intellectual proletariat" was spoken of also in France and in Germany.[11] But, apart from the fact that there were some capitalist countries – such as England, for example – that had no intellectual unemployment (which shows that this phenomenon was not so "universal"), it still remained to be determined whether, as many argued, the intellectual proletariat was much more widespread in Italy than elsewhere. Now, when Michels moved to an analysis of the data on Italy, he recognized the existence of a "very damaging disproportion" between supply and demand of intellectual labor in southern Italy, but he believed this phenomenon not to be present in central and northern Italy. To show that "Italy's reputation of possessing a superabundant 'intellectual proletariat' is a legend, at least if expressed in such a categorical form," he compared data on the number of persons who practiced any intellectual profession in Italy and in Prussia in 1901. Italy had at that time 24,196 lawyers, 22,168 doctors, and 813 dentists, compared to Prussia's 4,273 lawyers, 17,616 doctors, and 1,134 dentists. Moreover, the latter country had about a million and a half more inhabitants than Italy. Calculating the relation per thousand inhabitants (table 2.5), Michels discovered a very considerable difference "perfectly suited to support those who envision an enormous intellectual proletariat in Italy." But, according to him, this difference was only apparent, at least insofar as it concerned the lawyers. While, in fact, the data for Germany presented "only those who make the law their sole occupation," the Italian data included, in his

Table 2.5. Lawyers, Doctors, and Dentists per Thousand Inhabitants in Italy and Prussia, 1901

Professional Group	*Italy*	*Prussia*
Lawyers	.74	.12
Doctors	.68	.51
Dentists	.025	.03

SOURCE: R. Michels, *Proletariato e borghesia nel movimento socialista italiano,* p. 120.

opinion, also the laureati in law who succeeded their fathers in the management of their own firms or who dedicated themselves to journalism.[12]

Michels, in my view, committed two errors in his analysis. The first is of a "technical" nature. The Italian data on which he relied were those of the census of 1901, and it is well known that in this, as in all other censuses preceding 1936, the data on laureati surveyed concerned only the liberal professionals. The laureati employed as proprietors, managers, or employees of a business firm were included (without distinction as to field of study) among the personnel of those businesses. Thus the 24,196 lawyers surveyed in Italy in the census of 1901 were themselves as well "only those who make the law their sole occupation." This may be confirmed by a comparison with the data of 1882. In that year there were in fact 20,354 lawyers and 7,896 notaries, while in 1901 there were, in addition to the lawyers already mentioned, 6,253 notaries. Thus, over a period of twenty years, there had been an increase of just 3,800 lawyers and a decrease of nearly 1,600 notaries.[13] If one bears in mind that in those twenty years the Italian university had put onto the labor market about 20,000 new laureati in jurisprudence and at least 2,000 diplomati as notaries, it is clear that the data of 1901 were not at all exaggerated, and that a good number of these laureati either had remained unemployed or had had to accept a different occupation than that provided by their laurea, or finally, as we shall see, had been forced to emigrate.

The second mistake made by Michels is, in my opinion, of a more substantive nature. In the comparison that he made between the situation of Italian and German university graduates, he examined only the supply of intellectual labor, while he forgot, strangely, to make any observation on the differences in demand. Yet in 1901 Italy had a level of socioeconomic development much lower than that of Germany. As we saw, in fact, the percentage of the male population employed in agriculture was 58.9 in Italy and 35.7 in Germany, while that employed in industry was, respectively, 23.8 and 43.6. One can hardly imagine that these differences in socioeconomic development would not have been attended by great differences in the demand for intellectual labor. It is odd that Michels could have failed to take this into account, since he himself sought to explain the differences between the situation of doctors in the North and in the South of Italy precisely on the basis of the difference in demand determined by their levels of economic development.[14] In fact, then, both the data on which Michels relied and the differences certain to have existed between Italy and Germany in the demand for intellectual labor constitute further proof of the existence in Italy of widespread intellectual unemployment.[15]

The Attitude of the Italian Ruling Class

"The lawyers increase and multiply daily: they do so, if it weren't blasphemy to say so, like the proverbial grace of God. If aphids appear in a vineyard, everyone immediately takes care to treat the problem before it spreads; if locusts invade a field, everyone immediately goes to the attack to exterminate them. But no one worries or seeks remedies against this other breed of invaders which periodically, regularly, quietly, descend every year upon the *bel paese* from every Italian university."[16] So wrote Ettore Ciccotti in 1898. It would be mistaken, however, to draw from this or from similar declarations the impression that the Italian ruling class was indifferent to what was happening to the qualified labor market. Exactly the opposite was true. The Italian ruling class began to follow the phenomenon of intellectual unemployment with interest and anxiety from its very first appearance, and its awareness of this problem, and of the social and political consequences related to it, was very high by the last decade of the century. This is shown first by the numerous attempts made to forecast the relation between demand and supply of laureati; second, by the frequency with which parliamentary debates on education confronted this problem; and finally, by the steps that the government sought to take to cope with the situation.

The first attempt at forecasting the relation between demand and supply of laureati was made, about 1890, by the General Office of Statistics, which considered, however, only two groups: lawyers and doctors. Regarding the lawyers, the General Office forecast an annual demand for 364 laureati against a supply of 960. For the doctors, it calculated that there would be an annual demand for about 600 laureati against a supply of 900.[17] A second attempt at forecasting was made in 1897 by Carlo Francesco Ferraris, who pointed to the existence of a surplus especially of laureati in jurisprudence, medicine, engineering, and mathematics for teachers. To the training of a "learned proletariat," as Ferraris defined it, the overproduction of laureati in jurisprudence made a particular contribution. "This is evidently a dangerous crowd," he observed, "because the nature of the studies pushes the unemployed laureati in law more easily into the precarious profession of journalism or into the ranks of social and political agitators."[18]

The most systematic and documented attempt at forecasting the relation between demand and supply of laureati was made by Luigi Bodio and presented to Parliament in 1898 together with a bill on university autonomy.[19] By extrapolation from the existing data, Bodio's study showed that the situation of laureati in pharmacy and in veterinary science was not a cause for concern. As for the laureati in literature and philosophy, the supply was greater than the demand by the state schools and the *scuole pareggiate** but it was expected that the excess would find employment in the private schools. The situation of lawyers and doctors, on the other hand, was serious. Each year's supply was exactly twice the demand. It was estimated that there were in Italy 18,200 laureati in law (half of whom were employees of the Public Administration), and that the annual requirement would be 500 persons, while the university had been producing more than a thousand per year during the period 1888-96 (table 2.6). The same surplus was seen for doctors (supply: 900; demand: 500), of whom there were about 21,000, with a numerical ratio of 1 per 1,600 inhabitants. This was much lower, observed Bodio's study, than that of other European countries. As for engineers and architects, who numbered about 11,000 and of whom only 14 percent were employed in industry, a smaller imbalance between demand (300) and supply (350) was foreseen for the following years.[20]

The existence of a surplus of intellectual labor and the prediction that the imbalance between the school and the qualified labor market would grow worse deeply troubled the Italian ruling class, first of all because the difficulties of employment led diplomati and laureati to exert constant pressure to be absorbed in some way by the state. "We see the public administrations and the liberal professions," said the Hon. Lucchini to the Chamber of Deputies, "taken by assault and infested by a mob, if I may call it such, of moral parasites whose

**Scuole pareggiate*: "private" schools funded by the state whose curricula were "made equal to" the public schools' and whose diplomas had, therefore, the same value. Referred to hereafter as "semiprivate."

Table 2.6. Laureati in Some Faculties, 1888 to 1896

Year	*Law*	*Medicine*	*Veterinary*	*Pharmacology*	*Engineering*	*Literature and Philosophy*
1887–88	970	846	83	300	372	139
1888–89	987	874	95	310	304	112
1889–90	966	913	73	332	308	140
1890–91	968	950	79	300	331	150
1891–92	1,052	948	76	306	371	214
1893–94	1,243	941	86	279	403	206
1894–95	1,102	954	83	327	383	225
1895–96	1,275	959	117	346	376	216

SOURCE: F. S. Nitti, *La ricchezza dell'Italia.*

deficiencies and lack of ability are surpassed only by their capacity for intrigue."[21] But the greatest fear of the Italian ruling class was that the difficulties of employment might produce a political radicalization of the intellectual strata, who might leave the secondary schools and the university not as the faithful functionaries needed by the rulers to reinforce their own hegemony, but rather as dangerous subversives. This was a recurrent motif in many writings and speeches of the most authoritative exponents of the Italian ruling class.

> The most wretched and miserably paid positions [said Minister of Education Baccelli to the Chamber of Deputies] are competed for with an extraordinary frenzy by an enormous number of laureati. Professional practice becomes exceedingly difficult because of ruthless competition and a rancorous struggle for existence that is fatal to the dignity of the entire class of professionals. A plentiful band of misfits and malcontents is generated that constitutes a dangerous environment conducive to the growth of unhealthy germs. And these persons are all the more fearful because of their advanced learning and the fearlessness that attends their youth.[22]

Five years later, in a report which had very wide exposure, the Hon. Fusinato denounced the situation in these terms:

> All this annual overproduction, adding to that of preceding years, has created a veritable army of misfits who crowd into careers that require no university qualifications, or else remain unemployed. They are the ones whom the university has deceived; those who, *nourished on Greek and Latin, now die of hunger*; those who constitute that new form of *intellectual proletariat* which is even more miserable and threatening than the economic proletariat, and from which the extremist

political parties recruit many of their shrewdest, most active, and most dubious elements.[23]

It is not surprising, therefore, that already in this period the Italian ruling class sought to launch a defense. While from the debate in progress there gradually arose a plan to radically change the educational system (as we shall see in chapter 5), urgent measures were taken in the meantime to at least slow the growth of secondary and higher education. Regarding secondary education, Minister of Public Education Villari presented a bill of law on November 30, 1891 that provided for a considerable increase in the fees for the ginnasi and for the licei, and that was quickly approved by Parliament (Law no. 71, February 25, 1892).[24] In the report of the Central Office on this plan, one reads:

> In view of present conditions, considering that in the universities the training of professionals appreciably surpasses the need, every increase in the secondary school population represents an increase in the number of misfits. Under such circumstances, a combination of financial and didactic measures, capable of restricting attendance in the schools, must be considered truly progressive, because it would diminish the excessive and insane hastening after the by now overwhelmed liberal professions and after poorly paid government posts.[25]

Comparable measures were sought for the university. Acting on the conviction that one of the most important causes "of the excessive number of university students and of professionals in our country is the too easy access to higher education," because "university fees in Italy do not reach more than a third or at the most half of those of other nations,"[26] Minister of Public Education Baccelli presented a bill of law on December 6, 1894 to increase these fees. But if it had been easy to obtain the agreement of Parliament for the increase of secondary school fees, it took nine years to have the same provision passed for the university. Baccelli presented his bill of law, in fact, both in 1895 and in 1898. And two other attempts to increase fees were made by the Hon. Gianturco in 1897 and by the Hon. Gallo the year after.[27] Only the two bills presented in 1902, one by parliamentary initiative, the other by Minister of Public Education Nasi, achieved the approval of the two chambers, although against lively opposition.[28]

All these bills, with the exception of Gianturco's,[29] provided a very sharp increase of fees. For some faculties increments of 50 percent were proposed, but for others there were increases by a factor of five (table 2.7). This explains in part the deep hostility that each of these bills encountered. To increase fees, said Vincenzo Riccio to the Chamber of Deputies, meant one thing only: to raise "the sacrifices of poor families," that is, of the "small proprietors" and of the "small bourgeoisie that I have always considered the solid base of our governments." There was an even more important reason for opposition: the distrust that many held concerning the efficacy of such provisions for slowing the growth of higher education. There were many who thought, as Chimienti said, that "the misfits are produced in the secondary schools, not in the universities." But, it was observed, even admitting for the sake of argument that the increase of fees might block at least some of the students at the end of their secondary studies, this provision would do no more than shift the difficulty of employment from the laureati to the diplomati. "How is it," asked Vincenzo Riccio polemically, "that you intend to increase university fees and not make corresponding provisions for the entire educational order, and not make reforms? If you think that the increase in fees will impede the entrance of students to the university, then you will only have a greater number of students with the diploma from the liceo who will then constitute an even greater danger, since these will provide an even greater number of misfits."[30]

Intellectual Unemployment and the Economic Cycle

The data and the testimony that I have reported so far give rise to a question that is worth considering: was the intellectual unemployment that characterized Italy in the last two decades of the past century a conjunctural phenomenon, one tied to the course of the short-term economic cycle, or was it instead a long-term phenomenon due to other variables? This question can arise from even a summary acquaintance with the development of the Italian economy in these decades. It is well known that in 1880, concurrent with the first great world depression, an agrarian crisis began in Italy, one that struck the central and southern regions particularly and produced a sharp decline in the per capita level of consumption everywhere. But it is also known that from the following year and until 1888 there was a moderate growth of Italian industry – an average increase of 4.6 percent per year. From 1888 to 1896, on the other hand, the economy was hit by a very harsh crisis: industrial production overall registered an extremely low rate of annual growth, an average 0.3 percent with sharp decreases in the metallurgical and especially the mechanical sectors. Building construction, which had experienced a veritable boom in the years preceding, underwent a distinct drop in this period.

Table 2.7. University Fees in Effect until 1903 and Those Foreseen by Various Bills

Faculty	*Law in Effect until 1903*	*Baccelli Bill (1894)*	*Gianturco Bill (1897)*	*Gallo Bill (1898)*	*Bill by Parliamentary Initiative (1902)*
Jurisprudence	860	1,490	1,070	1,450	1,145
Medicine and surgery	860	1,820	1,070	1,450	1,365
Pure mathematics and engineering	860	1,705	1,070	1,450	1,175
Physical, natural, and mathematical sciences	450	960	520	750	845
Philosophy and literature	450	1,235	520	700	845
Chemistry and pharmacology	450	960	520	750	1,000
Notaries and attorneys	200	760	350	460	685
Pharmaceutical certification	200	870	200	350	560
Veterinary science	168	1,050	168	500	560
Agriculture	168	1,020	168	350	560

SOURCE: Atti Parlementari, Camera, *Documenti,* 21st Legislature, 2d Session (1902), Doc. no. 145.

It is likely that intellectual unemployment also felt the effect of the serious crisis undergone between 1888 and 1896. Luigi Bodio observed in his report, for example, that the drop registered in construction and the dwindling number of large public works threw quite a few engineers out of work. But while it is one thing to say that intellectual unemployment was aggravated in the period of recession, it is another to argue that it was due exclusively to the course of the economic cycle. We shall consider for a moment, therefore, the hypothesis that intellectual unemployment was an exclusively conjunctural phenomenon. To verify this hypothesis, it would be sufficient to show that, in the period from 1896 to the outbreak of the First World War, intellectual unemployment decreased sharply, to the point of nearly disappearing, since in 1896 there began what was to be more than simply an expansive period of the economic cycle. In that year the so-called "great leap" began, one of the most important periods of industrialization in Italian history. Industrial production grew by an average annual rate of 6.7 percent up to 1908 and by 2.4 percent over the following fifteen years.[31]

Bodio's study gives us a first, and negative, answer to the question of whether intellectual unemployment was a conjunctural phenomenon. Nevertheless, it is a partial and unsatisfactory answer, first, because the study was made only two years after the beginning of the "great leap," and second, because it was largely predictive in nature. What really happened during the period 1896–1913? Were Bodio's forecasts realized or not? Did intellectual unemployment persist or not in these seventeen years of economic expansion in Italy? With the utter lack of data on unemployment (and not only on that of intellectuals), there is only one way to answer these questions: to employ the data on intellectual emigration.

Intellectual Emigration

Before considering whether or not the data that we do have confirm the predictions made by Luigi Bodio, it is well to examine the general characteristics of the emigration of Italian intellectuals, a phenomenon as little known or studied as it is important. It may indeed be the clearest and most important manifestation of the contradictions of the educational system that followed from the Casati Law.

In the period from 1880 to the outbreak of the First World War, intellectual emigration was not only an Italian, but also to some extent a European, and particularly a French, English, and German phenomenon. The intellectual emigration of these countries had, however, different characteristics from Italy's. The university graduates of England, France, and Germany (even though for the last the argument is more controversial) did not abandon the "motherland" to escape unemployment, but departed simply because the countries to which they went (often in the employ or as representatives of their own country's big bourgeoisie) offered them a level of income and prestige even greater than that, already quite high, which they received at home. We know that a good number of French and English university graduates who emigrated went to the colonies of their own country. In particular, the English went mainly to the United States until 1890, and thereafter to the Dominions.[32] "The Germans," observed Nitti, "have reduced working class emigration to a minimum. In contrast, each year there set out, in victorious assembly, business agents who subsequently become bankers, doctors, engineers: it is the bourgeoisie that tends to emigrate and to extend its territory."[33] As has been noted, moreover, for these countries it is more precise to speak of the "circulation" rather than the emigration of intellectuals.[34] In 1890, while some university graduates from England left the country for the United States or for the colonies, the business houses of London were invaded by German graduates. In 1901, while some French graduates left the country, there numbered in France almost 4,000 Italian graduates who practiced liberal professions.[35]

The characteristics of Italian intellectual emigration were completely different. The laureati who left Italy to reach other European or overseas countries did so exclusively to escape unemployment. This can be adequately demonstrated by the following extract from a report presented in 1900 (thus, four years after the "great leap") to the Ninth Congress of Italian Engineers and Architects:

> The subject we are considering bears directly on the very difficult solution of the other quite complex problem of emigration in general. We do not think it necessary to repeat here the historical reasons that have provoked it. We shall say only that for the Italians, the one true cause of this reality is to be found primarily in the economic malaise that troubles everyone, from the workers to the professional. . . .
>
> . . . Many engineers, having emigrated without a clear objective, have had to adapt themselves in order to make a living to jobs that were not always becoming to their social standing.
>
> In Italy, more than elsewhere, the glut of engineers is such as to cause serious concern. Consider that we have seven post-graduate schools and that each provides the country with an average of fifty engineers a year! We are interested in neither the reasons for this rapid growth in the number of laureati nor the means which

> would be required to preserve the conquest of the laurea only for the best, nor are we concerned even that the industrial revival which seems to us to be occurring today in our country should bear fruit, although we bet it will; for we believe that, as great as the revival may be, it will never be sufficient for all the present-day unemployed, which are augmented every year by new arrivals. Given the abnormal and very difficult situation in which young professionals find themselves today, we think it would be providential for these to endeavor beyond the confines of our country.[36]

The fact that in many cases Italian laureati had to content themselves, as the report just quoted indicates, with jobs abroad much different from those for which they had prepared in their university studies shows that these graduates, in contrast to those of the other European universities that we have seen, were not drawn abroad by particularly advantageous work conditions.[37] Nor did they emigrate in the employ or as representatives of the industrial or commercial bourgeoisie of their own country. Rather, they sought only to escape unemployment. To give only one example, the Labor Information Office for Italians of New York advised in 1906 that Italian laureati and diplomati "rarely succeed in finding employment suitable to their aptitudes. . .especially if they do not have practical knowledge of the English language. All these people, emigrating to the United States, meet bitter disappointments and are often forced by necessity to adapt themselves to lowly, difficult, and not always well paid occupations."[38]

Therefore, in contrast to the other countries, there cannot be said to have been a "circulation" of Italian intellectuals. Italy's was an emigration pure and simple, an exportation of unemployed intellectuals to which corresponded no form of importation of qualified labor. The data that we have in this regard confirm this assertion. In 1901, at the time of the census, there were in Italy exactly 37,762 foreigners "in regular residence" and 23,844 "in occasional residence." Among neither the former nor the latter were teachers, lawyers, or engineers to be found. The only foreign university graduates that we find in that year are 209 doctors with regular residence and 144 with occasional residence.[39]

In contrast to the insignificant number of foreign graduates that were found in Italy, there was an enormous number of Italian laureati who were forced to emigrate. If Nitti complained that the number of Italian laureati which emigrated each year was too scanty ("hardly two thousand") and argued that "if Italy could send abroad each year a large number of engineers, industrialists, doctors, teachers, and above all businessmen, it would give the colonies an extraordinary element of endurance and strength,"[40] it was probably because he shared the opinion of the Italian ruling class, which saw no other way out than the emigration of "misfits," the exportation of the potential leaders of a revolutionary movement. "If one fears the outbreak of popular uprisings because of the shortage of work," observed Angelo Landra "and, in the public interest, one views the emigration of workers as a safety valve, a precautionary measure, why shouldn't the effects of an academic proletariat be feared even more, and why shouldn't a way out of this predicament be equally sought?" Even though recognizing that they were "treated a little harshly" in the countries to which they went, he thought there was no other solution than to encourage to the utmost the emigration of qualified labor. "These misfits, who in Italy would become revolutionaries, finding abroad a secure and steady wage, could not help but learn how to manage the mass of workers judiciously and how to exercise a beneficial influence, thereby making good use of the sway that their education gives them over the masses."[41]

The data which we possess show, in fact, how little justified was Nitti's judgment on the scantiness of Italian intellectual emigration. The first three columns of tables 2.8 and 2.9 report the number of emigrants "in liberal professions" from 1876 to 1920. This group includes doctors, pharmacists, lawyers, engineers, teachers, and midwives.[42] Actually, a close examination of these two tables may raise doubts as to the reliability of the data concerning women, whose number at first seems excessive. But besides the fact that midwives and teachers were included among the liberal professionals, we must also keep in mind the custom of attributing to women the profession of the husband.[43] Excluding women from the analysis,[44] the data from the two tables give us some indications of no little interest.

In the first place, they show us that the emigration of intellectual labor had imposing dimensions. It would be a mistake to conclude, having seen from the two tables that in the period from 1876 to 1920 the percentage of emigrants "in liberal professions" fluctuated from 0.30 to 1.30, that intellectual emigration was a phenomenon of scant quantitative importance. To estimate exactly what was known by the unfortunate expression, the "propensity to emigrate" of various social groups, it would be necessary to compare the composition by occupation and by educational qualification of the emigrant population with that of the population remaining in Italy. Unfortunately, with the data we possess this comparison is impossible. If, however, we bear in mind that in 1951 (the first year for which the compositon of the population by educational

Table 2.8. Intellectual Emigration, 1876 to 1899

Year	Emigrants in Liberal Professions*			Total Emigrants of All Occupations			% of Emigrants in Liberal Professions			Geographic Origin of Emigrants in Liberal Professions			
	M	F	M & F	M	F	M & F	M	F	M & F	North	Center	South	Total
1876	–	–	559	–	–	100,993	–	–	0.55	51	13	36	100
1877	487	58	545	78,533	10,191	88,724	0.62	0.57	0.61	59	5	36	100
1878	677	72	749	75,893	10,614	86,507	0.89	0.68	0.86	55	11	34	100
1879	638	86	724	91,767	14,735	106,502	0.69	0.58	0.67	57	9	34	100
1880	544	136	680	92,903	15,009	107,912	0.59	0.90	0.63	36	10	54	100
1881	546	48	594	109,152	14,504	123,656	0.50	0.33	0.48	63	11	26	100
1882	849	188	1,037	126,879	19,071	145,950	0.67	0.98	0.71	52	8	40	100
1883	668	135	803	138,062	18,000	56,062	0.48	0.75	0.51	44	14	42	100
1884	632	109	741	117,677	16,511	134,188	0.54	0.66	0.55	47	21	32	100
1885	760	104	864	117,059	22,111	139,170	0.65	0.47	0.62	55	7	38	100
1886	705	128	833	123,295	24,489	147,784	0.57	0.52	0.56	53	6	41	100
1887	896	158	1,054	154,685	32,685	187,370	0.58	0.48	0.56	58	10	32	100
1888	706	114	820	179,257	55,298	234,555	0.39	0.21	0.34	56	11	33	100
1889	1,125	218	1,344	159,280	32,069	191,349	0.71	0.68	0.70	65	10	25	100
1890	832	350	1,182	159,547	30,058	189,605	0.52	1.16	0.62	52	7	41	100
1891	1,288	345	1,634	189,217	52,270	241,487	0.68	0.66	0.67	53	6	41	100
1892	783	161	944	157,792	35,143	192,935	0.50	0.46	0.48	74	5	21	100
1893	1,332	274	1,606	173,524	39,629	213,153	0.77	0.69	0.75	57	6	37	100
1894	832	343	1,175	158,581	34,755	193,336	0.53	0.99	0.60	64	12	24	100
1895	1,225	300	1,525	189,635	52,261	241,896	0.64	0.57	0.63	50	5	45	100
1896	1,425	405	1,830	207,209	49,885	257,094	0.69	0.81	0.71	36	9	55	100
1897	1,426	463	1,889	197,040	52,111	249,151	0.72	0.89	0.75	39	14	47	100
1898	1,169	287	1,456	202,510	42,583	245,093	0.58	0.67	0.59	43	14	43	100
1899	1,640	548	2,188	232,700	40,467	273,167	0.70	1.35	0.80	42	13	45	100

*Doctors, pharmacists, midwives, lawyers, engineers, teachers.

SOURCE: Elaboration of data taken from General Commission of Emigration, *Annuario statistico dell'emigrazione italiana dal 1876 al 1925* (Rome: Poliglotta, 1926).

Table 2.9. Intellectual Emigration, 1900 to 1920

Year	Emigrants in Liberal Professions*			Total Emigrants of All Occupations			% of Emigrants in Liberal Professions			Geographic Origin of Emigrants in Liberal Professions			
	M	F	M & F	M	F	M & F	M	F	M & F	North	Center	South	Total
1900	1,644	462	2,126	269,139	48,732	317,871	0.62	0.95	0.66	43	16	41	100
1901	2,442	901	3,343	399,241	77,744	476,985	0.61	1.16	0.70	45	12	43	100
1902	2,302	732	3,034	410,015	73,333	483,348	0.56	1.00	0.62	40	18	42	100
1903	2,643	682	3,325	392,831	68,576	461,407	0.67	0.99	0.72	48	12	40	100
1904	1,114	225	1,399	356,886	63,906	420,792	0.31	0.35	0.31	52	19	29	100
1905	1,692	329	2,021	557,244	92,716	649,960	0.30	0.35	0.31	59	10	31	100
1906	2,006	385	2,391	592,201	112,191	704,392	0.34	0.34	0.34	56	14	30	100
1907	1,964	490	2,454	530,400	102,038	632,438	0.37	0.48	0.38	57	13	30	100
1908	1,570	262	1,832	372,000	66,207	438,207	0.42	0.40	0.41	64	14	22	100
1909	1,736	313	2,049	467,984	93,302	561,286	0.37	0.34	0.36	51	22	27	100
1910	2,040	434	2,474	487,296	94,681	581,977	0.42	0.46	0.42	37	37	26	100
1911	1,836	303	2,139	396,845	81,599	478,444	0.46	0.37	0.44	67	11	22	100
1912	2,521	380	2,901	534,685	104,270	638,955	0.47	0.37	0.45	56	22	22	100
1913	2,117	367	2,484	654,969	128,244	783,213	0.32	0.28	0.31	50	21	29	100
1914	1,906	395	2,301	348,038	73,333	421,371	0.55	0.54	0.54	66	14	20	100
1915	1,255	312	1,567	76,525	41,538	118,063	1.64	0.75	1.32	66	22	12	100
1916	714	228	942	64,298	49,856	114,154	1.11	0.48	0.82	60	26	14	100
1917	244	144	388	16,920	21,328	38,248	1.44	0.67	1.01	62	26	12	100
1918	166	104	270	13,808	10,944	24,752	1.20	0.95	1.09	71	16	13	100
1919	1,255	445	1,700	146,020	74,356	220,376	0.86	0.60	0.77	59	14	27	100
1920	595	341	936	409,411	151,306	560,717	0.14	0.23	0.16	47	15	38	100

*Doctors, pharmacists, midwives, lawyers, engineers, teachers.

SOURCE: See table 2.8.

Table 2.10. Average Annual Number of Male Laureati and Emigrants in the Liberal Professions

Periods	*Emigrants*	*Laureati*
1881–1890	772	2,912
1891–1900	1,278	3,681
1901–1910	1,950	3,951
1911–1914	2,095	3,955
1881–1920	1,315	3,791

SOURCES: Elaboration of data taken from General Commission of Emigration, *Annuario statistico dell'emigrazione italiana dal 1876 al 1925* (Rome: Poliglotta, 1926); ISTAT, *Sommario di statistiche storiche italiane, 1861–1955.*

qualification is known) laureati constituted 1 percent of the population, we can readily see that those "in liberal professions" were not underrepresented among the emigrants. But the most persuasive comparison is something else again. If we consider the forty-year period from 1881 to 1920, we see, in fact, that there were an average of 1,315 *male* emigrants per year "in liberal professions," while over the same period the university produced an average of 3,791 male laureati per year. As crude and approximate as these comparisons may be, they are more than sufficient to show the validity of the assertion that intellectual emigration was of considerable proportions.

In the second place, the data of tables 2.8 and 2.9 show us not only that the migratory flow of intellectual labor was considerable but also that, instead of decreasing, it actually increased over time. The number of intellectual emigrants increased, first of all, in absolute terms. The two tables indicate that, from between 500 and 600 initially, the number increased to more than 1,000 in 1891 (1,634 if women are included) and reached its highest point of over 2,600 in 1903 (3,343 including women). And this was six years after the "great leap" of the Italian economy had begun. But the increased absolute number may have limited significance, given that during the period considered the number of laureati increased steadily as well. It is worthwhile, therefore, to compare the average yearly number of male emigrants "in liberal professions" with that of male laureati who issued from the universities of Italy. Certainly this procedure has many limitations, and a comparison between these two series of data requires the utmost caution. Still, an examination of table 2.10 at least upholds the claim that intellectual emigration was constant in time, and therefore little or not at all affected by the course of the economic cycle.

In the third place, the data at our disposal allow us to disprove Michels' assertion that the "very damaging disproportion" between supply and demand

Table 2.11. Distribution by Area of Origin of Male Emigrants in the Liberal Professions and Distribution of the Population

Areas	Emigrants				Population		
	1877–80	*1881–90*	*1891–1900*	*1901–14*	*1881*	*1901*	*1911*
Northwest	36.19	39.90	29.35	39.36	26.86	26.72	27.15
Northeast	16.63	15.25	19.90	15.85	17.56	17.18	17.90
Center	9.25	10.78	11.62	15.93	16.25	16.86	16.66
South	37.93	34.07	39.13	28.86	39.33	39.24	38.29
Total	100.00	100.00	100.00	100.00	100.00	100.00	100.00
(N)	(2,346)	(7,719)	(12,784)	(27,889)			

SOURCE: See table 2.8 for emigration; for population, SVIMEZ, *Un secolo di statistiche italiane: Nord e Sud (1861–1961).*

for laureati concerned only southern Italy. Table 2.11 reports, in the first part, the distribution of male emigrants in the liberal professions by geographic area of origin and, in the second, the distribution of the Italian population. In this case also the greatest caution is necessary in examining the data.[45] One must not, for example, attribute undue importance to the fact that intellectual emigrants coming from the Northwest are overrepresented and those of the Center underrepresented with respect to the distribution of the population. All the same, from the comparison between the two distributions, it is at least legitimate to draw the conclusion that emigration affected not only the laureati of the South but also those of the other regions.

In spite of their limitations, the data reported in this section provide at least a partial answer to the question raised earlier. They show that intellectual unemployment affected not only the South, and that it persisted even during the seventeen years of economic expansion in Italy, thus demonstrating that it was not a conjunctural phenomenon tied only to the course of the economic cycle. It is now clearer where the origins of this phenomenon must be sought. The data that we have seen give us at least an approximate idea of the loss to Italy of "intellectual capital" during the period considered.[46] Clearly, if a country with such a high rate of illiteracy undergoes for at least forty years so constant and violent a hemorrhage of the intellectual cadres produced by its universities, then this country must have an educational system with profound contradictions.

Unemployment Within Various Intellectual Categories

Even if the data on emigration indicate that the phenomenon of intellectual unemployment persisted throughout the period from 1896 to the outbreak of the First World War, they say nothing, unfortunately, on its distribution by groupings according to the area of study in which the laurea was taken. If we depend on the testimony of the publicists of the period, we are often left with the impression that intellectual unemployment struck all the categories of laureati. "There is a multitude of doctors eager to win for themselves a municipal post," wrote Nathan in 1906, "of lawyers who argue over each other's clients and who exert the strength of oarsmen to acquire cases, of university graduates who employ every means to secure themselves employment, from state positions to the humbler ones in local and private concerns."[47] Yet even in the period from 1896 to the outbreak of the First World War, the group hardest hit by unemployment was that of laureati in law. Carlo Francesco Ferraris, the period's most important and extensively documented scholar of higher education, who in 1903 repeated Luigi Bodio's attempt of five years before to forecast the relationship between demand and supply of intellectual labor, observed that the phenomenon of disproportion between demand and positions offered continued to exist at all concorsi held for jurists. He predicted for the future "an enormous excess" of laureati in jurisprudence as well as of notaries and prosecutors furnished by the universities.[48] Ernest Nathan observed as well:

> As the laws increase and multiply, so too increases the number of those who make their profession in the interpretation of these laws. The utility of each is dubious when the former are put together carelessly and approved hurriedly; they are comprehended, assimilated, and above all put into effect slowly. It is certain, in any case, that while the Chamber of Deputies feels the need to justify its legislative power by modifying, increasing, and tangling the laws that govern us, the country could do without the extraordinary multiplication not of bread and fishes to feed the multitudes, but rather of fish that each day require more bread and accompanying stores, seeking and catching them in both clear and murky waters."[49]

In fact, in the period which concerns us, students in the area of legal studies, who had always in the preceding decades represented the majority of enrollments, increased even further. While the number of those enrolled to become notaries and prosecutors remained stable or actually fell after 1902–3, those in jurisprudence increased constantly, from 5,996 in 1895 – 96 to 9,851 in 1910 – 11. Consequently the number of laureati also increased steadily. From a thousand per year over the period examined by Bodio it increased to 1,600 – 1,700 (table 2.12). At the end of this period, examining the data on enrollments and laureati in jurisprudence, Ferraris considered the difficulties

Table 2.12. Laureati by Faculty, 1904–5 to 1910–11

Faculty	*1904–5*	*1905–6*	*1906–7*	*1907–8*	*1908–9*	*1909–10*	*1910–11*	*1913–14*
Jurisprudence	1,676	1,552	1,641	1,614	1,636	1,646	1,778	1,663
Medicine	862	801	771	669	644	672	676	656
Mathematics and physics	54	34	36	58	60	58	57	—
Chemistry	109	123	112	108	115	112	71	166*
Natural sciences	62	54	48	34	32	28	39	—
Literature and philosophy	240	224	219	244	234	208	305	297
Pharmaceutical chemistry	88	83	80	66	71	72	71	—
Pharmacy	543	597	574	496	493	494	329	291
Engineering	368	368	484	449	473	485	453	683
Veterinary	182	152	171	135	144	152	176	63
Agriculture	103	99	102	103	115	113	92	98

*Also includes laureati in pharmaceutical chemistry.

SOURCES: C. F. Ferraris, "Statistiche delle Universitá e degli Istituti superiori," *Annali di statistica,* 5th ser. (1913), vol. 5; ISTAT, *Statistiche dell'istruzione superiore nell'anno accademico 1945-46* (Rome, 1946).

of employment for this group still very great.[50] In one of his best-known books, Piero Calamandrei compared the data of 1880 with those of 1913 and pointed out that even though judicial work offered increasingly less opportunity for income to legal professionals, there had been a very sharp increase of "this *forensic proletariat* which every year is debased by its growth in numbers, like an overflowing river which becomes dirtier the more swollen it gets." Thus "the 'lawsuit' represents for the lawyer not at all the normal material of professional work, but the exception, the choice morsel, the stroke of luck."[51] The imbalance between supply and demand of laureati in law was especially strong in the South, since, among those in existence, the faculties of jurisprudence which supplied the largest annual contingents of laureati were those of Naples and Palermo. Thus, among the five appellate court districts with the highest number of lawyers per inhabitant, three were in the South (Naples, Catania, and Palermo).[52] According to Michels, in 1870 there were 7 lawyers for every ten thousand inhabitants in the North, and 12 in the South. By 1911 there were still only 7 in the North, but the count had risen to 15 in the South.[53]

The difficulties of employment for the laureati in medicine were also very great in this period. In contrast to what was seen to have happened to legal studies, enrollments in the medical area, which had grown slowly form 6,521 in 1893 – 94 to 6,919 in 1896 – 97, began the year after to decrease, finally reaching a low point of 4,517 in 1910 – 11. Thus the yearly number of laureati also remained stable or actually fell (table 2.12). Bodio's forecasts were shown to be accurate, however, and the market was unable to absorb the new doctors. In 1903, even noting the drop that had occurred in the number of enrollments, Ferraris argued that there was "still a surplus in the production" of doctors.[54] Ten years later, analyzing the statistics on higher education, he observed that the relationship between demand and supply of doctors had by then reequilibrated itself, owing mostly to emigration.[55] And, in fact, it is likely that a good number of the laureati in medicine who left the university during this period were part of the large contingent of graduates which, as was noted, left Italy each year in search of work in other European countries or overseas. The census data confirm this for us. There were 22,168 doctors in Italy in 1901, and 23,361 in 1911. In a decade, therefore, there had been an increase of little more than a thousand, while in the same period the university had put onto the labor market almost 7,000 new laureati in medicine. Even estimating at 2,000 the number of doctors who had left the profession by death or retirement (actually an excessive number), there still remain 4,000 doctors (or 57 percent of the laureati in this period) who had to emigrate.

The difficulties of employment for the laureati in the area of engineering were not as great. If, here too, we examine the course of enrollments and of laureati, we see, first of all, that enrollments in the first two years of study, after various fluctuations recorded in the preceding years, increase constantly at an annual rate higher than that of the faculties of jurisprudence, increasing from 1,032 in 1896 – 97 to 3,227 in 1913 – 14. Quite strong as well was the increase recorded for enrollments in the subsequent three-year period of study. These rose, in the same years, from 1,300 to 3,105. There were, however, some differences between the two branches of engineering, civil and industrial, both according to the course of enrollments and to the greater or lesser difficulty of finding work. Enrollments in civil and hydraulic engineering underwent a distinct drop up to 1902–3 and then began to rise in the following year. Laureati in this branch had, at least up to 1905 – 6, considerable difficulty in finding employment and were sometimes forced to emigrate ("our abundant emigration abroad will continue to expand," wrote Ferraris in 1903). From 1906 on, however, the demand for engineers in the building trade increased because of the increase in public works and the expansion of railway lines, and a good number of the new laureati were absorbed by the State Corps of Civil Engineers and by the State Railroad Administration. Enrollments in the industrial branch, on the other hand, grew constantly. To give a more precise idea of the distribution of enrollments between the two branches in the final three-year period of study, it will suffice to say that while in 1893–94 enrollments in the industrial branch were only 20 percent of the total 1,300, by 1911–12 the percentage of those enrolled in that branch had reached 50 percent of the total 2,400. Thus, both the lesser yield of industrial engineers (compared to those in civil construction) over the first part of the period considered and the greater demand for this type of labor provoked by industrial growth meant that industrial engineers did not encounter the difficulties of employment that the other laureati had known.[56]

Expansion of the Bureaucracy

To complete the analysis conducted so far of the characteristics of intellectual unemployment over this period, we must pause briefly to examine a phenomenon that was often, with good reason, linked to intellectual unemployment: the expansion of the bureaucracy. It happened that, before resorting to emigration, laureati just out of the university sought refuge in the Public Administration, against which they mounted a veritable assault.

From 1882 to 1911 the employees of the Public Administration increased from 98,000 to about 260,000. Even recognizing that the data for 1911 include the nearly 117,000 employees of the railroad and telephone systems (which had not existed in 1882), there had been, altogether, an increase over thirty years of close to 165,000 employees, or 68 percent. To illustrate the process, as it was termed in those years, of "organicomania,"* it suffices to recall that from 1904 (the year in which the power to alter the administration was transferred from the government to Parliament) to 1907, there were fifty-five laws approved to enlarge the various branches.[57] Such growth of the bureaucracy not only continued but accelerated over the following decade. From 1911 to 1923 the number of Public Administration employees doubled from 260,000 to over half a million.

This enormous growth was due, naturally, to various causes. Certainly, it arose partly from the requirements of the dominant classes, who began intervening as never before and by means of various state apparatuses in the broader

*_Organicomania_: roughly, a "hiring spree."

social life of the nation and needed, therefore, to create a large and articulate body of reliable functionaries. As Amilcare Puviani wrote, from the fact that "property obtained without work and work deprived of property increasingly attracted public attention and provoked criticism," there followed "an increasing need for the state to recruit members for the defense of the legal order, against which a growing part of public opinion revolted." However, Puviani continued, intellectual unemployment also contributed somewhat to the expansion of the Public Administration. "As the demand for public services determined the supply, so too that supply, whenever it was excessive, provoked the demand."[58]

No data exist, unfortunately, on the academic qualifications of employees of the Public Administration in the period considered. All the same, it is interesting to note that management positions increased from 4.06 percent of the total in 1882 to 6.75 percent in 1914. Moreover, the testimony of scholars of the time leaves no doubt that this monstrous growth was also due to the need to cope with unemployment in general and with that of intellectuals in particular. One of the most important researchers of the problems of the bureaucracy, the representative Giovanni Abignente, wrote: "There are too many laureati today who find nothing on the market for independent activity to satisfy their hunger: a crowd of misfits that rushes to the conquest of public offices and does not always reach them, even though it fills them with mediocrity and deficiency." In fact, according to Abignente, the relationship between intellectual unemployment and bureaucratic expansion was so close that he himself came to the naive conclusion according to which a reform of the Public Administration would have positive effects on the former by discouraging enrollment in the university.[59]

This assault on public offices on the part of unemployed intellectuals was effected primarily by putting pressure on local representatives in Parliament. It is not surprising that these pressures were often effective, considering the social and political situation in those days, the influence exercised by intellectuals, and especially the fact that the right to vote was still restricted to a very low percentage of the population (7 percent in 1895, 9 percent in 1909, 23 percent in 1913).

> This intellectual proletariat, [wrote Lolini] made up in large part of the sons of the impoverished bourgeoisie or the destitute small bourgeoisie, was forced in order to make a living to follow the one way open to it, given the cultural and economic conditions of the country; namely, that of public employment – the only

remaining anchor against starvation. Among the electoral clienteles of every representative, the most enterprising and brash are made up of these very misfits who, with all the force that comes from being unemployed, pressure their political patrons (representatives, powerful constituents) to secure even the most modest employment in public administrations. Created in large part artificially by the state and put in the tragic position of having to depend on it almost exclusively for employment suited to its cultural, academic, literary, and theoretical preparation, this wretched intellectual proletariat has for nearly half a century exerted a silent, hidden, but irresistible pressure on political men and on rulers so that new concorsi for state jobs might be held and the number of offices increased and extended, even if no one could give a plausible reason for their necessity."[60]

The various phases of the process of absorbing the unemployed laureati and diplomati into the bureaucracy are described by Nitti in his chapter "The Italian Budget Is the Civil List of the Bourgeoisie."[61] In the first phase, unemployed laureati pressure to be taken on as temporary employees, in the second to be employed permanently, and finally in the third they fought to obtain salary increases. This process was particularly evident in the South. "Every university graduate, upper-secondary graduate, or dropout endeavors to obtain a state job and thus to assure himself any income whatever at the expense of the local budgets. There is not a single position for municipal clerk, medical inspector, school teacher, school inspector, accountant, town comptroller, secretary, municipal guard, or janitor that does not have two or three suitors,"[62] wrote Salvemini with reference to southern Italy. But the same process took place, although to a lesser extent, in all other parts of Italy and for all the intellectual occupations.

CHAPTER THREE

Formation of the National System of Education

"Italian public education finds itself in peculiar circumstances. With regard to the number of schools and students, Italy leads all other nations for the abundance and the incidence of institutions of higher and technical education, and it is among the first for the number of students in the secondary school that prepares for university studies as well as in the special institutes and those of the fine arts. On the other hand, among the peoples of long-standing civilization, it has the lowest number of popular and primary schools, even though after the proclamation of the new kingdom it led all others for the relative increase of schools and of students in elementary education. This overabundance of scientific, literary, and artistic institutions, combined with the deficiency in schools for the people and for workers, reveals to us one of those innermost contradictions that explain our past history and indicate the extent of our present difficulties."[1]

So wrote Cesare Correnti, who was to become Minister of Public Education in 1866, fifteen years before the phenomenon of intellectual unemployment manifested itself in Italy. To what were these "peculiar circumstances" of the Italian education system due? What were the characteristics of its internal structure? How was it formed? It is these questions that I will try to answer in this chapter in order also to explain the phenomenon of intellectual unemployment. I shall do so by examining first higher and then secondary education. In both cases I will attempt to confront the complex problem of the relationship between the school and the dominant classes and of the actual capacity of the latter to establish educational institutions corresponding to their own interests.

The statement of Cesare Correnti quoted above indicates the extent of the problems that must have faced the organic intellectuals* of the dominant classes in formulating and implementing an educational policy for the new nation-state. On the other hand, the analysis that I have developed in the preceding chapter leads, in my view, to the conclusion that an educational system such as the Italian, which produced the largest surplus of laureati in a country with such high rates of illiteracy, did not fully correspond to the interests of the dominant classes from either an economic or a political point of view: not economically, because the considerable flow of intellectual emigration which it caused constituted a distinct loss of "human capital," and little need be said on what this meant for such an economically backward country; not politically, because, as all the observers of the period asserted unanimously, it introduced an important element of instability, furnishing freely, by a massive production of "misfits," a large number of intellectual cadres to the movements and the struggles of the subordinate classes.

Higher Education

To determine whether there might be a connection between the characteristics of the Italian system of higher education and intellectual unemployment, it is necessary to consider a hypothesis that was advanced repeatedly toward the end of the last century in the course of a debate, or more precisely an encounter, on the problem of the number of Italian universities, their distribution, and their financing.[2] Two basic positions emerged from this debate: that of the "abolitionists," who maintained that there existed an excessive number of universities in Italy and demanded the closing of the lesser ones and the concentration of scarce available resources in the development of the larger ones; and that of the "preservationists," who defended the status quo, and fought to preserve the threatened universities, because – as was pointed out, paraphrasing Bismarck –

**Intellettuali organici:* "organic" intellectuals. A term developed by Antonio Gramsci to suggest the relationship (an "organic" and reciprocal one) between intellectuals and the social class from which they arose and which they serve to articulate. "Every social group . . . creates together with itself, organically, one or more strata of intellectuals which give it . . . an awareness of its own function . . . in the economic [and] the social and political fields." Quintin Hoare and Geoffrey Nowell Smith, eds., *Selections from the Prison Notebooks of Antonio Gramsci* (New York: International Publishers, 1971), p. 5.

"we still haven't learned that to better illuminate the streets an effective remedy may be that of abolishing the little lamps."[3]

There were many lines of argument that the abolitionists and the preservationists brought forward in support of their proposals and their interests.[4] Among these, the one that interests us for the present discussion concerns the relationship between the number of universities and intellectual unemployment. That the latter might have depended also, or even exclusively, on the existence of an excessive number of universities in Italy was argued several times by the abolitionists: "with so many universities, we cannot help but produce an endless number of lawyers without cases, doctors without patients, engineers without work, of misfits, in short, who increase the social disequilibrium, the useless ballast of the great ship of state."[5]

On the other hand, the preservationists denied that there was any connection whatever between the number and the distribution of Italian universities and "respectable poverty,"[6] or they actually denied that in Italy there was real intellectual unemployment.[7]

If we seek to test the hypothesis advanced by the abolitionists on the existence of a casual relationship between number of universities and intellectual unemployment, it is clear first of all that, in comparison with the other European countries, Italy certainly had a very high number of universities with respect to the population. Even disregarding the so-called free universities (Camerino, Ferrara, Perugia, and Urbino), Italy presented by 1890, with its seventeen state universities, a much lower ratio of population to universities than that of Germany, Austria, or France, and one only slightly higher than that of little Belgium (table 3.1).

It is more difficult to verify the hypothesis that the acutal presence of numerous universities and their diffusion on Italian territory influenced the relatively high number of university students in Italy by encouraging (or hindering less than in other countries) those who finished secondary schools to continue higher studies. The statistical elaborations that were made both by the preservationists and by the abolitionists suggest that there was such an influence, though a limited one. The elaborations made both by the preservationist Mozzani on data for 1891[8] and by the abolitionist Ferraris on data for 1894[9] showed, in fact, that the more numerous the universities in a region, the higher was the number of university students with respect to the resident population in that region. Thus in 1894, Tuscany, Sicily, and Emilia, which had three universities each, presented a higher number of university students relative to their

Table 3.1. Population and Number of Universities in Selected Countries, 1890

Country	*Population (in thousands)*	*Universities*	*Population per University (in thousands)*
Germany	49,428	20	2,471
Austria	23,895	8	2,986
Italy	30,158	17	1,774
France	38,343	15	2,556
Belgium	6,136	4	1,544
Holland	4,621	4	1,155

SOURCE: F. Martini and C. F. Ferraris, *Ordinamento generale degli istituti d'istruzione superiore.*

population than Veneto and Piedmont, which had only one university apiece. Still more illuminating were the data concerning Sardinia, which, in spite of its very low level of development, achieved a higher relative number of students (with its two universities) than Lombardy, which possessed only one university.

An analysis of this type may be criticized, however, from a methodological standpoint, since given the considerable geographical mobility of the university population, an examination of data which uses the region as the unit of analysis has only limited value. On the other hand, the significant variations in the number of university enrollments during the first fifty years of Italian national unity (see chapter 4) cannot, certainly, be explained by the widespread diffusion of university centers. On the whole, then, it seems to me it can be argued that the effect of this variable was rather limited, and that to understand the dynamics of university enrollments, and hence of the supply of intellectual labor, it is much more important to examine the characteristics of the educational system at the secondary level (which I will endeavor to do in the next section) and the course of the economy (a subject that I will take up in chapter 4).

But there seems to be another connection between the diffusion of university centers and the contradiction between intellectual unemployment and illiteracy. The available data show us that the presence of so many universities on Italian territory caused a waste of the scarce financial resources assigned to public education and influenced their distribution in a manner profoundly unfavorable to primary education. That the high number of universities caused a waste of resources – as the abolitionists argued at length – is a certain fact. Comparisons with the data of other countries showed that Italy spent "as much or more for stunted and anemic institutions than did Germany for its magnificent centers of learning."[10] How this came about appears clearly from an analysis of the data in table 3.2. There were in fact six or seven universities that assembled such a small number of students that the enrollee-teacher ratio was incredibly low. Even limiting ourselves to the number of full professors (then, as now, these professors often had responsibilities outside the university), there were universities with an average of six students per instructor, which means that in certain faculties (as, for example, that of the physical, mathematical, and natural sciences at Cagliari) there was one teacher for every student.[11] No wonder, then, that in these universities the state and local governments' expense per student was incredibly high.

The costs that the state and local governments sustained to have these "stunted and anemic institutions" survive were clearly to the detriment of primary education. Regarding the state, it suffices to say that about 1860 it spent only 500,000 lire for primary education and more than 5 million for higher education,[12] while in 1887 – 88, following the efforts made by various ministers of public education to develop primary education, the costs were, respectively, 5 and 12 million lire.[13] As for local governments, it suffices to say that they contributed to a considerable extent (as much as 50 percent at times) to costs sustained for the higher studies. Furthermore, this happened almost exclusively in the case of the smaller universities, that is, those which – as Ferdinando Martini and Carlo Ferraris observed –[14] found themselves in provinces with among the highest rates of illiteracy.

Naturally, this does not mean that the presence of so many universities was the primary obstacle to the process of making the Italian population literate, because, as I will have cause to say further on, the variables that retarded this process were quite different. It means simply that the extraordinary diffusion of university centers, even though it may not be the most important variable, can certainly help us to understand the sharply contradictory situation in which public education found itself over the first several decades of Italian national unity. This is so if for no other reason than that it constituted one of the constraints with which the Italian ruling class had to reckon in choosing which model of the educational system to construct.

The presence of so many universities was not, in fact, desired by the Italian ruling class, whose educational policy was resolutely directed toward the reduction of their number. In fact, when the intellectuals of the historical

Right* sought to structure the Italian educational system according to a comprehensive plan, they had to reckon immediately with the preexistence within the nation's territory of a great many universities. "Among the many and greatest benefits that unification of the Italian provinces into one Kingdom has rendered to the common fatherland," wrote Carlo Matteucci, Minister of Public Education, "is not, unfortunately, to be counted the inheritance of many universities."[15] And if, after so many oscillations between autonomy and centralization, they succeeded, for better or worse, in implementing a centralized organizational model for the educational system, they were never in a position to reduce the number of universities.

The program of educational policy that the Italian ruling class sought in vain to realize aimed at reducing the number of universities for at least three reasons. First, this would allow the concentration of available resources into a few efficient university centers. "The whole plan," declared Matteucci, "is based on the conviction that to arrange our higher studies according to the intentions that we have adopted in view of the current conditions of the Peninsula, a few, complete centers of high education must be established in which from now on the best elements would assemble, drawn by the natural effectiveness of these institutions: namely the most celebrated teachers, the most magnificent collections, the most ample yearly endowments for the professional and the scientific schools."[16] Second, reduction of numbers would make it possible to divert part of the budgeted expenditures from higher education to the primary schools, which found themselves in the conditions already noted: "If for at least ten or twelve years, Italy were to spend on popular education...the two or three million lire which, to the advantage of these studies, could, be saved on the universities, boarding schools, girls' seminaries, and academies of fine arts, this would be a bargain and a deed well done."[17] Third, as Matteucci observed with impressive foresight, reducing the number of universities was the only

**Destra storica:* the "historical Right" of the Risorgimento and of National Unification (1815-1870), so-called in order to distinguish it from the "new" or "nationalist Right" of the early part of the twentieth century. The former is the best represented by Camillo Cavour and by Quintino Sella and Marco Minghetti, each to varying degrees politically and economically liberal and socially conservative. The *Sinistra storica* or "historical left" was so-called to distinguish it from the subsequently socialist and communist Left and is best represented by the opposition to Cavour's Right first in the pre-unification Piedmontese parliament and then in the Italian parliament, and particularly by Giuseppe Mazzini and Giuseppe Garibaldi. See the chapter by Salvatore Saladino in Hans Rogger and Eugen Weber, eds., *The European Right: A Historical Profile* (Berkeley and Los Angeles: University of California Press, 1966), pp. 208-260.

Table 3.2. Enrollments, Teachers, and Costs of Italian Universities, 1891–92

University	*Enrollments*	*Total Cost (lire)*	*Cost per Enrollee (lire)*	*No. of Teachers*	*Enrollments per Teacher*	*No. of Full Professors*	*Enrollments per Professor*
Macerata	156	36,860	236.28	15	12.0	9	17.3
Sassari	121	130,462	1,078.20	33	3.7	19	6.4
Siena	220	244,973	1,113.15	37	5.9	25	8.8
Parma	306	333,469	1,089.77	48	6.4	37	8.3
Modena	337	320,542	951.16	53	6.5	34	9.9
Messina	345	282,580	819.07	57	6.1	38	9.1
Cagliari	164	163,304	995.76	37	4.4	27	6.1
Catania	612	332,333	543.03	54	11.3	37	16.5
Pisa	697	652,960	936.81	82	8.5	53	13.5
Genoa	943	472,595	501.16	73	12.9	39	24.2
Pavia	1,106	508,375	459.65	70	15.8	50	22.1
Palermo	1,153	625,107	542.15	65	17.7	44	26.2
Padua	1,127	674,222	598.24	76	14.8	53	21.3
Bologna	1,323	619,671	468.38	73	18.1	53	25.0
Rome	1,434	949,133	661.88	97	14.8	70	20.5
Turin	1,979	699,022	353.21	86	23.0	60	33.0
Naples	4,741	890,293	187.79	96	49.4	72	65.8

SOURCE: Elaboration of data taken from F. Martini and C. F. Ferraris, *Ordinamento generale degli istituti d'istruzione supeiore.*

way to combat "that shifting to which the various social classes are themselves already disposed, in their often disappointed expectation of rising from industrial careers to those of the so-called liberal professions."[18]

But local interests and political clienteles effected such stubborn resistance that all the efforts made by various ministers of education to reduce the number of universities were futile. This resistance already manifested itself in full strength soon after the promulgation of the Casati Law, which had decreed the abolition of the University of Sassari. The repeated protests of political and cultural groups, the resignations in the municipality, the petitions to the Chamber of Deputies, and above all the action taken in Parliament by Pasquale Stanislao Mancini, who had been elected to that body after having committed himself to battle for the local cause, forced the Chamber of Deputies and Senate to approve in record time a bill of law (May 31, 1860) that restored to Sassari its university.[19]

This first defeat, however, did not prevent Senator Carlo Matteucci from presenting the Senate, in the summer of 1861, with a Bill of Law for the Reordering of Higher Education, which aimed precisely at the reduction of the number of universities. In view of the difficulties encountered in having it approved, Matteucci, once having become Minister of Public Education, took advantage of the discussion over the bill on university fees to introduce into it an article that gave the minister power to prepare "an administrative regulation to be approved by royal decree" that would establish "the uniform regulation of studies." It is precisely on the basis of this article that Matteucci was able to have promulgated the notorious regulation of September 14, 1862 that aimed at a gradual reduction in the number of universities by limiting the right to examine and to confer the laurea to only six universities. But this time, as well, the wide protest provoked by the regulation forced Matteucci's successor at the Ministry of Public Education, Michele Amari, to revoke the most controversial articles.

Many were the failed attempts, after Matteucci's, to reduce the number of universities: from that of Minister of Public Education Cesare Correnti, who considered it necessary "to close the deserted schools, abolish the little-attended faculties, to cut the dry branches,"[20] and who proposed to abolish those faculties that in the period 1861–70 had not reached an average student-teacher ratio of 8 to 1; to three bills of law introduced in 1882, 1885, and 1889 by Minister of Public Education Baccelli, the first of which sought to have the less thriving universities die a natural death by conceding them their autonomy; to the Hon. Turbiglio's proposal in January 1891 to reduce the universities "to a number no larger than ten"; and finally to that of Minister of Public Education Ferdinando Martini, who prepared, with the collaboration of Carlo Ferraris, a bill of law to abolish the universities of Messina, Modena, Parma, Siena, Sassari, and Macerata.[21] Upon each of these proposals there followed without fail an extremely violent reaction by those whose interests were threatened (a most varied group, considering that, among the various delegations which presented themselves to Martini, there was even one that represented the landladies and proprietors of eating establishments who lived off the university students), and very strong pressure was exerted on local representatives.

The repetition of these failed attempts showed only, as Cesare Correnti said diplomatically, that "it is one of the most singular, or rather portentous facts of our national resurgence that the suppression of the regional capitals was achieved more easily, in fact infinitely more easily, than the removal of the universities."[22]

Secondary Education

That the educational system founded upon the Casati Law and the Mamiani By-law,[23] revised but never fundamentally reformed until the Gentile Law, was an elite one that was of use to the dominant classes in maintaining their own hegemony over the subordinate classes is something that can hardly be denied. Even a superficial familiarity with the publicity that preceded and followed the Casati Law will show that even the official documents, with a candor that is certainly hard to find in those of today, made no secret of the fact that the school's function was to reproduce the profound differences between the social classes as they existed then. The most interesting thing – which escapes the many scholars who are intent on showing the anti-popular character of the Casati Law – is that the educational system provided by this law, if compared with others in existence in Europe and with those that followed it in Italy from 1923 on, was relatively "open." It had, that is, an internal structure which favored the influx of a relatively high number of students into the university. The relatively open character of the education system of Casati did not, however, escape Antonio Gramsci, who on several occasions gave it a distinctly positive judgment.[24]

The fact that the educational systems we know today have and in the past century had among their manifest functions that of selecting students does not mean that they are all identical. If we compare the various educational systems, we see that, although they are all characterized by a certain level of specialization and of differentiation in their internal structure, they differ greatly as to the nature of this differentiation and the level at which it begins. This difference is neither secondary nor irrelevant, as some would think, but has profound consequences for the functioning of the whole educational system. Recent comparative studies on various educational systems have demonstrated, for example, the influence their internal structures on the levels of aspiration of students.[25] Educational systems with internal structures that differentiate very early, and provide dead-end schools at the lower-secondary level, strongly depress the students' levels of apsiration, training them from the start to make more "realistic" plans regarding future occupation. On the other hand, systems in which internal differentiation begins later and which are not supplied with dead-end schools have a stimulating effect on the students' levels of aspiration, encouraging higher educational and occupational aspirations to emerge – at times, in fact, too high relative to the opportunities offered by the system of social stratification and by the labor market. This is true, in my view, of the educational system that issued from the Casati Law.

Examining the educational system of Casati we note, in the first place, that at the primary or elementary level it introduced no internal differentiation. While at the same time France and Germany had one school for children of the subordinate classes (called "primary" in the former country and "popular" in the latter) and another for those who were to continue their studies (called, respectively, "elementary" and "preparatory"),[26] Italy had a single elementary school. But the relative openness of the Italian educational system could also be found at the secondary school level. Having finished elementary school, the student could "choose" to enter the ginnasio, which lasted five years, from which he could pass to the liceo, which was three years in length, and hence to the university. This was, naturally, the main road for one who was able and willing to dedicate himself to the higher studies. But even for one who did not enter the ginnasio there was, theoretically, the possibility of reaching higher studies by another route, that of enrolling in the *scuola tecnica,** which lasted three years. This school, which in contrast to the former was free of charge, was not a dead-end school, but allowed the student to enroll either in the *scuola*

**Scuola tecnica:* lower-secondary school with tecnical curriculum the sections of which (agricultural, industrial, commercial, for example) gave access to the upper-secondary *istituto tecnico,* itself divided into similar sections.

*normale,** which lasted three years and granted the elementary school teacher's diploma, or in the *istituto tecnico* (three years also), which in its turn opened access to some university faculties since the physics-mathematics section of the istituto tecnico gave access to the faculty of physical, mathematical, and natural sciences and to that of engineering. In other words, to become a lawyer or a doctor it was necessary to pass through the classical studies of the ginnasio and the liceo, while to become a professor of mathematics or an engineer one could take the more manageable route of technical studies. Therefore, not only did the Italian system postpone internal differentiation until after the elementary school, whereupon the secondary was bifurcated into a classical and a technical branch, but even this technical branch allowed access to higher studies.

As was often observed, the Casati Law followed the German model as far as secondary education was concerned. The ginnasio and the liceo were, in fact, similar to the German *Gymnasium,* while the scuola tecnica and istituto tecnico were an imitation of the *Realschulen*. But with respect to this model, the Italian legislator had introduced some important innovations. The first is that the law granted a certain freedom in the teaching of the istituti tecnici, in both the subjects taught and the number of sections, which corresponded to curricular subdivisions, so that these institutes could respond to the socioeconomic needs of the provinces in which they were founded. The second and most important for the purposes of this discussion is that the Casati Law did not provide for the types of dead-end schools known in Germany as the *Bürgerschulen*. This means that at the secondary level the Italian educational system, in contrast to those of other countries, did not provide for any type of blind-alley school; or, to use Aristide Gabelli's expression, it had no "dumping school" that was meant to protect the others (those for students who "had to" continue their studies) from the danger of being "crushed by the mob."[27] It is in this sense that one can say that the educational system of Casati was, at the secondary level, relatively open, enough so that the subsequent attempts at changing it — from Gentile's to that of Bottai — always aimed at its closure, and that we will have to wait until 1962 (the year that the scuola media unica is established) to find a similar one.

What were the reasons for the relative openness of the Italian educational system, and what was the relationship between this and the various social classes? One of the variables which is usually taken into consideration to

**Scuola normale:* upper-secondary school for the training of elementary school teachers.

explain the greater or lesser openness of an educational system is the capacity of the excluded social classes to exert pressure. This variable is undoubtedly a factor, as we shall see, in bringing about the changes made after the Second World War, but it is not of much help in explaining the characteristics of the educational system established by the Casati Law.[28]

To understand the reasons for the relative openness of the Italian educational system, it is necessary, in my view, to determine first what was the program of educational policy of the ruling class, and what were the general objectives it sought thereby to achieve; and second, what constraints the social and economic situation of Italy at that time placed on the feasibility of this program. Only by starting from an analysis of the complex relationship between this plan and the objective difficulties of its realization, and therefore of the influence that these difficulties had both at the time of its formulation and in the period of its realization, is it possible to understand the contradictions and internal imbalances of the Italian educational system.

The Policy of the Italian Ruling Class

To succeed in understanding the program of educational policy of the historical Right and Left, one must first of all free oneself from the idea, as false as it is still widely circulated, that the Italian ruling class, afraid that the diffusion of education was a dangerous element of subversion, aimed to keep the masses in their state of illiteracy. As is well known, in the other continental European countries, such as Denmark and Prussia, popular education arose and was spread in the eighteenth century by the initiative of enlightened sovereigns who had discovered in it an instrument of extraordinary effectiveness for reinforcing their own authority. So too in the pre-unification Italy of the first half of the nineteenth century, beside the old model of social control through the ignorance of the people, little by little there emerged one of social control through education. The antithetical character of these two philosophies of education can be well illustrated by comparing the two following documents, the first drawn from a periodical of the Papal State, the second from a memorandum addressed to the Grand Duke of Tuscany:

Social Control through Ignorance

If likewise one diffused education in minute proportions, it would inevitably happen that the people would lose their primitive ingenuity and simplicity, they would become estranged from their traditions, and they would no longer love the force of authority above all else; it is of little use to teach the people to read and write, and it can bring grievous results.[29]

Social Control through Education

Where there is more Education for the masses, the People are better-mannered and more tranquil: they respect their governors, they carry out the laws that civil society constitutes and preserves, appreciating their advantages and recognizing the necessity of constraint. Examples of enlightened Submission are Scotland and the Northern Departments of France, where primary elementary Education is extended as widely as possible to the humble People: and the Magnanimous Maria Theresa and her Venerable Successors, having worked wisely to spread elementary education about the Hereditary States, have reaped abundant fruits of tranquillity and loving subjection.[30]

Now, it was certainly to the second of the two models that the Italian ruling class turned after unification. And indeed, if the political objectives set by the ruling class included secularization, the creation of a national consciousness, and the unification of the different cultures and traditions of the Italian regions, and if it aimed to have the new social and political system accepted throughout the Italian territory and by all the classes, it could not, certainly, do without the diffusion of elementary education.[31] There are many facts that could be cited in support of this assertion. Besides the various attempts I have already mentioned by various ministers of public education to divert a part of the budgeted expenses from higher to primary education, it must be recalled that it was the Casati Law that established for the first time the compulsory and gratuitous nature of primary education, a principle that "was still controversial in other European nations."[32] On the other hand, the ongoing disputes and the repeated attempts over the first few decades after unification to put the obligation into effect by applying severe penalties to noncompliers, as well as the struggle for control of the school against a Church that considered the "knowledge" imparted by the lay schools "ruinous and cruel for the people," are clear signs of the awareness of the Italian ruling class regarding the importance of elementary education.

The document that best demonstrates this awareness is perhaps the Preface to Plans for the Elementary Schools of 1888 (reprinted partially herein). It is, in fact, an eloquent testimony not only to the importance attributed by its promulgators to the school as an agent of political socialization (whose function of ideological training was actually considered more important than the transmission of the "knowledge of the letters of the alphabet"), but also of their

Preface to Plans for the Elementary Schools, 1888

The educational power of the school is proportionate to the moral dispositions and to the demeanor of the teachers. He [the teacher] will do admirably who chooses a reader in which there is no lack of moral stories, commenting on them and having the pupils repeat them. But this exercise will not produce large effects if he does not have inside himself the sentiments that can inspire others. If he praises virtue and shows himself to be evil, if he commends gentleness and is petulant, or courtesy and behaves rudely, or punctuality and is absent or arrives late to school, it is very certain that his treatises will produce not one effect, this precisely because of his objective method, since actions penetrate the memory much more deeply than words.... It is not so much a matter of being aware of duties as of becoming accustomed to and fulfilling them.... What these duties are, one learns from all the life that surrounds us; what life does not give us is the strength to discharge them. Now, it is precisely this strength that the child must be made to acquire, demanding without softness and without compromise the exact fulfillment of the duties appropriate to his age and to his situation. When he has acquired this valuable attitude within the restricted circle of the duties of his age and situation, he will very probably carry it with him at subsequent ages and conditions, extending it almost unconsciously to these more important duties. It will not help, therefore, to teach him, let us say, that he must not be absent from roll-call, if he has not in the meantime been accustomed not to be absent from school; nor to speak to him of the respect due the King, if first of all he does not salute the teacher. It is important that children not consider themselves adults, and that they become accustomed to submission and deference toward relatives, teachers, and elders. The exact fulfillment of the duties that they have as children, as students, and as youngsters, is the least uncertain guarantee that one can have of the respect that they will have subsequently for their duties as men, fathers and citizens. All this amounts to saying that it rests in the hands of the teacher to instill in the pupil the attitude of carrying out his duties. Above all to a people's traditional discipline, strong and unswerving, which holds everywhere, from the royal palace to the hovel, are due the envied miracles of other nations and the deeds both ancient and recent that have sufficed to render ours a glorious and now respected tradition. It is necessary, however, that the teacher pay attention and not allow himself to be deceived by certain appearances, since it can happen that a certain material order, a certain tranquillity, certain gestures of subordination and of deference do not entirely correspond to the dispositions of the mind, as often happened in the old school....When this very simple truth is made to penetrate deeply into our population, it alone would suffice, so fertile is it, to irrigate the country with youthful blood and to amplify mutual confidence, the spirit of association, trust, work; and the school would thereby render a service much more valuable than the propagation of knowledge of the letters of the alphabet.

extraordinary awareness of the very functioning of such processes of socialization, described, by modern sociologists, as *interpersonal transfer* (by which the student "will very probably carry with him at subsequent ages and conditions" an attitude of "submission and deference toward relatives, teachers, and elders," and will transfer it into an attitude toward the employer and the state) and *role distance* (which emerges from the fear that "certain gestures of subordination and of deference do not entirely correspond to the dispositions of the mind").

The Italian ruling class did all it could to ensure that the process of political socialization in the elementary schools would be realized in the way it wanted. Great care was taken, for example, in the choice of textbooks, and for some time it experimented with the option of centralization.[33] On the other hand, it was preoccupied with the principal agent of this political socialization—the *maestro**—and whether he would fulfill his task adequately. First, by recruitment: while before unification, in order to teach it was necessary to obtain a certificate of morality from the religious authorities, the Casati Law provided that "to be appointed maestro in a public elementary school" it was necessary to have a certificate of morality granted "by the mayor of the town in which the candidate has last resided" (Articles 328 and 330). Second, by putting the teacher under a strict system of controls: the newly hired had, in fact, to undergo a trial period of three years, at the end of which time he became permanent but not irremovable. The Casati Law and those following made clear that as long as he stayed in service the teacher could be dismissed at any point and for many reasons. It established, moreover, that the role of the elementary teacher was not specific but diffuse, that his behavior was subject to control not only inside but also outside the school, that is, in his personal as well as his professional life. It said, in fact, in Article 106, "The reasons that may lead to suspension or dismissal are: to have by dishonorable acts incurred the loss of public esteem; to have by teaching or writing impugned the truths upon which the religious and moral order rests, or attempted to undermine the principles and guarantees that are placed at the foundation of the civil constitution of the state."[34]

Far greater, however, was the importance attached to secondary education by the ruling class. When in 1851 Domenico Berti stated that "the law for secondary education interests all parties so vitally, and surpasses in importance

**Maestro:* elementary school teacher.

that of primary education, even though it applies to an infinitely smaller number of persons,"[35] he grasped one of the most important aspects of the program of educational policy of the ruling class, and one to whose definition Berti had contributed considerably. The measures taken before the Casati Law by Farini, Cibrario, and Lanza, as well as the work completed by the commission nominated by Minister Gioia (to which Berti, Boncompagni, and Rayneri belonged),[36] bear witness to the weight the Italian ruling class assigned to "middle-string" education and the efforts it made to modernize and open the educational system at the secondary level. Then too, after unification the ruling class allotted the scarce financial resources mostly to secondary and higher education, while it assigned to local governments the very heavy task of providing for the elementary schools.[37]

The extraordinary importance attributed by the ruling class to secondary education is explained by the fact that to it was entrusted the realization of a crucial political task: the training of the middle class. In the same 1851 essay, Domenico Berti remarked:

> The law for secondary education has for its object the education of the less deprived classes of society, or rather of those classes which, because of their special condition and fortune, are called upon to influence directly the destiny of a nation. And if this is so, speaking generally for all nations, it is even truer for ours where, due to the nature of the government and the special circumstances of the country, it is from these classes that the majority of the national guard, of expert lawyers, electors, representatives, public magistrates, and functionaries belonging to the various administrative branches is constituted. On the education of these classes, therefore, depends in large part the honor, prosperity, greatness, and, in a word, the future of a nation. For this reason, the law which provides for them must be considered not only a pedagogical law, but also a political law of the greatest moment.[38]

In the same vein, one of the most authoritative Piedmontese scholars of educational problems, Giovanni Maria Bertini, wrote two years before the Casati Law that "the purpose of secondary instruction is and must be to provide for the need for education and learning of the majority of the youth of that class which, by being midway between the dregs of society and the opulent class, and by its numerical strength, its enterprise, and the power of its opinion, constitutes the backbone of the nation and holds its destiny in its hand."[39]

That the formation of a large and articulate middle class was a crucial political objective for the Italian ruling class is easily understandable. Many

Table 3.3. Civil Status of Administrative and Teaching Personnel of Ginnasi, Licei, and Scuole Techniche (State and Semi-private), 1862–63

Type of School	*Administrative Personnel*		*Teaching Personnel*	
	Lay	*Clerical*	*Lay*	*Clerical*
Ginnasi	204	299	1,037	1,117
Licei	47	36	467	223
Scuole tecniche	114	60	861	200

SOURCE: *Annuario dell'Istruzione Pubblica del Regno d'Italia pel 1865–66* (Florence, 1866).

times in recent years, on the basis of analyses of various societies conducted both by sociologists and by anthropologists, the importance of the formation of so-called horizontal segments or brokers has been demonstrated — that is, of those intermediate social groups able to work as channels of transmission of the center's requirements and ideology to the more peripheral groups and communities.[40] This was, in fact, the political objective that the Italian ruling class sought to achieve by training, as Pasquale Villari said, "that large social class which remains between the people and those who are at the head of the country, in politics as well as in science." "Through them," he observed, "ideas filter down, as it were, continually from the higher orders to the lowest; through them, those who lead public opinion have a hold on the people, understand them, and take an interest in them. In a word, they are like the cement that gives unity and keeps intact the body of the nation."[41]

It was necessary to fashion, through the ginnasi and the licei, "civil servants of a certain rank."[42] But still more complex and binding was the problem of the training of teachers. Concerning these latter, in fact, it was not only a matter of creating the personnel for the new schools but also of replacing the old staff who were poorly qualified or, even worse, had an ideological outlook in conflict with the values and political orientations that the ruling class sought to spread throughout the nation through, among other institutions, the schools. It suffices to say that in 1862, a good part of both the teaching and the administrative personnel in the secondary schools consisted of priests (table 3.3).

The situation with regard to the elementary teachers was even worse: almost a third of the maestri in service in 1862 were, in fact, priests.[43] Moreover, nearly half were without the diploma and taught by "temporary certificate" (table 3.4). The task of training new elementary teachers, assigned to the scuole normali, was, therefore, truly critical.

Table 3.4. Civil and Legal Status of Elementary School Teachers in 1862–63

	Public Schools			*Private Schools*		
	M	*F*	*Total*	*M*	*F*	*Total*
Civil Status						
Lay	7,705	8,056	15,761	2,609	3,959	6,568
Religious	6,729	1,190	7,919	561	612	1,173
Legal Status						
Permanent certificate	7,964	5,321	13,285	1,180	2,305	3,485
Temporary certificate	6,470	3,925	10,395	1,990	2,266	4,256

SOURCE: *Annuario dell'Istruzione Pubblica del Regno d'Italia pel 1864–65* (Milan: Stamperia reale, 1864).

Report to S.M. from the City Council of Biella" in Ministry of Agriculture, Industry and Commerce, *Gli istituti tecnici in Italia* (Florence: Barbera, 1889), p. 31.

Sir,

Whoever passes through our workshops, and especially those relative to industries that depend on recent advances in the physical, chemical and mechanical sciences, must make the painful observation that, while the Italian born and talented factory manager is not absent and there is no want of the expert engineer graduated from one of our advanced technical schools, to find skilled foremen one must usually look abroad, or at least our own leave much to be desired. The industrial flank in Italy today could be described as an army in which brave soldiers abound and there is no lack of expert captains, but where there is a shortage of lesser officials. And the soldiers, however ingenious, sometimes experience insuperable difficulties in advancing through the ranks, because of the total absence or the insufficiency of their instruction.

Thus the general complaint, in these recent days so eloquently and authoritatively supported by the Congress of the Chambers of Commerce of Genoa: that there is a shortage in Italy of schools for artisans, schools directed at those who, once having learned to read, write and do arithmetic, intend to devote themselves to a skill, and which give them that basic knowledge of the applied sciences which pertains to that skill. . . .

There is today, especially, in the small centers of population, a nearly absolute dearth of institutions that lead the worker from the elementary school to the workshop by furnishing him with the knowledge indispensable for correct practice of his skill and that are as convenient for the youngsters as for the adult workers. . . .

No less important to the program of educational policy of the ruling class was the function assigned to technical education. At the lower-secondary level — in the scuola tecnica — it was to prepare the head workmen for which some northern entrepreneurs felt a great need (as shown by the document approved by the city council of Biella, and partially reprinted here). At the upper-secondary level — in the istituti tecnici — intermediate technicians were to be trained especially for industry. Actually, given the backwardness of the Italian economy, the demand for these technicians was nearly nonexistent. Nevertheless, the creation and expansion of these institutes were intended to anticipate and stimulate such demand, and in this way to facilitate maximally the emergence of industries.

Difficulties in Realizing the Policy of the Ruling Class

The objective difficulties for the realization of the program of educational policy of the ruling class were enormous. It is not difficult to grasp why, in a social reality such as Italy's at the time, educational institutions were not easily established. Italy was what today is called a traditional society, with a structure and organization based on foundations profoundly different from those which have accompanied and favored the expansion of education: a strong prevalence of the primary sector of the economy, an extremely rigid system of social stratification, a very low level of horizontal and vertical mobility, a scant differentiation between the family unit and the productive unit, and the existence of other educative institutions.

Besides enormous financial problems, the ruling class had to face two other kinds of difficulty in the realization of its plan. First, there was strong resistance from reactionary groups, at the center but especially at the periphery. The model of social control through education that the ruling class had largely adopted was still too little diffused throughout the country for the resulting educational policy not to encounter resistance. Second, the demand of families for education was still quite limited.

The lack of demand for education was particularly evident at the level of elementary schooling. The slowness of the process of bringing literacy to the population was due not only to the fact that the Casati Law had assigned to the local governments the task of providing for the establishment and maintenance of elementary schools and that in many of these localities the model of social control through ignorance still prevailed, but it followed also from the living conditions of the lower social classes, from the frightful poverty in which they lived, and from their need to avail themselves of the child labor. In a well-

Table 3.5. Reasons for Truancy in the Province of Bologna, 1874–75

	M	*F*	*M & F*
Obliged to Attend	26,479	25,012	51,491
Truants	12,389	14,075	26,464
% Truant	46.78	56.27	51.39
Reasons for Truancy	*M*	*F*	*M & F*
	%	%	%
Poverty	20.92	19.13	19.97
Distance	19.97	28.09	24.28
Work	29.32	25.59	27.33
Illness	1.79	1.59	1.69
Negligence	28.00	25.60	26.73
Total	100.00	100.00	100.00
(N)	(12,389)	(14,075)	(26,464)

SOURCE: Elaboration of data taken from "Censimento scolastico della Provincia di Bologna nell'anno 1874–75," *Bollettino officiale della Publica Istruzione* (March 1876), pp. 255–61.

known article, Pasquale Vallari, one of the most tenacious advocates of education, wrote: "I am told: We have opened elementary schools, technical schools, schools of design, nursery schools! But this is ironic. What does learning the alphabet matter to a person who has neither air nor light, who lives in dampness and stench, who must keep his wife and his daughters on the highway all day?"[44] And, in fact, one of the few inquiries conducted on the elementary school showed that over three-quarters of the children who were truant missed school because of "poverty," "work," or the "negligence" of parents (table 3.5). Considering that this research was conducted in the province of Bologna, it is easy to imagine what the situation must have been in the southern regions of Italy.[45]

The situation was undoubtedly much different at the level of secondary education. All the same, even here the demand for education was not wholly satisfactory. If living conditions prevented the lower classes from even approaching the elementary schools, the aristocracy and the middle classes were not yet sufficiently attracted by the secondary schools. There were certainly few cases like that of the Tuscan Ridolfi, who before unification had established on his estate of Meleto a model school to train, as he said, "the two classes of farm hands and owners ... the one a class of dependent men, the other independent,"[46] aware as he was of the need to train a new class of landowners and to base their power on new principles of legitimation. In general, the landowners had to overcome not a little resistance before agreeing to send their own sons to an institution that sought to replace the titles of nobility with others like the laurea or the diploma, which conferred privileges on those who acquired them and thus questioned the principles that legitimated their own power. As Tarozzi wrote, recalling this period, "when the law assigned to the *scuola classica** that eminent and isolated position by which, almost alone, it represented the secondary school, it was intended for the training of the ruling bourgeoisie, since higher education was reserved almost exclusively for them; the feudal aristocracy proudly abstained from it. But little by little their children were seen to enter higher education and thus the scuola classica which they had formerly disdained; the count then felt the need to become the lawyer."[47] And no less was the resistance of the ceti medi (except for the intellectual bourgeoisie which was itself the product of the school), which did not yet see in educational institutions a channel of social mobility or a new means of social promotion, different from and in certain respects more effective than the traditional ones.

This explains why, even by 1861, the secondary schools were little attended. According to the date reported in an article of 1865 by Giovanni Maria Bertini (table 3.6), in the ginnasi, licei, and scuole tecniche there was a relatively low average of students per class, with the highest number in northern Italy and the lowest in Sicily. Thus, as things stood, Bertini could rightly note, "that it is not the students who lack schools, but rather the schools that lack students."[48]

It was from the encounter between the program of educational policy of the Italian ruling class and the difficulties of creating in the people an adequate demand for education that the Italian educational system was born. In facing the selection-socialization dilemma in the creation and use of educational institutions, the Italian ruling class clearly chose the second horn; it did not create mechanisms of early internal selection and differentiation, for the simple reason that the social and economic conditions of the country and the educational policy that the ruling class sought to realize were so divergent that it had absolutely no need for these mechanisms. In other words, if the Italian ruling class created a relatively open educational system and introduced some important innovations over the German model, if it provided no "dumping school," this was because of the importance it attributed to the secondary school in

**Scuola classica:* that is, the ginnasio and the liceo (the majority of which had strictly classical curricula) in contrast to the scuola tecnica and the istituto tecnico (which were not even considered "secondary" but rather "technical" schools by the Casati Law).

Table 3.6. Schools, Students, and Students per Class by Geographic Area, 1861

Type of School	North			Center			South		
	Schools	Students	Students per class	Schools	Students	Students per class	Schools	Students	Students per class
Ginnasi	117	7,926	13.5	43	1,800	8.36	17	1,327	15.61
Licei	40	2,282	19.0	19	523	9.17	14	326	7.76
Scuole tecniche	85	6,211	24.3	44	1,171	8.86	7	123	5.85
Type of School	**Sicily**			**Sardinia**			**Italy**		
	Schools	Students	Students per class	Schools	Students	Students per class	Schools	Students	Students per class
Ginnasi	29	1,095	7.55	12	714	11.9	218	12,862	11.80
Licei	7	120	5.71	2	111	18.5	82	3,362	13.66
Scuole tecniche	18	521	9.65	3	242	26.9	157	8,268	17.55

SOURCE: Elaboration of data taken from G. M. Bertini, *Per la riforma delle scuole medie* (Turin: G. Scioldo, 1889).

building the new nation-state and in giving firm bases to its own hegemony. So great were the difficulties to be overcome in order for this institution to take root in the society of the time that the last thing needed was a dead-end or blind-alley school that would protect the others. If there was a danger, at least at the time the Casati Law was promulgated, it was certainly not that the schools would be "crushed by the mob" (to use Gabelli's expression), but that they would remain half deserted.

The First De-Professionalization of the Technical Institutes

The relative openness of the educational system and especially, as we shall see in the next chapter, the nature and course of the Italian economy, brought about radical change in the condition of secondary and higher education in the course of three decades. The secondary schools, relatively little attended before unification, grew considerably and in time put onto the labor market an increasing number of diplomati. While in the case of the maestri demand was greater than supply for the entire second half of the nineteenth century, there was a surplus supply of youth coming out of the licei over the period 1880–1900. The inadequacy of demand was felt even earlier for youth from the istituti tecnici, causing, in the five years 1871–76, certain small but significant changes in the educational system. Before examining the quantitative evolution of the secondary schools, it is worthwhile to pause a moment on these changes. Examination of the characteristics of the istituti tecnici and of the small reforms of 1871–76 allows us, first, to appreciate the difficulties that the Italian school encountered in taking hold, with regard both to the demand for education and to the opportunities for absorption of the personnel trained by secondary education; second, it allows us to note that the ruling class responded to these difficulties by opening rather than closing the educational system; and third, it shows us, how "advanced" the secondary educational system was in comparison with the socioeconomic conditions of the country.

The regulation of September 1860 putting the Casati Law in force provided that the istituti tecnici articulate themselves in four sections: commerce-industry, agriculture, chemistry, and physics-mathematics (also called mechanics and construction), of which only the last opened access to university studies. The first important thing to observe is that in the first years the chemistry section "remained deserted: which shows either that the country had not understood its utility or that somehow *it was in advance of the needs of the country under the current conditions of industry*."[49]

In October 1865 there was thus a first reordering of the istituti tecnici which brought the number of sections from four to nine with the addition, in part by bifurcation of existing sections, of those for industrial chemistry, mechanics, physical chemistry, precision mechanics, merchant marine, mineralogy-metallurgy, and accounting, "in vain hope," as was written some decades later "of encouraging the rise of various industries, even where they had not begun."[50] And, in fact, many of these sections were never even opened because of the absolute lack of students. According to the statistics for 1868–69, only three of these sections had found even relative success: the commercial, with about 1,300 students, which granted a diploma that helped in obtaining employment in the public administrations; the agricultural, with over 1,400 students, which was attended especially when it started training surveyors who could find work in public enterprises; and, finally, the physics-mathematics section, with its 1,700 students, which attained the greatest success, not — plainly enough — because its diplomati found work easily but because it opened access to higher studies.

From this situation the "little reforms" of 1871 and 1876 were born. The ordinance of 1871 lengthened the course of studies from three to four years and reduced the number of sections to five: physics-mathematics, agriculture, commerce, accounting, and industry. As far as the first was concerned, in the preparatory material of the reform of 1871 one could read: "It serves two classes of students: those who advance to higher studies to become engineers and those who, not advancing, dedicate themselves to the mechanical and chemical industries and form around the engineers a lower order from which the industries draw important services. This second class of persons, who lie midway between the head of the workshop and the engineer, is still few in number in Italy and little sought after because of the general conditions of our industry, whereas it is very much sought after in other nations where industry is quite advanced. Thus it is that, under present conditions, the students of the mechanics and construction section aim to secure the laurea in engineering by advancing in their studies, rather than the diploma of the 'mechanics and construction technician.'"[51] Mindful that the relative success of the physics-mathematics section was not due to a demand for that "class of persons who lie midway between the head of the workshop and the engineer," but rather to the access it opened to higher studies, the reforms of 1871 and 1876 decreed its de-professionalization, sharply reducing the technical-scientific content of its instruction and increasing its emphasis on "general education." This section then became the veritable workhorse of all technical secondary education. "I believe, therefore," wrote Marco Minghetti, "that that which is termed the physics-mathematics section in the Law of 1859 is like the principal trunk of the tree, and that the instruction which is bestowed there must have, yes, a scientific nature and character, but also a general, and, if I may say so, more humane one, insofar as it is the basis of many types of careers."[52] And, in fact, with the Law of 1871 the five sections were all to share the first two years, which were nothing less than the "more humane" first-two-year course of study of the physics-mathematics section.

Thus technical educational, which was born with the dual objective of preparing intermediate cadres and constituting a preparatory school for university studies, had taken its first steps in an economic situation so backward that it succeeded primarily because of the second rather than the first objective. The reforms of 1871 and 1876, which began the de-professionalization of the istituti tecnici, were no less than the legal recognition of this situation. Forty years later, an economist would write, commenting on these reforms:

> Technical education cannot prosper by the will of the legislator where economic development is lacking. One cannot create skilled workmen for the textile industry in a country where there are no workshops in which these workmen may be employed. . . . Once there is a prime substratum and a favorable environment, the technical education that develops in it will become a motive force that brings about, so to speak, geometric growth of the economy: but where the environment is not favorable, where the professional school does not correspond to the real conditions of the country, there it remains barren and deserted; or else it must adapt itself in order to live and must assume a different function than that which the founders had originally assigned to it.[53]

The Development of the Secondary Schools

The data that we have on the number of enrollments in secondary schools in the second half of the last century are not very satisfactory[54] and must, therefore, be used with a certain caution. With all their limitations, however, the data reported in tables 3.7 and 3.8 give us a precise enough idea of the course of primary and secondary education from unification up to the First World War. As may be seen from table 3.7, elementary education, after a sharp bound forward in the first decade, grew at a slower pace in the following period. In spite of the fact that the Law of July 15, 1877 reaffirmed compulsory schooling and that the three laws of July 18, 1878, June 8, 1888, and July 15, 1900 allocated subsidies for the establishment and maintenance of elementary schools to local governments, the number of enrollments in following decades increased very slowly.

Quite different was the development of secondary education. After the difficulties of the first years, enrollments grew constantly at a rather sustained pace. For the ginnasi and the licei, the strongest growth occurred in the twenty-year period 1870-90, while in the following period the number of enrollees remained practically stationary (in the licei) or actually declined (in ginnasi). As for the scuole tecniche, the istituti tecnici, and the scuole normali, the increase in enrollments continued at a rather sustained pace for the entire fifty-year period following the promulgation of the Casati Law (tables 3.7 and 3.8).

The data that we have seen show, therefore, that the Italian educational system, if it did not succeed in creating a sufficient demand for education among the lower social classes, was successful with the ceti medi.

> Owing to a number of causes in part spontaneous and old, in part artificial and new [wrote Aristide Gabelli in 1888], democracy expands day by day with greater speed. Thence comes a multitude of phenomena good and bad, but among others the rising into the professions of an ever-increasing number of youth who have in their families no examples or traditions of study. The son of a grocer wants to be a doctor, that of a carpenter sets off to become a lawyer, that of a shoemaker wants to be an engineer. It is a good thing, if they have the necessary will and the talent. But, unfortunately, in the majority of cases this shifting of social condition represents an additional obstacle for the school. The shoemaker, the grocer, the carpenter, and with these so many others, who have had nothing to do with books, have no appreciation of studies except for their direct and immediate utility. Their concern is academic status, because it opens the door to a profession and provides a living.[55]

But if the shoemaker, grocer, and carpenter of which Gabelli spoke foresaw the possibility of shattering the traditional, hereditary transmission of the professions, if they had hoped for a "shifting of social conditions" for their own sons, for their social ascent, this was possible also because of the particular structure of the Italian educational system, because of its relative openness, and especially because of the existence, next to the classical secondary, of a technical secondary school.

Unfortunately, we have data on the social composition of secondary school students only for 1862. Though these data concern the period when the secondary schools were still not developed, they are sufficient to show the differences between the classical and the technical branches at the secondary level. As may be seen from table 3.9, three years after the promulgation of the Casati Law the

Table 3.7. Enrollments in Elementary and Lower-Secondary Schools, 1862 to 1922

Year	Elementari (1000s)	Ginnasi				Scuole tecniche			
		State	*Semi-Private*	*Private*	*Total*	*State*	*Semi-Private*	*Private*	*Total*
1862–63	1,109	7,543	4,912	10,304	22,759	2,823	3,339	2,669	8,831
1870–71	1,605	8,277	14,475		22,752	5,631	12,742		18,373
1881–82	1,976	13,785	6,417	22,609	42,811	7,510	8,653	8,670	24,833
1891–92	2,454	25,380	8,360	23,785	57,525	21,411	8,636	4,197	34,244
1901–02	2,733	24,081	7,208	17,000*	48,289	27,825	11,049	6,000*	44,876
1912–13	3,387	34,899	5,032	9,853	49,784	74,692	16,086	9,199	100,147
1922–23	4,167	53,935	5,988	15,574	75,497	109,058	17,962	14,209	141,299

*Estimated data.

SOURCES: For the elementary schools: ISTAT, *Sommario di statistiche storiche italiane* (Rome, 1958); for the secondary schools up to 1880: Ministry of Agriculture, Industry and Commerce, Director General of Statistics, *Statistica dell'istruzione per l'anno scolastico 1880–81* (Rome, 1883); for the remaining years: ISTAT, *Annuario statistico italiano.* The choice of years was imposed by the availability of data (in many cases, those concerning the private schools are lacking).

Table 3.8. Enrollments in Upper-Secondary Schools, 1862 to 1922

Year	*Licei*				*Istituti tecnici*				*Scuole normali*			
	State	*Semi-Private*	*Private*	*Total*	*State*	*Semi-Private*	*Private*	*Total*	*State*	*Semi-Private*	*Private*	*Total*
1862–63	3,339	365	908	4,672	—	—	—	1,787	—	—	—	4,310
1870–71	3,645	2,113		5,758	—	—	—	1,797	—	—	—	6,130
1881–82	6,623	1,167	4,600	12,390	5,555	1,684	619	7,858	5,969	2,180	1,267	9,416
1891–92	9,371	1,246	5,096	15,713	7,840	1,114	438	9,392	14,229	1,877	1,923	18,029
1901–02	10,983	1,955	3,000	15,938	8,525	1,479	300	10,304	15,680	3,585	1,108	20,373
1912–13	12,366	1,366	1,404	15,136	20,208	2,561	993	23,762	40,923	5,874	3,536	50,333
1922–23	17,186	1,850	1,838	20,874	32,689	4,010	3,300	39,999	48,051	6,781	4,873	59,705

SOURCE: See table 3.7.

overwhelming majority of secondary school students were sons of "landowners." Nevertheless, the percentage of youth coming from these families varied according to the type of school and geographic area, and reached its highest point in the licei and lowest in the scuole tecniche (particularly in those of central and northern Italy). The latter schools, on the other hand, had a higher percentage of children of merchants and of "non-owners."

From the start, therefore, it was toward the scuola tecnica that the ceti medi: oriented their children. Entering this school, in fact, there was always the possibility, at least on paper, that they might actually reach the university, besides studying a year less than those who followed the classical branch, and that they might become teachers of mathematics or engineering. But even if they abandoned their studies before the university, they would find themselves in any case with "an occupation in hand" (an occupation socially more elevated than the father's) and a "piece of paper" in the pocket.[56]

From the point of view of those who wanted to send their children in that direction, technical education had a great advantage over classical: it had as Gabelli said, a "market value." Classical studies

> lack a direct and immediate applicability at a time when most people seek the useful; they are necessarily intent on profit and aim to acquire certain aptitudes and abilities in order to put them to use and to obtain their yield. Every day, the people go to schools in greater numbers; but on what condition? To find there what they need: not only schools that lead to the minor professions without having to pass through the long and costly apprenticeship of classical learning, but also schools of all forms, varied, numerous, and ever more appropriate to the variety and multiplicity of practical intents, ever more applied, more directly profitable. And not only such, but schools from which it is possible to leave after a brief interval with something relatively complete and finished in one's head, sufficient to open the way to an occupation or position of some sort; something, in other words, with a market value.[57]

From the standpoint of the social system and its stability, the superiority of technical education consisted in the fact that classical education, lacking "a direct applicability," could more easily create "misfits," that is, individuals who, if they did not succeed in continuing their studies to the end, became "full of contempt for material occupations but still inept at any other kind, removed from any precise goal and therefore unhappy all their lives." The result was that "sooner or later need creates pressures, and soon the throng is thrusting itself this way and that, pushing and shoving; hence that troubled crowd which

Table 3.9. Social Composition of Enrollments in Secondary Schools by Geographic Area, 1862–63

Social	*Ginnasi*				*Licei*				*Scuole tecniche*			
Condition	*North*	*Center*	*South*	*Italy*	*North*	*Center*	*South*	*Italy*	*North*	*Center*	*South*	*Italy*
Land-owners	69	51	69	65	78	69	75	76	44	36	52	44
Merchants	21	26	13	20	14	19	15	15	34	30	21	31
Non-owners	10	23	18	15	8	12	10	9	22	34	27	25
Total	100	100	100	100	100	100	100	100	100	100	100	100
(N)	(6,391)	(2,959)	(3,335)	(12,685)	(1,659)	(725)	(749)	(3,133)	(5,119)	(1,306)	(977)	(7,402)

SOURCE: Elaboration of data taken from *Annuario dell'Istruzione Pubblica del Regno d'Italia pel 1865–66* (Florence, 1886).

knocks on every door and is not less of a social peril than that of the unemployed workers for which it prepares instigators or leaders."[58]

Therefore, in order to "take off" in so difficult a situation, "to attract to itself, by a practical utility obvious to all, the inert material that rose from below, to rough it out, and to return it to society transformed,"[59] the new educational system, to which the Italian ruling class had assigned functions of such importance to the achievement of its political goals, was established without many overt mechanisms of internal differentiation, without dumping schools, so as to give all those who approached it the illusion of its being the new and safest channel of social mobility. The consequence was that it continued to have little success among the lower social classes, while it began to succeed too well with the ceti medi. An educational system was formed, that is, in which those who entered were few and relatively many of these remained to the end of their studies: a sort of creature with an oversized head and trunk and two incredibly small feet.

CHAPTER FOUR

Education, Industrialization, and Economic Dualism

To explain the course of secondary and higher education in Italy, I have so far analyzed as the independent variable the internal structure of the educational system, attempting to show, in contrast to the image which has traditionally been offered, that it was relatively open and in many ways more advanced than the socioeconomic conditions of the country. I have tried, in addition, to interpret these characteristics of the Italian school by considering the complex relationship between the program of educational policy of the ruling class and the difficulties encountered in its realization. But the internal structure of the Italian educational system is neither the only nor the most important variable to consider in explaining the development of secondary and higher education in the period under consideration. As Minister of Public Education Gallo observed, speaking of the phenomenon of intellectual unemployment, "one who attributes such a sorry state of affairs to the school reasons like those who, for example, attributed the evil of beggary to the institutions of social security and employment for the poor."[1]

In effect, to understand fully the "peculiar circumstances" of Italy's educational system, denounced already in 1866 by Cesare Correnti and forty years later by Ernesto Nathan, one must first of all refer to the nature and to the pattern of Italian economic development. But to succeed in explaining these "peculiar circumstances," it is necessary to free oneself from the prevalent idea that between economic development and the course of enrollments there is always and only a positive relationship.[2] The hypothesis of a direct relationship between economy and education may be adequate at the level of primary education, though it requires further qualification. But it is of no use whatever as far as secondary and higher education are concerned. At this level, in fact, the information we possess, however unsatisfactory, would show that in the period which interests us, either there is no relationship between economy and education or there is actually an inverse one.

Formulated in a loose and simplified way, the hypothesis with which I propose to interpret the existing information and which I will use in this chapter is the following: the expansion of secondary and higher education that occurred in Italy in the second half of the last century was due not to the growth but to the backwardness of the economy, not to the improvement but to the increasing precariousness of the socioeconomic situation of some classes, not to the rise in the demand for qualified labor at the middle and lower levels but to the difficulties of employment encountered by the labor force. What I shall try to show is that, if the shoemaker, the grocer, and the carpenter of which Gabelli spoke sent their children to scuole and istituti tecnici with increasing frequency, hoping that they might become engineers or at least *impiegati*,* if the ginnasio and the liceo were invaded by youth from families of the large and medium landowners in an incessant search for a laurea in medicine or jurisprudence, this was due to the backwardness of the Italian economic system and to the absence of a broad and prosperous productive middle class, which made the school, right from the start, the only channel of social mobility.

The hypothesis of an inverse relationship between economy and education was argued even by some of the men responsible for Italy's educational policy. These, even if only partially and in a confused manner, intuited that backwardness and underdevelopment had to be the most important sources of the expansion of secondary and higher education. In the report mentioned earlier, Minister of Public Education Gallo observed that the growth of education "is to be imputed instead to the economic conditions of the country, the imbalance among the various provinces in terms of levels of prosperity; to the obstacles that here and there impede the natural development of labor and of industry, by the weakness of capital, by the clash of competition, and by the crisis that is everywhere produced."[3] Some years before, in the introductory report to the Bill of Law on University Autonomy, Minister of Public Education Baccelli wrote:

> The statistics on Italian university students have shown in recent years an excessive rise in their numbers. They have reached the point of nearly twenty-one

**Impiegato:* salaried employee or, roughly, "white-collar worker" involving the more or less routinized "mental" labor, often office work, pertaining to the "new" middle class.

> thousand, equal to or even a little higher than that of German university students, even though the population of the Italian Kingdom is only a little more than three-fifths that of the German Empire. Despite the evident difference of proportion, even there many are concerned about the excessive increase of professionals, which is no longer in relation to the real needs of the nation. This phenomenon manifests itself all the more seriously in Italy and demonstrates the truth of that *theory which attributes it to the abasement of economic conditions,* by which the young, avoiding industry and agriculture, prefer the apparently more secure careers of clerks and professionals.[4]

Naturally, the interpretive hypothesis that I have proposed must be articulated and translated into terms capable of being put to the test. First, with regard to the dependent variable: the growth of schooling. On this subject, as has already been said, a distinction must be made according to the level of the educational system – primary, secondary, or higher. Second, with regard to the independent variable: the pattern of Italian economic development, which, as is well known, presents two basic characteristics. The first is the considerable delay with which the modern process of economic development began in Italy in comparison with other European countries. The second is the dualistic nature of this process, which took place exclusively in a few regions of northern Italy and thereby aggravated all the more, by the end of its first phase, that North-South difference already manifest at the time of unification.

Keeping in mind the basic characteristics of the Italian pattern of economic development, the relationship between economy and education may be examined in time and space. That is, one may hypothesize that there are significant variations: 1) in the course of education in correspondence with the course of the economic cycle; 2) in the rates of enrollment* according to the level of development reached by the various geographic areas; and that these variations might be different according to the level of the educational system considered.

Verification of the interpretive scheme of the economy-education relationship that I have proposed encounters significant difficulties, due substantially to the scarcity of relevant information. Not only, in fact, is it practically impossible to quantify the intervening variables, especially per capita income and the demand for qualified labor at various levels (from the elementary school certificate, which was then no small thing, up to the diploma of the upper-secondary schools), but there are also large gaps in the data on education. Even

*"Rate of enrollment": the number of enrollments at a particular level of the educational system divided by the population in that relevant age group.

with all these limitations, which must be kept in mind in reading what follows, it seems to me that it is possible to use the proposed scheme in the interpretation of the available data.

The Relationship Between Economy and Education Over Time

An examination of the relationship between economic and educational development is almost automatically limited to the period from 1881 to the outbreak of the First World War. While data and analyses on the twenty-year period 1860–80 are still rather scant, there is considerable agreement in the historical-economic literature on the course of the Italian economy for the following thirty years and on its periodization into three phases. The first, from 1881 to 1888, is characterized not only by the start of the agrarian crisis, but also by a moderate growth of industrial activity; the second, from 1888 to 1896, is marked by a general crisis of the economy which reaches its most acute phase in 1893–94; and the third, from 1896 to 1913, witnesses a very rapid growth (the so-called great leap) during which the foundations of modern industry were laid.[5]

Primary Education

In a recent study, Giovanni Vigo has confronted the problem of the relationship between the economy and primary education in Italy over the period 1870–1910.[6] Comparing the growth index of national income with the growth index of school enrollment, Vigo has pointed out that "two contrasting tendencies" presented themselves in this period. While, in fact, in the twenty-five-year period 1871–95 there was a relatively marked growth of schooling and a modest increase in income, in the fifteen-year period 1896 – 1910 there was a relatively strong increase in income and a rather modest expansion of education.

If, however, we restrict the analysis of growth in these two areas to a more limited period of time than that examined by Vigo (namely, for reasons already stressed, to the thirty-year period, 1881–1913), we see somewhat different results. As may be observed from table 4.1, there was a stronger rise in elementary education in the two phases of economic development (the first and the third) and a weaker one in the phase of crisis (the second). Therefore, at least for the period 1881–1913, it can be said that the course of primary education shows some significant variations that correspond to the course of

Table 4.1. Enrollments in Elementary Schools, Percentages of the Population 5–15 Years of Age, and Average Annual Increases

Year	*Enrollments (in thousands)*	*% of Inhabitants Age 5–15*	*Period*	*Increases*	
				Enrollments	*% Inhabitants Age 5–15*
	(a)	(b)		(a)	(b)
1881	1,976	34.6			
1888	2,326	37.6	1881–88	2.5	1.2
1896	2,564	38.2	1888–96	1.3	0.2
1913	3,484	46.9	1896–1913	2.1	1.3

SOURCE: For this table and for subsequent tables and figures in this chapter where source indication is omitted, see *A Note on the Data Used* at the end of the chapter.

the economic cycle and also that between these two phenomena there is a direct relationship.

But if it is true that in the period considered there is a direct relationship between the course of the economy and that of education, we must also recognize that the growth rate of elementary education in the two phases of economic expansion, though clearly higher than that of the crisis phase, remains throughout somewhat restrained and lower than we would expect, knowing on the one hand what profound changes the Italian economy had undergone in this period and, on the other, how low the rate of enrollment still was. How can this fact be explained?

Although in many ways a critical problem, the question of the relationship between the course of the demand for labor (qualified or not) and the course of education in the take-off phase of industrialization has been much neglected, and only in recent years has it received growing attention on the part of English social historians. A large part of the efforts of these scholars has been concentrated on reconstructing, over the period of the industrial revolution, the course of the dependent variable, education and particularly elementary education. Examining the data gathered on a sample (certainly not representative) of English urban and rural centers, Lawrence Stone has sought to show that the rate of illiteracy constantly declined over the period 1760–1835, even if the greatest advances were registered not in urban but in rural communities.[7] Notwithstanding these data, a series of investigations on the course of primary education in Lancashire, the central area of the industrial revolution, allows one to say that industrialization acted more as a restraint than as a stimulus to the process of bringing literacy to the English population.[8] On the basis of numerous indicators, Michael Sanderson has shown, in fact, that Lancashire, after a marked growth in the first half of the eighteenth century, experienced a slowdown in its primary education over the following decade and an actual decline in the period 1790–1820. There are many intervening variables that account for the negative influence exercised by the English industrial revolution on the advance of literacy: a reduction in the level of wages of textile workers that occurred after 1790, the increased geographic mobility of huge masses of the population, the weakening of the system of family authority and the consequent phenomenon of youth vagabondage. All the same, the most important variable was that the factory system created "a whole range of new occupations which required even less literacy and education than the old ones,"[9] and utilized increasing quotas of female and child labor.

Even with all the differences between England at the end of the eighteenth century and Italy a century later, this interpretive scheme is applicable as well to the Italian situation. It is true that some scholars have argued that "one of the most serious limiting factors of Italian industrialization in this period is shown to be the scarce availability of adequately qualified manpower, especially in the decisive industrial machine sector,"[10] but it seems to me that, however scanty, the relevant information that we possess does not vidicate this assertion. Italian industry too was born and grew through the exploitation of huge quotas of child and female labor.[11] The massive employment of this labor force was due not only to its low cost and to that "Jacobin liberty of labor that the State assured to our industries" spoken of by Rodolfo Morandi,[12] but was made possible also by the fact that the development of industry created, in addition to a certain number of working-class functions at a high level of specialization, a large quantity of new work positions that required no type of qualification whatever. To "run after a winder or tie a thread" in the processing of silk, the "small stature and manual dexterity" of little girls was incomparably more important than their having learned to read and write.[13] The studies that we possess on the composition of the Italian working class in the period of its formation leave us no doubts in this regard.[14]

The extensive employment of female and child labor, the very rapid rate of aging and replacement of the working class, the persistent migratory flow from the countryside toward the cities, and, finally, the predominance of small- and medium-sized enterprises at a low level of mechanization are all clear indicators of the low level of qualification required by the new work positions created by industry. This level varied considerably also according to sector, and it was certainly much higher in the machine and metalworking industry than in the textile industry.[15] But, on the whole, it can be said that industrial development produced a proletariat which, along with limited nuclei of craft-trained workers, presented a large mass of absolutely unqualified workers.

Thus industrialization favored, on the one hand, the birth and development of professional schools in response to the new demand for highly skilled workers;[16] but by creating a large quantity of work positions that required no qualifications and by employing child labor, it hindered, on the other hand, the development of elementary education. Certainly the agricultural labor of children also had a profound effect on school attendance, the rhythm of which was punctuated in many areas of the country by work in the fields. Even in 1895 one could read in an official report: "In the administrative district of Susa, school attendance is greatest in the winter; it is reduced to the least in other seasons, when rural jobs commence. An inspector recounts: 'I visited schools which in the summer had only one student, while in the winter they numbered over fifty.'" But if agricultural labor restricted school attendance to the winter months, industrial work rendered it totally impossible. "The inspectors of Bergamo, Lecco, and Como" reads the same report, "note how unexceptional is the case that children, and especially the little girls, having permission cards granted by the mayor, leave school before having taken the elementary leaving exams in order to enter the factories – primarily spinning mills."[17]

The most important data for testing the interpretive scheme used by the English social historians are, however, those regarding education. If we analyze accurately the course of enrollments in Italy for the period under consideration, we see that the picture presenting itself is rather different than the one we would expect using the traditional interpretive schemes. Table 4.2 reports the percentage of enrollments in elementary schools in the age bracket 6 – 14, broken down by sex and region, from 1881 to 1921. At first inspection, these data reveal well-known facts: that both at the beginning and at the end of the period considered there is a direct relationship between the level of economic development of the regions and their rate of enrollment and that this relationship holds for both males and females. But, if we distinguish between the regions of the Northwest (Piedmont, Lombardy, and Liguria) and the others, that is, between areas affected and not affected by the process of industrialization, we see that the course of elementary education is somewhat different. While, in fact, in the latter areas there was a constant increase in the enrollment rate, in the regions that were industrializing (above all in Piedmont and Lombardy), the percentage of enrollments in elementary schools grew very slowly or actually fell in the period 1901–7.[18]

The data that we have seen, therefore, show that the growth rate of elementary education in the two phases of economic expansion, however clearly greater than that of the crisis phase, was overall rather restrained. In effect, as far as elementary education is concerned, industrialization put in motion two counteracting processes. On the one hand, it produced a rise in per capita income and therefore included a growing number of families to send their children to school. But on the other hand, similarly to what had occurred a hundred years earlier in England, it created a large number of positions that required no qualification, permitted a massive utilization of child labor, and therefore checked the growth of elementary education. Nor was it enough, evidently, to attenuate the effects of this second process that some industrialists realized the importance of elementary education for socializing the nascent working class to subordination – or in the words of the industrialist Pietro Gavazzi of Como, for immunizing "the ignorant working class" from the danger of being "easily persuaded by persons without faith who preach all the virtues but remove from them the indispensable religious faith; and having forgotten the comforts that can be drawn from it, of receiving fanatically everything these charlatans are selling. Hence hatred for masters, known little or not at all, against whose comfortable and joyful life one compares with rancor one's own hardships and suffering."[19] In the conflict between the exigencies of the short and the long term, between interests that led to the utilization of an illiterate work force and those that counseled its instruction and political socialization (by means of the kingdom's elementary schools) prior to entry into the new regimen of the factory, the Italian industrialists preferred by far the former.

Secondary Education

While the hypothesis of a direct relationship between economy and education is shown to be substantially valid for the elementary schools (allowing for the stipulations mentioned above), it is of no use whatever for the secondary schools. "At the doors of the university," wrote Arangio-Ruiz in 1902, "the misfits have already been created: the university doesn't make them, it acknowledges them: the ginnasio produces them, the liceo baptizes them, the university confirms them, and society judges and dispatches them." If the secondary schools expanded and produced those "misfits" that the university then "con-

Table 4.2. Students Enrolled in Elementary Schools in Some School Years by Sex and Region per 100 Inhabitants, 6–14 Years of Age

Region	*1881–82*	*1901–2*	*1907–8*	*1921–22*
		Males		
Piedmont	71.0	74.4	71.2	73.0
Liguria	57.8	64.9	72.7	69.2
Lombardy	64.9	66.9	65.5	72.0
Veneto	61.6	64.5	61.2	78,0
Emilia-Romagna	50.0	58.4	68.2	74.0
Marche	36.0	43.8	51.5	67.7
Tuscany	35.5	46.4	53.3	66.7
Umbria	39.0	46.7	53.6	69.0
Latium	48.5	52.5	59.6	58.7
Abruzzi and Molise	38.1	39.7	47.3	61.2
Campania	38.3	39.2	40.3	48.2
Puglia	24.3	32.1	39.8	48.2
Basilicata	30.3	32.5	36.6	49.6
Calabria	29.2	28.5	35.1	30.1
Sicily	24.7	33.1	43.1	44.1
Sardinia	37.6	37.9	45.7	54.4
Italy	46.3	50.7	54.8	59.4
		Females		
Piedmont	68.0	71.3	68.8	70.6
Liguria	56.3	62.8	71.2	67.6
Lombardy	63.0	64.3	63.3	70.5
Veneto	51.9	56.9	54.2	69.6
Emilia-Romagna	46.6	53.7	63.6	68.6
Marche	31.5	35.6	44.7	63.0
Tuscany	32.0	43.6	49.5	61.4
Umbria	33.3	39.3	45.9	62.0
Latium	54.2	53.2	58.4	56.3
Abruzzi and Molise	31.0	32.5	40.6	53.8
Campania	36.5	33.7	35.6	43.3
Puglia	25.4	32.2	38.8	46.0
Basilicata	24.0	25.9	31.0	44.9
Calabria	21.0	20.3	27.1	24.5
Sicily	23.4	34.2	44.3	43.7
Sardinia	31.8	35.9	44.3	53.0
Italy	43.1	47.3	51.5	55.8

SOURCE: F. Noble, "Istruzione scolastica," in ISTAT, *Sviluppo della popolazione italiana dal 1861 al 1961,* vol. 17 of *Annali di statistica* (Rome, 1965).

firmed," it was certainly not, according to Arangio-Ruiz, because of economic development and the rise in per capita income. On the contrary, the "rise of the student body" was, in his own view, caused by the "social question," namely the crisis of the middle to upper classes and the difficulties that the young coming from these classes encountered in finding occupations "suitable" to their social origins and their expectations.

> Rural and urban property, capital, has been depreciating to the point that it now yields little interest. Even the wealthy – but prolific – families are not able, because of rising costs and falling income, to increase their property which, divided among many children, ceases to be wealth and becomes poverty. The families that descend from proprietors or professionals can hardly be expected to adapt to the situation by sending their sons off to become shoemakers or tailors, because in these fields as well the positions are already taken. Many try the way of higher studies, rather than halting at the lower levels, because they find nothing better. Having obtained the laurea, and convinced of thereby finding things less difficult, they set off to find a more lucrative and promising living.[20]

It is certainly not the case that this analysis was shared by the majority of scholars of the problems of education at the time. Nevertheless, what I have reported was not an isolated view. According to Giuseppe Tarozzi, the expansion of secondary and higher education was definitely not a result of economic growth. It was his view that "the capital holdings of a large part of the bourgeoisie" were revealed over time to be "insufficient to fulfill their purpose," namely that of assuring their possessors a relative comfort, that of being transmitted to their sons "as an income with which to live and to speculate," and finally of being partly assigned as dowries to their daughters so as to "maintain them in a social position at least equal to that into which they were born." In this situation, "for the sons, professional income became an absolute necessity...and the dowry of daughters became increasingly uncommon because decreasingly sufficient for growing needs. This had to and did produce (along with other effects) an extraordinary crowding into the so-called liberal professions and into university studies."[21]

The limited nature of the information that we possess makes the task of testing this hypothesis very difficult. Nevertheless, even with all necessary caution, an analysis of the growth over time of secondary school enrollments shows its essential soundness, at least for some types of schools.[22]

Let us consider first the lower-secondary schools: the scuola tecnica and the ginnasio (tables 4.3 and 4.4). On the basis of the average yearly increase in

Table 4.3. Enrollments in the Scuola Tecnica and in the Ginnasio, 1881–1913

Year	*Enrollments*		*Per 1,000 Inhabitants Age 15–20*	
	Scuola tecnica	*Ginnasio*	*Scuola tecnica*	*Ginnasio*
	(a)	(b)	(c)	(d)
1881	24,833	42,811	9.42	16.25
1888	30,836	51,286	11.01	18.32
1895*	37,305	59,578	12.86	20.54
1913	108,044	53,163	33.42	16.44

*1895 was taken because for 1896 there are no data on enrollments in the private schools.

Table 4.4. Average Annual Percentage Increase of Enrollments in the Scuola Tecnica and the Ginnasio

Period	*Enrollments*		*Per 1,000 Inhabitants Age 15–20*	
	Scuola tecnica	*Ginnasio*	*Scuola tecnica*	*Ginnasio*
	(a)	(b)	(c)	(d)
1881–88	3.4	2.8	2.4	1.8
1888–95	2.9	2.3	2.4	1.7
1895–1913	10.5	−0.6	8.9	−1.1

school enrollment (table 4.4, columns c and d), we see that, both for the ginnasio and the scuola tecnica, the values are similar in the first and the second phases. However in the third phase, that of the "great leap," the course of enrollment in the two lower-secondary schools is completely different: there is a very strong increase in enrollments in the scuola tecnica and a clear drop in those of the ginnasio. Therefore, while the course of technical education as offered by the scuola tecnica seems to have been affected positively by economic growth, that of the classical instruction offered by the ginnasio seems to have been negatively affected.

Much clearer are the data concerning the two upper-secondary schools: the liceo and the istituto tecnico (tables 4.5 and 4.6). Here too, examining the average yearly increase in school enrollment (table 4.6, columns c and d), we note some differences between the course of technical education and that of classical, in that in the third phase there occurs a relatively strong expansion of the former and a contraction of the latter. Still, considering all three phases, we notice that, both for the istituto tecnico and for the liceo, the rate of average yearly increase is stronger in the crisis phase (the second) than in the phases of economic expansion (the first and the third).

Table 4.5. Enrollments in the Istituto Tecnico and the Liceo, 1881–1913

Year	*Enrollments*		*Per 1,000 Inhabitants Age 15–20 years*	
	Istituto tecnico	*Liceo*	*Istituto tecnico*	*Liceo*
	(a)	(b)	(c)	(d)
1881	7,858	12,390	2.98	4.70
1888	6,538	13,846	2.34	4.94
1895	10,274	17,689	3.54	6.10
1913	25,189	14,670	7.79	4.54

Table 4.6. Average Annual Percentage Increase of Enrollments in the Istituto Tecnico and the Liceo

Period	*Enrollments*		*Per 1,000 Inhabitants Age 15–20*	
	Istituto tecnico	*Liceo*	*Istituto tecnico*	*Liceo*
	(a)	(b)	(c)	(d)
1881–88	−2.4	1.7	−3.1	0.7
1888–95	8.2	3.9	7.3	3.4
1895–1913	8.0	−1.1	6.7	−1.4

In conclusion, of the four types of secondary school examined, there is one, the scuola tecnica, whose rate of enrollment shows a direct relation to the course of the economy, while the other three show an inverse relation. This inverse relationship is very distinct in the case of the liceo, but it is to be found also for the ginnasio and even for the istituto tecnico. Therefore, the hypothesis that the principal cause of the expansion of secondary education was the backwardness and not the growth of the economy would hold not only for classical studies but also, although in lesser measure, for the istituti tecnici.

It is, in my view, a mistake to interpret the increase in enrollments at the istituti tecnici simply as a consequence of the enhanced demand for diplomati produced by industrialization.[23] The data that we have would instead lead us to think that this increase was at least in part due to the difficulties of graduates of the scuola tecnica in finding employment and to the consequent need to continue studies. Our data do not, unfortunately, allow calculation of the rate of passage from the scuola tecnica to the istituto tecnico. Nevertheless, I have calculated the rate IT/ST, namely the percentage produced by dividing enroll-

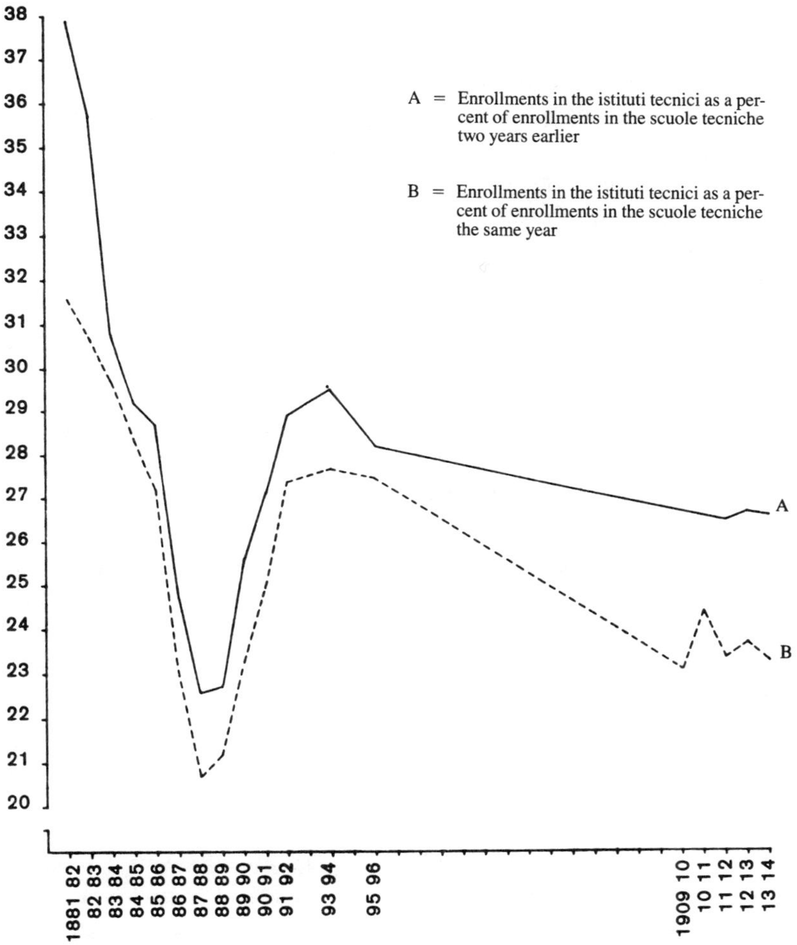

Figure 4.1. Enrollments in the istituti tecnici as a percent of enrollments in the scuole tecniche from 1888 to 1913.

ments in the istituti tecnici by the enrollments in the scuole tecniche for the same year (curve B in figure 4.1) and for two years earlier (curve A).[24] As may be seen, these two curves have a substantially analogous course and one exactly opposite to that of the economy: falling in the first phase of expansion, rising in the second phase of crisis, and again falling in the third phase of expansion.

There is only one way, it seems to me, to interpret this course of the IT/ST rate. In the phases of economic expansion demand for youth who have completed the scuola tecnica increases, and consequently the percentage of those who continue studies in the istituti tecnici decreases. In the periods of depression, on the other hand, demand contracts, and consequently the number of those who, lacking anything better, continue their studies increases.

A proof of the validity of this interpretation is provided us, moreover, by the educational policy carried out in these years by the ruling class. For the purpose of "reducing the truly extraordinary and superabundant number of aspirants to administrative jobs" coming from the scuole tecniche, it was decided, with Royal Decree no. 488, to restructure a certain number of these schools.[25] With the conviction that training "youth truly suited for commercial firms and for agricultural and manufacturing industries" would facilitate their absorption by the labor market, the technical-professional character of the curriculum was accentuated, and graduates of the reformed or "re-professionalized" scuole tecniche were required to take a supplementary examination in order to enter the istituti tecnici. Nevertheless, such a conviction was shown once again to be entirely without foundation. Re-professionalization of the curriculum actually affected very few scuole tecniche, and even in these few, students and teachers demanded and obtained entrance to the istituto without a supplementary examination. "Which means," observed Salvemini and Galletti, "that the students do not find in the school an institution that assures them immediate employment in industry, and they aim, therefore, to keep open the supply lines to the Istituto."[26]

Higher Education

In the case of the university as well, it is quite difficult, starting from the hypothesis of a direct relationship between economy and education, to reach an understanding of what happened in the period that interests us. It is true, in fact, as may be seen from table 4.7, that the increase of university students in the first phase is greater than that in the second. Nevertheless, it must be noted that the sharp increase for the eight years 1881–88 is no more than a result of the very strong growth of the licei that characterized the preceding decade.[27]

On the other hand, if we analyze the course of enrollments in the two succeeding phases, we notice that it is entirely opposite to what we would expect on the basis of the hypothesis of a direct relationship of economy to education. As may be seen from figure 4.2, while in the phase of economic crisis there is a steady climb of the curve, in the seventeen years of the "great leap" the number of enrollments remains almost stationary. What happened, then? Simply this: that, as Carlo Francesco Ferraris wrote:

Table 4.7. University Students, Students per 1,000 Inhabitants from 20–25 Years of Age and Average Annual Increases

Year	*Enrollments*	*Per 1,000 Inhabitants Age 20–25*	*Period*	*Increases*	
				Enrollments	*Per 1,000 Inhabitants Age 20 to 25*
	(a)	(b)		(a)	(b)
1881	12,481	5.10			
1888	17,584	6.95	1881–88	5.9	5.2
1896	24,318	9.39	1888–96	4.8	4.4
1913	28,026	9.62	1896–1913	0.9	0.1

> The professions of a more strictly economic nature, directly inclined, that is, to the production of wealth, exercised a stronger attraction by offering higher and quicker gains than many of the so-called liberal professions. . . . Thus many, rather than procure those academic qualifications for which the pecuniary income came later and was less outstanding, preferred to become agriculturalists, industrialists, and businessmen. To the more intense activity of industry and commerce was dedicated a larger troop of active forces who deserted some of the higher studies in order to attend to others of a professional economic nature and to enter into business directly after the intellectual preparation that it required.[28]

All this does not mean, necessarily, that in the third phase the difficulties of employment for youth coming out of the secondary schools had completely disappeared. I know of no data that would illustrate this point, but some facts suggest that these difficulties persisted, although certainly to a lesser degree, even during the "great leap." Figure 4.2 indicates that after decreasing in the preceding phase, the percentage of enrollments in engineering increased sharply, from 10 percent at the beginning of the century to 22 percent in 1913. This important change in the composition of the student body was certainly due to the increase in the demand for engineers that occurred during the period of industrialization. However, one must not attribute the increase of enrollments in engineering solely to the demand for laureati, because, as we have seen, intellectual unemployment persisted even for engineers for many years after the start of industrialization.

It is then probably more precise to say that this change was a consequence of the analogous one that occurred in the composition of the flow of diplomati. In the third phase there was, in fact, a decrease in the diplomati produced by the licei and a sharp increase in those from the istituti tecnici. It was probably just this occurrence that put in motion, and brought to completion, that process of de-professionalization of the upper-secondary schools initiated three decades

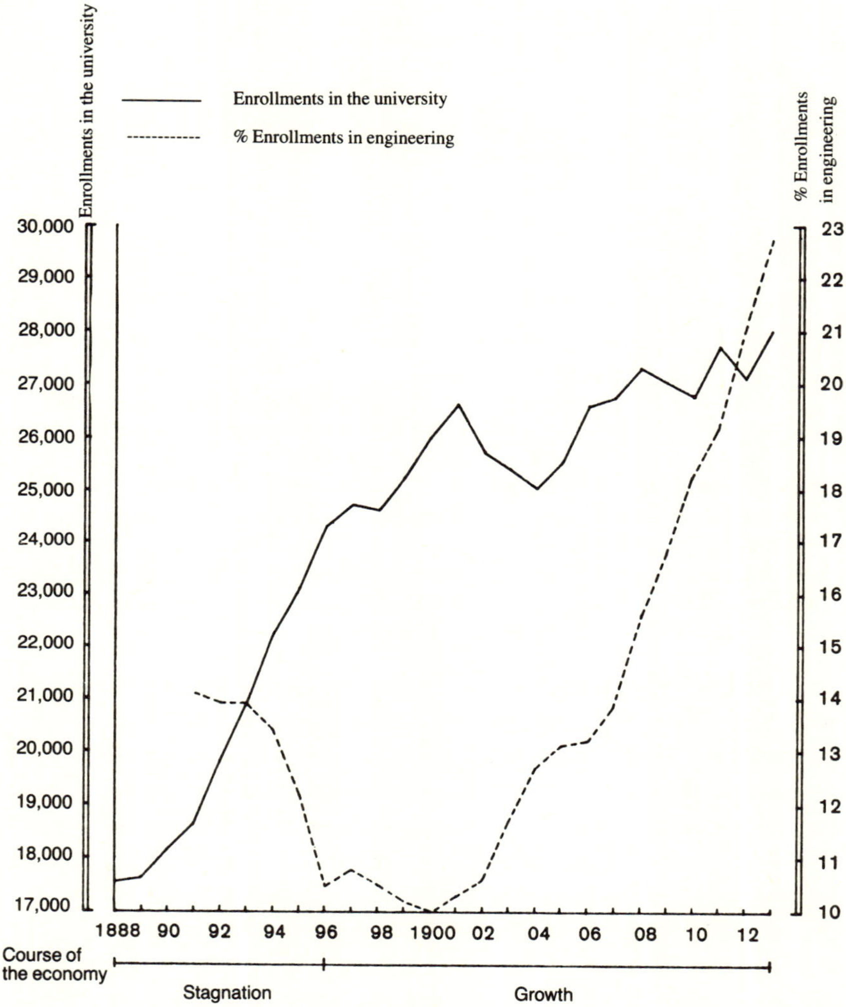

Figure 4.2. University enrollments and percentage of enrollments in engineering from 1888 to 1913.

earlier. That is, the pressures of diplomati to force an opening in the "supply lines" (to use Salvemini's expression) eventually broke down many of the protective barriers of the university. The diplomati of the industrial section came to be admitted to the faculties of business, agriculture, and pharmacy. The diplomati of the agricultural, land-surveying, accounting, and commercial sections obtained access, in addition to these three faculties, also to veterinary science. Finally, those coming out of the physics-mathematics section were able to pass directly after the first two years of science to the third year of philosophy.[29] The completion of the process of de-professionalization of the upper-secondary schools produced by the strong pressures of diplomati to gain entrance to the university (so strong that, for the first time, the temple of the *Humanae litterae* was opened to them) would lead us to believe that the difficulties of employment persisted, though to a reduced extent, even in the third phase. But, as I have said, with the information at our disposal, this remains pure conjecture.

What is clear and worthy of emphasis, on the other hand, is that in the "great leap" phase of the economy the growth of higher education was halted completely. The importance of this fact may be still better understood by comparison with the situation in other countries. It has already been recalled in chapter 2 that over the decade 1881–91 Italy was, among the six European countries considered, one of those with the highest rate of university students to population. As may be seen from table 4.8, in 1901 the situation had not changed in this regard. By its rate of university students, Italy was in second place, after Germany and before Belgium, France, Holland, and Switzerland. On the other hand, the situation changed radically in the following period. In only twelve years, Italy passed from second to next-to-last place among the countries considered. But in order for Italy to lose its preeminence in the relative number of university students, it had to accomplish its "industrial revolution," which coincided with that long period of rapid development which extended from the very end of the century to the outbreak of the First World War. Is this contrast by itself not enough to show that the expansion of higher education which took place in Italy before the "great leap" was none other than the outcome of its economic backwardness?

The data we have seen, therefore, show that Italy's situation was in many respects similar to that of several other European countries in the first half of the nineteenth century. In this period intellectual unemployment also struck France and Germany, although it spared England. This was not due, however, so much to existing differences in demand as to those in the supply of university graduates, as is shown by the fact that the rate of university students to population was higher in the former two countries than in the third.[30] Since it was England that was the most developed economically, it seems clear that the rush toward education that occurred in France and Germany was due above all to the shortage of professional outlets for youth of the middle and upper social

Table 4.8. University Enrollments per 100,000 Inhabitants in Selected Countries, 1901 and 1913

	1901	*1913**
Italy	81	80
Germany	90	121
Belgium	79	104
France	72	126+
Holland	58	78
Sweden	53	90

*The data on education are for the academic year 1913–14; those for population, 1911.
+Includes foreign students enrolled in French universities; the number would be 108 if these students were excluded.

SOURCE: Elaboration of data taken from: M. C. Kaser, "Education and Economic Progress: Experience in Industrialized Market Economies"; V. Castrilli, "L'affollamento universitario in Europa," in *Studi in onore di M. Barillari* (Bari: Cressati, 1937).

classes.[31] More precisely, one can say that the fundamental characteristic of these two countries, like that of Italy in the second half to the nineteenth century, was that "the growth of the absolute bureaucratic state preceded that of large-scale industry. The state's need for an educated class encouraged professionalism, while the economic basis of the country did not provide extensive economic opportunity for the trained and the ambitious."[32]

The Relationship Between Economy and Education by Geographic Area

The second basic element of the pattern of Italian economic development was its dualistic nature, the progressive accentuation of the North-South difference and of the subordinate position of the *Mezzogiorno*, or in short: the *questione meridionale.** It remains to be seen, therefore, what consequences these phenomena produced for the nature and development of education.

In 1911, Gaetano Salvemini compared the conditions of education in Lombardy and in Sicily and observed that while in the former the scuole tecniche were more widespread, in the latter the ginnasi predominated. The reason for this difference, he believed, was that in the Mezzogiorno

> agriculture, industry, and commerce, given the poverty of the country and the sluggishness of economic life, demand only a very limited specialized personnel,

**Mezzogiorno:* southern Italy. *Questione meridionale:* the problem of what to do with the less-developed South. The *Settentrione* refers to northern Italy.

and offer almost no possibility of productive employment to that class which is neither rich enough to live on interest nor poor enough to accept voluntarily what it regards as the degradation of manual work. Under such conditions all the families of middle and small landownership are led to send their sons almost exclusively toward the liberal professions and clerical jobs."[33]

With the data available it is possible today to expand Salvemini's analysis. As we shall see, in fact, the difference between northern and southern Italy was not limited to the different distribution of lower-secondary schools, but ran much deeper.

For this analysis, one can start from the data contained in tables 4.9 and 4.10, elaborated from those gathered on the occasion of the 1911 census.[34] We are confined to the choice of this year by the fact that, because of the way the preceding censuses were collected and presented, it is not possible to submit them to the same kind of elaboration. But fortunately the 1911 census, situated as it was at the end of the period of industrialization, is in a certain sense the ideal year for the kind of analysis I intend to conduct. It is in this year, in fact, that the accentuation of North-South differences reached its highest point.[35]

Table 4.9 reports the rates of enrollment for the age cohort 10–15 years, that roughly corresponding to the last years of the elementary schools and to the lower-secondary schools. The positive relationship that one expects to find between economy and education emerges clearly: the enrollment rate decreases sharply from North to South both for males and for females, but for the latter the differences by geographic area are much more pronounced than for the former.

The discussion becomes more interesting, however, when we consider the data of table 4.10, which reports the rate of enrollment for the age cohort 15–21 years, which covers the upper-secondary schools and a part of the university sector. If we reasoned according to the traditional interpretive schemes we would expect to find also at this level the same positive relation encountered in the lower schools; indeed, we would expect to find it even more marked. Starting, in fact, from the extraordinary differences in per capita income between North and South in 1911, we would expect that in the North the number of families that had their children continue studies to the end of the lower-secondary school was much greater than in the South. Then, too, the profound economic transformations that took place in the preceding thirty years had produced some important social changes which are generally thought to affect positively the demand of families for education.

Table 4.9. Active* and Nonactive Population 10–15 Years of Age by Sex and Geographic Area, 1911

Area	*Agriculture*	*Industry*	*Other Activity*	*Total Active*	*Total Nonactive*	*Of Which Students*	*General Total*	*N*
				Males				
North	31.61	15.31	2.21	49.13	50.87	49.07	100	829,052
Center	39.85	12.02	1.77	53.64	46.36	42.44	100	301,485
South	40.83	14.01	2.11	57.05	42.95	33.87	100	731,200
Italy	36.57	14.31	2.10	52.98	47.02	42.03	100	1,861,737
				Females				
North	20.85	13.62	2.17	36.64	63.36	46.01	100	820,725
Center	21.73	10.21	1.60	33.54	66.46	37.47	100	292,163
South	17.50	4.72	2.34	24.56	75.44	22.20	100	695,189
Italy	19.71	9.65	2.14	31.50	68.50	35.48	100	1,808,077
				Males and Females				
North	26.26	14.47	2.19	42.92	57.08	47.55	100	1,649,777
Center	30.93	11.13	1.69	43.75	56.25	40.00	100	593,648
South	29.46	9.54	2.22	41.22	58.78	28.18	100	1,426,389
Italy	28.26	12.01	2.12	42.39	57.61	38.80	100	3,669,814

*That is, employed or in search of first employment

SOURCE: Elaboration of data taken from Ministry of Agriculture, Industry and Commerce, General Directory of Statistics and Labor. *Censimento della popolazione del Regno d'Italia al 10 giugno 1911* (Rome, 1915), vol. 5, *Popolazione presente, di età superiore ai dieci anni, classificata per sesso, età e professione o condizione.*

Table 4.10. Active and Nonactive Population 15–21 Years of Age by Sex and Geographic Area, 1911

Area	*Agriculture*	*Industry*	*Other Activity*	*Total Active*	*Total Nonactive*	*Of Which Students*	*General Total*	*N*
				Males				
North	44.22	38.71	9.25	92.18	7.82	6.65	100	836,330
Center	50.27	30.72	8.32	89.31	10.69	8.51	100	312,527
South	50.84	27.02	6.56	84.42	15.58	9.42	100	721,417
Italy	47.79	32.87	8.06	88.72	11.28	8.03	100	1,870,274
				Females				
North	30.27	30.11	6.85	67.23	32.77	5.30	100	889,472
Center	25.65	20.44	6.03	52.12	47.88	4.79	100	332,397
South	21.95	9.69	4.27	35.91	64.09	3.62	100	774,927
Italy	26.27	20.58	5.71	52.56	47.44	4.56	100	1,996,796
				Males and Females				
North	37.03	34.28	8.01	79.32	20.68	5.95	100	1,725,802
Center	37.58	25.42	7.14	70.14	29.86	6.59	100	644,924
South	35.88	18.05	5.38	59.31	40.69	6.41	100	1,496,344
Italy	36.68	26.52	6.85	70.05	29.95	6.24	100	3,867,070

SOURCE: See table 4.9.

In spite of all this, in examining table 4.10 we see that in the 15 to 21-year-old cohort there is an inverse relationship between economy and education. Considering together students of both sexes, we see that the rate of enrollment is higher in the South than in the North. For males the rate increases from North to South, while for the females it has exactly the opposite course, even though the differences are far less than those encountered in the younger cohort.

The picture that emerges from these data is rather clear. Compared to the North, the South presents a lower rate of enrollment at the elementary and lower-secondary levels and a higher one at the upper-secondary and university levels. The Mezzogiorno has concurrently the highest rates of illiteracy and of intellectual unemployment. Therefore, the South found itself in relation to Italy in the same position in which Italy found itself in relation to Europe. And in effect, comparing it with the other European countries, one could have said of Italy what Ettore Ciccotti wrote of the Mezzogiorno: "there the school does not arise spontaneously, as in a more advanced industrial country, where it responds to an urgent need and an immediate usefulness; in the South it is deliberately imported like an external requirement."[36]

The reasons for the "peculiar circumstances" of the Italian educational system, denounced by Cesare Correnti and by Ernesto Nathan, seem clearer to us now. Intellectual unemployment and illiteracy are no less than two faces of the same coin: the condition of education in an underdeveloped country. It can be said, in other words, that both the educational system of a developed country and that of an underdeveloped country may be represented geometrically by a pyramidal trunk, but with a basic difference: that the latter presents a polygon much narrower at the base and much wider at the vertex.

Economy and Education over Time and by Geographic Area

It is now possible to expand the preceding discussion by following the progress of education over the course of that process of dualistic development which, as shown above, characterized the Italian economy. It is possible, that is, to conclude by examining the course of education over time and by geographic area. In this case as well one may start from 1881 and employ that three-phase periodization which has already been used. Without entering into the controversies over the point at which the North-South imbalance began, it can safely be said that in 1881 a critical period commenced for the industrialization of several northern regions and the subordination of the Mezzogiorno. While, in fact, at the time of unification the industrial sector was larger in the South than in the North (though weaker and more backward insofar as it was constituted by family-run craft enterprises), in the period beginning in 1881 there occurred simultaneously a moderate growth of industry in the North and a crisis of that in the South.[37]

I have already sought to follow, by examining the data of table 4.2, the course of elementary education by geographic area from 1881 to 1920. This type of analysis is not possible for higher education. Carlo Francesco Ferraris, calculating the percentage of university students over inhabitants by geographic area in the period 1896 – 1912, observed that it was lower in the North than in the South (especially for the faculties of medicine and surgery and for those of jurisprudence) and attributed this fact to the "greater economic progress of the region, especially industrial and commercial, which allows or impels many to turn to practical economic professions and to those liberal professions of a technical character."[38] This constitutes a further element of proof for the hypothesis of an inverse relation between economy and higher education. But beyond this, unfortunately, it is not possible to go with the data that we possess.[39]

On the other hand, analysis of the course of education by geographic area beginning in 1881 is possible for the secondary schools. If we consider, in particular, the schools of the classical branch we can see clearly the effects of the dualistic development of the Italian economy on education. As may be observed from figure 4.3, at the beginning of the period considered, it is the regions of the Center and the Northwest that have the highest number of enrollments in the ginnasio compared to population, while the South is in third place. Then, however, things change radically. There was occasion to observe, in the preceding pages, that the average yearly increase of enrollments in the ginnasio in all areas of the country was comparable in the first and second phases (in fact, that of the first phase is slightly higher than that of the second). An analysis of the data disaggregated by geographic area now allows a deepening of the discussion. In the first phase, there was an expansion of the ginnasi in the regions of the South, Center, and Northeast, but not in those of the Northwest: that is, where the process of industrialization begins, as it does in Lombardy, Liguria, and Piedmont, there is a drop in enrollments in the ginnasi. The strongest expansion of ginnasi occurs, on the other hand, in the Mezzogiorno, which at the end of this first phase passes from third to second place in number of enrollments. However, in the second phase, namely that of economic crisis, the expansion of the ginnasi characterizes all regions, even those of the Northwest. Finally, in the third phase, the curve declines for all areas, but even here the drop is stronger in regions undergoing industrialization and weaker in the Mezzogiorno. So it is that at the end of the "great leap" the Mezzogiorno moved to first place in the number of enrollments.

The course of enrollment in the liceo is analogous (figure 4.4). In this case as well, at the beginning of the period considered the South is in third place in number of enrollments, after the Northwest and the Center. But the depressing effect of economic growth on school enrollments is here much more easily perceptible. In the first phase, the number of enrollments decreases sharply in the regions of the Northwest and the Center, remains practically stationary in those of the Northeast, and rises only in the Mezzogiorno. Thus in 1888 the South moves from third to second place for number of enrollments. The growth of the licei picks up, on the other hand, at an accelerated pace during the period of economic crisis in Italy, not only in the South but in all regions, including those of the Northwest. Finally, in the period of the "great leap" the curve rises slightly in the Center, drops slowly in the South, and falls sharply in the North, particularly in the regions most closely involved with the process of industrialization. Thus in 1911 the regions of the Northwest move from first to third place for number of enrollments.

As far as technical education is concerned, it is worthwhile to examine together the two figures (4.5 and 4.6) of enrollments in the scuole and istituti tecnici. The data examined above have already led to the conclusion that the sharp increase of enrollments in the istituti tecnici that occurred in the third phase was not simply an effect of increased demand for diplomati produced by industrialization, but was due, at least in part, to the difficulties of graduates of the scuole tecniche in finding employment. Now, the analysis of data by geographic area offers additional elements of proof for this hypothesis. As noted from figure 4.1, the IT/ST rate rises during the phases of crisis and falls in the phases of economic expansion. In other words, in the phases of economic expansion the rate of growth of the istituti tecnici is more rapid than that of the scuole tecniche. But this difference in the two growth rates is not identical in all areas of the country. The disaggregated data show, in fact, that the difference in growth rate is much smaller in the South than in the Northwest. What does this mean? Simply that *also in the third phase* the scuole tecniche in the Mezzogiorno grew at a much more rapid rate than the demand for the qualified labor produced by these schools and, therefore, a greater number of students had no

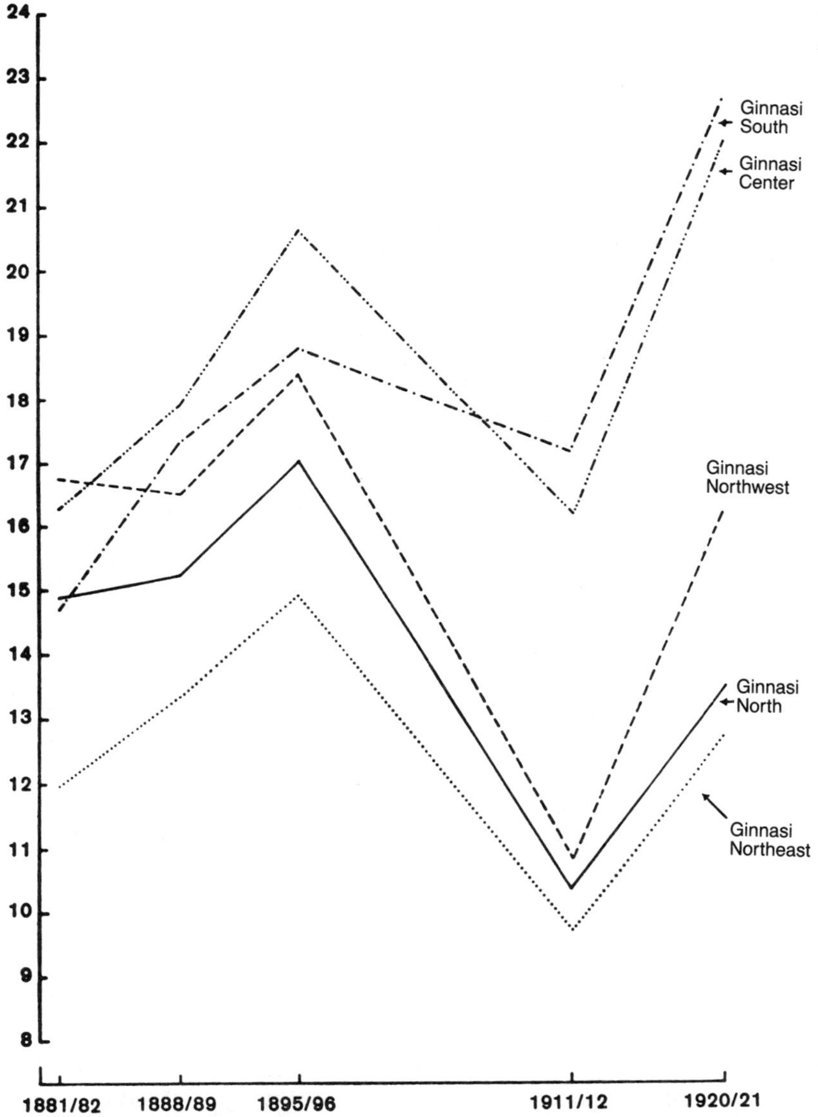

Figure 4.3. Enrollments in the ginnasio per 10,000 inhabitants, by geographic area, 1881 to 1920.

choice but to continue their studies. The validity of this hypothesis may be demonstrated even more fully by calculating the IT/ST rates for the various regions and comparing them with the percentage of employees in industry over the entire male labor force of the respective regions.[40]

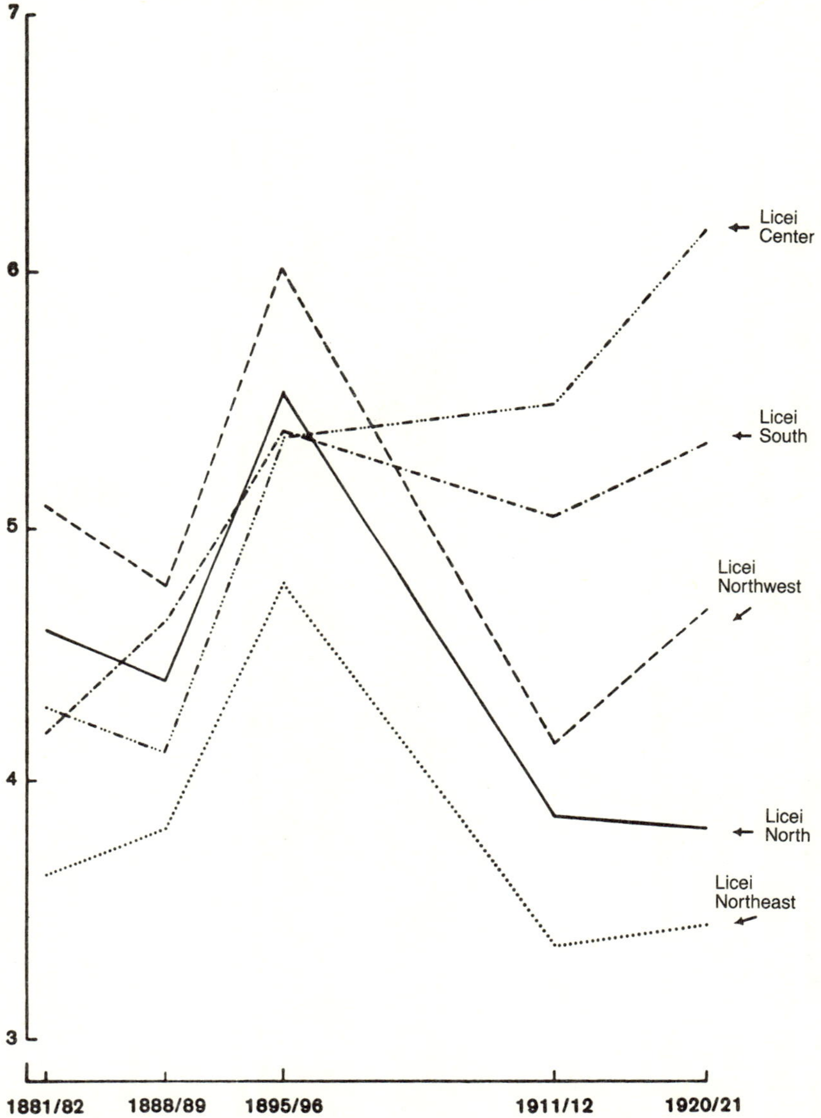

Figure 4.4. Enrollments in the liceo per 10,000 inhabitants, by geographic area, 1881 to 1920.

As may be seen from table 4.11, the value so obtained is positive but extremely low in 1882 and becomes negative in the following years. This means that as the dualistic process establishes itself, and the differences between

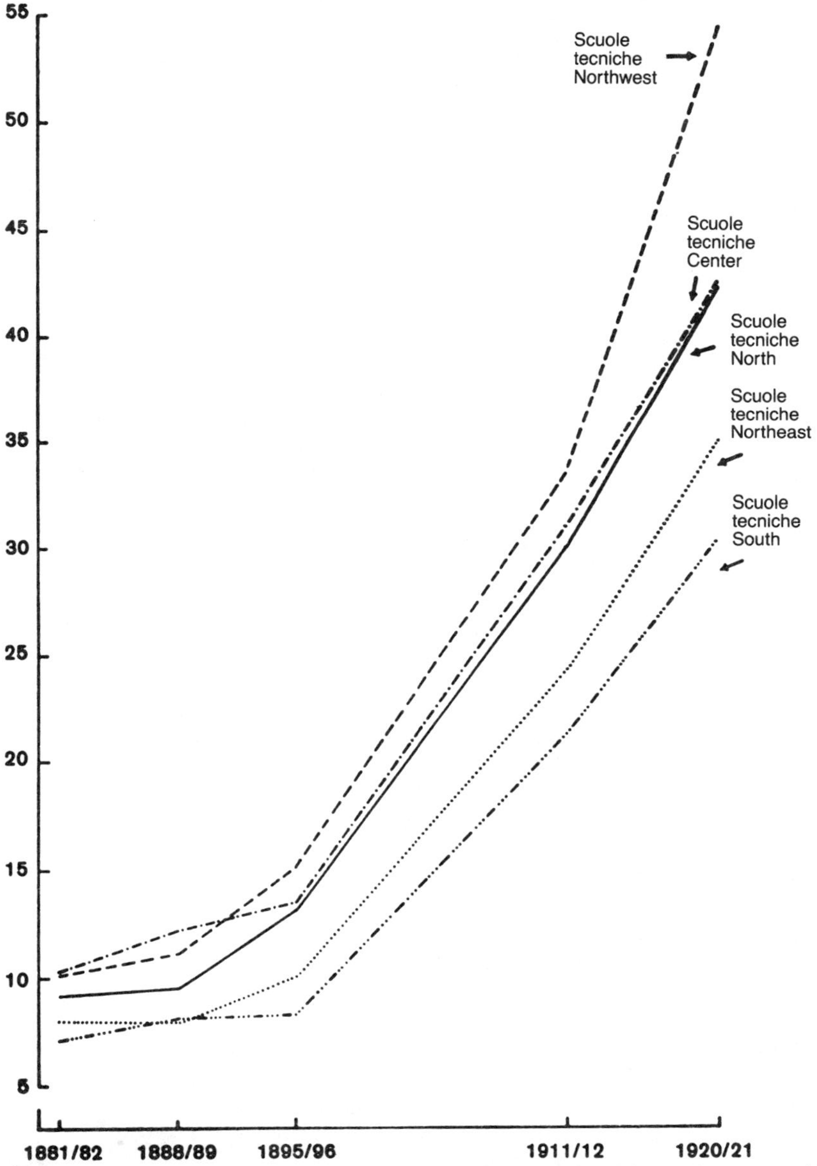

Figure 4.5. Enrollments in the scuola tecnica per 10,000 inhabitants, by geographic area, 1881 to 1920.

North and South increase, a negative relationship is brought about between the level of economic development reached by the various areas of the country and the percentage of graduates of the scuole tecniche who continue their studies.

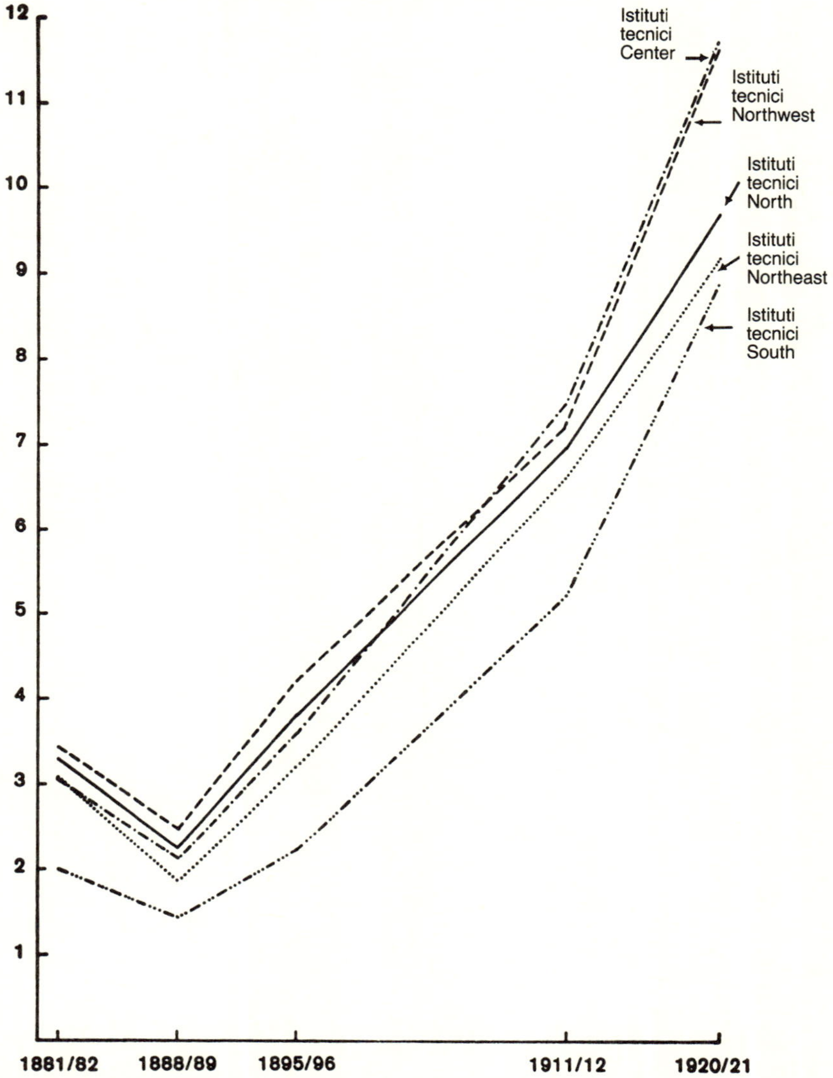

Figure 4.6. Enrollments in the istituto tecnico per 10,000 inhabitants, by geographic area, 1881 to 1920.

A Note on the Data Used in the Tables and Figures

Some indication is now necessary on the sources of data used in this chapter and the criteria that I have employed both in the choice of years and in the data

Table 4.11. Correlation Coefficients on a Regional Basis Between the Percentage of Employees in Industry of the Male Labor Force and the Ratio IT/ST (*N* = 16)

Year	*r*
1882–83	0.20
1895–96	−0.45
1911–12	−0.41
1920–21	−0.76

elaborations carried out.

1. For tables 4.1, 3, and 5, the data are taken from the *Annuario statistico italiano* (various years). There are slight differences between these and the disaggregated data by geographic area of tables 4.12 and 13, which were taken from other sources (see below). The data on population by age cohort were taken from Istituto di Statistica (ISTAT), *Sommario di statistiche storiche italiane, 1861 – 1955* (Rome, 1958). For the years 1888 and 1895 the population 15 – 20 years of age was estimated. For 1913 the data for the population in 1911 were used.

2. The rates of enrollment for the elementary schools by geographic area (table 4.2) are those calculated by ISTAT for the age cohort 6 – 14 years. Other scholars, such as, for example, Vigo in *Istruzione e sviluppo economico in Italia nel secolo XIX,* have calculated the rate of enrollment for the age cohort 6 – 12 years. Both these produce some distortions with respect to the actual enrollment rate: the first under and the second overestimating. But for the analysis that I have conducted in this chapter, one does not arrive at substantially different results by following one rather than the other criterion. (Vigo, for example, arrives at the conclusion, on the basis of his calculations, that from 1881 to 1901 the rate of enrollment in the regions of the industrial triangle "did not increase appreciably").

3. For figure 4.1, the percentage relationship between enrollments at the istituti tecnici and enrollments at the scuole tecniche was not calculated, for lack of information on the enrollments at private schools for some years (those not marked on the horizontal axis of the graph). For other years, the data concern both public and private schools and were taken from the *Annuario statistico italiano* for 1905–7 and for 1913, and from Ministry of Agriculture, Industry, and Commerce, General Directory of Statistics, *Statistica dell'istruzione per l'anno scolastico 1880–81* (Rome: Elzeviriana, 1883).

4. For figure 4.2 the data were taken from ISTAT, *Sommario di statistiche*

Table 4.12. Enrollments in the Secondary Schools by Type of School and Geographic Area, 1881–82 to 1920–21

Type of School	*Year*	*North*	*Northwest*	*Northeast*	*Center*	*South*	*Italy*
Ginnasio	1881–82	18,796	12,809	5,987	7,525	16,490	42,811
	1888–89	21,617	14,151	7,466	9,471	20,198	51,286
	1895–96	24,308	15,981	8,327	11,298	23,972	59,578
	1911–12	16,224	10,188	6,036	9,376	22,806	48,406
	1920–21	24,709	15,932	8,777	13,724	32,181	70,614
Liceo	1881–82	5,709	3,891	1,818	1,991	4,690	12,390
	1888–89	6,244	4,102	2,142	2,183	5,418	13,846
	1895–96	7,895	5,224	2,671	2,937	6,857	17,689
	1911–12	5,998	3,909	2,089	3,166	6,703	15,867
	1920–21	6,987	4,597	2,390	3,843	7,569	18,399
Scuola tecnica	1881–82	11,920	7,893	4,027	4,872	8,041	24,833
	1888–89	14,113	9,634	4,479	6,559	9,532	30,204
	1895–96	19,019	13,268	5,751	7,418	10,868	37,305
	1911–12	47,312	31,959	15,353	18,003	28,716	94,031
	1920–21	78,147	53,916	24,231	26,656	43,039	147,842
Istituto tecnico	1881–82	4,176	2,637	1,539	1,415	2,245	7,836
	1888–89	3,191	2,144	1,047	1,130	1,682	6,003
	1895–96	5,454	3,656	1,798	1,978	2,842	10,274
	1911–12	10,894	6,780	4,114	4,322	6,965	22,181
	1920–21	17,739	11,388	6,351	7,281	12,605	37,625

storiche italiane 1861–1955 (Rome, 1958). The percentage of enrollments in engineering was calculated only beginning in 1891, because for the preceding years enrollments in engineering are not distinguished from those of the science group.

5. For figures 4.3, 4, 5, and 6, which concern enrollments at the various secondary schools, both public and private, data on education were taken from: Ministry of Agriculture, Industry, and Commerce, *Statistica dell'istruzione secondaria e superiore per l'anno statistico 1881–82* (Rome: Elzeviriana, 1885), *Statistica dell'istruzione secondaria e superiore per l'anno statistico 1888–89* (Rome: Elzeviriana, 1891), and *Annuario statistico italiano* for 1900. Data on population were obtained from S. Somogyi, *"Evoluzione della popolazione attraverso il tempo,"* in ISTAT, *Sviluppo della popolazione italiana dal 1861 al 1961, Annali di statistica* (Rome, 1965), vol. 17. For 1891 I referred to data

Table 4.13. Enrollments in the Secondary Schools per 10,000 Inhabitants by Type of School and Geographic Area, 1881–82 to 1920–21

Type of School	*Year*	*North*	*Northwest*	*Northeast*	*Center*	*South*	*Italy*
Ginnasio	1881–82	14.87	16.76	11.98	16.27	14.37	15.04
	1888–89	15.24	16.47	13.35	17.87	17.31	16.46
	1895–96	17.05	18.41	14.92	20.64	18.81	18.34
	1911–12	10.38	10.82	9.72	16.23	17.18	13.96
	1920–21	13.50	16.23	12.70	22.01	22.69	18.24
Liceo	1881–82	4.51	5.09	3.63	4.30	4.19	4.35
	1888–89	4.40	4.77	3.82	4.12	4.64	4.44
	1895–96	5.53	6.02	4.78	5.36	5.38	5.44
	1911–12	3.84	4.15	3.36	5.48	5.05	4.57
	1920–21	3.82	4.68	3.45	6.16	5.33	4.75
Scuola tecnica	1881–82	9.43	10.32	8.06	10.54	7.18	8.73
	1888–89	9.95	11.21	8.01	12.38	8.17	9.70
	1895–96	13.34	15.29	10.30	13.55	8.52	11.48
	1911–12	30.28	33.95	24.73	31.16	21.63	27.12
	1920–21	42.72	54.94	35.05	42.76	30.34	38.19
Istituto tecnico	1881–82	3.30	3.45	3.08	3.06	2.00	2.75
	1888–89	2.25	2.49	1.87	2.13	1.44	1.92
	1895–96	3.82	4.21	3.22	3.61	2.23	3.16
	1911–12	6.97	7.20	6.62	7.48	5.24	6.39
	1920–21	9.69	11.60	9.18	11.68	8.88	9.72

reported by Cassa per lo Sviluppo Mezzogiorno (SVIMEZ), *Un secolo di statistiche italiane: Nord e Sud (1861–1961)* (Rome, 1961). Data on enrollments at the various secondary schools used for constructing the graphs are reported in table 4.12 in absolute figures and in table 4.13 per 10,000 inhabitants.

CHAPTER FIVE

Changing the Educational System: The Gentile Reform

Few and unsatisfactory are the analyses conducted until now of the Gentile Reform, certainly the most important and fundamental attempt at changing the Italian system of education from unification to the present. It is curious that most historical studies on fascism devote few lines to "the most fascist of reforms" (as Mussolini was to call it), and that many do not speak of it at all. On the other hand, the educational historians,[1] while they have served to elucidate the profoundly reactionary character of the Gentile Reform, have, for the most part, limited themselves to a reconstruction of events, without, in my view, offering an adequate interpretation of them.

There are, quite plainly, two explanations of the Gentile Reform furnished by these studies. The changing of the Italian educational system is attributed: 1) to the cultural, or rather, ideological current that preceded it; or 2) to the urgent need of the nascent regime to train, more than ever, future citizens in the most complete subordination. The second interpretive line is doubtless correct and accounts for the changes introduced into the educational system regarding the *mechanisms of socialization;* namely all those innovations of the reform of 1923 that strongly accentuated the hierarchical and authoritarian character of the Italian school. However, this is not enough in itself to explain the Gentile Reform, and in particular it does not account for all those changes (certainly no less important) introduced in 1923 regarding the *mechanisms of selection*. The first interpretation is, in contrast, completely inadequate. In fact, to reconstruct the thought of Gentile and his followers, to analyze the political and pedagogical program that proceeded therefrom, to ask whether, by moving to the historical embrace with fascism, the idealists renounced their conception of the world or did no more than coherently develop its premises, serves very little to explain the reform of 1923, just as it serves little, in general, to begin from the history of ideas to explain political and social history.

Paradoxically, one could say that Giovanni Gentile, the "philosopher of the cudgel," the abstract and proud theoretician of the Spirit and of its manifestations (the man who, to give only one example, produced pedagogical propositions such as: "If education is the growth of the spirit and the growth of the spirit is the proper object of philosophy, then pedagogy insofar as it is a science is nothing if not the philosophy of the spirit"), sometimes made use of interpretive schemes less idealistic than those used to explain his reform by some of the radical or Marxist historians. Speaking before the *Consiglio Superiore** of the Ministry of Public Education on November 15, 1923 of the reforms that he had launched a few months before, Gentile maintained:

> The schools were not of the type or the number necessary for the needs of the country, not of the sort to provide for the spiritual, scientific, and economic needs of national life, which needs are the only arenas in which the individual can usefully employ his own assets. From the licei, from the universities, from the scuole normali there left every year a number of graduates of each that was enormously higher than what was needed: and the great majority of these youths had sought in the school the diploma rather than learning. The educational population grew each year at a much more rapid pace than the population of the kingdom. The schools overflowed. . . .[2]

Indeed, if one wanted to interpret adequately that complex and fundamental program of change in the Italian educational system which goes under the name of the Gentile Reform, and if in addition to the innovations concerning mechanisms of socialization one wanted also to explain those regarding mechanisms of selection, it would be necessary to examine the existing relationship between school and labor market. The interpretive hypothesis of the Gentile Reform that I propose and that I will employ in the following pages is that it was *also* a reactionary response to the existing imbalance between school and labor market (which was manifested above all in a growing overproduction of intellectual labor) and to the social and political tensions that this imbalance produced. Before considering the content of this response, I will examine the conditions that made it possible. These were: 1) the elaboration of an ideology and an

**Consiglio superiore della pubblica istruzione:* academic body advisory to the minister of public education, in three sections corresponding to the primary, secondary, and tertiary levels of the educational system.

organic program of change in the Italian educational system; 2) the rise of intellectual unemployment and, more generally, a sharp loss of status by the ceti intellettuali; 3) a process of political mobilization of these strata and the activation of processes of reconversion and reequilibration of status; and 4) the changing of power relations between the classes.

The first of these conditions was already present long before the outbreak of the First World War. The program of change in the Italian educational system did not arise, in fact, by improvisation out of Gentile's head, but was prepared in the course of analysis and discussion conducted for some twenty years by a particularly large group of minds (some of which were "progressive") to offer a solution to the "new problems" of the Italian school, particularly those related to intellectual unemployment. The other three conditions, on the other hand, appeared only after the war. The second was the result of the accentuation of the economy-education "scissors,"* of the reduction of the income of the ceti intellettuali (and of the ceti medi in general), and of the economic, social, and political progress of the proletariat. These conditions brought about a process of mobilization of the ceti intellettuali, directed generally at altering the existing sociopolitical order, and in particular at transforming the institution most "responsible" for their status imbalance: the school. Finally, the change in power relations occurred with the defeat of the workers' movement and the advent of fascism.

The Conditions of Change: I. The Elaboration of the Program

The plan for altering the Italian educational system was the result of a long and, in some ways, tormented process which began a few years after the phenomenon of intellectual unemployment appeared in Italy. As secondary and higher education expanded, as the supply of intellectual labor increased, and as the imbalance between school and labor market was aggravated, there developed among the creators and interpreters of "public opinion" a process of reaction that called into question even the very bases of the educational system left by the Casati Law. The debate on the school, which had actually never

*The economy-education "scissors" refers to the phenomenon in which the supply curve for educational qualifications and the demand curve of the economy for those qualifications approach, intersect, and then glance off each other, so that a graph of these two curves roughly resembles an opened pair of scissors.

ceased, became more intense and lively and above all confronted problems and showed the existence of anxieties that were new. Few were the optimists, those who offered a positive analysis of the situation. These, even deploring "the large numbers of those who, having completed a few years of study, often with great sacrifice, flock into jobs with the state or large firms, while they could have been excellent industrial or agricultural workers," believed this to be "a natural product of the diffusion of learning," a sort of price paid upon the altar of progress. They even discerned some positive aspects in intellectual unemployment, foreseeing that it would make "the aversion for so-called manual labor" disappear and lead to a situation of redistribution and rotation between study and productive activity, manual and intellectual labor.[3]

The most acute observers, however, discerned behind the phenomenon of intellectual unemployment profound imbalances of a structural nature, and reached the conclusion, albeit with some confusion, that the expansion of secondary and higher education which had occurred in Italy was due not to prosperity but to underdevelopment and poverty. To those who maintained "higher studies for the needy classes to be especially harmful because they take hands away from agricultural and industrial work," Giuseppe Tarozzi replied drily: "This is certainly not the moment to demand that the number of unemployed workers and migrant peasants grow." "If by precluding instruction you want to cure the plague of misfits," he observed, "first consider whether you will not, on the contrary, multiply the hungry, whether you will not find yourselves before a tough alternative: either learned misfits or ignorant poor."[4]

But the majority accused the school of having become a factory for misfits and consequently a "cell of rebellion." In the diagnoses of the pessimists was present in part the old diffidence and the old fear of the old reactionaries over the diffusion of education. But only in part. In reality their diagnoses and their charges were the product of rather different fears and anxieties. Even an analysis of their language alone, which reveals the frequency with which they used expressions like *spostati, fuorviati, disillusi, spostamento delle condizioni, spostamenti dolorosi,** would suffice for understanding that what worried these observers was not the diffusion of education, but the fact that the school, rather than regulating the processes of social mobility, rather than defusing their potentially explosive load, had rendered them even more difficult and danger-

*"Misfits," "those gone astray," "disenchanted," "displaced by circumstances," "wretched drifters."

ous. "It is sad to confess," said Giorgio Arcoleo "that this imbalance of individuals and of classes, far from diminishing, has increased with greater and more widespread education, so that the school, rather than filling the cracks that the revolution opened among the groups that constitute society, rather than composing souls to the changed order of things, seems itself a source of dicontent, disorder and unhappiness."[5]

The school, it was argued, did not regulate but accelerated the processes of upward mobility, did not depress but stimulated aspirations and occupational expectations. One did not enter it to satisfy the "thirst for knowledge," but to get a piece of paper, to rise on the social scale, to seek social promotion. The observers of the time, partly because they were bound to an aristocratic conception of study as "disinterested activity," partly because they were worried by the growing imbalance between school and labor market, inveighed against the instrumental attitude of students and their parents regarding the school, attitudes which, because of its own structural characteristics, this institution could not help but produce. Galletti and Salvemini noted ironically that "the man and the citizen takes the licenza of the scuola media to have done with studies, just as he takes first communion to have done with the faith, just as he will take a wife to have done with love."[6] Speaking of the university, Fusinato wrote:

> Together with its ancient customs, the university is losing its character and function. Students, families, the public no longer consider it a school of independent scientific research, which has for its purpose the disinterested cultivation of the spirit, but rather, a state establishment through which it is necessary to pass in order to obtain in some fashion a diploma which gives access to careers. Not the preoccupation with study, but with examination is the anxiety, and the obtaining of practical result by the quickest routes.[7]

That the diagnoses and the charges of the great majority of scholars and politicians were not so much the product of the old aversions to the diffusion of literacy but rather arose from the anxiety that the school, instead of regulating, accelerated and rendered more dangerous the processes of upward mobility, is shown by the fact that these diagnoses and charges came as well from intellectuals who passed and still pass today (rightly or wrongly) for "progressives." Augusto Monti inveighed against the

> flank of betrayers of the hoe and of the trowel, who for some years now have been

crowding into our secondary schools: ill-mannered, ignorant, clamorous, excitable, and supported by worthy relatives who yearn for their little dunces to advance at any cost to the conquest of the 'licenza' and then of the 'position.' Before, when these people, whether for physical ineptitude or material ambition, deserted the stable or the workshop, it was the seminary that received them. Now instead they all run to the scuola media which gives them the 'licenza,' the qualification for employment, and there they stay, tough, brutish, eating like wolves and understanding *nothing*, conducting strikes and beating up teachers.[8]

Similarly, some years later, Piero Gobetti laid the blame on those "who have to win lauree because mamma, grandpa, or papa wants it so," especially because "these people harbor a purpose, but, in fact, as regards means and follow-through, blessed idleness is proclaimed." In his view the only solution was that of blocking "the road to the indolent, the future misfits, and quickly. We will have fewer lawyers and fewer lecturers but more seriousness and more honesty. The current students of the liceo could be eliminated in eighty cases out of a hundred."[9]

In addition to accelerating the processes of upward mobility, as was claimed, the school was the principal cause of processes of downward mobility, or at the least it made more accute the frustrations that derived from these. Having entered the school to "shift" their own circumstances, a part of those who carried on to the end became permanent "shifters," incapable of finding the work for which they had studied so much and at the same time unable to return to their fathers' work. The effort to "surmount the embankment," to "rise ever higher," provoked according to Arcoleo a "movement of retrogression": "all the passive residues of the higher circles sink downward to prevail over the active residues of the lower circles. When even lowly concorsi are opened, the excess product of the university constitutes a barrier for those others who, poorer in condition but richer in intellect, would have the right to these positions."[10]

It is from this analysis of the school and of its relationship to Italian society that the program of change arose. Many were the debates and very many the articles and books that advanced more or less concrete proposals for resolving the existing problems. All the same, the two decisive contributions to the formulation of a fundamental program of change for the educational system came from the work of the Royal Commission for the Ordering of Italian Secondary Studies and from the Congress of the National Federation of Secondary School Teachers (FNISM).

The Royal Commission, instituted by decree on November 19, 1905 by Minister of Public Education Leonardo Bianchi, began its work in December of the same year. Made up of some of the most prestigious scholars of educational problems that Italy had, such as Galletti, Salvemini, and Vitelli, it worked for a good four years, gathering a large quantity of statistical material on the material condition of secondary education and seeking by means of a broad survey to gain as precise a picture as possible of the attitudes and proposals for change which came from those principally responsible for the administration of the secondary schools. It is impossible here to record the debates that went on within the commission, the polemics and conflicts that led some of its most authoritative members to resign, nor even the principal results of the survey. For the purposes of this discussion, it suffices to say that the Royal Commission arrived at the conclusion that it was necessary to revise and restructure completely the educational system left by the Casati Law, rendering it more closed and selective at the secondary level by "opening new schools that would be, let us say, safety valves for the impetuous fervor of modern life,"[11] namely by instituting those dumping or dead-end schools which, as was noted earlier, thecountry lacked.

Two objectives were sought in proceeding with the institution of these dumping schools: first, that of raising the level of studies. Separating right from the start, with a reform of the secondary schools, those who "intended" from those who "did not intend" to pursue studies all the way to the university would clear "the schools of erudition of all the useless and cumbersome elements;" "the annual production of misfits and of malcontents" would be reduced, and thus "the, today, far too abased dignity of studies" would be raised. Second, "the crowd that stirred to the assault of public offices and of so-called administrative careers" was judged "undignified, and too dismal the condition of abandonment, especially in some regions of Italy, in which the countryside is left and the professions of the industries and agricultural trades are deserted." Only the creation of dead-end schools could reverse this tendency, "lifting the toil of the fields, the labor of the workshop, the activity of the trades to the rank of noble purpose, and restoring to such living and indispensable forms of social activity the many minds and many energies that today, exhausted by the vain search for distant unattainable goods, constitute a dangerous obstacle and perhaps a serious threat to our society."[12]

The second major contribution to the formulation of the program for altering the Italian educational system came from the National Federation of Secondary

School Teachers. This group, which brought into its ranks men like Gaetano Salvemini, Ernesto Codignola, Giovanni Gentile, Giuseppe Kirner, Concetto Marchesi, Rodolfo Mondolfo, Giuseppe Lombardo Radice, Giuseppe Tarozzi, confronted in its congresses all the most important problems of the Italian school.[13] Various were the political ideas of its constituents, various the analyses made of the situation of the school and of Italian society, and various the remedies proposed. Concerning the problem of intellectual unemployment in particular, there were those, such as Gaetano Salvemini, who pointed out that "the plethora of misfits" was a typical "condition" of capitalist society, independent of the existing educational arrangement and therefore not eliminable from that society ("intellectual labor, like manual labor, has and always will have its unemployed").[14] There were others, such as Giovanni Gentile, who argued:

> Our society is crammed with lawyers and doctors out of work, with so many people with a laurea framed and hung in the most honorable place in the house. They have completed, and very badly, their university studies, in the same way that they made it badly through the secondary, complaining about the excessive burden each day with every teacher, requiring special exam sessions every year, always shouting against having to learn Greek. And we wish to reform the school in favor of these? What's the use? These people were not born to studies; on the contrary, *fruges consumere!** They are numerous; and they have no right to become doctors and lawyers. A state of ruin will be what assists them on the way to the practice of liberal professions which, for being professions, presuppose scientific cultivation.[15]

But beyond these differences, which today appear truly nonessential, there was a broad agreement on many things among the majority of the men of FNISM. They were, in the first place, convinced that the Italian ruling class was by now in an advanced stage of decadence and corruption, because the machine that served to produce it – the school – was completely unfit to fulfill its function (however, if one considers Salvemini's statements, his analysis of the parasitic charcter of the southern intellectual bourgeoisie, his denunciation of the overabundance of classical schools in the Mezzogiorno, one realizes that in reality he was not always faithful to his affirmation of principle that the "plethora of misfits" was not eliminable from capitalist society). In the second place, they thought that the most urgent task was that of replacing the most important pieces of that machine, of radically transforming the educational

*Latin: Let them eat lightly.

system left by the Casati Law. In the third place, beyond the differences of detail between the "classicists" ("intransigents" and "moderates") and the "modernists," with the Conference of Cremona in 1903, with that of Milan in 1905, with the publication in 1908 of the fundamental book by Galletti and Salvemini, *La riforma della scuola media,* and finally with the Conference of Florence in 1909, a wide consensus was developing on the key point of the program of change: the need for closing the educational system at the secondary level by establishing that "outlet of the training schools," as Salvemini wrote, which could both satisfy "the devouring frenzy for education and learning that exhausts the popular classes today"[16] and, at the same time, protect the secondary schools and the university from these classes.

The Conditions of Change: II. The Growth of Intellectual Unemployment

Having been attenuated, at least for certain categories, in the last phase of the Giolittian age, and reabsorbed completely with the start of the First World War and the conversion of unemployed laureati and diplomati into soldiers, intellectual unemployment exploded again with more strength than ever at the end of the war. The economy-education scissors, which had characterized the quarter-century preceding the war, was accentuated to the point of becoming dramatic. On the one hand, the economy entered into a severe crisis: the production apparatus was in pieces; industry had to undergo a process of reconversion; agricultural production decreased; the cost of living rose at a dizzying rate. But, above all, the number of unemployed, which in November 1919 reached two million, grew immensely. On the other hand, the secondary schools and the university, having grown abnormally during the war years, threw onto the market a great mass of laureati and diplomati. Compared with the prewar period, the graduates of the liceo increased by 46 percent, those of the scuole normali by 191 percent, and those of the istituti tecnici by an extraordinary 256 percent (table 5.1).

Very sharp also was the increase of laureati, which doubled when compared to the preceding period, increasing from 4,197 in 1913–14 to 8,464 in 1919–20 (table 5.2).

The accentuation of the economy-education scissors caused very serious unemployment among diplomati and laureati. Regarding the former, there are data only on diplomati in elementary school teaching. In four years from

Table 5.1. Diplomati for Selected Years, from 1909 to 1920

Year	*Scuole normali*	*Istituti tecnici*	*Istituti nautici**	*Licei*
1909–10	4,099	2,942	361	4,952
1911–12	5,434	3,463	338	4,826
1912–13	6,362	3,929	357	5,389
1913–14	7,671	3,865	325	4,725
1917–18	10,664	3,326	756	4,832
1918–19	11,917	7,108	349	7,226
1919–20	11,488	10,473	598	6,109
1920–21	9,383	7,132	796	5,617

*Nautical Institutes.

SOURCE: ISTAT, *Annuario statistico italiano* (1909, 1911, 1915, 1919, and 1921).

1917 – 18 to 1920 – 21, more than 40,000 new maestri graduated, while the number of those employed increased from 94,000 to 105,000, up by only 11,000.[17] If one considers the fact that besides the new diplomati there were thousands of maestri demobilized from the front, it is clear how high their rate of unemployment must have been. A thorough inquiry made by the most important elementary teachers' periodical of the time, *I diritti della scuola,* showed how dramatic the situation was. The number of those preparing to be licensed in 1916 – 17 (column 6 of table 5.3) was 9,523 persons, but because of the high number of independent students who presented themselves at the examinations during the war there were more than 10,000 diplomati. Since the positions offered by concorso were 1,797, there was a surplus each year of almost 9,000 diplomati, with the highest points in Sicily, Lombardy, and Piedmont (column 9). This means that the yearly percentage of absorption of supply was around 16 percent, with even lower points in Campania, Sicily, and Sardinia (column 10). "For thirty or forty positions," observed the same review some months later, "the number of aspirants is nine hundred, a thousand, even two thousand; the mass becomes more imposing every hour and is actually forming an army of misfits, on whose fortunes it is necessary to reflect with due concern."[18]

The situation for laureati was no different. At the end of 1921, pinpointing the situation, Federico Mastrigli observed that the increase in the number of laureati had

Table 5.2. Laureati by Faculty, 1913–14 to 1922–23

Academic Year	*Juris-prudence*	*Economics and Commerce*	*Political Science*	*Naval Institute*	*Literature and Philosophy*	*Education*	*Medicine and Surgery*	*Veterinary Science*	*Engineer-ing*	*Archi-tecture*	*Mathe-matical, Physical and Natural Sciences*	*Pharmacy*	*Agriculture*	*Total*
1913–14	1,663	203	14	—	297	57	656	63	683	6	166	291	98	4,197
1914–15	1,306	52	12	—	204	76	841	62	410	3	178	305	64	3,513
1915–16	1,137	67	11	—	243	89	511	88	213	1	150	224	44	2,778
1916–17	1,061	75	9	—	228	78	218	81	145	2	114	164	27	2,202
1917–18	1,230	116	9	—	217	124	221	32	179	3	136	118	20	2,405
1918–19	2,366	503	30	—	503	119	1,086	42	623	12	306	169	135	5,894
1919–20	2,700	843	59	—	719	233	1,247	88	1,435	12	477	347	304	8,464
1920–21	2,136	762	45	—	692	191	1,484	140	2,045	15	546	332	266	8,654
1921–22	1,937	645	52	—	595	206	1,278	181	1,932	13	591	470	210	8,110
1922–23	1,992	587	43	24	620	271	1,905	197	2,154	37	669	462	213	9,174

SOURCE: ISTAT, *Statistica dell'istruzione superiore nell'anno accademico 1945–46* (Rome, 1948).

Table 5.3. Supply and Demand for Maestri: Teacher Population, Those Preparing to be Licensed, and Those Licensed, 1916–17, and Teaching Positions Offered by Concorso in 1920

Region	*Teacher Population (1916–17)*			*Number Preparing to be Licensed (1916–17)*			*Number Licensed (1917)*	*Positions Offered by Concorso (1920)*	*Surplus Diplomati (ann. avg.)*	*% Annually Absorbed*
	M	*F*	*MF*	*M*	*F*	*MF*				
Piedmont	280	4,007	4,287	105	820	925	1,315	227	1,088	17.26
Liguria	103	1,549	1,652	40	382	422	352	57	295	16.19
Lombardy	345	4,994	5,339	121	1,304	1,425	1,516	233	1,293	15.37
Veneto	100	2,987	2,997	32	841	873	908	323	585	35.57
Emilia	168	3,539	3,707	41	854	895	1,072	129	943	12.03
Tuscany	171	2,118	2,289	72	468	540	759	218	541	28.72
Marche	131	1,516	1,647	48	418	466	505	47	458	9.30
Umbria	55	643	698	20	176	196	235	52	183	22.12
Lazio	126	1,629	1,755	38	393	431	483	50	433	10.35
Abruzzi and Molise	88	895	983	33	215	248	237	126	111	53.16
Campania	283	3,210	3,493	42	772	814	838	67	771	7.99
Puglia	266	1,651	1,917	92	470	562	571	60	511	10.50
Basilicata	136	317	453	23	90	113	100	71	29	71.00
Calabria	123	805	928	37	145	182	290	60	230	20.69
Sicily	558	3,739	4,297	175	1,033	1,208	1,291	71	1,220	5.49
Sardinia	71	309	380	28	195	223	242	16	226	6.61
Italy	3,004	33,818	36,822	947	8,576	9,523	10,714	1,797	8,917	16.77

SOURCE: Elaboration of data taken from: "Produzione e fabbisogno di maestri in una nostra inchiesta," *I diritti della scuola,* April 2, 1922.

> devalued academic qualifications in such a way that lawyers who are not functionaries of public welfare, second lieutenants of the Royal Guard or assistant secretaries of the Post Office, engineers who have not been able to find an opening in the state corps of civil engineers or with the state railroad, doctors who have not finished in time to secure a corner in the central or provincial administrations, struggle desperately in the confines of unemployment, twenty-five or thirty years old and still dependent on their families, disillusioned with life before even having lived it, exhausted by a struggle that they still have not won; misfits in spite of themselves, victims of the romantic illusions of those who have put them onto a mistaken path.[19]

Unfortunately, there are no precise data that allow us to appraise the unemployment rate for laureati exactly, much less that for their various categories. Nevertheless, the data that we have on the course of supply of the labor force and the analysis provided by the various professions' publications allow us to say that this phenomenon assumed truly impressive proportions. It was noted that in the fifteen-year period before the war the supply curve of laureati in jurisprudence had risen steadily, reaching its highest point of 1,663 in the year 1913–14. After the natural drop recorded in the war years, it began to rise again. Compared to 1913 – 14, the laureati of 1918 – 19 increased 42 percent. In five years, from 1919 to 1923, the faculties of jurisprudence put onto the market more than eleven thousand new laureati. How could all these persons be absorbed? The Public Administration, which had been in the preceding period the biggest provider of work for laureati in law, was unable to adjust its capacities of absorption to the new rate of increase in supply, so that a large part of the new laureati remained unemployed. No better, on the other hand, was the lot of those who entered the independent profession of attorney.

> In Italy today [observed Piero Calamandrei in 1921] the number of legal professionals is enormously higher than is warranted by social needs; this pathological elephantiasis of the forensic orders brings with it as a natural consequence the unemployment and economic hardship of the great majority of professionals, and therefore the progressive intellectual and moral abasement of the profession, of which public opinion, even without exactly understanding the causes, takes account with such harsh judgment.[20]

In the case of doctors, it was noted earlier that the supply curve had taken a slightly downward course in the fifteen years before the war, reaching its lowest point in the year 1913 – 14 with 656 laureati. It began, however, to rise quickly after the war, reaching 1,905 in 1922–23. In five years the university threw onto the market 7,000 new laureati who found themselves facing no little difficulty fitting in. What must have been their work situation at that time emerges clearly from a reading of the profession's publications.

For example, the *Federazione medica* wrote in October 1921:

> Now that the equilibrium between demand and supply is completely broken, the situation of the medical class is, without fail, worse in comparison with that of the other categories of intellectuals. A whole crowd of individuals without any calling, and indifferent to the professional path ahead, was, in the torrid days past, drawn to medicine on the basis of a false illusion and a yearning for greater protection of its own well-being.[21]

According to the *Federazione medica,* there were two causes of the surplus of doctors, one "ordinary," the other "extraordinary." The ordinary cause consisted in the fact that the faculty of medicine offered the "deceptive illusion" of reaching a high level of income by completing studies that were much quicker and easier than those that the aspirants to other liberal professions had to face. The "extraordinary" one was an effect of the war:

> the war, for reasons which needn't be illustrated here, has pushed an enormous number of youth toward the medical faculties, which have seen their enrollments triple, quadruple, and even quintuple. Moreover, the war, as everyone knows, has enormously simplified exams and has lowered the level of studies and created in our youth illogical pretensions with an atmosphere of dionysian, careless, simplistic arrivism which helps maintain the indiscipline and the bewilderment of relations characteristic of this political moment.[22]

The same analysis was made by the *Policlinico,* which dwelt more fully on the consequences of this "plethora of doctors":

> It is probable that in our society the demand for medical work will undergo a continual increase. But the growing requirement will never be sufficient to absorb the enormous heap of new laureati, which surpasses every availability of professional employment. The superabundance of doctors with respect to the effective needs of the population is the cause, in many respects, of problems and dangers. For doctors, the clearest and most obvious harm they experience from the displacement of the equilibrium is the related unemployment. Professional earnings are reduced not only because they are divided among a greater number of competitors, but also by the law of supply and demand: the supply of services results in their becoming cheaper. The excess of doctors cannot help compromising also the morality, or at least the dignity, of the entire profession, since it prevents a certain number from living comfortably by their work: they are induced to resort to tactics

> of more or less unfair competition, to more or less censurable practices. By depressing the ethical level of the profession, not only is its prestige obscured, but also its efficiency is reduced.[23]

Yet the group most struck by unemployment was that of the engineers. The supply curve, which had moved up in the prewar period, began to rise at the close of the war at a much more sustained rate. Among all laureati the engineers showed the largest increase compared to the prewar period. In the six years 1904 – 10 the faculties of engineering put onto the market about 2,500 new engineers, while in the four years 1919 – 22 they produced more than 8,000 laureati, with the difference, moreover, that the former period was characterized by expansion of the economy, by the birth of new industries, and by an intense activity of the building trade, while the latter was a period of crisis.

The magnitude of the employment difficulties for engineers is also quite apparent from the profession's publications. The journal of the National Association of Italian Engineers (ANII), *Ingegnere italiano*, commenting on a law to combat unemployment which facilitated the financing of works "of public interest" in order to give work to farm laborers and unskilled workers, complained that to this cure for working-class unemployment there corresponded no similar concern, on the part of the government or of entrepreneurs, for intellectual unemployment:

> Generally speaking [it bitterly observed] it is always and only a question of the manual laborer. . . . Industry and capital in their initiatives, on the one hand, and the state in the development of its program of applying the law against unemployment, on the other, have not been concerned until now in any way with another category of unemployed persons which must likewise make its weight felt in the general economic budget. We are speaking of technicians in general and of engineers in particular. While it is true that by now the greater part of the class of engineers consists of employees of the public administrations or in large private firms (with more or less, and rather less than more, satisfactory economic treatment), it is also true that not a few independent professionals do not find adequate room for the development of their enterprise, which must, therefore, content itself with remaining latent. Many young laureati, while recognizing the necessity of practical apprenticeship in entering the profession, are forced to accept, if they are lucky, functions and duties that are often very inferior to their learning and preparation, even given its theoretical nature.[24]

The ANII became intensely active in confronting the situation. It established, first of all, employment offices with the task not only of receiving requests for engineers on the part of employers but also of soliciting them.[25] It also pressured the government to make the concession of funds to public entities or private enterprises dependent on their appointment of a certain number of engineers.[26] It fought for the swift creation of land reclamation associations, on the condition, naturally, that these would absorb unemployed engineers.[27] Above all, it sought to do everything possible to encourage the exportation of engineers. To this last objective the journal of the National Association of Italian Engineers had recourse many times, attempting to demonstrate to the relevant authorities that the emigration of engineers was not only "an outlet for the unemployment of intellectual workers, which is certainly no less serious than working-class unemployment," but that it could also serve very well to "discipline proletarian emigration," and thus prevent the working class, which had "a very simplistic mentality," from forming "the conviction that abroad things fared better than in Italy."[28]

These pressures to encourage intellectual emigration, and in particular the attempt made in 1923 to export at least a small part of the surplus of engineers, show better than anything else how serious the unemployment of these laureati must have been. In 1923, in fact, the Italian ambassador to the United States, engineer Gelasio Caetani, concerned himself with arranging for the emigration of a certain number of Italian engineers, in spite of the new policy against immigration inaugurated by the American government. After making contact with numerous enterprises, he was assured by Ford, United States Steel, General Electric, and Anaconda Copper that they would hire a number of Italian engineers as *workers* with the future prospect of "promoting them to draftsman, superintendent, engineer, etc. . . . according to the skill which they will have to demonstrate and especially to their ability to command and direct workers." These engineers, whose number was fixed at fifty for the first year, had to have a certain knowledge of the English language, to possess various certificates and testimonials, sufficient money for the voyage, and room and board up to the day of the "first payment for work." Moreover, it could not appear "in any way that the youths came to the United States under a work contract, because otherwise they would not be allowed to embark, given the current emigration laws in force."[29]

"In what way can the dignity of a person of very civilized origins and customs," asked engineer Caetani, rhetorically, in expounding the successes obtained by his initiative, "be considered lessened if, in order to complete his technical and scientific education, he voluntarily mixes with a different social category for a limited period of his life?"[30] But the new Italian engineers had absolutely no need of sermons to be convinced. Even though nothing more was offered than emigration to another country for the job of a worker with, to say the least, uncertain future prospects, and although the requirements (such as knowledge of English) were not then very widespread, the Association received an avalanche of applications from newly trained Italian engineers who wanted to emigrate – so many that to reassure and to calm the applicants, to cope with the pressures and the letters of introduction that it received, the general presidency of the association, entrusted with selection, often intervened with press releases declaring its "perfect understanding of the agitation, the impatience, and the fear that has invaded the spirit of our colleagues who aspire to a career. He among us who has passed through unemployment knows what such a delay means."[31]

The Conditions of Change: III. Mobilization of the Intellectuals

The peculiarity of the political behavior of Italian intellectuals during the Giolittian era* in contrast to those of other countries was often noted, and frequent mention was made of their restlessness, their extremism, the instability of their orientations. Yet, no serious systematic attempt has ever been made to explain the influence of the phenomenon of intellectual unemployment on this behavior.[32] As was noted earlier, the politicians and the scholars of the time argued repeatedly that unemployment provoked a considerable political radicalization of the intellectuals and furnished cadres for subversive movements. Antonio Gramsci was of this view as well, writing that "Italian political parties. . .were always made up of 'volunteers,' in a certain sense of misfits, and never or almost never of homogeneous social blocks." He saw in the presence of an "unhealthy number" of intellectuals of a rural background (in addition to the diffusion of the subproletariat and to the apoliticism of the popular masses) the principal cause of "voluntarism," namely of that restlessness of the ceti intellettuali which led them to form, to the right or the left, "vanguards without support troops," "shock troops without infantry or artillery," whose verbal

*From 1901 to the eve of the First World War, the presiding force in Italian politics was Giovanni Giolitti (1842–1928), a progressive liberal and five times premier from 1892 to 1921.

extremism was inversely proportional to the number and the strength of the ties that they had with the great masses.[33]

On the relationship between unemployment and the political behavior of the intellectuals, not all, however, were in agreement. To give one notable example, Robert Michels denied (with very unconvincing arguments, in fact) that the leadership of the socialist party was recruited from among the "intellectual proletariat," and argued that the radicalization of the ceti intellettuali was, at least in the Mezzogiorno, a phenomenon not of the left but of the right: "This enormous intellectual proletariat of the Mezzogiorno. . .is the great preserve not of socialism but of reaction."[34]

However things may have been – and only systematic and deeper research would give us a clear picture – there was broad agreement on the fact that the political behavior of the intellectuals changed appreciably in the postwar period. Actually, as concerns the period following the First World War, the political behavior of the ceti medi as a whole was analyzed more than that of the intellectuals in particular. The thesis is by now sufficiently shared that the sense of relative deprivation of the ceti medi grew during this period in an extraordinary manner because there occurred at the same time a rise in expectations due to the war experience and a loss of status caused both by the economic crisis and by the victories of the proletariat.[35] It was precisely this imbalance between aspirations and reality, or this intensification of the sense of relative deprivation, that led the ceti medi, according to this thesis, to embrace the movement and the ideologies of fascism in hope of a reequilibration of its own status and of a demobilization of the working class.

But a specific analysis of the political behavior of the intellectuals, a history of their organizations and of their struggles is yet to be made even for this period.[36] Without having any intention of doing this analysis and this history here, I will limit myself – in order, above all, to analyze the conditions that made possible the alteration of the Italian educational system – to a brief examination of the process of mobilization of the intellectuals that took place in the postwar period, concentrating on two groups which I consider in many ways particularly important: the maestri and the engineers. The particular importance of these two groups lies in the fact that they were hit harder by unemployment than all other categories of diplomati and laureati. In the case of the engineers, however, it can be attributed to two special reasons: 1) the fact that at least some found themselves deeply immersed in an objectively difficult position – in the violent struggles that hit the Italian factories; and 2) the peculiarity of their course of training, which rendered them more dissatisfied than other laureati and therefore more inclined to demand changes in the educational system.

The process of mobilization of the maestri began long before the First World War, and, to be exact, in 1901, the year in which the National Union of Italian Maestre and Maestri was founded, which in 1902 assumed the name of National Elementary Teachers Union (UMN). Because of the pressures exerted at both the national and the local levels on representatives of the most diverse tendencies, who in a situation of restricted electoral suffrage could not but be sensitive to the demands of a wide and influential band of the electorate,[37] the UMN succeeded quickly in achieving some remarkable successes especially in regard to the problems of pensions and the juridical status of maestri. All the same, it remained faithful until the outbreak of the war to the line which came out of its Congress of 1902: apoliticism, the refusal to join the chambers of labor or to avail itself of the methods of struggle of the workers' organizations ("the teachers' strike," said President Luigi Credaro in his report, "from whatever angle it is considered, appears as a childish and, I would almost say, insane idea. The method to follow must be *persuasion*").[38] Nevertheless, at the end of the war, the process of mobilization of the maestri accelerated sharply. In June 1919 it reached the point of proclaiming a strike that lasted nine days and saw a very high participation of maestri despite the threats of superiors and cries of scandal from the moderate press. A good number of maestri were, moreover, presented in various lists at the political elections of 1919, "and for the first time something happened which was not afterward to be repeated: a small group of maestri entered the Chamber of Deputies."[39]

The process of mobilization of the engineers, on the other hand, began after the First World War. Before that there did exist a Federation of Brotherhoods of Engineers, but this, in contrast to the UMN, never succeeded in establishing itself either among the engineers or with its opponents (employers and government). It was the new situation established in the postwar period that caused a rapid advance in aggregation and mobilization of the engineers.[40] In January 1919, a gathering of Italian engineers met in Milan and laid the foundations of the National Association of Italian Engineers (ANII). In the approved agenda one read:

> The Assembly of Italian Engineers (which constitutes itself the promoter of the

> ANII), convinced of the importance assumed by the class of engineers in every manifestation of modern civilization and in clear contrast to the scarce appreciation of them and of their work which is offered by the authorities and by the country, and considering the pressing necessity that the engineers assume that role in national life which is their due as exponents and interpreters of the economic and productive activity of the country, as well as the duty that they have to provide the best protection for their qualification and professional decorum. . . .[41]

On the other hand, the engineers had a role of the greatest import in the founding of the Italian Confederation of Intellectual Labor, which its promoters intended to be "a third Estate" or "a third front" between the capitalists and the proletariat. Observing, in fact, that "the tumult of desires, aspirations, and claims of the economically most powerful or politically and syndically most organized classes leads to an ever greater superimposition of the interest of these more enterprising classes on the interests of the others, to the point where the way of reestablishing a just equilibrium is no longer sought,"[42] the engineers came to argue that "what the industrialists and the manual workers have already accomplished or are accomplishing must be accomplished by the intellectual workers, on penalty of seeing themselves increasingly deprived of every importance and every influence in the economic-social order."[43]

But what were the political tendencies of this process of mobilization of the intellectuals? If one considers, in order to answer this question, the variable "employment-unemployment," then it is no longer sufficient, in the case of intellectuals, to speak simply of a loss of status, as for the other components of the ceti medi. It is much more precise to say that there were at the same time two situations: one of partial downward mobility, the other of blocked upward mobility. The first was the situation in which the already established intellectuals who remained unemployed found themselves, especially those who had returned from the front; the second that of the youth, new laureati and diplomati, who did not succeed in finding work. One may hypothesize that both these situations produced a process of mobilization of the intellectuals to modify the existing order and to reequilibrate their status, but while the first pushed them to the right, the second led them to the left. The fact is, however, that together with unemployment, we find in the same period other factors, such as inflation and the advancement of the proletariat, which strongly attenuate the results of the second situation (blocked upward mobility). The devaluation of the currency, observed Mondolfo, "put them in the condition of the 'new plebes' of which Treves speaks, because of the descent toward a poverty no less marked than that of the proletariat; but it does not generate in them so much a brotherhood of pain and a solidarity of consciousness with the proletariat, as a sense of vexation which translates itself sometimes into resentment against the new neighbors and spiritual detachment from them, as of fallen nobility which does not know how to reconcile itself to its new companions."[44]

If one wished to explain this complex situation in terms of the theory of "relative deprivation" or of "reference groups,"[45] it could be said that the intellectuals' sense of being relatively deprived arose from several contrasts, each one of which had different consequences for their political behavior. For the young the contrast between the promised and hoped-for professional situation and the real one; for the already established intellectuals the contrast between the past professional situation and the present one; finally the contrast, for everyone, between the situation of their own group and that of the proletariat.

It was said that there were several fascist expeditions led by maestri of the UMN, and even that "there were chambers of labor set on fire with the complicity of their unionists."[46] But to understand the political orientation of the great majority of maestri, it is enough simply to glance through their professional publications. The most recurrent motif that we find there is resentment for the conquests of the proletariat, which are viewed as "usurpation of status" (to use Germani's expression). The two principal periodicals of the maestri, *La scuola* and *I diritti della scuola,* return constantly, in sketches and articles, to the same themes: while the maestri are unemployed and those employed earn starvation wages, the wages of the workers rise, because the political authorities devote all their attentions to the latter, so much so that between manual and intellectual proletarians, the real ones had by now become the latter:

> We observe that workers are paid on average above what impiegati in general are paid. We maestri, we who are at the bottom of the intellectual proletariat, even though we are first in social importance, do we not perhaps look with envy on the payment of the smith, the mason, the tailor, etc...., not to mention that of the worker of the large workshop, who all draw for their work a remuneration double or triple that which we receive? Is not an apprentice dressmaker paid more than a schoolmistress? Everyone knows these things.[47]

Even at the announcement of the increase in salaries of the maestri, *La scuola* could not help taking up its usual commentary:

> The salary increases granted to elementary teachers, following the Berenini decree, are still, for the greater part of maestri, on paper. Only a few willing local governments and some provinces have paid the teachers back payments and pay them the new salaries. Therefore a gloomy consideration leads us to compare our class with that of the other workers. If we were workers, railway employees or whatever, in any case not maestri, we would not have to wait eight months for an increase in wages after it was granted us. With maestri. . . ![48]

The principal reference group for the engineers was also the working class. In their professional press we find the same resentment, the same moral indignation, the same envy against the proletariat in ascent:

> the salaries which it [the state] offers the engineers prove once again that a mason, a machine worker, a sergeant of the Royal Guard, a typesetter, a brakeman for the railroad, and even a public roadsweeper receive wages always much higher and sometimes even double not only the salary offered the *Engineer General* in Brussels, but also that of our own Public Administration and often as well of Italian industry. The proletariat of intelligence, however, is required to have diplomas, competitive exams, office hours in excess of six, and all in exchange for the guarantee of poverty.[49]

On the occasion of the railway strikes of 1920, these "proletarians of intelligence" not only acted as strike breakers, inveighed furiously against the workers' struggle, and accused the government of weakness, but came to complain that the antistrike premium granted to workers was of the same amount as the technicians' and that even in the remuneration for strike breaking the sacred hierarchies were ignored:

> The bonus pay in favor of nonstrikers, they say, will be "uniform," between officials and workers. An engineer will receive a bonus in equal measure to a laborer, or nearly so. Blessed equality! Impenitent demagogy![50]

The engineers had further reasons, moreover, to be dissatisfied and resentful. Placed as usual between the conflicting expectations of capitalists and workers,[51] they felt role conflict acutely at the moment when class conflict most polarized Italian society. Unable to make the class leap, to pass over to the other side of the barricade, the engineers became the object of bitter attacks by workers, and, with the occupation of the factories, many of them were "made the target of personal violence, and of abductions."[52] On the other hand, the feeling that the services they rendered government and industry were not valued and repaid in adequate measure spread within their numbers. And – it should be emphasized – this was probably an accurate feeling, because the dominant economic and political groups were far too preoccupied with holding their own against the proletariat to be able to interest themselves, with the appropriate supportive therapies, in the morale of the intellectuals. Under these conditions, their feeling of being situated "between the anvil and the hammer" increasingly gained ground:

> The engineer remains a wage earner, but a wage earner of uncertain value and stripe. For the worker, he is the long hand of the "boss," if not the taskmaster working for the boss or for himself. Against the "chief" the barbs and even on occasion the assaults of the workers and their organizations are turned. Workmen in the various trades have little regard for us; they are suspicious of us. The owners and the state remember the engineer only when they're in distress and when they can't do without us. All this recalls only too well the often repeated yet expressive image of the man who stands between the anvil and the hammer.[53]

The presence of so many circumstances that pushed the mobilization process of the intellectuals to the right did not completely annul the single condition that led them to the left. In 1919 there was a schism to the left in the National Elementary Teachers Union. At the origin of this split, according to its promoters, was "the revolutionary phenomenon of the proletarianization of the ceti medi": "the ceti intellettuali detach themselves from the bourgeoisie and draw nearer to the proletariat, making common cause with it. The function of the bourgeoisie is reduced to its least tolerable expression."[54]

The programmatic bases of the new group, the Italian Elementary Teachers Union (SMI), were set in Milan in April 1919. The principal objectives of the SMI were: 1) attachment to the General Confederation of Labor; 2) the choice of the "method of class struggle" in the resolution of economic problems; 3) support of the proletariat and of its organizations; 4) an intense propaganda effort within the proletariat to urge the question of the school and the ongoing commitment "to spread learning for the purpose of emancipation among the laboring classes."[55] All the same, the group was very small, and the new SMI never succeeded in establishing itself among the maestri. "We were very few in number," wrote the official organ of the new union in 1919, "and we are still very few, but we are not alone; a whole world is with us. . . ."[56] And three years later the directors of the SMI affirmed: "There are few of us now, but this is the destiny of the vanguard minorities."[57]

The influence of partially blocked upward mobility on political behavior is even more apparent in the case of the engineers than in that of the maestri. In the process of their mobilization, which, as was noted earlier, was one of the most important moments for the establishment of the National Association of Italian Engineers, there were considerable tensions between two different groups or currents of engineers. The professional press announced, scandalized, that at their conference in Naples in 1920 the expression "class struggle" was used for the first time, and hastened to add that this unpleasant incident was due exclusively to the presence of Romita and Bordiga.[58]

In reality, the tensions and conflicts that existed within the association of engineers were due to the different professional situations in which these found themselves. The proof of this fact is that tensions arose from the activity initiated by the so-called young engineers,[59] who were hit much harder than the others by unemployment, and that they reached maximum intensity in Rome and Naples, the two cities where the problems of employment for new laureati were greatest.[60] While in Rome the dissidence subsided with the majority's conquest of the directorate of that section of the ANII,[61] in Naples the group of "young engineers" separated itself from ANII, joined the General Confederation of Labor, and began publication on May 1, 1922 of the *Giornale del Sindacato Ingegneri Italiani* which, in its first editorial, after polemicizing violently against the "bourgeois engineers," "watchful sentry of capital," confirmed that it wanted to struggle alongside the proletariat for the "revitalization of the forces of intellect."[62]

The process of mobilization of the intellectuals was not aimed only at transforming the existing socioeconomic order. To reequilibrate their own status, they also aimed at changing the institution which most often appeared to them as the most responsible for the situation in which they found themselves: the school. The maestri sought especially to obtain some measures against unemployment capable of producing immediate effects, namely of influencing the demand for work: the establishment of new elementary schools, effective enforcement of the law on compulsory attendance, the division of large classrooms into two, the reform of pensions so as to facilitate the retirement of older teachers.[63] As for measures capable of affecting the supply of labor, the maestri concentrated their demands on the reduction of the number of scuole normali.[64]

More ambitious, on the other hand, was the attempt of the engineers to reduce the supply of intellectual labor, and much more systematic was the program of change of the Italian educational system that they sought to have passed. This is easily explainable. First, the engineers were, as mentioned earlier, the hardest hit group of laureati in terms of unemployment, and thought that this situation was "caused not only by the war and by the critical period through which industry and commerce are passing, but also by the excessive trust that youth and their families have in a magnificent and brilliant future obtainable in the profession of engineering." In order fundamentally to resolve this problem, it was necessary according to them to put back in to question the mechanisms that regulated the supply of intellectual labor and therefore, "to put pressure on the government to obtain as quickly as possible a limited enrollment of students in our schools."[65] Second, the particular course of instruction of the engineers, who, as we have seen, were the only ones among the classical professional figures who were able to reach the higher studies by passing from the scuole and istituti tecnici, led them into continual comparisons with the other groups of laureati, especially the lawyers and doctors, who enjoyed greater prestige, greater power (the engineers' complaints of being underrepresented in Parliament compared to lawyers were continuous in this period), and greater possibility of employment, and thus accentuated engineers' sense of relative deprivation.

To realize the importance of the engineers' particular course of instruction in accentuating their sense of relative deprivation compared to the other laureati, it is worth examining the data of the only inquiry conducted on university students in the pre-fascist period. From table 5.4, which reports data on the social origin of students by faculty, it may be seen that in 1911 the relative majority of university students, 37 percent to be exact, came from families of landowners. The other two large contingents came from the families of intellectuals (29 percent considering diplomati and laureati together, rows 4 and 3, respectively) and impiegati and merchants (21 percent together), while students from the lower social classes barely reached 7 percent. Nevertheless, the composition of the student body by social origin varied according to faculty. Thus, while the percentages of sons of landowners were higher than the general average for those who attended the faculties of agriculture, pharmacy, law, medicine, and also literature and philosophy, they were much lower for the students who arrived at the university from the secondary schools of the "second path," who enrolled more frequently in the faculties of education, economics and commerce, science, and engineering and who came more often from families of the middle class.

The program elaborated by the engineers for changing the educational

Table 5.4. University Students by Father's Occupation and Faculty, 1911

Father's Occupation	*Law and Notary*	*Literature and Philosophy*	*Medicine*	*Pharmacy*	*Sciences*	*Engineering*	*Agriculture*	*Veterinary Science*	*Economics and Commerce*	*Education*	*Orienting Institutes*	*Total*
Landowners	40	39	42	43	26	24	53	42	15	13	49	37
Industrialists	1	1	2	1	2	5	1	2	6	—	1	2
Liberal professionals	24	17	26	30	26	30	20	19	19	38	16	25
Elementary teachers, accountants, surveyors	3	7	3	3	6	5	3	2	5	5	4	4
Impiegati	12	19	7	7	16	14	8	9	14	22	11	11
Merchants	9	6	9	8	9	11	10	11	28	—	10	10
Armed service	2	2	1	2	3	3	1	2	3	19	3	2
Workers, assistants, odd-jobbers, service personnel	6	6	5	3	6	5	2	2	5	—	5	5
Farmers, peasants, farmhands	2	2	4	2	3	1	2	9	2	—	1	2
Not ascertained	1	1	1	1	3	2	—	2	3	3	—	2
Total	100	100	100	100	100	100	100	100	100	100	100	100
(N)	(3,606)	(240)	(1,622)	(327)	(254)	(1,574)	(300)	(98)	(235)	(37)	(566)	(8,859)

SOURCE: Elaboration of data taken from: ISTAT, *Indagine sugli studenti iscritti nelle Università e negli Istituti superiori nell'anno accademico 1931–32* (Rome, Failli, 1936).

system was officially sanctioned in the works and activities of the Commission for the Reform of Studies in Engineering, appointed in 1919 by Minister of Public Education Baccelli, in which the directors of the university polytechnical institutes and faculties of engineering in the various cities of Italy took part. The report of the Baccelli Commission identified two basic objectives to be achieved by reform of the educational system: 1) "to elevate the tone of studies currently imparted in the faculties of engineering"; 2) "to uncrowd the faculties of engineering, from which every year there now graduate a number of diplomati much greater than the capacity of our national, industrial, and professional life to absorb."[66] To achieve these objectives it was proposed, first, that the polytechnical institutes, which then had only a three-year course of study which had subsequently to be followed by two years of study at a mathematics faculty, should include "the whole complex of five years in course"; second, that university enrollment fees should be increased; third – and much more important – that the physics-mathematics section of the istituti tecnici be abolished and the possiblity of access to the university polytechnical institutes be granted only to students coming from the liceo so that there would be "no difference between the secondary preparation of engineers and that of doctors and lawyers": "The general education of the engineer must be no different from that of the doctor or lawyer. In life, lawyers, doctors, and engineers are continually in contact: from their ranks must emerge the leaders of the public life of the country; they must be able to participate with equal resources in the discussions of assemblies of every type."[67]

Characteristics of the Gentile Reform

Recalling the Gentile Reform some years later, Mussolini wrote: "the mill ground continually, producing in great number the kind of men that ended up for the most part obtaining jobs in the bureaucracy. The functioning of the public administration was thus lowered by deadened personnel, deprived of life. The university created other dummies in the so-called 'liberal arts' such as jurisprudence and medicine. It was time that such a delicate mechanism that exercised so much influence on the spiritual life of the nation was renewed in a precise, definitive, and organic manner. We had to expel from the secondary schools the negative and arrogant elements. . . ."[68] Indeed, once it had seized power, the Fascist Party paid the debts that it had contracted with the two most important social groups to which it owed its success: the big bourgeoisie and the ceti medi. If in favor of the big bourgeoisie it issued all those measures of political economy with which we are familiar, from the abolition of registration of share titles to privatization of telephone networks and of insurance, it was no less grateful to the ceti medi. It took a series of measures favoring the various categories of artisans, limited the awarding of licenses to favor the merchants, and launched the Gentile Reform to favor the ceti intellettuali.

There were, however, other good reasons to change the educational system. In addition to the desire to create mechanisms of socialization more in keeping with the ideology of the new regime, it was necessary to radically overcome that imbalance between school and labor market which was so dysfunctional to the needs of whatever group was in power, and therefore of the fascists as well. In the first place, intellectual unemployment brought about constant pressure on the government by the various organizations of intellectuals to increase the demand for work.

> This system could not be allowed to continue indefinitely [wrote Balbino Giuliano, one of Gentile's closest collaborators and later Minister of Public Education] playing with the destiny of the nation and its students. It could not be allowed to continue sending forth diplomati and laureati whose lives ended up in the condition of one who finds himself in an orchestra with a flute without knowing how to play. It could not be allowed to go on enlarging every day the ranks of disabled who confront the government with the choice of abandoning some of them to poverty or creating useless positions for them.[69]

In the second place, unemployment produced that radicalization of the ceti intellettuali which, if it had largely worked in favor of the fascists before the March on Rome, could have turned against them now that they had conquered power. Recalling the period preceding the reform, the same Balbino Giuliano wrote: "I experienced the distressing sensation of seeing children playing with weapons; and more than once I said to myself that the most dangerous illiteracy was not that of the poor people who knew neither how to read nor write, but was that of the well-educated classes."[70]

The Gentile Reform was, in substance, a fundamental plan for changing the mechanisms of socialization and selection of the educational system of Casati. It aimed at two different objectives: the training of students to the most complete subordination, and the reduction of the supply of intellectual labor. Leaving aside the investigation of changes concerning the mechanisms of socialization, which besides already being familiar do not concern the present discussion, it is well to consider the transformations brought about in the mechanisms of selection. First of all, series of examinations at various levels of the educational system was introduced: for admission, eligibility, promotion, up to the qualifying exams for the practice of a profession, all of which were to function as filters and regulators of the flow of students. But these were certainly not the most important changes. At the level of higher education, Gentile again confronted the problem of the number of universities, espousing the thesis of the abolitionists. However, facing the unfailing and very strong resistance of the holders of threatened interests, he was forced to give way to a strategy in some ways reminiscent of that devised in his time by Minister Baccelli: "slow suppression by anemia."[71]

The law of September 30, 1923, in fact, divided the universities into three categories: A, B, and C. The universities and higher institutes of type A were under the complete care of the state, those of type B were maintained by agreements between the state, local governments and private bodies, while the "free" universities of type C were exclusively supported by local governments and private interests and received no assistance from the state. If by this distinction Gentile aimed in the long run to suppress by natural attrition the smallest universities, for the time being he not only was unable to reduce their number but was actually forced to increase it. Milan, Bari, Florence, and Trieste became seats of universities, while new faculties were granted to the already existing universities of Cagliari and Messina.

The most important innovations, those that radically altered the internal structure of the Italian educational system, were introduced at the secondary level. In the classical branch, the so-called supplementary classes were abolished and a limit on enrollments was introduced. In the other branches, the scuole normali, which were renamed *istituti magistrali,* were reduced drastically in number (as the maestri had demanded–from 153 to 87). But the biggest change took place in the technical sector, where the scuola tecnica was abolished and replaced by another school without outlet: the *scuola complementare.* In short, under the reform of 1923 the student who finished the elementary school and wanted to continue studies found himself facing these schools: the ginnasio-liceo, the liceo scientifico, the istituto magistrale and the istituto tecnico (each of which now had a lower-secondary course), and, finally, the scuola complementare (besides the *liceo femminile* in which girls could enroll at age fourteen). But while as before the liceo (which now added a distinctly scientific section) gave the student access to the entire university, and the istituti tecnici allowed access only to the faculties of economics and commerce or statistics (and no longer science, mathematics, engineering, etc.), the new scuola complementare and the liceo femminile were entirely closed.

Gentile never made a mystery of the objectives motivating these changes. In August 1923, two months after launching his reform, he expressed himself in these terms in an interview in the *Giornale d'Italia:*

> To the somewhat irate question, "How will we find employment for all the students?" I answer: Positions need not be found for all. Let me explain myself. The reform aims exactly at this: to reduce the scholastic population which, in recent years, by universal recognition, has increased to the point of plethora, with obvious damage to both students and teachers. A little while ago I read in a newspaper the statistical news: in three years 1,500 engineers received the laurea in Milan. What will they have to do, and where can they find work? Until last year, the average yield of diplomas for elementary school teachers was about 15,000 a year, while the need was for 2,000 or 3,000. Naturally, the exorbitant number only puts pressure on the public administrations for finding jobs, in whatever manner. Now, one of the fundamental criteria of my reform aims directly at avoiding such pernicious defects.[72]

The model of the educational system created by the reform of 1923 is clear enough. At the *upper-secondary* level, by closing access to the istituti tecnici to almost all university faculties, Gentile reversed the tendency of the preceding twenty-year period and re-professionalized the secondary schools, which reached, indeed, a level of professionalization much greater than that foreseen by the educational system of Casati. In other words, for Gentile, the istituti tecnici were to perform almost exclusively the function of training intermediate professional cadres and not, as had happened before, university students. At the *lower-secondary* level, Gentile replaced the relatively open system provided by Casati with a closed one, introducing even two dead-end schools: the complementare and the liceo femminile. Gentile's objective at the level of the scuola media, it must be pointed out, was not simply to decimate the number of students, but to reduce the number of students in the schools that permitted access to the university and to redirect the others into the two dumping schools. In fact, had he chosen the straightforward exacerbation of selection, by clearing out altogether some part of the students from the educational system, he would have removed them from scholastic socialization just at the time when the nascent regime had an extraordinary need for educational instruction in order to transmit its own ideologies and to consolidate its consensus. The two dumping schools constituted, in a certain sense, a way out of the selection-socialization dilemma. The liceo femminile, "a school fit for the intellectual and moral needs of young ladies," served to absorb and block the demand for instruction of the female students, and put the istituto magistrale under protection.[73]

But the most important was the scuola complementare, to which was entrusted the fundamental task of looking after the socialization of the subordinate masses while at the same time preventing these from forming a "too elevated" level of aspiration and "encumbering" the schools that opened access to the university. "The complementare," said Senator Tamassia with exemplary clarity, "the only one in the poor villages, had to swallow the student and restore him saturated with a measured and reduced knowledge, and that is all. Undoubtedly, in order to prevent the creation of misfits, lawyers, lettered men, philosophers, that school cut a long story short."[74] And a year later, speaking of this school, Hon. Meriano affirmed: "The criterion that presided over its establishment was the same one that led to the reduction in the number of istituti magistrali: the criterion of practicality, of uncrowding the market for impiegati. Instead of a small bourgeoisie that renders the state plethoric and mechanical, a new small bourgeoisie, a class of artisans, of workers, of peasants passably educated – in short the true people's school, the true post-elementary school, the practical school."[75] The scuola complementare had, therefore, a role of the highest import in the model provided by the reform of 1923: it was to grow larger, to become "one of the fundamental ganglia of Italian public education,"[76] so much so that it was the only school for which no limit on enrollments was foreseen.

The program of change that Gentile sought to realize was thus very similar to that elaborated in the preceding twenty-year period by the most prestigious Italian intellectuals. Speaking to the Senate, Gentile was able, therefore, to point out the precedents for his reform in Galletti and Salvemini's *La riforma della scuole media* ("a book dedicated to Turati")* and in the Report of the Royal Commission for the Ordering of Secondary Studies. Nor may one argue that he was misleading when he affirmed, "I can say that I have invented nothing," and when, considering the activities of his predecessors, he added, "the ideas remained in the books. There, Honorable Senators, they would have

*Filippo Turati (1857–1932): socialist leader elected to parliament in 1896 and leader of the reformist section of the socialists that urged abandonment of revolutionary methods.

always remained without fascism, which has likewise given to the Italian State this energy which for too many years was called for: I mean the faith and the strength necessary to translate into action all those ideas of the commission which could and had to be carried out."[77] In effect, if the reactionary program of change which had been elaborated by the idealist intellectuals and by their allies had never been carried out before then; if after so many years of discussion the critical problem of the secondary school had not been resolved; if in consequence the imbalance between school and labor market had worsened, this was due exclusively to the fact that the power relations between the social classes of that time had not allowed it. Only the defeat of the working class and the advent of fascism, by changing these power relations, had established the conditions for the realization of the educational program of the idealists.

The Gentile Reform produced its effects quite promptly. The number of enrollments in the secondary schools underwent a virtual collapse. Figure 5.1 shows the course of enrollments of all the secondary schools of the lower and upper level from 1913 – 14 to 1926 – 27. The upper curve indicates that the number of enrollments, which had risen continually from 260,000 in 1913 – 14 to 337,000 in the school year 1922 – 23, underwent a reversal of this tendency beginning in that year and reached the lowest point (around 237,000 enrollees) in 1926 – 27. The collapse of enrollments is even sharper if the students of the two dumping schools (the complementare and the liceo femminile) are excluded from the total. In this case, the number of enrollees who could, theoretically, continue their studies up to the university level declined enough to reach a much lower level than in 1913 – 14.

Table 5.5, on the other hand, shows the effects of the Gentile Reform at the university level. Here the number of enrollments, which had reached it highest point of 53,000 in the first two years of the postwar period (under very particular conditions, therefore), had stabilized at 44 – 45,000 in the following years. Beginning from 1926 – 27, the first year in which the effects of the Gentile Reform could have been felt, they decreased by a rate of 5 percent in the first year, and 1 percent and 4.8 percent in the two following years, reaching in 1928 – 29 a level of 40,000. But even more than on the number of enrollments (the reduction of which was, for reasons that I will discuss shortly, much lower that Gentile's objectives had established), the Gentile Reform of 1923 produced important effects on the composition by faculty. From table 5.5 it can be seen, in fact, that the decrease of enrollments occurred generally in those faculties such as that of mathematical, physical, and natural sciences, and of engineer-

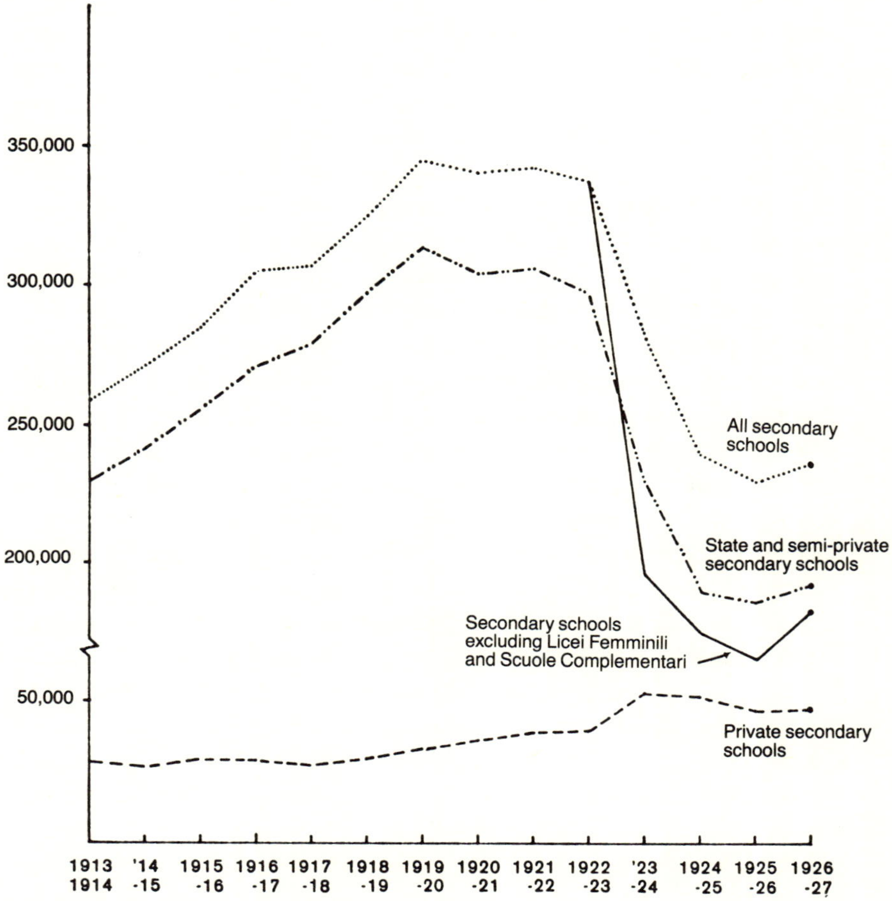

Figure 5.1. Course of Enrollments in the Secondary Schools from 1913–14 to 1926–27.

ing, which in the past were entered through that scuola tecnica which the reform had replaced with a dead-end school, the complementare.

In particular, the reform had very profound effects on engineering, first, regarding the number of enrollments, and second, regarding the social origin of students. The burden of enrollments in engineering, which had risen constantly, from 10.47 percent of the total in 1896–97 to 23.25 percent in 1921–22 (with a high point of 25.88 percent in 1917–18), began a steady decline from that year on, decreasing to 11.15 percent in 1931–32, and directly to 8.21

Table 5.5 Students Enrolled in the Universities from 1913–14 to 1929–30 by Faculty

Faculty	1913–14	1914–15	1915–16	1916–17	1917–18	1918–19	1919–20	1920–21	1921–22	1922–23	1923–24	1924–25	1925–26	1926–27	1927–28	1928–29	1929–30
Jurisprudence	9,382	9,009	8,450	8,479	8,627	10,036	10,225	9,766	8,566	7,991	8,288	8,864	9,391	8,871	8,933	8,835	9,864
Economics and commerce	1,379	1,631	1,075	1,289	2,554	3,791	5,792	7,212	6,161	5,453	4,814	4,369	5,209	5,886	5,902	6,687	7,745
Political science	130	134	92	84	75	118	131	170	195	224	255	423	510	444	490	636	886
Naval institute	—	—	—	—	—	—	—	61	116	135	125	205	242	189	204	228	207
Literature and philosophy	1,908	2,232	2,248	2,618	3,109	3,538	3,631	3,586	3,278	3,067	2,765	2,595	2,551	2,501	2,397	2,378	2,546
Education	282	502	588	783	800	1,112	1,165	941	747	749	597	907	1,038	1,070	1,064	1,139	1,322
Oriental Institute	—	—	—	—	—	—	—	—	—	—	11	119	60	105	208	400	541
Medicine and surgery	5,342	5,663	6,193	8,006	8,645	9,170	10,524	10,208	9,957	10,080	9,429	9,105	9,126	8,865	9,497	8,985	9,990
Veterinary medicine	290	360	335	341	313	519	881	1,068	916	919	826	832	984	909	1,000	748	704
Engineering (except 2 yr. prep. course)	3,105	3,684	3,879	4,204	4,951	5,442	8,025	7,946	7,100	6,203	4,877	5,075	4,892	3,807	3,437	2,308	2,489
Engineering (2 yr. prep. course)	3,227	3,159	3,129	3,754	5,030	6,229	5,665	4,416	4,207	4,062	2,978	3,194	2,892	2,760	2,154	1,864	2,083
Architecture	29	35	26	39	30	75	61	94	116	143	152	149	178	144	181	184	241
Mathematical, physical, and natural sciences	1,325	1,534	1,473	1,651	2,765	3,402	4,000	4,030	4,155	3,838	4,181	3,825	3,851	2,906	2,801	2,146	2,318
Pharmacy	1,080	1,151	992	1,075	1,167	1,547	2,109	2,350	2,586	2,816	3,080	3,309	3,424	3,228	3,076	2,732	2,770
Agriculture	547	530	488	559	625	1,135	1,461	1,391	1,034	881	757	789	860	1,027	950	983	1,009
Industrial chemistry	—	—	—	—	—	—	—	—	—	—	—	—	—	152	156	126	135
Total	28,026	29,624	28,968	32,882	38,691	46,114	53,670	53,239	49,134	46,561	43,235	43,760	45,208	42,864	42,450	40,399	44,940

SOURCE: ISTAT, *Statistica dell'istruzione superiore nell'anno accademico 1945–46* (Rome, 1948).

Table 5.6. University Students by Father's Occupation and Faculty, 1931–32

Father's Occupation	*Law*	*Political Science*	*Literature and Philosophy*	*Medicine*	*Pharmacy*	*Mathematical, Physical, and Natural Sciences*
Proprietors and well-to-do	14	14	6	13	12	11
Managers and entrepreneurs	4	5	3	5	4	8
Liberal professions	33	27	30	28	35	26
Elementary teachers, accountants, surveyors	4	3	6	3	5	4
Impiegati	23	24	28	19	20	25
Merchants	10	9	9	17	11	11
Army	2	5	4	1	1	2
Artisans, workers, wage earners	2	—	3	3	2	3
Farmers, tenant farmers, leasing peasants	4	7	5	6	4	4
Pensioners and other occupations	4	6	6	5	6	6
Total	100	100	100	100	100	100
(N)	(8,555)	(609)	(2,247)	(9,358)	(2,040)	(3,322)

Table 5.6. (continued)

Father's Occupation	*Engineering*	*Architecture*	*Agriculture*	*Veterinary Science*	*Economic and Commercial Sciences*	*Education*	*Oriental Institute*	*Naval Institute*	*Total*
Proprietors and well-to-do	8	16	17	16	8	7	9	21	11
Managers and entrepreneurs	10	9	5	4	6	3	2	5	5
Liberal professions	28	27	23	15	12	15	27	—	26
Elementary teachers, accountants, surveyors	4	2	5	4	4	6	7	—	4
Impiegati	22	22	15	15	31	27	25	32	24
Merchants	11	6	11	16	20	12	12	15	14
Army	3	1	1	1	2	4	2	7	2
Artisans, workers, wage earners	2	3	2	4	4	6	—	—	3
Farmers, tenant farmers, leasing peasants	4	7	15	16	4	8	2	6	5
Pensioners and other occupations	8	7	6	9	9	12	14	14	6
Total	100	100	100	100	100	100	100	100	100
(N)	(2,671)	(373)	(736)	(471)	(6,912)	(1,271)	(367)	(121)	(39,053)

SOURCE: Elaboration of data taken from: ISTAT, *Indagine sugli studenti iscritti nelle Università e negli Istituti superiori nell'anno accademico 1931–32* (Rome: Failli, 1936).

percent in 1936–37. From the data given in table 5.6, it can also be seen that in 1931 – 32, in contrast to the situation twenty years earlier, the percentage of students in engineering belonging to the upper social classes (proprietors and the well-to-do, managers and entrepreneurs) was equal to that of the students in law or medicine. The same can be said for the faculty previously attended by students coming from the scuole tecniche, namely the mathematical, physical, and natural sciences.

Table 5.6 shows as well that, with the Gentile Reform, a good part of the cost of the contradictions of the Italian educational system was once again unloaded onto the shoulders of the working class. Comparing the data of table 5.6 with those of table 5.4, even with all the caution required by the use of different occupational categories, one can see the changes undergone in the social composition of the student body from 1911 to 1931. These changes reflect, first of all, those that occurred five or ten years earlier in the social stratification of the country. It is in this light that the decline in students who were the children of landowners, which decreased from 37 percent to 11 percent, and the increase of those coming from families of managers and entrepreneurs, must be interpreted. The same can be said, at least in part, of the very sharp increase in the percentage of offspring of impiegati, which passed from 10 percent to 24 percent. But these changes are also a consequence of the changes undergone by the internal structure of the educational system under the Gentile Reform. This is demonstrated by the fact that the percentage of students who were the children of workers decreases from 5 percent to 3 percent even though in twenty years the numerical weight of the industrial proletariat had grown sharply in the occupational composition of the active population. The data regarding the last occupational group are of limited significance, because it is not possible to determine how large a part was constituted by farmers who owned their own land.

All this does not mean that the Gentile Reform did not encounter resistance. The opposite is true. In spite of the fact that power relations had changed and the political situation, as noted earlier, was the most suited for a restructuring of the educational system, the reform of 1923, by its nature, could not help encountering hostility from a large number of people. Demonstrating considerable foresight, Piero Gobetti had written in 1919:

> Certainly it will not be easy to succeed in a reform so seriously and intelligently revolutionary – and not only because of the deficiencies of Minerva. Even if

> Giovanni Gentile were at the Ministry of Education, as we would wish, there would be at the least a struggle with that eighty percent of the students eliminated and with their fathers, grandfathers, and uncles, who would not submit to seeing sons and grandsons in the workshop. Not to mention the fact that there would also be reaction from the teachers who would find themselves without enough state schools and with nowhere to teach.[78]

Resistance to the reform manifested itself already at the stage of its preparation, from the moment that Gentile, as noted, had to retract the idea of reducing the number of universities. But the sharpest resistance occurred at the time of the reform's implementation.[79] If the National Association of Italian Engineers gave its enthusiastic approval to the reform because it aimed to "raise again the level of learning and reduce the numbers of the proletariat of intelligence by a severe selection,"[80] as the Baccelli Commission had demanded, the very many parents of students who were cleared out of the secondary schools that gave access to the university were not of the same opinion. The most clamorous example of resistance (a veritable textbook case in the sociology of education which illustrates perfectly the relationship between school and social promotion) is furnished us by the reaction of parents to the new scuola complementare. That school to which Gentile assigned such an important role in the new educational system was, in fact, completely deserted. As shown by the data in table 5.7, from the 141,000 students in the scuola tecnica of 1922 – 23 only 83,000 students passed to the scuola complementare in the following year.

> The frightening off of families [wrote an expert from the Ministry of Public Education] and their crowding at the doors of the scuola complementare to withdraw their young produced a situation comparable to that in which a distrusted bank, even if unjustly, finds itself in danger and under siege by its depositors who reclaim their money. Financial men are acquainted with the *run*, this earthquake that can shake in one blow even the most solid institution if it has not prepared itself to face it.[81]

The operation undertaken by Gentile to attempt to alter the course of a large number of students by means of a "cul-de-sac" school, as Turati described it[82] (a school that could look after their socialization without permitting the continuation of studies, thereby convincing them that schooling and social promotion were, at least for them, two very different things) was shown in practice to be much more difficult than foreseen. When, some years later, a colleague of Gentile observed that "the secondary school was and is threatened on several

Table 5.7. The Course of Enrollments with the Transformation of the Scuola Tecnica into the Scuola Complementare

School Year	*Number of Schools*			*Number of Students Enrolled*						
	State	*Semi-private*	*Private*	*State and Semi-private Schools*			*Private Schools*			*All Schools*
				Male	*Female*	*Total*	*Male*	*Female*	*Total*	
					Scuole tecniche					
1920–21	314	108	190	84,462	48,980	133,442	11,635	2,507	14,142	147,584
1921–22	324	114	237	86,471	44,561	131,032	12,905	3,414	16,319	147,351
1922–23	341	107	208	87,158	39,862	127,020	11,597	2,612	14,209	141,229
					Scuole complementari					
1923–24	334	96	174	50,226	24,429	74,655	5,326	2,818	8,144	82,799
1924–25	340	91	183	39,800	18,098	57,898	3,928	2,764	6,692	64,590

SOURCE: ISTAT, *Annuario statistico italiano.*

sides: families still attached to the 'diploma disease,' to the conquest of the diploma with little or no heed to the authentic, actual learning of their young, have threatened it and threaten it now . . . ,"[83] he grasped the most important reason for the partial failure of the reform of 1923. While it might have been possible to start out with an educational system equipped with a dumping school, which carried out the socialization of students without allowing them to continue studies, it was not easy, once the open education system of Casati had been established and had put down roots, to march in reverse. Once the school had affirmed itself as the real channel of social mobility, it was quite difficult to persuade the people to send their children to school only "for authentic, actual learning," also because those whom one wished to persuade were precisely those who had to send their children to the complementare, namely to that school which by definition would have separated them from this learning forever.

CHAPTER SIX

Education and Labor Market in the Fascist Period

Was there or was there not considerable intellectual unemployment during the fascist period? This is the first question for which I will seek an answer in the pages that follow. In truth, it is still an entirely open question because either it has never been confronted (I know of not one historian of fascism who has ever considered it) or it has been confronted in a completely unsatisfactory manner. In particular, Walter Kotschnig, in a book that can be considered, at a distance of thirty-five years from its publication, the most important study of the problem of intellectual unemployment in over twenty countries between the two world wars, denies that this phenomenon concerned Italy.[1] Basing his argument albeit on "official" information, he claimed that there was no widespread intellectual unemployment in Italy for three reasons: first, because of the "low number of university graduates in comparison to other countries" produced each year by the universities (about 9,000) and because of the fact that almost a third of these were absorbed by the Public Administration; second, because of the "rapid economic development" that characterized Italy after the First World War and that manifested itself especially in the birth of numerous new industries; finally, because of the Ethiopian War of 1935–36, which had eased the labor market by keeping a good number of Italian youth "employed" under arms.

In reality, the situation of the intellectual labor market during these years was profoundly different. What I shall try to show in this chapter is that, in spite of the Gentile Reform and the economic growth that characterized the first phase of the fascist period, the phenomenon of the intellectual unemployment persisted until it found, with the outbreak of the Second World War, a temporary solution with the conversion of the unemployed into soldiers.

Besides seeking to document the existence of considerable intellectual unemployment during the fascist period, I will attempt to analyze its causes by considering three variables that seem to me particularly important. In order not of importance but of presentation, they are: 1) the characteristics of the educational system, and in particular, the partial failure of the Gentile Reform, namely of what was – in my view, as I have noted – the most important reactionary attempt to resolve the existing imbalance between school and labor market; 2) the course of the international market for intellectual labor, which reduced the possibility of emigration by closing what had been, before fascism, the principal safety valve for the surplus of laureati; 3) the course of the Italian economy, especially from the year 1929 when, as is well known, the great crisis occurred and the Great Depression began. The first of these variables affected the course of secondary and higher education and, therefore, the supply of intellectual labor; the second affected demand; finally the third, besides influencing demand, as is obvious, also affected the course of education, and thus the supply.

The Educational System: Partial Failure of the Gentile Reform

It is best to begin with the course of secondary and higher education during the fascist period. Concerning secondary education, I have already pointed out that the Gentile Reform led to a sharp drop in the number of enrollments, which reached the lowest point in 1925 – 26 and remained practically stationary for the following three years. However, beginning in 1929, there was an exceptional expansion in all four branches of secondary education: in ten years, enrollments in the istituti tecnici doubled, and those in the ginnasi and the licei classici and scientifici grew by over two and a half times. But the strongest growth was realized in elementary teachers' education, which in a decade quintupled its enrollments (table 6.1).

Regarding higher education, the Gentile Reform, as has been seen, led to a much more moderate drop in the number of enrollments, which reached its lowest point in 1928–29 at 40,000. Even at this level, however, starting in 1929 the curve began to rise again at a very sustained pace, so much so that in ten years the number of enrollments had more than doubled (table 6.2).

We may bettter account for the course of higher education during the fascist period by comparing the Italian data with those of other European countries, as

Table 6.1. Course of Enrollments in the Secondary Schools (State and Non-State), 1926–27 to 1939–40

Year	*Ginnasi and Licei Classici*	*Licei Scientifici*	*Istituti Magistrali*	*Istituti Tecnici*
1926–27	83,458	5,921	27,139	74,865
1927–28	82,864	6,263	27,178	70,736
1928–29	83,098	6,179	28,202	71,576
1929–30	88,617	6,271	32,935	76,657
1930–31	90,837	6,300	37,878	73,227
1931–32	104,781	6,619	48,155	84,811
1932–33	124,422	7,239	62,507	92,558
1933–34	137,718	7,561	79,757	84,787
1934–35	149,721	7,994	99,578	86,756
1935–36	171,133	8,601	123,969	89,447
1936–37	190,145	9,887	154,168	95,542
1937–38	196,542	10,209	159,254	117,115
1938–39	208,078	12,039	168,743	134,122
1939–40	222,039	14,074	167,799	147,552

SOURCE: ISTAT, *Annuario statistico italiano 1942* (Rome, 1942).

we have already done for other periods. It was noted in fact, in chapter 2, that in the last two decades of the nineteenth century Italy had not only the highest rate of illiteracy among the European countries but also the highest number of university students relative to population. It was noted in chapter 4, on the other hand, that as a consequence especially of the economic growth that characterized the Giolittian period, Italy lost the latter distinction by becoming, in 1913 – 14, one of the countries with the lowest relative number of university students.

With the First World War, however, the expansion of higher education in Italy picked up again vigorously. In spite of this, as one can see from table 6.3, at the beginning of the fascist period, or more exactly in 1924 – 25, Italy had eleven students per ten thousand inhabitants, that is, a lower ratio than that of Germany, Sweden, France, and Holland, and higher only than Great Britain's. The Gentile Reform, provoking a sharp slowdown in the growth of higher education, had further accentuated the distance between Italy and the other countries, so much so that in 1930, as may be seen in the same table, the number of university students relative to population in Germany had become exactly twice that of Italy. Beginning in that year, however, the situation changed once again. Italy recovered, in about nine years, a good part of the distance. In 1938 – 39 it

Table 6.2. Students Enrolled in the University by Faculty, 1930–31 to 1941–42

Faculty	*1930–31*	*1931–32*	*1932–33*	*1933–34*	*1934–35*	*1935–36*	*1936–37*	*1937–38*	*1938–39*	*1939–40*	*1940–41*	*1941–42*
Jurisprudence	10,073	10,310	11,515	12,149	12,998	13,331	14,097	14,052	13,583	14,245	20,937	22,346
Economics and commerce	8,285	8,490	9,191	9,601	10,623	11,414	13,008	13,222	13,115	13,388	23,011	27,479
Political science	806	770	856	914	944	1,130	1,211	1,413	1,414	1,664	2,958	3,489
Statistical science	—	17	17	15	16	41	87	129	122	129	309	198
Naval Institute	179	170	249	302	355	386	359	316	312	295	665	872
Literature and philosophy	2,709	2,829	3,571	4,046	4,981	6,312	7,756	8,871	9,752	11,447	15,779	18,163
Education	1,456	1,746	1,964	2,910	3,698	4,291	6,229	7,803	10,061	11,905	13,800	13,871
Oriental Institute	656	484	598	537	696	992	1,198	1,866	2,617	3,359	7,986	8,814
Medicine and surgery	9,991	11,168	13,231	14,298	14,803	14,152	13,829	12,492	10,909	11,020	13,781	16,140
Veterinary science	673	593	660	669	723	690	729	858	873	899	1,242	1,476
Engineering (excluding first two years)	2,658	2,382	2,618	2,671	2,475	2,391	2,573	2,619	2,687	2,725	3,809	5,367
Engineering (first two preparatory years)	1,632	1,724	1,555	1,573	1,586	1,666	1,899	2,316	2,349	3,186	5,522	6,769
Architecture	233	473	647	728	754	737	794	870	844	803	1,114	1,506
Mathematical, physical, and natural sciences	2,269	2,192	2,520	2,519	2,921	3,155	3,347	3,707	4,425	5,737	8,840	10,410
Pharmacy	2,734	2,560	2,904	2,786	2,718	2,427	2,266	2,180	2,051	1,896	2,567	3,146
Agriculture	1,130	934	933	899	992	1,204	1,382	1,305	1,244	1,467	2,533	3,142
Industrial chemistry	121	92	97	96	77	82	127	151	207	266	450	585
Total	46,262	47,614	53,672	52,294	62,020	64,944	71,512	74,909	77,429	85,535	127,058	145,793

SOURCE: ISTAT, *Statistica dell'istruzione superiore nell'anno accademico 1945-46* (Rome, 1948).

had a ratio of seventeen students to ten thousand inhabitants, distinctly higher than that of Germany (which, because of the introduction in 1933 of the numero chiuso, underwent an actual collapse in university enrollments), Great Britain, Holland, and Belgium, equal to that of France, and lower only than that of Sweden and Switzerland.

Now, to understand the course of secondary and higher education during the fascist period it is necessary to examine first of all the characteristics of the educational system after what I have defined as the partial failure of the Gentile Reform. In speaking of a "partial failure," I am certainly not referring to all those "inovations" introduced to reinforce the authoritarian character of the Italian school, because with the passage of time – that is, as fascism showed its true face – these took root to such an extent that they survived fascism and are still in part present in the current educational system. I am referring rather to those modifications, introduced especially at the secondary level, that aimed to reduce the level of aspiration of students and the number of those able to reach the university without reducing (indeed, increasing) the number of youth who were to undergo the socializing activity of the school.

I have already alluded to the fact that the most dangerous opposition to the Gentile Reform came not from political actors but from the silent and yet very perceptible resistance of those most directly interested: the parents of those children whom the reform sought forcibly to channel into the dumping schools. The collapse of enrollments in the scuole complementari put Gentile once again before the very socialization-selection dilemma that he had sought to resolve with the establishment of these schools. The reactions of parents affected by the reform showed that in the attempt to resolve the problem of selection (and consequently that of the school – labor market imbalance) one ran the risk of aggravating that of socialization, namely, of losing a segment of the age group from 11 to 14 years old just at the moment when the new regime had a desperate need of the school's activity to transmit its values and ideology. It was exactly to avoid running this risk that Gentile touched up the educational structures that he had only just created with a provision that was to be considered temporary. If the reason for the flight from the complementari was, as Senator Tamassi said, that this school "merited the verse: Abandon all hope, O ye who enter here,"[2] then in order to conquer the resistance of the parents, it was necessary to reestablish, if only temporarily and in a very attenuated from, that link between school and social promotion which the very institution of the scuole complementari had sought to cut.

Table 6.3. Students (Male and Female) Enrolled per 10,000 Inhabitants in Nine Countries, 1924–25 to 1949–50

Academic Year	*Germany*		*Great Britain*		*France*		*Holland*		*Belgium*		*Sweden*		*Switzerland*		*Spain*		*Italy*	
	A	*B*	*A*	*B*	*A*	*B*	*A*	*B*	*A*	*B*	*A*	*B*	*A*	*B*	*A*	*B*	*A*	*B*
1924–25	14	9	10	—	13	11	13	9	—	—	14	12	—	—	—	—	11	8
1930–31	20	14	10	—	16	15	15	12	13	—	16	13	15	12	16	15	10	7
1938–39	11*	—	10	—	—	17	14	11	12*	—	18	14	21	18	—	—	17	9
1948–49	—	—	16	—	—	30	27	19	17‡	—	22	14	28	21	19	18	36	21
1949–50	24†	16†	—	—	—	—	29	20	—	—	24	15	27	20	—	—	31	—

A = Students enrolled in universities and other higher educational institutions.
B = Students enrolled only in universities.
* 1937.
† German Federal Republic.
‡ 1947.

SOURCE: Elaboration of data taken from: 1) V. Castrilli, "L'affollamento universitario in Europa," in *Studi in onore de M. Barillari, Annali del Seminario Giuridico Economico della Regia Università di Bari* (Bari: Cressati, 1937); 2) V. Castrilli, "Lo sviluppo della studentesca universitarià nell'ultimo ventennio," *Il giornale dell'universitá* (March 15, 1951), 3:67-72; M. C. Kaser, "Education and Economic Progress."

Thus it was that Gentile instituted, only for the period 1923 – 27, some courses of integration at the end of the scuola complementare which gave the possibility of access to the istituto tecnico and to the liceo scientifico.[3] It was a matter, as was stated very clearly by a Ministry expert, of "a wise delaying practice to give the administration time to reassure families about the vitality of the scuola complementare."[4] In reality, not even these provisions were enough to make the number in the scuola complementare pick up again, so that the law of January 7, 1929 decreed the abolition of this school and its replacement. More precisely, this and the successive laws of October 6, 1930 and June 15, 1931 rearranged lower-secondary education by instituting, in place of the scuola complementare, a *scuola secondaria avviamento al lavoro** which was only partially a dead end, in that it provided some possibility of transfer to the istituti tecnici and the magistrale.[5] It was the official recognition of the partial failure of Gentile's attempt. The new revised and corrected educational arrangement doubtless had a much more closed internal structure than that of Casati. Nevertheless, the fascist ruling group had not fully succeeded in carrying out the plan to establish the dumping school which was to have served to socialize students from the subordinate social classes while preventing them from continuing their studies.[6]

The Course of the International Market for Intellectual Labor

In the period preceding the First World War, the international market for intellectual labor was substantially "free." In almost all countries, legislation regarding immigration of intellectuals was much more open than that which regulated the migratory currents of unqualified labor. There were, indeed, some nations which did not consider the intellectual an immigrant but assimilated him as "a tourist, of independent income,"[7] and consequently did not put him under the general prescriptions of control that applied to foreigners upon entering the country. The few data available show in fact that the migratory currents of intellectuals reached considerable proportions. Besides the data that I have already reported for Italy, I shall mention that, of the total intellectual labor force, foreigners constituted 31 percent in Argentina (1914), 30 percent in

**Avviamento:* from the verb *avviare,* to set going, start, send off. Thus the *scuola secondaria avviamento al lavoro* or *avviamento* was the secondary school that got one started working.

Canada, 15 percent in Brazil (1920), 10 percent in Switzerland, and 6 percent in France.[8]

The situation changed profoundly, however, after the First World War. In the period between the First and Second World Wars, the exceptional expansion of higher education that took place in many countries of the world, but especially in Europe, caused a sharp imbalance between supply and demand for intellectual labor, an imbalance which was aggravated by the Great Depression following the crisis of 1929. To give only some indication of the seriousness of intellectual unemployment in this period, it will suffice to recall that in Japan, the number of university graduates who remained unemployed increased from 24 percent 1925 to 34 percent in 1928, and rose to as much as 46 percent in 1931. In Bulgaria and Finland unemployed intellectuals reached, after 1930, 35 percent and 59 percent, respectively.[9]

Certainly more interesting for the purposes of this discussion is the situation of two countries which for evident reasons (geographical proximity and the lesser difficulty of fitting in from the linguistic point of view) probably had an important role in the absorption of a part of the surplus of Italian laureati: France and Switzerland. Both these countries were characterized in the period between the two world wars by considerable intellectual unemployment. For France, as for most other countries, precise data are lacking. The single exception regards the engineers, for whom it is known that in 1934 about 14,000, or 25 percent of those who practiced this profession, were unemployed.[10] It is certain, however, that unemployment concerned not only engineers but all French intellectuals, and in particular the teachers, lawyers, and journalists. The situation was no different in Switzerland. There, a survey conducted in 1935 on a sample of university graduates in the preceding fifteen year period revealed the proportion of unemployed at 5.6 percent. The same investigation showed, however, that a high percentage of "employed" graduates, found themselves in a situation of underemployment or of hidden unemployment. Then too, beginning in 1935 the Swiss employment office reported that of a total of 20,000 graduates in engineering and architecture, about 7,000 were unemployed.

The immediate consequence of this situation was a sharp reduction of the migratory currents of intellectual labor. To the growing difficulties of intellectuals in emigrating to countries where they had to confront a much sharper competition than before, there were added legal restrictions of various types. The professional organizations of countries that suffered from intellectual unemployment succeeded at times, in cases where licences for practice depended exclusively on them (as was the case, for example, with the medical profession in Switzerland and Great Britain), in blocking the migratory flow. There was no need, therefore, for the political authorities to intervene directly. In other cases, these organizations exerted strong pressure (aided as well by the future unemployed, the students, who contributed by staging harsh strikes) for the enactment of truly restrictive laws. Thus, for example, in France the Armbruster Law of 1933 and those of 1934 and 1935 practically closed the borders to foreign intellectuals. In still other countries, as, for example, Holland, the problem was confronted "upstream" by prohibiting the enrollment of foreign students in national universities. But even more than by special laws, "protection" against foreign university graduates came "by way of a more severe enforcement of already existing provisions on residence and work permits."[11]

The new situation that was developing had immediate consequences for Italy as well. Giacomo di Giacomo, the leader of the Fascist Corporate Association* of Professionals and Intellectuals, founded in 1923, hoped in 1927 "that soon, from our ports humming with trade may set sail, by craft both heavy and light, not only our workers and peasants but also the captains of our ingenuity, of our own genius, to achieve new civil conquests, with the heart of our ancients and the new spirit that Fascism has given us."[12] It was clear, nonetheless, what lay behind this rhetoric. Moreover, two years earlier, di Giacomo had written: "There exists another problem that concerns not only individuals but also the national collectivity, that of intellectual emigration. Connected intimately with that of unemployment, it leads us, because of the economic crisis and the disproportion between supply and demand for intellectuals produced, to consider indispensable the placement of professionals and of technicians abroad, especially in the younger and richer countries."[13]

And, indeed, the pre-fascist and fascist governments sought to do everything possible to assist the exportation of surplus laureati. In 1920, the lawyer Valerio De Sanctis had set up a Foreign Placement Office for intellectual workers under the supervision of the Italian Colonial Office, and had visited Romania and Germany. Next the problem was addressed by the General Commission for Emigration, which established a special commission to consider the problem. Finally, the Corporate Association of Professionals and Intellectuals took up

*_Corporzione sindacale fascista:_ see _Carta del Lavoro_ in the glossary.

the question. But naturally, given the international situation, these efforts yielded no result, and the number of intellectuals who left Italy each year decreased sharply. Unfortunately, there are precise data on this subject only up to 1925, reported in table 6.4. It follows from this table, first that the number of emigrated intellectuals, which had diminished considerably in the years of the First World War, rose again in 1919. But from that year forward it began to fall, reaching the lowest number in 1925. On the other hand, this table shows also an interesting change in the geographic destination of intellectuals, which is not found for the other emigrants. In the eleven years considered (unfortunately, there are no data for destination before 1915), we note a constant increase in the percentage of intellectual emigrants to countries overseas and a corresponding reduction in the percentage of emigrants to other European countries. This accords with the fact that it was, above all, the European countries that were hit in this period by intellectual unemployment.

Regarding the data for the following period, reported in table 6.5, we must bear in mind that beginning in 1926 the criteria for classification of emigrants by profession were modified. While previously the category "emigrants in liberal professions" included exclusively "doctors, pharmacists, midwives, lawyers, engineers, and teachers," beginning in 1926 other groups of intellectuals were included in this category: "painters, sculptors, draftsmen, photoengravers" and "theater artists and musicians."[14] If we bear in mind the fact that in the preceding forty-year period these latter two groups, if taken together, had always been much larger in number than the professionals in the strict sense, it can be estimated, on the basis of the data from table 6.5, that the number of laureati who left Italy from 1928 to 1937 was about 500–600 a year. Therefore, the data of this period too, though inexact, would show a sharp drop in intellectual emigration with respect to the period preceding the First World War.

There is no doubt, however, that the sharp reduction of the emigratory flow was not due to a decline in intellectual unemployment. This the same fascist unionists were to recognize, though with their unfailing rhetoric.

> Our country's lack of emigration of intellectuals [the lawyer Cornelli observed at the First Congress of the Provincial Corporate Association of Milan of the Fascist Unions of the Intellectual Professions] is not a sign of prosperity for our intellectual classes. The lack of emigration is caused by various other conditions and considerations, and in large part by the almost impassioned attachment that the intellectual categories feel for the Mother Country. In Italy, it can be safely affirmed, there is a

Table 6.4. Destination of Emigrants in Liberal Professions and of All Emigrants, 1915–1925

Year	*Emigrants in Liberal Professions*				*Total Emigrants*			
	Continental Countries	*Overseas Countries*	*Total*	*Number Cases*	*Continental Countries*	*Overseas Countries*	*Total*	*Number Cases*
1915	88	12	100	1,567	59	41	100	118,063
1916	85	15	100	942	51	49	100	114,154
1917	84	16	100	388	76	24	100	38,248
1918	88	12	100	270	88	12	100	24,752
1919	75	25	100	1,700	60	40	100	220,376
1920	57	43	100	936	66	34	100	560,717
1921	46	54	100	384	26	74	100	215,980
1922	61	39	100	447	51	49	100	222,802
1923	52	48	100	830	49	51	100	314,185
1924	30	70	100	471	62	38	100	294,101
1925	36	64	100	353	60	40	100	236,535

SOURCE: Elaboration of data taken from: General Commission for Emigration, *Annuario statistico dell'emigrazione italiana dal 1876 al 1925* (Rome: Poliglotta, 1926).

Table 6.5. Emigrants in Liberal Professions (in the broad sense), 1928–1937

Year	*Continental Countries*			*Overseas Countries*			*Total*		
	M	*F*	*MF*	*M*	*F*	*MF*	*M*	*F*	*MF*
1928	549	348	897	553	175	728	1,102	523	1,625
1929	1,078	462	1,540	296	115	411	1,374	577	1,951
1930	1,315	398	1,713	317	70	387	1,632	468	2,100
1931	1,285	390	1,675	180	75	255	1,465	465	1,930
1932	625	200	825	112	45	157	737	245	982
1933	981	310	1,291	140	47	187	1,121	357	1,478
1934	706	266	972	209	50	259	915	316	1,231
1935	779	278	1,057	72	29	101	851	307	1,158
1936	495	142	637	107	69	176	602	211	813
1937	622	221	843	107	37	144	729	258	987

*For the definition of this category, see the text.

SOURCE: Elaboration of data taken from ISTAT, *Statistica delle migrazioni da e per l'estero* (Rome, 1933–1938), vols. 1-8.

> plethora of intellectual workers. We unionists who experience the torment and the tragedy of the working masses, we who, through the highs and lows of the crisis of production, are accustomed to feeling the pulse of the Italian economy, can with steady assurance affirm that the scanty emigration is neither a sign or an index of prosperity for the intellectual categories.[15]

The Course of the Economy

As important as the revisions and rearrangements of the Italian educational system left by the Gentile Reform of 1923 may have been, they are not enough to explain the course of secondary and higher education and, therefore, the variations recorded in the supply of intellectual labor during the fascist period. Perhaps the most important independent variable, in my view, is the course of the economy during this period. As regards the fascist period as well, if we referred to the traditional conception according to which there is always a positive relationship between the course of the economy and that of education at all levels, we would not succeed in understanding much of what happened. A superficial examination of trends in the economy and education in the fascist period does seem to confirm the validity of this conception, since the available data indicate, in fact, that from the end of 1922 until the outbreak of the Second World War, there occurred simultaneously an increase of per capita income and a growth of education at all levels. A closer analysis, however, shows us that this interpretive hypothesis is substantially mistaken. In reality, to understand something of what happened in the twenty-year fascist period, it is necessary to introduce several distinctions, as was done in the analysis of the preceding period, concerning both the course of the independent variable (the economy) and that of the dependent variable (education).

Without entering here into a detailed analysis of the course of the Italian economy during the twenty-year fascist period, it suffices to mention, for the purposes of this discussion, that two subperiods may be clearly distinguished: one that runs from the advent of fascism until 1929, and a second that runs from 1929 to the outbreak of the Second World War. Starting in 1922–23, the Italian economy entered a phase of expansion: the new regime limited workers' salaries, while in industry a sharp increase in productivity was registered; unemployment fell, from 380,000 in 1922 to 112,000 in 1925; national income grew, from 102 billion lire in 1922 to almost 125 billion in 1929. The second subperiod was characterized, on the other hand, by a deep depression: industrial production grew at an extremely low average yearly rate (1.2 percent), and national income fell so far that only in 1935 did it reach the level touched in 1929. Most important, however, unemployment expanded extraordinarily, from 300,000 in 1929 to over 1,000,000 in 1933. In particular, the difficulties of employment for the young population became severe.[16]

As far as education is concerned, however, it is necessary to distinguish primary from secondary and higher education. The course of primary education showed a positive relationship to the course of the economy. The number of enrollments in the elementary schools fell between 1921 and 1926, and rose steadily in the fifteen years following (table 6.6). This was due, however, to the sharp reduction of births that occurred in the war period.[17] If we examine the enrollment rate (namely, the number of enrollments in the elementary schools divided by the population 6–14 years of age), we see that it increased in the period of economic expansion, and remained constant or actually fell in the period of the great crisis (table 6.7).

It is more difficult to interpret the course of education at the two other levels of the educational system. Here, in the first period characterized by economic expansion, a drop or a stagnation of enrollments both at the level of secondary instruction and at the university level is recorded, while in the second period of economic depression a very considerable growth of secondary and higher education is encountered. According to Minister of Public Education Balbino Giuliano, the most important factor in the expansion of secondary education begun in 1926 was population growth, and in particular the fact that in the immediate postwar period there was a sharp pickup in the birthrate.[18] All the same, even a superficial analysis of the existing data shows that this type of explanation is completely without foundation. As may be seen, in fact, from tables 6.8 and 6.9, from 1931 to 1936 there is not only an increase in the absolute number of enrollments but also an even sharper increase in the rate of enrollment.[19]

On the other hand, to pronounce, on the basis of what has been said, the existence of an inverse relation between economic and (secondary and higher) educational development during the fascist period is not methodologically correct because of the lack, in the two subperiods considered, of a condition of *ceteris paribus*. We have seen that the two subperiods in question differ not only in the course of the economy, but also in the internal structure of the educational system, and it was observed that the sharp reduction in the number of enrollments in secondary schools and in the university that was recorded in the first

Table 6.6. Enrollments in the Elementary Schools, 1920 to 1940 (thousands)

Year	*Students*	*Year*	*Students*	*Year*	*Students*
1920–21	4,166	1927–28	3,838	1934–35	4,841
1921–22	4,267	1928–29	4,052	1935–36	5,074
1922–23	4,167	1929–30	4,340	1936–37	5,187
1923–24	3,981	1930–31	4,595	1937–38	5,051
1924–25	3,759	1931–32	4,762	1938–39	5,095
1925–26	3,622	1932–33	4,799	1939–40	5,149
1926–27	3,635	1933–34	4,818	1940–41	5,213

SOURCE: ISTAT, *Sommario di statistiche storiche italiane (1861–1955)* (Rome, 1958).

Table 6.7. Enrollments in the Elementary Schools as a Percentage of the Population 6–14 Years of Age

Area	*1921–22*	*1931–32*	*1932–33*	*1933–34*	*1934–35*	*1935–36*	*1936–37*	*1937–38*	*1938–39*
Northwest	71.05	82.24	80.59	79.21	78.01	77.81	81.12	78.16	77.70
Northeast	60.46	81.00	81.00	80.49	80.18	80.23	83.34	81.39	81.55
Center	63.07	74.63	73.23	72.63	72.04	73.61	78.29	74.78	74.21
South	45.07	62.45	62.19	67.34	60.41	60.53	63.62	60.30	59.69
Italy	57.61	73.03	72.29	71.41	70.57	70.82	74.20	71.18	70.73

SOURCE: Elaboration of data taken from F. Noble, "Istruzione scolastica," in ISTAT, *Sviluppo della popolazione italiana dal 1861 al 1961, Annali di statistica* (Rome, 1965), 17:295–320; F. Noble, "Per una più esatta determinazione della popolazione in età scolastica," *Annali di statistica* (Rome, 1940), 6:479–97.

Table 6.8. Enrollments in the Secondary Schools (excluding istituti tecnici) by Type of School and Geographic Area, 1931 and 1936

Area	*Ginnasio*		*Liceo classico*		*Liceo scientifico*		*Istituto magistrale*		*Total*	
	1931–32	*1936–37*	*1931–32*	*1936–37*	*1931–32*	*1936–37*	*1931–32*	*1936–37*	*1931–32*	*1936–37*
Northwest	18,270	31,750	6,008	8,039	1,738	2,136	12,689	41,661	38,705	83,586
Northeast	13,005	23,784	3,979	5,108	2,020	2,942	11,897	34,232	30,901	66,066
Center	17,878	34,051	5,775	7,831	1,186	1,542	9,511	32,427	34,350	75,851
South	35,197	64,941	10,995	14,641	2,539	3,267	15,493	45,848	64,226	128,697
Italy	84,350	154,526	26,759	35,619	7,483	9,887	49,590	154,168	168,182	354,200

SOURCE: Elaboration of data taken from ISTAT, *Statistica dell'istruzione media per l'anno scolastico 1931–32 e notizie statistiche per gli anni scolastici dal 1927–28 al 1930–31,* (Rome, 1936), and from *Annuario statistico italiano.*

Table 6.9. Enrollments in the Secondary Schools (excluding Istituti tecnici) per 10,000 Inhabitants from 15-25 Years of Age by Type of School and Geographic Area, 1931 and 1936

Area	*Ginnasio*		*Liceo classico*		*Liceo scientifico*		*Istituto magistrale*		*Total*	
	1931–32	*1936–37*	*1931–32*	*1936–37*	*1931–32*	*1936–37*	*1931–32*	*1936–37*	*1931–32*	*1936–37*
Northwest	90.39	193.89	29.72	49.09	8.59	13.04	62.77	254.42	191.49	510.46
Northeast	72.39	154.11	22.15	33.10	11.24	19.06	66.22	221.81	172.02	428.10
Center	130.56	279.88	42.17	64.37	8.66	12.67	69.46	266.53	250.86	623.46
South	131.17	270.34	40.98	60.95	9.46	13.60	57.74	190.86	239.35	535.74
Italy	107.17	227.26	34.00	52.38	9.51	14.54	63.01	226.73	213.69	520.92

SOURCE: Elaboration of data taken from ISTAT, "Sviluppo della popolazione italiana dal 1861–1961," in *Annali di statistica,* vol. 17 (Rome, 1965), and from sources noted in table 6.8.

phase could be explained on the basis of the Gentile Reform. It can be advanced, however, by way of hypothesis, that the most important source of the growth of secondary and higher education that occurred in the second phase of the fascist period was the Great Depression and the marked unemployment it produced. And, indeed, the data that we possess seem to confirm the validity of this hypothesis.

Let us begin with secondary education and analyze its development over time and by geographic area. Even if we lack disaggregated data for the years immediately preceding the great crisis, from a comparison between the situation of 1931 – 32 and that of 1936 – 37 it appears clearly how much youth unemployment influenced the growth of schooling. Again in 1931, two years after the start of the great crisis, we find, naturally quite attenuated, that inverse relationship between the level of economic development reached by the various geographic areas and their enrollment rates (table 6.9). Once again, that is, the regions of the South had a higher rate of scholarity than those of the Northwest and especially the Northeast. Even so, it took five years for the situation to reverse itself. From 1931 to 1936 the growth of secondary education was very considerable in all areas of the country, but it was extraordinarily more rapid in the regions of the North (especially in those industrialized) than in those of the South. The significance of this change is evident: the Mezzogiorno, after having held for so long the record for rate of enrollment, loses it. But it loses it exactly at the moment when, with the great crisis, unemployment (youth and otherwise) spreads throughout the country and becomes massive, therefore, also in the industrialized areas.

Female Education

A separate discussion of elementary teachers' education, or more generally female instruction, is worthwhile for the purpose of bringing some further element of verification to the hypothesis that the development of secondary education during the period of the Great Depression was due to the difficulties of youth in fitting into the labor market.

In order to explain the very strong expansion of teachers' education, and more generally of female instruction, that occurred in this period, one could examine, together or alternately, the following hypotheses: 1) that such growth was due to the existence of a strong demand for maestri in order to implement a policy of primary school expansion, in view of its importance for the socialization of children into the values of the new regime;[20] 2) that this growth was not peculiar to the period in question, but rather was part of a gradual tendency, begun many decades earlier, toward a progressive insertion of women into the educational system.

The groundlessness of the first hypothesis will follow clearly from what I will say in the next section on professional outlets for those certified by the istituti magistrali during the fascist period. In this section I will show, instead, the untenability of the second hypothesis, which is related to a conception of female instruction that is as widespread as it is superficial. It can be expressed in two points: 1) that historically there has been a slow but steady opening of the educational system to women, that is, linear and without reversals of tendency; 2) that this opening was due prevalently to cultural factors, that is, to change of the role definition of the woman in society, to the overcoming of antifeminist traditionalism, and the like. In reality, an analysis of the statistical data over a long enough period of time raises serious doubts as to the validity of this conception and pushes us, first, to revise the discussion of the course of the dependent variable, female instruction, and second, to seek independent variables other than cultural ones.

As regards the dependent variable it is necessary, first of all, to make a distinction according to the three levels of the educational system. At the university level, the thesis of linear increase, without reversals of tendency, of female education seems to be confirmed by the data. Examining, in fact, the forty-year period 1910–50, one observes a constant rise in the female percentage of total university enrollments, from 5.8 percent in 1913–14 to 26.3 percent in 1950. But at the other two levels of the educational system, things proceed in a much different fashion. At the level of elementary schooling, considering a time span of eighty years, the percentage of females in the total enrollment undergoes a very slight increase, from 44.3 percent in 1871 to 47.2 percent in 1891, and then remains constant in the seven following decades (in 1950 it is still 47.2 percent). But the most surprising and interesting data for the purposes of my discussion are those concerning secondary education. In fact, at this level one observes over the course of almost forty years[21] a series of fluctuations that definitely undermine the thesis of female education's linear increase without reversals of tendency, as well as that of the influence on this increase of cultural variables (figure 6.1).

Figure 6.1 shows a sharp increase, both in absolute number and in the percentage of female students, corresponding to the two world wars. Nevertheless, the events of the wars are not sufficient in themselves to explain the

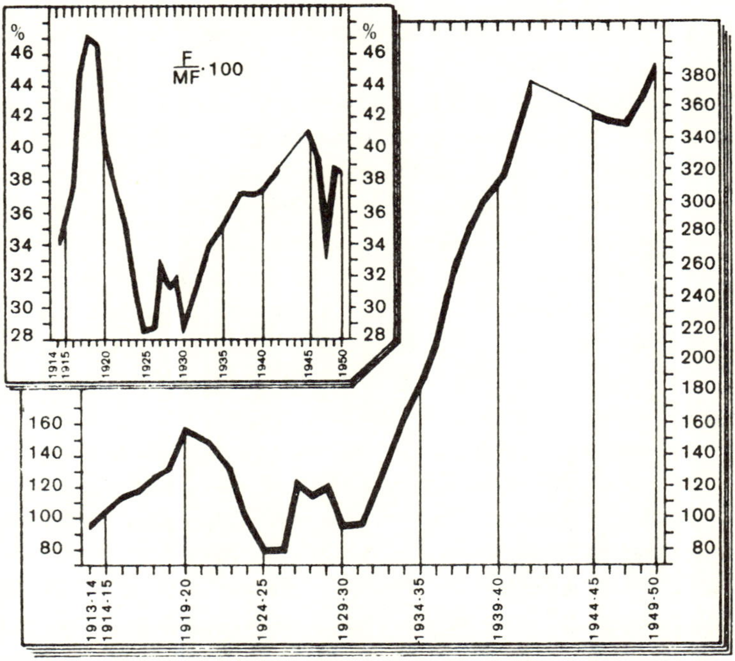

Figure 6.1. Female secondary school students from 1913–14 to 1949–50 (in thousands).

Source: T. Salvemini, *L'istruzione femminile in Italia secondo le statistiche dell'ultimo cinquantennio,* in Ministry of Public Education, *Accesso della donna all'educazione* (Rome, 1952), p. 39.

fluctuations that appear between 1913 and 1950. As can be seen from the same graph, a slight increase in female students occurs in 1926 and 1927, while there is a veritable explosion of female instruction beginning in 1930 and for the whole period of the Great Depression.

Indeed, these data show clearly that it is definitely not possible to explain the course of female instruction with variables of a cultural order, if only because it would otherwise be impossible to reconcile the fact that the explosion of female education took place during the fascist period (especially in the second phase) with the ferociously antifeminist orientation of the regime, which certainly reinforced the traditionalistic values of the Italian population regarding the work activity of women.[22]

To understand the course of female education one must, in my opinion, begin instead from an analysis of employment trends. Now, if we examine the period 1901–51 we see that while for males the rate of work activity decreased slightly from 66.7 percent to 63 percent, the reduction in the rate of such activity for women was very considerable, from 37 percent to 23.1 percent.[23] One might, at first view, explain the reduction of the rate of activity for women by the increase in *per capita* income. Or else one might argue that the data regarding the female population treated by various censuses are comparable only with difficulty, in that the concepts "active" and "nonactive" woman have changed in meaning with the shifting of the population from agriculture to industry and to the tertiary sector. While in fact in the case of agriculture there is no rigid separation between the roles of "housewife" and "female worker," in the sense that a woman can fulfill both, this separation holds very clearly for industry and for the tertiary sector, and forces a woman to dedicate herself to one or the other.

These attempts at interpretation are, however, insufficient. This can be seen clearly from a closer analysis of the data available to us. In the first place, examining the course of the rate of activity distinguished not only by sex but also by age cohort, we note that while for the cohorts under 25 and over 65 years of age, a reduction in the percentage of those active is recorded for both males and females, in the age cohort 22–44 the percentage of those active remains constant during the entire period for males, but undergoes a sharp reduction for females. In the second place, an analysis of the course of the rate of activity for females in various countries from 1920 to 1950 shows that in the other countries a much lower reduction is encountered than that noted for Italy, or there is actually an increase of this rate.[24] In the third place, in examining the rate of female activity according to economic sector, one observes that for the expulsion of the female labor force from agriculture there is no proportionate absorption of this labor on the part of industry and the tertiary sector.[25] All these facts would lead one to think, therefore, that the sharp reduction in the rate of female activity in the period considered is none other than a result of employment difficulties that certainly grew during the fascist period, both because of the insufficient development of industry and because of the reduction in migration abroad.[26]

Precisely these difficulties of insertion of the young into the labor market constituted one of the most important sources of the very sharp increase of female education that has been noted. In order, however, to offer some decisive elements of proof for this hypothesis it is necessary to examine as the independent variable not the rate of activity for females, which can serve only to appraise long-term "structural" unemployment, but rather a "conjunctural" instrument of analysis: the rate of female unemployment. Figure 6.2 shows precisely the course of the number of unemployed women from 1919 to 1934.[27] As may be observed, after having reached a high point in 1921, female unemployment decreased in the three following years. It rose again in 1926 and 1927 (two years of economic crisis, as is well known), fell slightly the following year (just when the crisis was being overcome), and rose very rapidly from 1930 onward. Now, if this is compared with figure 6.1, an impressive correspondence may be observed between the course of female unemployment and that of female education. In the case of female education as well there are, in fact, increases that correspond to the two economic crises, namely that of 1926–27 and that after 1930.

Unemployment of Diplomati and the Expansion of Higher Education

Verification of the hypothesis that the most important source of educational expansion was the Great Depression is relatively easier at the level of higher education, despite the fact that at this level also much of the relevant information that would be necessary to conduct a rigorous analysis of the existing relationship between the course of the economy and that of higher education over time and area are missing. In particular, basic and indispensable data are lacking for investigating the variations that occurred during the fascist period in rates of enrollment at the university level according to geographic areas at differing levels of economic development. To examine these variations it would be necessary to base our analysis, given the geographic mobility of university students, not on data regarding *sites of enrollment*, but on those for *residence of their families.* We have this information only for the academic year 1931–32, the only one in which a special inquiry was conducted by ISTAT. The data of this inquiry indicate that the number of students enrolled in the university (relative to population) was higher in the South than in the North, and they show, therefore, that in this year too, as in 1911, there was an inverse relationship between economic development and diffusion of higher education (table 6.10).

Even though information is lacking for the following years on enrollment rates at the university level according to geographic area, it seems to me that it may be possible to supply convincing elements of proof for the hypothesis that

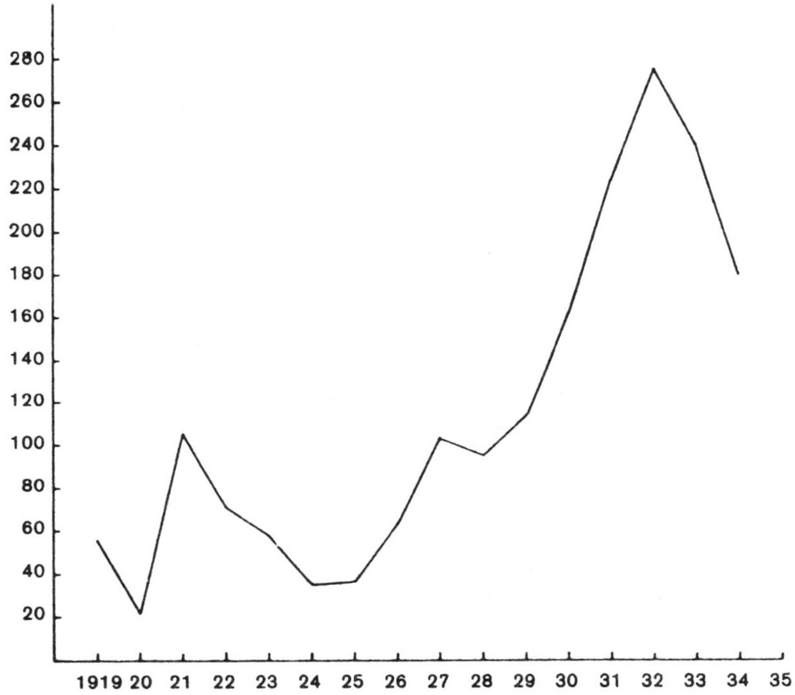

Figure 6.2. Course of female unemployment from 1919 to 1935 (in thousands).

Source: N. Federici, "Le caratteristiche e i problemi dell'occupazione e della disoccupazione femminile," in Parliamentary Commission of Inquiry on Unemployment, *La Disoccupazione in Italia* (Rome, 1953) vol. 4, Part 5, p. 100.

I have formulated. To do this it is necessary to begin with the situation in which the diplomati from the upper-secondary schools found themselves over the period that concerns us. The completely divergent development of the economy and of secondary education from 1929 on provoked, in fact, considerable unemployment among the diplomati who left the secondary schools.

I have reported in table 6.1 the overall number of enrollments in the istituti tecnici from 1926 to 1939. It is well, however, to mention now that the greater part of these students (about 50,000 in 1925 and 110,000 in 1939) attended the *istituti commerciali*, which trained accountants and surveyors; another considerable segment (14,000 in 1926 and 22,000 in 1939) was enrolled in the *istituti*

Table 6.10. University Students in 1931–32 by Site of Enrollment and Family Residence, and the Ratio of Students to Inhabitants by Geographic Area

Family Residence	Site of Enrollment of Students				Population (in thousands)	Students per 100,000 Inhabitants
	North	South	Center	Italy		
North	17,682	804	139	18,625	18,594	100
Center	741	8,085	213	9,039	7,197	125
South	1,307	2,556	13,974	17,837	14,518	122
Italy	19,730	11,445	14,362	45,501	40,310	111

SOURCE: Elaboration of data taken from ISTAT, *Indagine sugli studenti iscritti nelle Università e negli Instituti superiori nell'anno accademico 1931–32, Statistiche intellettuali,* vol. 13 (Rome: Failli, 1936), and SVIMEZ, *Un secolo di statistiche italiane; Nord e Sud (1861–1961)* (Rome, 1961).

industriali, which trained industrial technicians, while enrollments in the *istituti agrari* and *nautici* were relatively few. Unemployment, however, struck all categories of diplomati – accountants, surveyors, and industrial as well as agricultural technicians.

Even the National Secretary of the Fascist Union of Surveyors had to recognize, in his report on the work performed by the union in 1935–36, that

> unemployment is no little cause of anxiety and concern. More properly it should be called insufficiency of work. The phenomenon has been analyzed and widely referred to the confederation for study of provisions that could minimize it. A shrinkage of work is everywhere apparent which, in certain cases, comes close to total unemployment.[28]

He reported also that from twenty-nine provincial unions in 1935, 264 cases of unemployed surveyors had been noted and that the union had "given assistance to 45 surveyors with subsidies in the amount of L. 5,456." But these data, as we shall soon see, did not even hint at how widespread unemployment was among the surveyors: they only revealed the impotence of the union in dealing with the situation.

No different was the condition in which the accountants found themselves. These either remained unemployed or were forced to accept underpaid, subordinate jobs which had very little to do with their educational qualifications. Those who sought to be independent professionals certainly found themselves in no better a situation. This was revealed, in 1935, in the official organ of the National Fascist Union of Professional Accountants:

> For years we have seen all around us the *thinning out* of professional work. In more

> recent times the phenomenon has taken on more serious or, shall I say, without wanting to shock anyone, alarming aspects. And yet many youth continue to enlarge our ranks each year. What is worse, some arrive who have their own inherited wealth and therefore are able, even if professional practice renders them little, to scrape by.[29]

Three years later the same review wrote:

> There is no doubt that the greater part of us today are short of work. He who does not see this does not want to see it, or at the end of the month does not need to provide for the necessities of his existence and his family's with increasingly lean professional earnings. But among us one could find another subgroup: those who are indeed so deprived of work as to very often lack even the means to pay office rent, taxes, personnel, and telephone and (why not say it?) even the modest union dues.[30]

And even when, after having for some years covered a state of concealed unemployment with the label "independent professional," the accountant made up his mind to seek dependent employment via the *gerarca*,* the frustrations he encountered were even greater:

> Nothing is more painful than to watch a forty-five-year-old colleague – father of three or four children, no longer able in practicing a profession that he has carried out honorably for fifteen or twenty years to find the means to provide for the necessities of his family – request some position so that he might be allowed to procure such means. Well, nine times out of ten the step taken by the gerarca achieves the same result. And the words of complaisant and polite administrators and managers are always the same. . . . Virtually none of them is capable of understanding the *anguish* of the request, the *necessity* for a concern that must go beyond sterile and hypocritical assurances, the *humaneness* of a gesture which should be carried out, however small. . . . And it will be quite a sum indeed if, deigning to consider the request just to please the Mr. So-and-so who recommended our aforementioned forty-five-year-old colleague, father of three or four children, someone offers the splendid salary of L. 800, or at most 1000 a month![31]

The category of diplomati hardest hit by unemployment was, however, the industrial technicians, as we shall see shortly from the little data that we have. The employment difficulties that these faced were very considerable and induced the union to claim as a general right "whatever occupation, just so it is

**Gerarca:* Fascist party official present in every locality.

an occupation" for these technicians, even at the cost of their having to accept a "dequalification in the job classification":

> It is true. We know of a large metallurgical firm that has hired new laureati in engineering, assigning to them the control of a series of small departments; a function assigned in normal times to foremen who rise from the ranks. We know of a textile plant that has acted similarly by hiring diplomati in industrial technology. These are functions unworthy of either of these two professions, we agree, but meanwhile they offer a way for such technical personnel to solve their economic problem, to live in an environment suited to their aptitudes and to have the possibility of advancing in their field. If by necessity, therefore, this comes about as an exception, then let us make a virtue of necessity: let us organize this state of affairs by giving it a juridical imprint, such that *all industries should be obliged to hire only technical personnel for all, even the most simple, technical functions: apprenticeship, middle-level, and managerial functions. Likewise the diploma or the laurea should be required even for simple functions.*[32]

Although, as I have noted, the number of agricultural technicians who graduated from the upper-secondary schools was relatively low, unemployment spared not even this category of diplomati. An inquiry conducted on diplomati of the Istituto tecnico agrario of Imola from 1926 to 1929[33] revealed that 22 percent had found work in their fathers' business, 12 percent in other concerns, 9 percent were teachers, 23 percent performed military service, and as many as 34 percent were unemployed. Bearing in mind that the Institute of Imola served the provinces of Bologna and Ravenna, which were certainly among the most developed with regard to the agricultural economy and had, therefore, presumably one of the highest demands for agricultural technicians, we can imagine how high the unemployment rate must have been among these diplomati in the other parts of Italy. Moreover, the National Fascist Union of Agricultural Technicians estimated in 1940 that 31 percent of agricultural technicians were unemployed (table 6.11).

Therefore, not one of the categories of diplomati who left the istituti tecnici was spared from unemployment. This was also the finding of an inquiry on intellectual unemployment conducted in 1935 by the Fascist Confederation of Professionals and Artists. Although the survey was completed only for those enrolled in the Provincial Unions of the Confederation, the results – in the absence of other data – are of great interest. From this survey emerges the fact that the hardest hit category was that of the industrial technicians, who showed a percentage of unemployed at 25.14 nationally, 23.11 in the North, 23.28 in the

Table 6.11. Employment of University, Upper-Secondary, and Lower-Secondary Graduates in Agriculture, 1939

Occupation	*Laureati in Agronomy (University)*		*Agricultural Technicians (Upper-Secondary)*		*Licensed Agricultural Workers (Lower Secondary)*		*Total*	
	N	%	*N*	%	*N*	%	*N*	%
Employees of state and state-controlled agencies	1,000	29	900	21	—	—	1,900	15
Employees and managers of agricultural businesses	200	6	1,000	24	3,000	60	4,200	33
Practititioners of independent professions or managers of self-owned businesses	2,000	59	1,000	24	1,000	20	4,000	32
Unemployed	200	6	1,300	31	1,000	20	2,500	20
Total	3,400	100	4,200	100	5,000	100	12,600	100

SOURCE: Elaboration of data taken from: National Fascist Union of Agricultural Technicians, "La direzione delle aziende agrarie, la preparazione dei dirigenti e la difesa dei titoli professionali," *L'avanguardia rurale* (April 1940), p. 69.

Center, 27.15 in the South, and as much as 48.19 on the Islands. But even among the other categories of diplomati the percentages of unemployed were very high: 10.78 for the surveyors, 7.10 for the accountants, and 8.88 for the agricultural technicians.[34]

Yet even higher – incredibly high – was unemployment among the diplomati of the istituti magistrali. It is true that in 1926, speaking to the Chamber of Deputies, Meriano had sketched a rather optimistic picture of the situation, arguing that, because of the energetic measures taken by the Gentile Reform, unemployment of elementary teachers was being completely reabsorbed. "Where the pruning was courageous," he observed, "but guided by experience, as is the case of the istituti magistrali, the results are by now encouraging. Before the reform, the istituti magistrali conferred about 12,000 diplomas yearly, while the need did not exceed 3,500. Today the degree holders of the istituti magistrali are from 5,000 to 6,000, or only a few more than necessary."[35] All the same, as was noted, these institutes soon began to expand again and from 1929 onward actually underwent the most rapid expansion of all the upper-secondary schools, so that the imbalance between supply and demand for new diplomati became very sharp once again. A survey conducted by the Ministry of National Education revealed that in 1938 there were at least 100,000 unemployed maestri.[36] If one keeps in mind that in the same year there were about 119,000 employed maestri, one can imagine the unemployment rate of these diplomati. What had led to this situation? In contrast to the other diplomati, in the case of the maestri it is possible to arrive at some approximation of the course of supply and demand of the labor force. And this I have sought to do in table 6.12 by comparing, for a period of fourteen years, the number of those certified by the istituti magistrali with the number of employed maestri.

In order to reconstruct the course of demand, it is necessary also to take into account the number of positions made available because of death or retirement due to age limits; in the period in question these can be estimated at about 1,600 a year.[37]

Table 6.12 gives an idea of the imbalance between supply and demand for maestri. In the period in question (as has been noted, a considerable imbalance occurred earlier as well) about 133,000 diplomati came out of the istituti magistrali. The increase in employed maestri was about 23,000, to which may be added another 22,000 positions made available by death and mandatory retirement. This means, in other words, that about *two-thirds* of the new maestri did not succeed in finding work in this period.

If it is true that the fundamental cause of the unemployment of diplomati was the completely opposite course of an economy in the midst of depression and of a secondary education system in the midst of considerable expansion, it can also be said that the phenomenon was further aggravated by a new form of competition that the diplomati had to face: that of the laureati who, given the impossibility of finding work in the professions for which they had prepared during their university studies, invaded, so to speak, occupations of a lesser grade on the social scale, namely those traditionally reserved for diplomati. The attention of the union organizations was concentrated, understandably, on this sort of relationship between the unemployment of laureati and that of diplomati:

> There is a connection, I would almost say of cause and effect, between the situation of the university professionals and of the middle professionals.... The excess of the university population, having gone beyond virtually all possibility of profitable employment for the university-graduate professionals, has impelled these laureati toward the lesser activities, has forced them to compete for the work of the middle professionals, to try to replace them even in public jobs and in the most lowly occupations (just recently seven engineers competed for a non-management positions as municipal surveyor).[38]

> And it happens that if, for example, a concorso is held for a certain number of surveyor positions, three-quarters of the candidates who present themselves will have the laurea in engineering, which leads to the consequence of abasing the work of laureati in engineering to the more restricted ambit of that of the diplomati in surveying and taking away from the surveyors a certain number of positions that were to be reserved for them.[39]

As exaggerated as these analyses may have been, there is no doubt that the competition of laureati further aggravated the difficulties of employment for the diplomati. This can be confirmed by examining the case of maestri, the one group of diplomati for which there are precise data. Table 6.13 shows, in fact, that both in 1926–27 and ten years later there was a sizable number of laureati among the employed maestri,[40] and that the phenomenon of the "invasion" by laureati or their "*declassamento*"* concerned males much more than females.

**Declassamento:* loss of professional and social status, downward mobility.

Table 6.12. Graduates of the Istituti Magistrali, Enrollments in the Faculty of Education, and Employed Maestri, 1926 to 1939

Year	*Graduates of the Istituti Magistrali*	*Enrollments in Education Faculty*	*Employed Maestri*	*Increase in Employed Maestri over Preceding Year*
1926–27	3,126	1,070	98,674	1,174
1927–28	3,139	1,064	100,488	1,874
1928–29	3,245	1,139	101,669	1,181
1929–30	3,423	1,322	101,311	– 357
1930–31	3,422	1,456	105,195	3,884
1931–32	4,864	1,746	107,749	2,554
1932–33	5,911	1,964	108,686	937
1933–34	8,192	2,910	109,800	1,114
1934–35	10,034	3,698	111,378	1,578
1935–36	11,630	4,291	117,469	6,091
1936–37	13,654	6,229	122,796	5,327
1937–38	14,474	7,803	117,423	–5,373
1938–39	19,003	10,061	119,866	2,443
1939–40	28,855	11,906	121,964	2,098

SOURCE: Elaboration of data taken from: 1) ISTAT, *Statistica dell'istruzione superiore nell'anno accademico 1945–46* (Rome, 1948); 2) ISTAT, *Statistica dell'insegnamento medio per l'anno scolastico 1936–37* (Rome, 1940); 3) ISTAT, *Statistica dell'istruzione media nell'anno scolastico 1945–46* (Rome, 1950); 4) ISTAT, *Sommario di statistiche storiche dell'Italia (1861–1965)* (Rome, 1968).

Table 6.13. Maestri in Public Elementary Schools by Qualification and Sex, 1926–27 and 1936–37

<table>
<tr><th rowspan="3">Qualification</th><th colspan="6">School Year 1926–27</th><th colspan="6">School Year 1936–37</th></tr>
<tr><th colspan="2">M</th><th colspan="2">F</th><th colspan="2">MF</th><th colspan="2">M</th><th colspan="2">F</th><th colspan="2">MF</th></tr>
<tr><th>N</th><th>%</th><th>N</th><th>%</th><th>N</th><th>%</th><th>N</th><th>%</th><th>N</th><th>%</th><th>N</th><th>%</th></tr>
<tr><td>Laurea in education</td><td rowspan="2">2,416</td><td rowspan="2">12</td><td rowspan="2">4,620</td><td rowspan="2">6</td><td rowspan="2">7,036</td><td rowspan="2">8</td><td>370</td><td>2</td><td>910</td><td>1</td><td>1,280</td><td>1</td></tr>
<tr><td>Other laurea</td><td>1,800</td><td>8</td><td>4,740</td><td>5</td><td>6,540</td><td>6</td></tr>
<tr><td>Diploma from istituto magistrale</td><td>17,555</td><td>87</td><td>67,254</td><td>93</td><td>84,809</td><td>91</td><td>19,927</td><td>89</td><td>81,755</td><td>93</td><td>101,682</td><td>92</td></tr>
<tr><td>Qualification lower than diploma from istituto magistrale</td><td>284</td><td>1</td><td>406</td><td>1</td><td>690</td><td>1</td><td>338</td><td>1</td><td>706</td><td>1</td><td>1,044</td><td>1</td></tr>
<tr><td>Total</td><td>20,255</td><td>100</td><td>72,280</td><td>100</td><td>92,535</td><td>100</td><td>22,435</td><td>100</td><td>88,111</td><td>100</td><td>110,546</td><td>100</td></tr>
</table>

SOURCE: Elaboration of data taken from ISTAT, *Statistica dell'istruzione elementare nell'anno scolastico 1926–27* (Rome, 1931), and ISTAT, *Statistica dell'insegnamento elementare per l'anno scolastico 1936–37* (Rome, 1941).

Still, the most important relationship between the unemployment of diplomati and that of laureati intersects, so to speak, the hypothesis that I formulated at the beginning of this section. This hypothesis can now be reformulated in the following terms: given the impossibility of finding work, a growing number of diplomati from the istituti tecnici and magistrali pursued their studies by entering the university. It is in this sense that one can say that the sharp expansion of enrollments in the higher studies was due to the economic depression.

The available data confirm the validity of this hypothesis. Table 6.2 shows that the expansion of university enrollments, even if very strong overall, did not concern all groups of laurea. Indeed, enrollments in scientific and engineering groups, after having registered a sharp drop, reached the level of 1923 only in 1929. The groups of laurea that registered an increase were the medical, agricultural, and juridical, and above all those in economics and literature – in other words, the groups that involved such faculties as economics and commerce, and education. Now, it is well known that only diplomati of the istituti magistrali could have access to the education faculty. And even though students who came out of the licei were allowed to enroll in the faculty of economics and commerce, in fact for the most part those who did so were the diplomati from the istituti tecnici.[41] Thus it was that enrollments in the education faculty grew from 1,300 in 1929 to almost 12,000 in 1939, and those in the economics and commerce faculty from 7,700 to over 13,000. A sharp increase was recorded also for enrollments in the Istituto Orientale* (from 540 to 3,300), to which all diplomati had access, and those in the agriculture faculty, which beginning in 1931 was open to agricultural technicians.

For a more rigorous proof of the hypothesis I have advanced, it is necessary to examine the rates of passage of diplomati to the university (that is, the percentage who continued their studies) in the various years. On the basis of existing data it is possible to calculate the rates of passage only for 1931 and then beginning in 1935–36. For an appropriate reading of the data contained in table 6.14 it must be borne in mind that the rates of passage for graduates of the istituti tecnici were calculated on the basis of first-year enrollments in the faculties of economics and commerce, statistical science, and agriculture, and in the university naval institute in Naples; while those for the licei graduates

**Istituto Orientale:* university-level institution located in Naples with courses, among others, leading to the laurea in Islamic studies, philosophy, and literature.

were calculated on the basis of enrollments in the remaining faculties (excluding education). This means that while the total rates of passage and those of the graduates of the istituti magistrali may be considered exact, the other two series of rates of passage are only approximate. Even with these limitations, which are not very significant, the data of table 6.14 allow us to verify the hypothesis advanced.

Considering the total rate of passage (the third column of the table), we see that it reaches the very high level of 67.73 percent in 1931, but then decreases slightly in the following years, to rise once again with the outbreak of the war. Nevertheless, in the period 1930 – 35 a change occurs in the composition of diplomati by qualification, in that the percentage of those coming from the licei decreases (from 50 percent to 35 percent) and, correspondingly, the percentage of those who come through the istituti tecnici and the istituti magistrali increases. This explains why, while the total rate of passage diminishes slightly in the first five years, that of the diplomati of the istituti tecnici rises from 48.90 percent to 68.47 percent, and that of the diplomati from the istituti magistrali rises from 16.16 percent of 27.91 percent. Therefore, a good part of the unemployed diplomati of the istituti tecnici are converted into university students. The process occurs to a much lesser extent for diplomati of the istituti magistrali. Aided probably by the fact that the unemployed who knocked at their doors were female, the faculty of education, although experiencing a very considerable growth of enrollments, managed with the admission examination (which functioned more or less as a sort of numero chiuso or quota system) to keep out a good number of unemployed maestri who were seeking, through university studies, a way out of their situation.

This tendency toward the conversion of unemployed diplomati into university students was also acknowleged during the fascist period. Two scholars, politically very close to the regime, wrote in 1934:

> We have seen that the postwar period marked a phase of stasis or regression [in the number of university enrollments], and that the sharp increase took place beginning in 1927 up to the present, that is, concomitant with the economic crisis. Such an assertion allows us to realize how well founded is the hypothesis that the increase of students is connected to the reduction of employment opportunities and to the resolution that many students make to continue their studies either for the purpose of occupying their time or for that of procuring qualifications that may be of advantage to them in future competition. Such a hypothesis would also explain the very sharp increase in certain university centers (such as the faculty of education

Table 6.14. Rates of Passage from the Upper-Secondary Schools to the University, 1934 to 1948

Year	*Total Diplomati*	*Enrollments in 1st Level of University Studies in the Following Year*	*% Total Diplomati Who Continue Studies*	*Diplomati from Istituti Tecnici*	*Enrollments in 1st Level of University Studies in the Following Year*	*% of Diplomati (Ist Tec) Who Continue Studies*
1930–31	18,373	12,445	67.73	5,759	2,816	48.90
1935–36	29,915	19,944	66.66	7,638	5,230	68.47
1938–39	42,428	27,526	64.88	7,202	5,440	75.53
1939–40	69,612	54,507	69.61	13,534	14,503	107.15
1940–41	55,203	49,612	89.87	11,646	14,231	116.46
1941–42	55,866	51,890	92.88	12,754	17,506	137.25
1945–46	60,271	47,178	78.27	18,119	13,025	71.89
1946–47	58,038	41,885	72.16	19,611	10,671	54.41
1947–48	59,324	42,401	71.47	18,722	10,075	53.81
1948–49	58,516	36,367	58.51	17,603	7,601	43.18

Table 6.14. (continued)

Year	*Diplomati from Istituti Magistrali*	*Enrollments in 1st Level of University Studies in the Following Year*	*% of Diplomati (Ist Mag) Who Continue Studies*	*Diplomati from Licei Classici and Scientifici*	*Enrollments in 1st Level of University Studies in the Following Year*	*% of Diplomati (Liceo) Who Continue Studies*
1930–31	3,422	553	16.16	9,192	9,076	98.74
1935–36	11,630	3,246	27.91	10,647	11,468	107.71
1938–39	19,003	5,361	28.21	16,223	16,725	103.09
1939–40	28,855	9,250	32.05	27,223	30,754	112.97
1940–41	21,602	8,749	40.50	21,955	26,632	121.30
1941–42	19,698	5,218	26.48	23,414	29,166	124.56
1945–46	17,072	6,363	37.27	25,080	27,790	110.80
1946–47	13,204	4,785	36.23	25,223	26,429	104.78
1947–48	14,070	4,484	31.86	26,532	27,842	104.92
1948–49	14,910	3,474	23.29	26,003	25,292	97.26

SOURCE: 1) for the first year: elaboration of data taken from ISTAT, *Indagine sugli studenti iscritti nelle Università e negli Istituti superiori* (Rome: Failli, 1936); 2) for the other years: T. Salvemini, "La popolazione scolastica e il suo incremento in rapporto allo sviluppo demografico ed economico del Paese, "in Parliamentary Commission of Inquiry on Unemployment, *La disoccupazione in Italia* (Rome: 1953), vol. 4, part 2, pp. 201-66.

> and the advanced schools of commerce) that admit youth already licensed by secondary institutes that give sufficient qualification to practice an independent profession. The accountant and the elementary school teacher, finding difficulty in winning crowded state concorsi or in procuring employment, try to obtain a higher qualification in order to have greater possibilities of success.[42]

On the other hand, this phenomenon, besides bringing about a considerable growth of higher education, had another consequence of some relevance: that of determining a growing de-professionalization of those istituti tecnici which, as was said, the Gentile Reform had sought to re-professionalize, reversing the tendency of the previous ten years. This is demonstrated not only by the high percentage of diplomati who were enrolled in the university, but also by the pressure exerted by their unions to open access for unemployed diplomati to new faculties. *Il geometra italiano,* in fact, asked for the establishment of "a school for surveyors at the university, parallel to that for engineers, from which the surveyors could graduate with the laurea and with training and complete authority with regard to rural engineering." "This," it argued, "is the only way to save our class."[43] *Il perito industriale* accused the Gentile Reform of having "cut the ground out from under the young industrial technicians desirous of pursuing studies into the higher institutions and obtaining a laurea,"[44] and asked for the abolition of "the restriction whereby the qualification of industrial technician is a dead end. The studies of the industrial technicians render them more than fit to gain access to the higher schools, since such studies, by breadth and duration, are equivalent to those imparted by the other secondary schools."[45]

The Unemployment of Laureati

Having examined in the preceding sections the most important variables for explaining the course of supply and demand for the intellectual labor force, we must linger for a moment on the characteristics of the employment and unemployment of laureati during the fascist period. As has already emerged in large part in the preceding sections, unemployment during the fascist period concerned not only diplomati but laureati as well.

I had occasion to say that one of the groups hardest hit by unemployment before the advent of fascism was that of the engineers. But it was also seen that the Gentile Reform, by radically restructuring the educational order, produced a sharp decline in the number of enrollments in engineering, a drop that at no time during the entire fascist period was halted. Indeed, not even the subsequent revisions of the Gentile Reform reversed this tendency. The adjustments made in 1929 and 1931 influenced the course of enrollments in other faculties, but had no repercussions on the course of enrollments in engineering. These adjustments did give some possibilities of continuing studies to students of the lower-secondary avviamento, but they limited these possibilities to those upper-secondary schools that, after the Gentile Reform, no longer gave access to engineering. In spite of all this, the engineers continued to suffer from considerable unemployment for the entire fascist period.

In 1928 the National Confederation of Fascist Unions of Professionals and Artists conducted an inquiry on the work situation of their members. The survey revealed that the engineers numbered "3,000 unemployed of the 15,000 enrolled in the engineers' union, without counting the large number of poorly employed, at salaries little higher than those current for female typists."[46] Therefore, if there actually were 15,000 members of the union, the unemployed engineers would have been 20 percent in 1928. In reality, according to other sources, the number of engineers enrolled in the union did not exceed 10 – 11,000 in that year.[47] This would lead one to conclude that the percentage of unemployed engineers was much higher than officially indicated. On the other hand, according to the same union, many among the employed engineers were, in reality, underemployed or underpaid. It was observed, for example, that while typists, despite their low level of education, earned "salaries of at least 500 – 600 lire a month," there were industries that hired newly graduated engineers at the same level of pay, to bring them then, after many years, to salaries of 800 – 1000 lire a month, and there were others that offered 800 lire a month to engineers with three or four years of experience.[48]

It is not difficult to explain why considerable unemployment among engineers persisted despite the decline that was recorded in the number of enrollments in the faculties of engineering. In the first place, there had been, as was noted, a sharp reduction of emigration on the part of Italian laureati, including engineers, of course. The official organ of the National Fascist Union of Engineers continued to consider emigration the most important remedy for the unemployment of engineers but had to recognize bitterly that "in this endeavor little is actually accomplished. In fact, proportionately few engineers move abroad or to the colonies."[49] In the second place, even such a radical reform (at least for the faculties of engineering) as that of Gentile needed a certain number of years to produce effects of a certain import. Table 6.15 shows us, in fact, that the annual number of laureati in engineering, after having reached its highest

Table 6.15. Laureati by Faculty, 1923–24 to 1941–42

Year	Jurisprudence	Economics and Commerce	Political Science	Statistical Science	Naval Institute	Literature and Philosophy	Education	Oriental Institute
1923–24	1,406	775	57	—	17	557	226	7
1924–25	1,660	650	73	—	17	580	180	—
1925–26	1,572	692	84	—	18	623	205	—
1926–27	1,762	637	92	—	23	550	220	5
1927–28	1,918	721	93	—	26	565	273	24
1928–29	2,240	793	111	—	26	637	323	32
1929–30	2,197	1,014	166	—	31	633	267	25
1930–31	2,204	1,020	139	—	53	630	225	61
1931–32	2,292	1,069	182	8	29	632	231	75
1932–33	2,460	1,179	197	2	34	626	331	84
1933–34	2,525	1,307	159	2	27	782	403	101
1934–35	2,835	1,296	174	3	31	873	432	81
1935–36	2,748	1,434	222	6	54	941	476	65
1936–37	2,772	1,540	232	3	55	1,165	607	109
1937–38	2,902	1,459	223	12	55	1,467	754	103
1938–39	2,732	1,551	217	8	45	1,672	879	102
1939–40	4,705	3,633	429	25	79	2,647	2,326	251
1940–41	2,385	1,544	236	8	44	1,900	1,653	176
1941–42	2,176	1,097	194	20	26	1,944	1,670	173

Table 6.15. (continued)

Year	*Medicine and Surgery*	*Veterinary Science*	*Engineering*	*Architecture*	*Mathematical, Physical, and Natural Sciences*	*Pharmacy*	*Agriculture*	*Industrial Chemistry*	*Total*
1923–24	1,659	188	1,575	27	746	644	192	—	8,076
1924–25	21,362	160	1,451	16	623	637	203	—	7,612
1925–26	1,137	189	1,393	18	636	703	134	—	7,404
1926–27	1,391	180	1,408	22	642	768	156	—	7,856
1927–28	1,518	175	1,466	13	637	802	204	—	8,435
1928–29	1,581	198	1,091	22	758	804	197	—	8,813
1929–30	1,490	224	985	20	615	805	230	—	8,702
1930–31	1,363	193	1,041	29	548	801	299	—	8,606
1931–32	1,475	160	873	36	526	753	191	16	8,548
1932–33	1,698	140	924	73	563	830	189	19	9,349
1933–34	2,034	159	863	89	600	755	218	21	10,045
1934–35	2,167	180	885	113	625	704	168	30	10,597
1935–36	2,364	166	886	107	590	692	193	13	10,937
1936–37	2,309	161	822	108	574	626	230	16	11,329
1937–38	2,179	150	895	118	634	651	292	15	11,909
1938–39	2,046	181	902	117	628	681	263	20	12,044
1939–40	2,076	267	883	174	1,145	525	382	37	19,584
1940–41	1,713	168	618	64	690	457	246	32	11,934
1941–42	1,714	159	515	49	649	436	167	22	11,011

SOURCE: ISTAT, *Statistica dell'istruzione superiore nell'anno accademico 1945-46* (Rome, 1948).

point in 1922 – 23, decreased steadily, but only by 1928 – 29 did it manage to reach the not very low level of 1919 – 20. To these two factors must be added a third: the economic crisis that began in 1929 and that certainly provoked a reduction in the demand for engineers. In April 1929, *L'ingegnere* wrote:

> In the present state of affairs in Italy, there are several thousand unemployed engineers, to which must be added those who are employed with functions not suitable to the laurea in engineering and those who despite being professionals cannot rely on the continuity of professional employment.[50]

From then on, the same review could not help returning, at least every so often, to the problem of the unemployment of engineers.[51] To give only a few examples, in 1932 it defined the situation in these terms:

> Parallel to the unemployment of the working class is the even worse employment situation of engineers, who have faced the period with a great spirit of sacrifice; such unemployment, as a recent collection of statistics in *L'ingegneria* shows, is serious among the old professionals, but it is even more serious among the young, whose number grows every year by about a thousand new laureati. For these, as for the other professionals, not one provision has been taken so far, and most have supported themselves on savings, awaiting better, more hopeful times, and consoling themselves with the study of various questions that the unions themselves have often raised. But if this can boost their morale for a time, it will eventually be necessary also to provide them with work so that they can take up a normal life again, even though it be more modest in view of the changed conditions of the world and national economy.[52]

Six years later, the national secretary of the National Fascist Union of Engineers was forced to recognize the difficulties of employment still existing for the engineers:

> Youths come to us hardly out of the schools, youths of the G.U.F.,* with fresh energies and new hopes: they come to us thinking that they have reached the goal by winning the laurea and passing the state examinations. And here it is that quickly, at their first contact with the harsh reality of life, they receive their first, and alas, bitter disappointments. Difficulties of placement: where to situate them? A serious problem, sometimes dramatic when accompanied by urgent need. We must recognize that until now there has been no organization that could help the youth and direct their first steps into the profession. So much care for them as long

*Fascist Youth League.

as they are students, and now, just at the critical moment of their placement, nothing.[53]

It is difficult, at any rate, to say exactly how many unemployed engineers there were. According to the Hon. Bernocco, at the beginning of the 1930s, to an annual supply of about 900 engineers there corresponded a demand of 500. "Every year, therefore, there is a troop of almost 400 engineers who arrive to aggravate the already very grave fortunes of their fellow laureati."[54] According to other estimates, in 1935 more than 50 percent of Italian engineers were unemployed.[55] Finally, according to official data of the survey conducted in that year among the actual enrollees of the Fascist Confederation of Professionals and Artists, 11.36 percent of the engineers were unemployed.[56]

For the laureati who practiced the other two classical professions, doctors and lawyers, the difficulties of employment were great as well. In these cases, however, since they were for the most part independent professionals, one must speak of underemployment rather than of unemployment. As Giacomo di Giacomo noted in 1928, "in the absolutely independent professions, such as that of lawyer, there is unemployment, understood as a shortage of professional business, namely the lack of a suitable clientele to afford the professional a suitable living."[57] This means that for these professionals the estimation of unemployment or underemployment becomes even more difficult than in the case of engineers. Nevertheless, the analysis of their professional publications, which I have conducted for the whole fascist period, leaves no doubts about the difficulties of insertion into the world of work encountered over the entire twenty-year period both by doctors and by lawyers.

As for the doctors, the supply curve reached its highest point in 1922–23, the year in which the faculties of medicine and surgery put onto the market about 2,000 new laureati, but it was sharply reduced in the following four years, in large part because of the Gentile Reform. Starting from the academic year 1927–28, it began, however, to recover and once again exceeded the 2,000 mark by 1933. Regarding the decade 1930–40 it can be calculated that on the whole the faculties of medicine put onto the labor market about 20,000 new doctors. If it is borne in mind that, according to the census of 1931, professionally practicing doctors were fewer than 33,000, one can imagine the size of the supply of new doctors that occurred in the decade 1930–40.

The *Federazione medica,* which was until 1926 the official organ of the Federation of the Orders of Physicians and from that year on of the National

Health Corporate Association, devoted an impressive number of articles to the analysis of the so-called plethora of doctors, of its causes and its remedies. In order not to bore the reader with quotations from these articles, which do no more than repeat monotonously throughout the fascist period the same striking analysis of the situation, I will limit myself to quoting three pieces from 1924, 1927, and 1931:

> There are thousands and thousands of young doctors who languish unemployed in their districts, whose flourishing energies wither in an idleness that demoralizes and crushes them; these are youth who would have been able to expound, with love and ardor, all their knowledge on behalf of suffering humanity, but, against their will, are constrained to an idleness which, when it is not of the mind and the spirit, is of the body.[58]

> The professional arena is saturated and full like the chalice which one drop will make overflow. The doctors swarm in the cities, especially the seats of universities, are very numerous among citizens in provincial areas, and now begin to invade the countryside, so that in many little villages, where before the war there was only one doctor and he was more than enough, now there are even three or four of them. How do they live? This is really a mystery, so much the more since nowadays it is mostly the less prosperous classes who send their sons to that medical faculty which, because of the cost of studies, was once attended rather by the wealthy.[59]

> From time to time, in journals of high culture especially, there appear articles which are cries of alarm on the sometimes sudden appearance of an increase of professionals disproportionate to social needs. . . . Because of such an increase the followers of Hippocrates no longer easily find medical charges nor positions in hospitals or in university institutes or in sanatoria or in state administrations. They find wide open now only the military career, at which very few aim, because, it is pointed out, of its low pay and the limitation of freedom due to the severe discipline that it demands.[60]

According to the *Federazione medica,* the "plethora" concerned the doctors of the large urban centers in particular, since they, of course, had a potential doctor-client ratio much lower than that of the agricultural areas. Nevertheless, even the doctors paid by the small centers were not getting on very well if, according to the same source, it was not difficult in that period to find advertisements in the newspapers of this sort: "Fifty-year-old municipal doctor with small family, rich only in long, honest, hard practice, who can also provide modest artistic capacities (painting-literature), seriously seeks dignified employment, hopefully related to the profession, but which guarantees him a secure living or at least one less harsh that the present."[61]

An attempt to estimate the existing relationship between demand and supply was made in 1932 by the National Fascist Union of Doctors. Estimating at 900 the annual demand for doctors and at 2,200 the supply, the union foresaw a surplus of over 8,000 doctors over the next six years.[62] But the lack of closer surveys and the aforementioned difficulties of measuring as complex a phenomenon as that of the unemployment or underemployment of independent professionals does not allow us to say even approximately to what extent this estimate might be accurate.

As for the lawyers, the supply curve reached its highest point in 1919 – 20, when the faculties of jurisprudence graduated as many as 2,700 laureati, and then declined over the next six years. It begun to rise again, uninterruptedly, in 1926 – 27 and reached a record 4,700 laureati in 1939 – 40. For the decade 1930 – 40, one can calculate that on the whole the faculties of law threw onto the labor market about 28,000 new laureati. In this case as well, there are absolutely no data that allow an estimate of the dimensions of the surplus of supply of new laureati over demand. But also in this case an analysis of professional publications allows us to say that the "forensic professions" suffered "acute discomfort."[63] The figure of the aspiring lawyer, underemployed or forced to adapt to more unusual jobs, became, even within the tight limits placed upon information by the fascist regime, a recurrent motif of a part of the press:

> There are lawyers, as everyone knows, working as copyists, peddlers, movie impresarios, preachers. But they do not complain, do not protest, and aware of the hour that passes, are grateful indeed for the possibility of scraping a living by whatever happens to come by.[64]

In this period, besides the three classical professional figures that we have witnessed so far – lawyer, doctor, and engineer – we find a fourth: the research chemist. This new type of profession began to spread immediately after the First World War with the development of the chemical industry. It was, in fact, starting in 1920 that the chemical industry, which before the war had quite modest dimensions, began to grow. In conditions of considerable concentration, the chemical industry expanded rapidly: net value produced rose from 451 million lire in 1921 to 1,733 million in 1929, while employment rose from

50,000 employees in 1911 to 99,000 in 1927, reaching the level of 128,000 in 1937.[65]

The Italian school then furnished intellectual labor to the chemical industry at two different levels: the upper-secondary school produced industrial-chemical technicians, while the university prepared, by way of the science faculties, laureati in chemistry and pharmacy (there was in addition, in Milan and Bologna, a faculty of industrial chemistry).[66] Now, if we concentrate our attention at the university level, we see from table 6.15 that, in contrast to the case of the engineers, the number of research chemists and pharmaceutical chemists produced by the university, after having reached its highest point in 1923–24 (more than 700), decreased only in the two following years, and then began to rise again and to settle at 400–500 annually through 1935–36.

A good part of these chemists that came out of the Italian universities did not find work. The profession's publications of the period are full of articles on the problem of the unemployment of research chemists, though they do not furnish us with one single piece of evidence that would allow an appraisal of the size of the phenomenon. The organ of the National Fascist Union of Chemists opened, in fact, a referendum among its readers in 1935 on "the causes of the unemployment of the chemists." In response to just this referendum, one such chemist approaching retirement recalled that the unemployment of chemists was certainly not a recent phenomenon, a simple consequence of the economic crisis of 1929:

> Having received the laurea thirty years ago, I have been able to follow the story of chemists in Italy from when the universities granted annually four or five such lauree until the present, when there are so many of them! My thirty-year experience authorizes me to say that the chemist in Italy was always in crisis if one excepts the brief hiatus of the war and the immediate postwar period, for obvious reasons. In recent years, naturally, the general crisis has once more made acute a crisis that has always been chronic![67]

The female university graduates were the first to be pushed off the labor market. In this regard it must be noted that compared to medicine, law, and engineering, the faculty of chemistry was the only one to have a relatively high percentage of women students. In particular, it can be calculated that of 100 laureati in chemistry who came out of the faculties of science about 23 were women and that of the laureati in chemistry and pharmacy almost 50 percent were female. The first data that we have on the number of laureati who practiced

Table 6.16. Research Chemists in Italy by Sex and Position in the Profession, 1936

Professional position	*Males*		Females		Total	
	N	%	*N*	%	*N*	%
Independent professionals	263	6	36	6	299	6
Managers	557	12	34	5	591	12
Office employees	3,618	82	574	89	4,194	82
Total	4,438	100	646	100	5,084	100

SOURCE: 1936 census.

the profession of research chemist during the fascist period are those of the census of 1936. These data, reported in table 6.16, indicate that only 12 percent of the employed chemists were female. If we consider the fact that, taking research and pharmaceutical chemists together, more that 30 percent of those who came out of the university with this laurea were female, it can be estimated that at least two-thirds of the women chemists who appeared on the labor market were forced to renounce any form of professional activity and to withdraw into being housewives.

The alleviation of pressure on the labor market that the forced professional inactivity of the young female chemists caused was not enough, however, to permit a rapid absorption of the male labor force. After a period of "total unemployment" (to use an expression of the professional press) the young research chemist passed to a phase of "semi-unemployment," meaning that he had to adapt himself to a "dequalified" work position, to use a contemporary expression.

> If the members of the aforesaid profession may in general become unemployed following the total loss of their position, in very many cases the qualified technician, losing his employment, does not become entirely unemployed, since he accepts a job of lower rank that that to which his qualification would otherwise entitle him, or he devotes himself to independent practice. He will not, therefore, be "totally unemployed" in the true sense of the term but will come to find himself in a position of waiting that can be called *semi-unemployment*. Unemployment among the chemists is not too widespread if by such is meant the totally unemployed; but what is very high, nevertheless, is the number of those who are employed in positions of a lower rank than those to which the qualification they possess would entitle them. Another symptom of the abnormal situation is the permanence with which many are fixed in a lower professional situation.[68]

In some cases the new laureati in chemistry were forced to content themselves with whatever work they could find, even outside the industry:

> One enrolls in chemistry, sometimes, with the intention of taking the qualifying exam in teaching. . . but once having graduated it is annoying to sit for the necessary exam; one finds a way, therefore, by means of recommendations and contenting oneself with little – very little – of squeezing into some lowly penned-up job, which, nonetheless, is a job. Those who succeed in obtaining recommendations get jobs, thereby cheapening the profession; the others end up in occupations from shoe-polish salesman to servant-doorkeeper and worse. And I do not exaggerate at all.[69]

But usually the period of "semi-unemployment" was spent in the industry itself. Here the research chemist – as the professional press observed – who before the war performed only managerial functions had to resign himself to a "lower classification," to performing "dequalified" functions which once were carried out solely by his subordinates.

> Once, not long ago – for I am referring only to the immediate prewar period – there were, as there are today, laureati in pure chemistry and in chemistry and pharmacy on the one hand, and on the other diplomati in pharmacy and diplomati from several types of industrial schools who were specialized in special practical applications founded on chemical science. For example, the school for masters in dyestuffs at Prato, etc. . . . The laureati in chemistry were few, and a majority dedicated themselves to the career of university teaching or to other educational institutions or were employed in state technical laboratories. From these, generally, industries drew the few chemists that they then employed, and these few entered the industry in specialized and managerial positions. . . . No one would have thought to hire a chemist in order to reserve him exclusively for measuring the specific gravity of sulfuric acid on arrival or performing the series titrations that are often needed in industry. The chemist directed and the practical part was entrusted to head technicians or to specialized head workers provided sometimes by the professional schools. Thus also the chemist disdained to concern himself ordinarily with those small analyses of urine etc. . ., which were still in his sphere of competence, leaving them to the pharmacist as things of little importance to him. . . . After the war the enormous expansion in the development of applied chemistry (and not only this) induced a large number of youth to acquire the laurea in chemistry and a no less large number to hasten to the professional schools, which were also enlarged, improved, and encouraged in every way. . . . The chemist resigned himself to "descend the order," searching also in industry for those lower positions that consisted exactly in those series determinations or practical supervisions of equipment which before were calmly assigned to head technicians, head workmen, and sometimes even simple workers specially trained.[70]

CHAPTER SEVEN

The Corporate Associations of Intellectuals and the Carta della Scuola

What I have sought to show in the preceding pages is that even during the fascist period the school at least in part escaped the control of the dominant classes. Notwithstanding the undeniable success obtained by the regime in the fascisization of this institution through a profoundly authoritarian organization and the transmission of those values necessary to the formation of "fascist youth," a series of variables over which the regime could exercise no control (the reactions of students and parents to the Gentile Reform and the consequent failure of the scuola complementare, the closure of the safety valve of intellectual emigration, the great crisis begun in 1929) brought about a very sharp imbalance between school and labor market. In this sense, if one wanted to sum up in one sentence the history of the relationship between the school and the fascist ruling groups, one could say that the only bourgeois right that they did not easily succeed in abolishing or putting under control was the "right to study."

At this point, however, in order to expand this analysis, to show the partially dysfunctional character of the school with respect to the needs of the regime, and to understand the attempts at changing the educational system which – as we shall see – took place toward the end of the fascist period, it is necessary to examine the consequences that the imbalance between school and labor market had for the attitudes and the political and professional (namely, trade union) behavior of the intellectuals. More exactly, in order to illuminate the partially dysfunctional character of the school with respect to the needs of the regime, I propose to consider in this chapter: 1) whether the situation of status imbalance in which many intellectuals came to find themselves might have provoked attitudes and behaviors of detachment or actually of opposition toward the fascist regime; 2) which processes of conversion and of reequilibration of status they and their organizations put in motion, and in particular what pressures they exerted to influence the demand for and the supply of intellectual labor, and particularly to provoke change in the existing educational system.

It is from the attitudes and behavior of the intellectuals and their organizations – that is, from the most important result of the imbalance between school and labor market – that we must begin in order to understand the provisions adopted by the fascist government for regaining control over the situation in some manner. Thus, I will endeavor, in the second part of this chapter, to examine the measures taken by the fascist government to stimulate demand for intellectual labor. But above all I will seek to identify the measures it took to reduce supply, and therefore the changes it sought to bring about in the educational system.

The Demands of the Intellectuals

To offer an exact evaluation of the attempts made by the intellectuals and their organizations to influence the course of the demand and supply of laureati and diplomati, we must bear in mind that these organizations underwent some profound transformations during the fascist period. Like the workers, the intellectuals too were enrolled in the corporative organization of the period with the task, as Edmondo Rossoni said, "of being beside the workers, enlightening them, making known among them the idea and the necessity of fascist unionism."[1] The law of April 3, 1926 abolished the existing orders and replaced them with fascist unions which assumed all the functions of the former, including those related to the keeping of professional registers and to the discipline of members. They had legal status and legally represented all members of the category, even if not enrolled in the unions. Following this law, the number of intellectuals who joined the Fascist Confederation of Professionals and Artists increased rapidly, from 70,000 in 1928 to 130,000 ten years later, and to 152,000 in 1940 (table 7.1). If the official data reported in table 7.1 are accepted as sound, it can be said that at the end of the fascist period the rate of unionization of laureati and diplomati had reached 75 percent. The end of their organizational autonomy and the fitting into organizations rigidly controlled from above led to intellectuals' loss of the capacity to exert pressure externally, on the government and other state organs as well as to exert internal control

Table 7.1. Enrollments in the Unions of the Fascist Confederation of Professionals and Artists, 1928 to 1940

Unions	*Organized*				*Represented*
	1928	*1929*	*1938*	*1940*	*1940*
Architects	1,425	948	1,101	1,319	1,871
Authors and writers	1,000	820	1,645	1,878	2,646
Actuaries	—	—	165	181	198
Lawyers and attorneys	9,790	11,106	15,903	16,745	26,634
Fine arts	1,800	2,227	4,302	5,263	6,144
Research chemists	960	1,126	1,267	1,398	1,909
Laureati in economics and commerce	1,630	1,917	2,921	3,414	4,066
Pharmacists	8,115	8,760	11,595	12,113	14,854
Surveyors	4,750	5,261	6,394	9,113	11,869
Administrators of private educational institutions	—	—	—	448	—
Journalists	4,350	4,079	3,333	4,022	4,714
Nurses (diplomate)	—	—	554	1,674	1,700
Engineers	10,510	10,500	12,638	12,680	19,154
Teachers	—	915	1,812	3,651	5,820
Inventors	—	—	660	850	—
Doctors	15,650	17,635	27,180	29,731	38,171
Musicians	950	1,507	3,213	4,136	5,020
Notaries	2,500	2,800	2,988	3,003	3,507
Midwives	4,050	6,455	12,616	14,323	17,159
Legal representatives	—	269	539	944	1,612
Technical assessors and appraisers	—	2,000	2,021	2,557	2,924
Industrial technicians	—	2,011	2,643	4,458	7,555
Accountants	2,310	2,151	2,843	3,736	5,847
Directors and stage managers	—	—	397	546	759
Agricultural technicians	—	8,484	5,222	6,561	9,218
Veterinarians	3,000	3,166	3,259	3,600	4,035
Women artists and actresses	—	—	3,648	4,535	4,620
Total	70,790	95,711	130,859	152,900	202,006

SOURCE: F. Coscera, *Professioni ed arti nello stato fascista* (Rome, 1941), p. 41.

such as over access to the professions and over the behavior of those who practiced. In spite of this the difficulties of employment for laureati and diplomati were so great that they ultimately created more tension and conflict within the corporative fascist organization than one might have thought possible.

Pressure to Influence Demand

The pressure exerted by the intellectuals to influence the course of demand for their services was of two types: on the one hand, they sought to effect an increase in demand, and on the other they struggled fiercely among themselves, union against union, over its distribution. As I will endeavor to show, they produced in both the former and latter cases very sharp tensions and conflicts within the corporative organization, forcing the fascist political and union leaders to intervene and to mediate constantly:

> in all cities, the pharmacists and their assistants commonly sell medical advice along with the respective medicines, even in the presence of doctors, who tolerate it in order not to incur the wrath of the pharmacist; some who are even more shameless have established a consulting room in the back room of the shop for examinations and treatment, and perform hypodermic injections, treat wounds, look after eyes and venereal diseases etc., etc. . . . Everyone knows, both the doctors and the authorities, and no one is concerned about it. And this is not to mention the midwives, orderlies, bone doctors, healers, who freely exploit the public in the countryside and in the cities. One can imagine how large a number of patients would hasten to the doctors, if these defrauders were struck down.[2]

Passages such as this, of which the professional publications of the fascist period are full, give us an idea how violent was the struggle between the various organizations of intellectuals over the distribution of demand. Certainly, competition over the distribution of demand, the tendency to expand, or at the least to preserve, one's own area of intervention is a constant feature of the activity of intellectuals' organizations. All the same, it is especially at moments when the pie becomes smaller that the struggle over its division becomes more frenzied. Thus during the fascist period the various unions of intellectuals inveighed violently against each other, accusing each other by turns of "professional interference," "improper use of the profession," "amateurishness," "charlatanism"; the lawyers against the laureati in business and commerce, the architects against the engineers, the engineers against the surveyors, the surveyors against agricultural technicians, the doctors against the pharmacists, the midwives, and even the nurses. This is not the place to review the history of these contests, the victories and losses of the various corporative associations. What I wish to stress is that the conflicts were so violent and frequent as to necessitate – as the official organ of the Fascist Confederation of Professionals and Artists wrote – "a continual and patient, even if inconspicuous, effort by the Confederation, which must settle every difference by negotiation according to the principles of union law and if possible to the full satisfaction of the categories concerned."[3]

Naturally, the ways in which the various member unions of the Fascist Confederation of Professionals and Artists sought to bring about an increase in demand were different, and different too were the targets against which they directed their action. The engineers' first target was the local governments, accused of not adequately appreciating the importance of their professional services and consequently of each not having its own technical office. "There is not one rural *comune** in Italy, however small it may be," wrote the official organ of the National Fascist Union of Engineers, "which does not have a municipal doctor [but] the same cannot be said as far as offices for technical personnel are concerned."[4] The demand made repeatedly, therefore, was that of establishing in every comune (or by consortia among the smallest comuni)[5] technical offices headed by an engineer, which would provide not only for problems of the public services, of agriculture, or of the utilization of public resources, but also for the "education of representatives of the various trades" and for the "diffusion of the government's directives, close contact with the working classes, natural moderating and arbitrating functions in possible disagreements between capital and labor, and a dispassionate contribution to the collaboration of classes."[6]

The second target of the vindicative action of the engineers was the industrialists who, in spite of the sacred character which they had assumed by now, became the object of harsh attacks. If Italy's mechanical industry found itself in an inferior position compared to that of other countries, in spite of the "lower cost of manual labor," this was due, according to the engineers, to its scanty technologization, to the "irrational" way in which it was conducted – that is, substantially to the fact that the industrialists did not avail themselves sufficiently of the engineers' services:

> The general picture today of our mechanical industry. . .is that of numerous small workshops and even large ones which make a little of everything, imitate right and left, seek work frantically if only to watch their machines turn round, and lack a technical and economic program that could assure some probability of a decent future. Such workshops have four or five technicians per hundred workers, a

*The Italian *comune* or municipality is typically a city, town, or village together with the surrounding area up to the boundary of adjoining comuni. There are about 8,000 comuni comprising the national territory.

> number which they are afraid of increasing so as not to increase general expenditures.[7]

All this derived, according to the engineers, from the "retrograde and therefore antifascist mentalities"[8] of many industrialists. "There are firms and enterprises," they observed, "in which the most lively hostility prevails against the so-called technicians, where sometimes the managers even boast of being able to keep engineers at a minimum."[9] And even when the industrialists decided to rationalize their enterprises and to hire technicians, their preferences were for "diplomati from the secondary institutes, of little competence, but more adaptable than the conscientious engineer, often forced into secondary functions."[10] But apart from the attacks conducted in the professional press, which went so far as the threat to compile a "black book" of "firms conducted irrationally" (namely without their labor), the National Fascist Union of Engineers also made some very precise demands: to obligate construction firms that performed works above a certain scale to have an engineer as technical director and, likewise, industries that utilized machines "which required special technical knowledge to operate" to have laureati in engineering as directors and shopheads.[11]

As for the lawyers, the attempt to increase demand led, first of all, to a change in codes of conduct of those who practiced the profession, which, if not formally recognized, was nevertheless condoned by the union organizations. The "art of procuring the client" through "recourse to the service of so-called 'middlemen for cases,'"[12] which was denounced already in 1921 by Piero Calamandrei, was being perfected and institutionalized. The review of the Fascist Union of Lawyers and Prosecutors pointed out:

> Everywhere, in the prisons, hospitals, state offices, union associations, and charitable institutions, there are organizations, often in conflict with each other, actually directed to having the defense of a prisoner assigned to one counsel rather than to another; a case involving an automobile accident to counsel X rather than to counsel Y; or a case involving an on-the-job accident to that needy colleague who, if he wins, is likely to turn over a major percentage of the counsel's fees he receives to the person who procures it for him. There are brokers in every sector of social life; everywhere there are some who cut deeply into the fees of colleagues who resort to these brokering practices. . . .[13]

In the same way another practice denounced by Calamandrei was spread and institutionalized: "the delaying tactic. . . which succeeds in assuring long life to litigations by the generous nourishment of quibblings, by the same solicitous indulgence with which the peasant daily prepares the pasture for his only heifer in hopes of being able to milk it for many long years to come."[14] The review of the Fascist Union of Lawyers and Prosecutors itself attributed "the relative increase in litigation" to the "artificial prolongation of suits, charges, and useless interlocutory matters, caused by some needy lawyer to scrape a living" and showed all its sympathy "for colleagues who practice these methods."[15]

But more important for the purposes of this discussion are the attempts to bring about an increase in demand that were made by the same Fascist Union of Lawyers and Prosecutors, which, as far as we can tell, created sharp conflicts both for its corporative organization and for the Fascist Party. The principal cause of the "reduction of litigation," and therefore of the demand for their services, was attributed by the Fascist Union of Lawyers and Prosecutors to the system instituted by the Carta del Lavoro.* As is well known, one of the ways (although certainly not the most important) through which the fascist corporative organization that arose from the Carta del Lavoro sought to have the workers, as Salvemini said, "play the part of the animals in the Society for the Protection of Animals" was the obligation to try to settle controversies over work "amicably" by negotiation within the union before bringing them before the judiciary.

To perform this function, as well as to assist the member before the magistrate in the event of an unsuccessful agreement, the union organization established in-house legal offices. To give an idea of work carried out by these offices it suffices to report a few data: in 1934 there were 64,936 individual disputes resolved within the union and 9,842 by the judiciary; in 1935 there were respectively 63,959 and 9,043; in 1936, 54,894 compared to 7,752.[16] But the legal offices, according to the *Rassegna del sindacalismo forense*, little by little expanded "the sphere of their activity from the field of extrajudicial and judicial assistance in union matters to invading the fields of commercial, pension, criminal law, etc." To this cause of the reduction of demand there was added, according to the Fascist Union of Lawyers and Prosecutors, a second: the establishment in many urban centers of legal offices "in the various districts' Party sections. . .which lend their assistance *free* and not always only to the people who have need of such assistance." In these circumstances, the attempts

**Carta del Lavoro:* corporatist statute regulating labor relations under the fascist regime. See glossary entry.

of the Fascist Union of Lawyers and Prosecutors to increase demand ultimately led to questioning of the corporative organization itself and of the action of the Fascist Party. Discussions on the incompatibility of the independent profession of law with the system of corporative organization became increasingly frequent, and the feeling was increasingly widespread that, confronted with the activity of the latter, the lawyers became like the "unemployed coachmen who from the height of their ramshackle carriages watch the speeding automobiles and the thundering airplanes pass by."[17] Thus the Fascist Union of Lawyers and Prosecutors asked repeatedly that the legal offices established by the professional organizations be abolished and that the functions of those established by the Party be limited and controlled.[18]

Much of the effort of the National Fascist Union of Doctors to produce an increase in demand was directed at protecting and strengthening the monopoly situation of their members by redefining the codes of professional conduct. If the defense of a monopoly situation and the struggle against processes of demystification of professional stature and the spread of specialized knowledge are, as has often been observed,[19] a constant characteristic of intellectuals' organizations, it is equally true that this defense and this struggle become particularly bitter in moments of surplus supply. To give at least an idea of the efforts that the National Fascist Union of Doctors made in this direction, it will be enough to offer a few examples.

First, it tried desperately to reverse the tendency of doctors to abandon the practice of writing their own prescriptions by prescribing, instead, commercial preparations. In the report presented to the Third Congress, the commissioner of the union devoted much attention to this problem, saying among other things:

> Too easily we doctors prescribe commercial medicine, rather than write a prescription ourselves. This very often happens by laziness, sometimes because the doctor has lost the ability to prescribe or perhaps has not made the effort to learn it. . . . *From the practice of prescribing commercial medicine derives medical unemployment:* the patient, when he notices that the doctor takes the trouble to compose the suitable prescription, feels the need to rely on his work. If, on the other hand, he notices that the doctor prescribes only commercial medicine, he gets it by himself. We ourselves accustom patients to avail themselves of the pharmacist rather than the doctor. There is only one remedy and we hope to succeed in it! That the law compel the pharmacist not to sell such medicine if not under medical prescription.[20]

Second, besides attempting to revive the practice of prescription writing, the union concerned itself with the way in which the prescriptions were to be made. For a long time, and especially in 1930 and 1931, there took place within *La federazione medica,* the official organ of the National Fascist Union of Doctors, a debate over "the use of Latin in medical questions." Without entering here into the particulars of this debate, it suffices to mention that the use of Latin was advised especially in writing prescriptions in order to reinforce the sacred and inaccessible character of the medical profession in the eyes of the layman:

> One could in the meantime return to writing prescriptions in Latin. Our prescriptions could then be understood and mailed to every country in Europe. They would acquire a certain esteem with the educated and uneducated public, because, not being easily glossed and annotated, they would acquire an aura of superiority and mystery which is not the least factor in the success of the doctor's prescription. . . . The dignity, the prestige, and also, of course, the well-being of our class would certainly gain from it.[21]

Finally, the journal of the doctors' union attacked many times those forms of "diagnosis and therapy from a distance,"[22] from the advertising of medicines to the doctor's column in the newspaper, which were considered dangerous threats to the monopoly of knowledge by the corporate association and its members.

The National Fascist Union of Doctors, in its attempt to effect an increase in demand, also entered into conflict with the policy of the fascist government. It never hid, in fact, its profound hostility to all laws or provisions which, reducing the number of illnesses, would also have reduced demand:

> And we, general practitioners, no longer see any of the patients who once formed the fundamental basis of our practice: babies, sick persons, venereal cases. Now even patients with pulmonary tuberculosis report themselves less and less to the usual treatment, and after the application of the prudent law against tuberculosis, these will disappear completely from our treatments. The social legislation, which we ourselves composed and favored, is now turned against us. The next insurance against illness will certainly bring a further reduction of our practice. . . .[23]

From this bitter struggle to increase demand not even the "school inspectors," accused of having "brought a reduction in the practice," escaped:

> Many of these are true angels of decency, of faith and of charity, but there are others of them who turn themselves into veritable doctors advising this and that remedy or even suggesting this or that commercial preparation.[24]

Nevertheless, the two most important targets of the struggle of the National Fascist Union of Doctors to increase demand were the medical insurance companies and health clinics which, along with the spread of the commercial medicines, were considered the fundamental causes of medical unemployment. After having taken a sort of sounding among its members in 1931, the National Fascist Union of Doctors took an open position against the diffusion of medical insurance, which "from being an isolated fact is becoming a social phenomenon which can damage the material and moral livelihood of doctors."[25] Realizing, however, the irreversible character of this phenomenon and of the strong pressure exerted by the other unions for its diffusion, the leaders of the National Fascist Union of Doctors gave up the battle for abolition of these companies (despite contrary pressure from their membership) and posed instead two conditions for their continued existence:

> 1) that the number of patients entrusted to each doctor be small, namely so as not to tie up the doctor totally, and thus to allow him an independent practice; 2) that only the poor be enlisted, again, in order to leave room for independent practice.[26]

Much more radical was the battle conducted against the health clinics, accused of dashing "every hope of a dignified livelihood for a class that is still believed to be wealthy and thus quite eligible for taxation by the public treasury."[27] In this case, in fact, the union clearly aimed to prevent the health clinic from becoming widespread by using all its means:

> Can we prevent the rise of health clinics? [asked the Commissioner of the union in the report to the Third Congress]. Legally, no, because the law gives no authority to the union, but even so we might be able to, given the moral authority which the unions have as natural advisors of the prefects and of the provincial doctors, namely those who must give permission for the health clinics to emerge.[28]

Pressure to Influence Supply

The action of the various fascist unions of professionals and artists to overcome the imbalance between supply and demand for intellectual labor was concentrated on demands capable of producing effects in the short term. This explains, in the first place, why the pressures of the organizations of intellectuals aimed at influencing the course of demand more than that of supply and, in the second place, why the attempts at controlling supply – which we shall see were not absent – were addressed for the most part to influencing what could be called the terminal phases in the training of the intellectual labor force. The most important demands supported for many years by the unions of intellectuals were, in fact, the closure of the professional registers, the expulsion of foreign students (before and after the laurea) from Italy, and the establishment of the numero chiuso in access to higher education.

The demand for closing the register was advanced both by the lawyers' and the doctors' unions. The lawyers' professional publications confronted the question a number of times, and more or less always in these terms:

> A problem presents itself concerning the sharp reduction of work, and it is still necessary to face it even if at first view it may seem unpleasant (we shall see, in fact, that it is not so): the problem, that is, of closing the registers. It cannot be disputed that the registers are more than glutted compared to the quantity of work. Given this, is it logical to continue to add new members, with the result of dividing even more that work which is already much less than what is needed by those already enrolled, and with the result of creating misfits among the youth who, entering the new career, find themselves for this reason experiencing bitter disappointment when they thought they had achieved that coveted economic independence?[29]

On the other hand, the *Federazione medica* began to confront the subject in 1921, and even after the whole medical order at its congress in 1924 officially demanded that the register be closed, it continued to publish a large number of articles on this theme. While there was no absence of "liberal" voices championing open rolls and accusing the supporters of closed registers of "corporativism" and of "wretched egoism,"[30] the position of the great majority was that of the "protectionists":

> It is not pleasant, it is true! Those in Italy who take a university degree for the beauty of science are few. He who graduates does so for the most part to make his daily bread. . . from science, even from that baked in the oven. But *necessitas non habet legem*.* And then what better is proposed? Propaganda? Emigration? [These are] mild expedients, of little effectiveness, which, however, must not be ignored, since they can serve as accessories.[31]

> But then does the streetcar driver really commit a crime against liberty when he exhibits the notice "full up," and keeps clusters of people from dangerously piling up on the outer parts of the vehicle?[32]

*Latin: literally, "need does not constitute a legal right" or "necessity has no claim on the law."

There was actually one among the "protectionists" who proposed even more radical measures, namely taking "the pharmacists with the law on pharmacies" as a model and requiring "preferences in practicing for the sons of doctors, whose fathers are often able to leave nothing as an inheritance other than the advantage of their experience."[33]

The second demand, as I mentioned earlier, was to expel foreign students, before and after the laurea, from the national territory, and this was argued above all by the corporative association of doctors. The number of foreign students enrolled in Italian universities had increased considerably during the fascist period, from 487 in 1921–22 to 2,166 in 1926–27 to 1,897 in 1931–32. Of total enrollments foreign students constituted 0.4 percent in 1921 – 22, 5.1 percent in 1926 – 27, and 4 percent in 1931 – 32.[34] Of these, about half were enrolled, in the years indicated, in the faculty of medicine. It was not strange, therefore, that the association of doctors might also in this case have led the campaign against "the damaging penetration of foreign students who have succeeded and still succeed in scrounging, behind the presentation of false qualifications and after a few months of inadequate preparation, that *laurea* which Italian students arrive at after six years of hard study and natural sacrifice."[35] The *Federazione medica* argued that "the foreign invasion" came from those "countries where the closed register has been in effect for several years"; it implicitly accused the government of gathering "the excess material of other countries, giving the right to practice to persons who do not have it in their own country,"[36] and asked repeatedly that foreign students, once having graduated, not be allowed to undertake the state exam for certification to professional practice. From the Congress of the National Fascist Union of Doctors came, in 1931, a "more practical" proposal: that of posing as a condition of residence in Italy for foreigners who had received the laurea in Italian universities the payment of fees in arrears:[37]

> We know that the majority of foreign students are from the Balkan peoples and are rarely wealthy; if we were to require a few thousand lire for back fees, few would stay, and thus we would have solved the problem in absolute fairness and without touching on the political subject.[38]

The establishment of the numero chiuso for entrance to the university was demanded by all the most important unions of laureati, and in particular by the doctors, the engineers, and the lawyers. The lawyers debated at some length the radical proposal of closing the faculty of law for several years, and advanced as a subordinate proposal the reduction of the number of universities, and particularly of the faculties of jurisprudence, refusing, as they said, to consider Italy "an association of grand duchies, for the cultural prestige of which the little university inherited by each of them was necessary."[39] Among the doctors, the numero chiuso was considered an alternative solution to the closing of the register and was supported especially by those who maintained, with the usual delicacy, that "foeticide [was] better than homicide,"[40] or who considered that closing the register was "of dubious effectiveness" because it was equivalent to "shutting the stall after the bulls have escaped."[41] The most consistent supporters of this demand were, nevertheless, the engineers, who presented, at the beginning of 1930, a memorandum on intellectual unemployment to the Ministry of Corporative Associations with the request that the numero chiuso be introduced for access to the faculties of engineering.[42]

Pressures from the organizations of intellectuals to influence the course of supply were almost never, on the other hand, directed at producing changes at the secondary level of education. For many years, the publications of the unions of intellectuals demanded a more rigorous and severe selection at this level, but they never proposed fundamental reform programs for the secondary schools. This does not mean, however, that proposals of the sort advanced by members of the fascist government were not viewed positively by the unions of intellectuals. In particular, the *Rassegna del sindacalismo forense* unconditionally approved of Minister of Corporative Associations Lantini, who argued at the lawyers' national congress for the necessity of "having it understood by our good people that conducting a trade does not at all diminish the citizen, indeed it ennobles him before the brainy vagabondage of the many who do nothing of their own nor produce anything of use for the country." "To elevate oneself in life," observed this review, "does not mean becoming a lawyer rather than an artisan. To elevate oneself means, on the contrary, becoming a Luca della Robbia or a Stradivari among the artisans or an Irnerio among the lawyers."[43] But to convince "our good people" of the new meaning that was to be attributed to the expression "to elevate oneself in life," propaganda was certainly not enough. The functioning of the secondary schools had to be profoundly revised:

> It can rightly be observed that there exists in Italy a great disproportion between the number of ginnasi and licei, which prepare youth for the intellectual professions, and the number of scuole di avviamento, which must train the artisans and specialized technicians for agriculture, construction, industry, etc.... And this, while our country is saturated with doctors, lawyers, and accountants, whereas we

experience on the other hand a great shortage of artisans, technicians, and specialized workers, who are necessary especially now that for the colonization of the Empire we will need specialists in agriculture, forestry, building, mining, highways and other technical knowledge. To remedy this discord, therefore, it would be necessary to close some ginnasi and licei and open some training schools.[44]

The Government's Response

Pressed by the organizations of intellectuals and concerned over the possible consequences of the unemployment of diplomati and laureati in terms of loss of consensus among these important social strata, the fascist ruling group took several steps to confront the situation. Given the impossibility of questioning the foundations of the regime (the corporative order, relations with the industrialists), it sought to bring about an increase in the demand for intellectual labor by another route. Thus it reduced by five years the maximum age for remaining on the job for some categories of functionaries; it introduced, beginning in 1932, the forty-hour work week in offices; it forbade the accumulation of pension with public employment; it expelled some of the women from public jobs. Moreover, with the *Foglio disposizioni** of November 14, 1934, the secretary of the Fascist Party declared that 2 percent of expenditures supported by public entities for the construction of buildings had to be allotted for their "artistic embellishment" (that is, to employ members of the Union of Fine Arts) and that, for certain professional activities, the prefects of each province had to use not the work of their own functionaries but that of "competent" laureati and diplomati (graduates in business, lawyers, engineers, accountants, etc). The comuni had to make use of substitutes designated by the union, instead of municipal doctors in nearby localities, in cases of a short vacancy of the municipal doctor's post.

But above all the fascist ruling group sought to confront the situation by rapidly expanding the bureaucratic apparatus. If in the regime's first period of life the number of public employees remained constant or actually decreased slightly, beginning in 1930 it began to rise rapidly and at a much more sustained pace, doubling in about ten years (table 7.2). Nevertheless, neither these measures nor the much paraded new possibilities of work that were to be opened in the colonies for the intellectuals[45] sufficed even minimally to resolve the problem of unemployment for the intellectuals aspiring to become "depend-

**Foglio disposizioni:* sheet of directives.

Table 7.2. Growth of State Employment in Italy, 1923 to 1943

Year	*Total Personnel*	*Increase*
1-7-1923	509,145	—
1-7-1930	498,825	−10,320
2-7-1931	581,309	9,164
1-7-1932	638,329	129,184
1-7-1940	990,045	480,900
1-7-1941	1,239,374	630,229
1-7-1942	1,293,328	784,283
1-7-1943	1,430,060	920,916

SOURCE: F. Demarchi, "I laureati nella Pubblica Amministrazione," in *I laureati in Italia* (Bologna: Il Mulino, 1968), p. 222.

ents" or, much less, for those aspiring to become "independent" professionals. For these latter, as Cogliolo recognized sadly in his famous *Malinconie universitarie,* "not even the great genius of the Duce will find the way to mobilize clients and to make them come to us, forcing them to bring suits or to become patients or to order statues."[46]

New Attempts at Changing the Educational System

Unable to resolve the problem with measures that might profoundly influence the course of demand, the fascist ruling group sought to intervene once again in the mechanisms for training the intellectual labor force. Of the three demands supported by the unions regarding the control and regulation of supply, it ultimately adopted only one: the expulsion, in an amiable way, of the foreign university students. Adopting, in fact, the "practical" proposal of the corporative association of doctors, the secretary of the Fascist Party, with the Foglio disposizioni of November 14, 1934, established that foreign students, once graduated, who intended to practice a profession in Italy were obliged to pay fees "covering their entire educational career." It never accepted, on the other hand, the demand to close the professional registers, and, somewhat more surprisingly, it never resorted to the numero chiuso, despite the introduction of the measure in Germany in 1933 by the Nazi government.[47] It was Mussolini himself who responded negatively in the April 1, 1930 session of the

Chamber of Deputies to those who asked for a reduction in the number of universities, considered "factories of misfits, of intellectual misfits who are socially and politically the most dangerous element of all."[48] Replying to Senator Boccardo, who asked for the establishment of the numero chiuso in university access, Minister of National Education De Vecchi di Val Cismon maintained in 1935 that "the longing for knowledge and elevation of the young cannot be restrained according to a quota."[49] Then too, Bottai always opposed the idea that Italian universities should seek the "dangerous protections and unreliable shelters provided by the automatism of the numerus clausus."[50]

If the fascist government made no recourse to the numero chiuso, it was certainly not due to respect for the "longing for knowledge and elevation of the young." While this is a certain fact and has no need of further demonstration, it still remains to be explained, however, how an authoritarian regime such as the fascist, which had freed itself with such ease from the other bourgeois rights, did not succeed in doing likewise with the "right to study" by intoducing the numero chiuso. To answer this question it must be recalled, as was mentioned earlier, that during the fascist period unemployment had struck not only the laureati but also the diplomati, and that indeed one of the most important sources of the expansion of higher education which had occurred beginning in 1929 was, exactly, the unemployment of diplomati. In this situation, the introduction of the numero chiuso would thus have curbed the expansion of higher education, but it would also inevitably have increased the difficulty of employment for the diplomati. As Mario Attilio Levi observed,

> If with the concorso and admission exam the number of positions in the higher institutes and universities were limited, thereby proportioning it to the real possibilities of absorption. . . , the problem would remain of turning thousands of youth into misfits at eighteen years of age in order to avoid the risk of their becoming so at twenty-two or twenty-four, when, that is, they would have better capacities and better means for facing the struggle for a living and professional competition.[51]

To introduce the numero chiuso meant, therefore, to increase dangerously the already strong tensions existing at the level of the diplomati tecnici and magistrali and to create new problems for the graduates of the liceo classico and scientifico. "Considering the particularly serious case of the youth coming out of licei, the problem of their settlement would remain grievous. It being too late to become farmers, workers, shop clerks, many of them would seek to remedy their situation by procuring the diploma from the istituto magistrale or tecnico. Thus there would be a glut, namely greater unemployment, among the teachers, surveyors, accountants, and commercial and industrial technicians."[52] This is why the educational policy of the fascist government, in this regard, moved in a completely different direction from that desired by the organizations of engineers, doctors, and lawyers. Facing the problem of the unemployment of diplomati, the only answer that the fascist government could think of at first was that of deferring the insertion of diplomati into the work world by turning them into university students. That is, it did no more than juridically sanction the acutal tendency toward the de-professionalization of the secondary schools. Indeed the law of June 13, 1935 transformed the post-secondary institutes of education, of economics and commerce, and of agriculture into actual university faculties.[53]

But how could the problem of intellectual unemployment really be resolved? The debate that unfolded on this subject in the review *Vita universitaria* revealed that the university teachers as well proposed restrictive solutions of various types, but all at the level of higher education. Agostino Gemelli declared himself against the numero chiuso and argued that "the removal of the inept, the unsuitable, those who would end up being unemployed and weighing upon the community" had "to happen spontaneously and by means of self-selection."[54] To realize this plan he proposed that students *fuori corso** be eliminated and that attendance be made obligatory. Pier Paolo Luzzatto Fegiz proposed that those who, after a certain number of exams, had achieved an average lower than 20 out of 30 be dropped from the university.[55] Others recommended educational and vocational guidance and proposed as an example for imitation the guidance conferences promoted by the Rector of Padua for those qualifying in the licei.[56] Still others, such as Giuseppe Lombardo Radice, argued that, as well as making "propaganda against the glut by warning families," it was necessary to make "propaganda in our university surroundings, in order to arouse a stronger awareness of our *sacred* duty of social selection."[57]

Nevertheless, as time passed and the situation worsened, the fascist ruling group, and particularly Minister of National Education Bottai, grew convinced of the need to revise and modify the functioning of the mechanisms of selection at the level of the lower-secondary school. Many times it had been argued that overcoming the imbalance between school and labor market could be achieved

**Fuori corso:* not making steady progress in the normal sequence of courses and exams leading to the laurea.

only by making the mechanisms of selection more severe and efficient at the level not of higher studies but of the lower-secondary. To realize this plan, however, partial measures were not sufficient (the introduction of new exams, pressures from above on the teachers to be more severe, etc.). It was thought necessary to transform profoundly the internal structures of the educational system.

This is, plainly, the presupposition on which stands the Carta della Scuola of January 19, 1939 which, following Gentile's, constitutes certainly the most fundamental attempt made to modify the Italian educational system and to readapt it to the "exigencies" of the labor market. Bottai was convinced that "the problem of the school today finds its critical point in its middle sector," and that it was at this level one must intervene if one really wanted to transform that "fomenter of ambitions, creator of unemployed and dissatisfied masses, continual element of disorder and of disturbance, in the productive no less than the moral livelihood of the Nation," which he believed that school to be. He recognized that the avviamento had performed an important function in discouraging the educational and occupational aspirations of some students. Nevertheless, this function was much more limited than that assigned by Gentile to the scuole complementari. The crisis of the Gentile Reform and the replacement of the complementari with the avviamento had marked the change from a dumping school to a school which, on the contrary, offered "an incentive, even if indirect, to the young people to alter their own social condition." "If a criticism can be made of the present-day school," Bottai observed, "it is that it nourishes, with the crumbs of culture, illusory ambitions of fitting into the student ranks, which might offer an escape from manual work as the price for social elevation."[58]

The problem was therefore that of transforming the lower-secondary, and in particular of replacing the avviamento with a true dumping school:

> I also think that the scuola di avviamento had become distorted, and that, on the inclined plane of aspiration toward the scuola media, it has lost its rough and ready character of a school of the people, a school for the people. We shall align it once again with the elementary school. We shall return it, together with the elementary school, into the school of the popular classes, the great school of the masses in which a large part of Italian youth must find satisfaction of their professional and cultural needs, without coming to cherish facile illusions in the other sectors of the scuola media.[59]

The Carta della Scuola entailed at the lower level a division of the primary school into two cycles: the three-year elemenatry school and the two-year "school of labor." The second cycle was to be operated "in the name of work" in such a way as to socialize future manual workers to their role early by preventing the formation of "unrealistic" aspirations. At the end of primary schooling there were three possibilities: the *scuola media,* the *scuola artigiana,* and the *scuola professionale.* The scuola media (three years) was the only one that permitted access to secondary studies, and from there to higher studies. The scuola artigiana (three years), "typically rural or suited to the small localities" and aimed at training workers, artisans, and peasants, was "to make attachment to the Italian family's traditions of honesty and work take root in the children," and to internalize the "attachment to a trade" by accustoming them to manual labor and establishing the principle of the "school as workshop." These schools were to arise on the same educational terrain as the elementary schools and employ the maestri as teachers. The scuola professionale (three years), which could then be completed by a two-year scuola tecnica, was to arise in the large urban centers and to aim at training specialized workers or impiegati at a low level of qualification. It had as teachers not maestri but teachers with the laurea. What mattered more, however, is that, even though directed at two different strata within the subordinate classes and consequently presenting a range of different characteristics (consider only the different status of the teachers), the scuola artigiana and the scuola professionale had one fundamental thing in common: they were both dead-end schools, dumping schools.

At the upper-secondary level the Carta della Scuola foresaw the liceo classico, the scientifico, the istituto professionale for farmers, surveyors, and industrial technicians, the istituto tecnico for commercial and mercantile concerns, and the istituto magistrale. The most interesting thing is that for the diplomati of the istituti tecnici new points of access were provided to various university faculties formerly reserved only for students who came from the licei. In particular, the diplomati of the commercial istituti tecnici could enroll not only in the faculty of economics and commerce but also in political science; the agricultural technicians not only in the faculty of agriculture but also in the mathematical, physical, and natural sciences; the surveyors could enroll in the faculties of engineering and the sciences; and the industrial technicians were allowed to enroll in the faculties of engineering, industrial chemistry, and the sciences.

In what way did the Carta of Bottai seek to overcome the imbalance between school and labor market? First of all by the introduction into both the primary and the secondary school of "productive labor." Troops of pedagogues and philosophers, from De Ruggiero to Volpicelli, from Mazzetti to Valitutti,[60] were charged with producing the new ideology of the "school of labor," and the task of diffusing it was assigned to the mass media, especially the press. The subject most treated by the 1,573 writings – books and articles – which were published during a period of two years on Bottai's Carta[61] was that of productive labor in the school, of its training function, of its political significance. The people were to be convinced that the introduction into the school of productive work, which according to some was "rough," "harsh," "difficult to do," according to others "simple," aimed at a reconciliation of the social classes, at overcoming the division between manual and intellectual labor. The "man who knows so well how to sum up in images the essence of things" [Bottai] managed to say, "Finally a school is formed where 'the little gentlemen' will learn how to dirty their hands."[62]

But even if there was no lack of those who saw then, and see today, in Bottai's plan a "revolutionary" attempt to overcome the social division of labor,[63] there is no doubt that it was nothing more than a provision to overcome the imbalance between school and labor market – a provision, it should be noted, that had important precedents: for instance, that effected by the Nazi government, which, in order to "uncrowd" the universities and overcome intellectual unemployment, did not limit itself to introducing the numero chiuso, but also took other supporting measures, such as prescribing obligatory manual work service of a year's length for students who wanted to enroll in the university. Bottai himself often said clearly what he had in mind:

> When one considers that all Italian youth, after three years of elementary schooling, will have to attend the school of labor for two years, it is easy to infer that many youth, by effectively acquiring an interest in manual labor along with an awareness of its national functions and its high human dignity, will feel themselves drawn to it. And the humiliating shifting about between classes, provoked by the unreflective craze for continuing studies, will diminish.[64]

But even more important for overcoming the imbalance between school and labor market were the changes foreseen at the level of secondary education. At the upper-secondary level Bottai, by opening new points of access for diplomati to university faculties, did no more than take up De Vecchi's policy again and extend it; he codified the trend toward de-professionalization which, as we have seen, had been caused by extensive unemployment of diplomati, by their entrance en masse into the faculties to which they were allowed access, and by their pressure to obtain the opening of new university outlets. At this level, therefore, the course taken by Bottai was completely different from that followed by Gentile in his time, which had aimed rather at a re-professionalization of the upper-secondary schools. At the lower-secondary level, on the other hand, the Carta della Scuola aimed at the creation of a closed and profoundly hierarchical system with the establishment even of two dumping schools: the scuola artigiana and the scuola professionale. At this level Bottai thus imitated the Gentile model, by further accentuating its closed character.

Under circumstances that not only prevented him from blocking the way of diplomati to the university with the numero chiuso, but actually forced him to open new access for them, thereby turning the university into a large parking lot for unemployed intellectual labor, in order to regain equilibrium between school and labor market Bottai had to direct many of his efforts toward the lower-secondary level. Here, by creating two dumping schools, he sought once more to sever, at least for a part of the subordinate classes, the link between school and social promotion. Already in March 1937, speaking to the Chamber of Deputies on the national education budget, he clearly set forth the objectives of his program:

> If the scuola di avviamento is led to perform its function, which is to complete the elementary instruction of the people without any foolish, and likewise useless and dangerous, aspiration toward the scuola media; if it is shown capable of absorbing, therefore, increasingly large masses and preventing them from trying to "shift their lot" by means of the scuola media; if the scuola media, with its schools of technical and of classical studies, by a distribution of competencies from the lower to the higher levels regulated in a more unified manner, offers a more finished preparation for the young (who for many occupations and positions must now find in secondary qualifications valid passports for the livelihood of the country) thus avoiding the illicit craze to secure in the universities higher qualifications for lower tasks; [very lively applause] then these, the Universities, will finally be safe, in a zone where professional preparation is itself a science, has to be science, and must, on pain of irreparable decay, remain science."[65]

But how could Bottai have imagined success in realizing a restructuring of the lower-secondary school which had partially failed sixteen years earlier; and how could he have imitated Gentile's model if, hit by the silent opposition of students and their parents, it had remained alive in its original form for not even a year? To answer these questions, it is necessary to bear in mind that toward the end of the 1930s the selection-socialization dilemma in the use of educational institutions presented itself in very different terms than in 1923.

In the first part of this chapter, I sought to point out the consequences of status imbalance for the professional behavior of already established intellectuals who found themselves in this position and for their organizations. Now I wish to advance the hypothesis that this very imbalance produced consequences also for the political attitudes of the intellectuals, bringing about their detachment or actually their opposition to the regime. It can be hypothesized, in other words, that while the already established intellectuals were threatened by a process of partial downward mobility, and reacted by putting in motion those processes or requilibration of status already mentioned, that is, the pressure to influence demand and to modify the mechanisms regulating supply, the others, namely those who had yet "to arrive," the young laureati and university students, had instead to reckon with a process of partially blocked upward mobility, and also reacted, at least to some extent (in the presence of other conditions, naturally), with attitudes of detachment or of opposition to the regime.

Given the nature of the regime, it is not easy to bring elements of proof to this hypothesis. There are, however, several facts that show it to be at least reasonable. As is known, as the regime consolidated itself, but especially beginning in 1930, the "youth problem," or more precisely that of the students, came to light, since it was on them that attention was concentrated. The many writings that treated this problem at first denounced the apathy and indifference of the young and then little by little, and naturally with the required caution, denounced the diffusion among the young of antifascist attitudes.[66] We can safely say that this was not the usual dispute between academic and worldly people over the generational conflict. It reflected instead the anxieties of the fascist ruling group, since, as we know, this is the period in which a tendency to the left both inside and outside the party actually manifested itself among the young intellectuals.[67]

The emergence of the youth question and the advent of antifascist tendencies among the students have recently been interpreted by Gino Germani as the outcome of existing contradictions between the mechanisms of control and of mobilization of the elite. Without denying the validity of the interpretive hypothesis suggested by Germani, I think it can be argued that an important variable to examine in explaining this phenomenon is the position of status imbalance in which the intellectuals found themselves. The writings that dealt with the "youth question" from 1930 onward often emphasized that in reality the true problem was that of employment for young intellectuals. The contrast between aspirations and real possibilities of employment for young diplomati and laureati was not, certainly, a characteristic peculiar to the fascist period, but it became particularly acute in this period because of the continual exaltation of the young on the part of the regime and the oft-repeated affirmations of the necessity of revitalizing the fascist ruling class. The attitude of these youth, on the other hand, could be summarized, according to a contributor to *Critica fascista,* by the following words: "They have told us, in school and outside, in books and newspapers, that Fascism needs a young ruling class to replace the elders who are very often nonfascist or still freemasons in spirit, and now instead we find ouselves without a job or with one for which it was not worth the trouble to have studied so much."[68]

In any case, and whether or not the hypothesis I have advanced is valid, it is certain that Bottai's program of educational policy was based on it. That is, Giuseppe Bottai – the strongest ideologue of the regime, the editor of *Critica fascista,* which dedicated so much space to the youth problem – became convinced that between intellectual unemployment and the youth problem there was a cause-and-effect relationship, and this conviction certainly influenced his plan for altering the Italian educational system. This relationship showed in fact that, beyond a certain threshold, the existence of selection mechanisms of little efficiency would produce negative effects on processes of socialization.

The school system that Bottai had under his supervision had all the requisites for functioning splendidly as an agent of socialization. It had been progressively fascisized at all levels, from the elementary schools to the university, and it conveyed the beliefs and values necessary for training the "young Italian fascist." But the lack of efficient mechanisms of selection (besides the other factors mentioned, over which the fascist government could exercise no control), by aggravating the existing imbalance between school and labor market, risked making the work of socialization performed by the school completely useless. The young person who left after thirteen or seventeen years of school had received a complete fascist training and was therefore in the best condition for accepting without question the foundations of the new regime. But this training could enter into crisis if he found himself facing great difficulties in finding that work for which the school claimed to have prepared him. Of this Bottai was perfectly aware:

> The fascisization which has taken place until now has already made great progress compared to the professed agnosticism of a while ago. But it is not everything, because the question does not consist only of exciting the young with the political ideas of fascism. If its political task consisted totally in this, the school could not be viewed as indispensable to the ends of political education nor its problem so urgent.[69]

Even a totalitarian political socialization such as the fascist one could be inadequate or remain "abstract" if it were imparted by a school that produced more diplomati and laureati that the market was in a position to absorb.

> Not only the teacher [Bottai observed] who does not seek the "pretexts" to speak opportunely about politics is abstract; abstract as well is the school which, while the country needs engineers, supplies lawyers, while the country needs jurists, supplies orators, while the country needs men trained for modern life, remains ordered according to an outdated humanism (or, therefore, no humanism at all), [lively applause] although continually professing faith in fascism.[70]

But until then the problem of equilibrium between the two functions of selection and socialization performed by the school was not posed much differently from the way it had been in Gentile's time. The most important change that had occurred since 1923 was rather the different weight assumed by the school in the processes of socialization, or more precisely, the increased importance of other agents of socialization. The fascist regime had consolidated itself and had created a wide network of instruments of social control. The political socialization of the young was secured not only by the school, but also by the mass media, which themselves were completely fascisized, and still more by the fascist youth organizations. In particular, these last, which recruited and organized youth of all ages, from four to twenty-eight succeeded in performing a definitive role in the political socialization of the younger generations both by the extent of their diffusion and by the effectiveness of their instruction techniques.[71] In this situation, the selection-socialization dilemma therefore posed itself in much different terms. Bottai himself recognized this:

> If by chance little effort were expended in the school on political education, if no one sought there such "occasions," if no one were stirred on the bases and premises of politics, we would still have to agree that the young would still grow into the political ideals of Fascism. Life, the entire life of the nation, the family, the Fascist political groups, trade unions, and recreational bodies, the newspaper, the radio, the sports clubs, and above all the great historical events of our age of which the

young are spectators and empassioned actors as only they know how to be, would altogether educate them to these political ideals even if they were not to be found implicitly or explicitly in the school.[72]

If the school was no longer the only agent of political socialization which the regime could use, then the importance of selection among the two functions performed by the school could be accentuated, and the risk faced with relative calm which Gentile, in such a different situation, could absolutely not allow himself to run: that of losing with a restructuring of the lower-secondary a part of the students of the subordinate classes who, just as they had refused in 1923 to be transformed from students of the scuola tecnica into students of the complementari, would probably also have been opposed to being coerced into the scuole artigiane and professionali. Bottai understood this perfectly:

> The legislator of '23 –and we would be wrong to forget him today – first set out resolutely on this path. But he did so in a political and social world that was very different from our own. That world had yet to be systematized, regimented; and therefore, it lacked the relationships that are appropriate for this one – school to single party, school to corporative associations, school to Balilla* organizations. Are these not relationships that likewise renew the problem, that oblige us to persist, as on a work of reclamation, in order not to compromise or actually annul the work already done?[73]

As is well known, the outbreak of the Second World War allowed the realization of only a small part of the ambitious plan Giuseppe Bottai had elaborated for transforming the educational system. On the other hand, the insufficiency of the means at hand and the resistance of the teachers made completely ineffective even the first innovation implemented by the author of the Carta: the introduction of "productive labor" into the school. Thus, facing further expansion of university enrollments, which occurred with the outbreak of the war, the fascist government had to fall back on an emergency provision, and with the law of January 11, 1943 gave the Minister of Public Education the power to fix the ceiling number (the numero chiuso, in effect) of students who could enroll in some faculties.

**Balilla:* "Nickname of a Genoese boy, G. B. Perasso, who by throwing a stone at some Austrian soldiers started the revolution which drove them out of Genoa in 1746. . . . Fascist youth organization, 'Opera Nazionale Balilla,' for boys. . . . ." *Cambridge Italian Dictionary,* ed. Barbara Reynolds (Cambridge, Eng.: The University Press, 1962), 1:80.

CHAPTER EIGHT

Intellectual Employment and Unemployment, 1945–1973

Toward the end of the 1950s, in the midst of the economic boom, the thesis of a "shortage of qualified personnel" arose. Elaborated by *équipe* of prestigious experts, supported by the dominant economic and political groups, and spread throughout the country by a myriad of publications, conferences, and debates, this thesis had immediate success and continued to hold the field for almost a decade. That the forecasts made then were completely mistaken has been clear to all in recent years. All the same, analysis of the course and the interrelations of the phenomena that concern us and on which these forecasts too were based, has yet to be reconsidered critically.

Thus, for the last thirty years as well it is necessary to reconstruct the trends in intellectual unemployment, to determine whether and in which phases of this period there was a surplus of qualified personnel, and to estimate what dimensions intellectual unemployment assumed and which categories it struck. In this attempt at reconstruction I will employ an oft-used periodization of the last thirty years into three phases: 1945–1950, 1951–1963, and 1964–1973. The first is characterized by the post-war reconstruction; the second by the most rapid economic growth yet known in Italy; and the third by two severe crises. As we shall see, this periodization allows us to specify not only the principal turning points of the Italian economy, and therefore of the demand curve for intellectual labor, but also those of the supply curve.

The Period of Reconstruction

At the close of the Second World War there recurred the phenomenon of the demand-supply "scissors" for qualified labor which had occurred after the

First World War. On the one hand, the war had left the national economy in a disastrous situation, with a somewhat depleted productive apparatus, and with an unemployment rate that despite the freeze on firings, reached very high levels. On the other hand, the secondary schools and the universities, after the strong expansion recorded in the decade of the economic depression, were further swollen during the years of the war, as had happened in 1915–1918.

To adequately assess this process of higher educational expansion it is enough to refer back to table 6.3. It follows from the data in this table that, after having brought itself to third place in the ranking of European countries by number of university students in the decade of the depression, Italy reached first place in 1948–49. With a ratio of thirty-six university students per ten thousand inhabitants, it even surpassed by a considerable extent Switzerland and Sweden, not to mention Germany, France, Great Britain, Holland, Belgium, and, naturally, Spain. At the close of the war, therefore, the Italian secondary schools and universities threw onto the market tens of thousands of diplomati and laureati. In five years, from 1945 to 1950, about 300,000 new diplomati came out of the secondary schools. The production of laureati, which over the second phase of the fascist period had averaged 11,000 a year (reaching, however, the record point of 19,000 in 1939–40), underwent a very sharp increase. In the academic year 1945–46 as many as 27,000 new laureati came out of the university. In the five-year period 1945–1950 there were about 113,000 new laureati put onto the market. In this situation, intellectual unemployment, which had been reabsorbed only during the war years, exploded once again more strongly than ever.

The seriousness of the situation was declared already in 1945 by Adolfo Omodeo, Minister of Public Education in the Badoglio government, who observed that there were more enrollments in just the universities of Rome and Naples than in all of England. "The social evil," he wrote, "is troubling. The war has multiplied excessively the mass of misfits who orient themselves to the liberal professions." And in another article he predicted that "the crisis of overproduction of laureati, which was already manifested in the twenty years of fascism, will become harsher because of Italy's economic ruin."[1]

The Left's analysis of the situation was dramatic. The theoretical review of the Italian Communist Party (PCI), *Rinascita*, wrote:

> Every year, with the alarming pace, pressing and mechanical, of a machine that no one regulates or controls, the school puts out an ever increasing mass of misfits

> into the life of the country. It is not true that the school does not absorb the "impoverished" elements, especially of the small and very small urban and rural bourgeoisie. It absorbs them, pulling them away from their habitual work surroundings – the field, workshop, small production, sometimes the factory – not in order to return them there with higher qualifications or managerial capacity, but to turn them into unproductive persons who search for a *position,* a higher social standing – and possibly, by desperation or ambition, even into the black militia of adventurers and thieves.[2]

Concetto Marchesi, in those years the most prestigious and authoritative communist leader in the area of educational policy, pointed out, on the other hand, the peculiarity of Italy's educational system and identified clearly its most important contradiction: that of being hit by "a dual crisis of excess and shortage," of having at the same time "three-quarters of the population removed from the ordeal of intellectual activity" and "an enormous and ridiculous number of university graduates." "Italy has a plague that must be eradicated as soon as possible: the plague of graduates."[3] And although in less dramatic tones, socialist and communist deputies and senators continued during the entire period of reconstruction to accuse the government of inability to confront a situation in which, as the communist Silipo said, there were continually put into Italian society "counterfeit accountants, counterfeit doctors, counterfeit lawyers, counterfeit engineers, counterfeit teachers, namely, an extraordinary number of misfits, of *declassati*."[4]

Even the Christian Democrats themselves did not deny the existence of the imbalances denounced by the Left or even attempt to minimize their importance. Deputy Rescigno spoke, for example, of the "sense of sadness, melancholy, and perplexity of our youth when they come out of the university."[5] Bertola argued that "with the sharp disjuncture of these years between the number of maestri diplomati and the number of positions, there are many misfits created."[6] Donatini dwelt upon the extraordinary difficulties of employment for diplomati of the agricultural institutes: "I understand that there are cases of agricultural technicians who for years have worked as common laborers just to make a living."[7]

On the other hand, over the five long years in which he was Minister of Public Education, even Gonella never denied that intellectual unemployment was a very serious problem. It was he himself who, on October 29, 1946, opened a "campaign against the unemployment of intellectuals" with a dramatic speech on the radio in which he not only denounced the situation in which "hundreds of thousands of Italian" diplomati and laureati found themselves without work, but also warned of the political consequences that the process of "proletarianization" of the ceti intellettuali could produce.[8] And again in 1951, a few days before leaving his office to Antonio Segni, in the seventh cabinet of De Gasperi, he lamented "the inflation of academic qualifications" and "the evil of the so-called academic proletariat destined increasingly to aggravate the crisis of the ceti medi."[9] No different in this respect was the attitude of his successor, who in his first act as minister described the presence of a considerable surplus of laureati and diplomati with respect to demand as "a phenomenon of considerable seriousness."[10]

In the absence of precise data it is difficult, however, to say what the rate of unemployment for diplomati and laureati was during the period of reconstruction. The estimates credited in those years indicate the number of unemployed intellectuals at 350-400,000 (or even 600,000).[11] But these are quite exaggerated data.[12] Among the diplomati, one of the categories hardest hit by unemployment was that of the maestri, just as after the First World War and in the second part of the fascist period. It was estimated that the average annual absorption of maestri was about 6,000 compared to a supply of about 10,000 of these diplomati.[13] It happened however, that at the concorso held in 1947 for 25,000 positions, 87,000 competitors presented themselves: "An enormous caravan of the unemployed," wrote *I diritti della scuola*, "of which scarcely one section will succeed in reaching the riverbank, while the 'bulk' will be driven back into the desert of its desolation." "The war," observed this review, "has certainly aggravated unemployment among the maestri with the slowdown of the normal growth of classes; but the phenomenon goes back a long way, and the blind, culpable stupidity of the government has let it increase in plain view; it has even encouraged this march of the deceived and the hungry with great indulgence and toleration.[14]

Not one of the categories of laureati was saved from unemployment. Of the 20 universities that replied to an inquiry conducted by the Ministry for the Constituent Assembly, 13 indicated their faculties of law and medicine as "excessively crowded" compared to the possibility of employment, 7 indicated the same for their literature faculties, 4 for their faculties of pharmacy and of economics, 3 for engineering, 2 for education and veterinary science, and 1 for mathematics and architecture.[15]

The most interesting data that we possess for this period are those concerning the state concorsi held from 1945 to 1952. The information gathered in table 8.1

not only shows clearly that the assault on the Public Administration by unemployed intellectuals, which had practically never ceased since the end of the nineteenth century, began again with greater force than ever during the period of reconstruction; but it also gives us at least an approximate idea of the extent of the imbalance between demand and supply of labor at all levels of qualification. Considering all the concorsi held, we see that for each position offered there was an average of 16 applications. Excluding from the analysis the data regarding the Ministry of Public Education,[16] we observe that the imbalance between demand and positions offered, although it has a decreasing course progressing from the lower to the higher categories, remained very strong even in the concorsi that required the laurea and the diploma (groups A and B, respectively). For each position offered in the former group there were in fact 6 competitors, and almost 9 for those in the latter. Nor can it be said, on the basis of the data of table 8.2, that such an imbalance spared some categories of diplomati and laureati as an old thesis, so dear to the supporters of educational and vocational guidance, would have it, according to which intellectual unemployment concerned exclusively students who came from the humanistic schools and faculties, and not those with technical-scientific training, from industrial technicians to engineers and research chemists.[17]

In this situation, facing the difficulties of acquiring a position corresponding to their educational qualifications, a certain number of candidates tried to enter at the next lowest level. This process of declassamento involved all categories: the laureati presented themselves at concorsi for diplomati, the diplomati at those that required the lower-secondary licenza, etc. However, it was much more pronounced for the diplomati than for the laureati (table 8.3).

The Situation in 1951

Some information on the employment situation for intellectuals in the postwar period can be drawn from the data collected on the occasion of the census of November 1951. It is worth pausing to consider these data, both because the 1951 census was the first to provide information on the composition of the population by level of education (and therefore also on that considerable part of the intellectual labor force which entered the market during the fascist period) and because its results have never been fully analyzed as far as the problem that interests us here is concerned – probably because they were published only in 1957 when, rightly or wrongly, the debate over intelletual unemployment had lost its interest.

Table 8.1. State Concorsi Held from 1945 to 1952 by Category

Categories	*Ministry of Public Education*			*Other Administrations*		
	Positions	*Applications*	*Difference*	*Positions*	*Applications*	*Difference*
Group A (laurea required)	5,806	115,500	109,694	6,722	41,662	34,940
Group B (diploma required)	637	3,646	3,009	12,937	113,940	101,003
Group C (licenza required)	779	9,319	8,540	10,803	187,072	176,269
Subordinates	1,520	11,259	9,739	11,094	315,817	304,723
Total	8,742	139,724	130,982	41,556	658,491	616,935

SOURCE: "Indagine sui concorsi banditi dalle amministrazioni statali," in Parliamentary Commission of Inquiry on Unemployment, ed., *La disoccupazione in Italia* (Rome: Chamber of Deputies, 1953), vol. 1, part 2, pp. 307–32.

Table 8.2. State Concorsi Held from 1945 to 1952 by Educational Qualification Required (excluding Concorsi for the Ministry of Public Education)

Qualification	*Positions*	*Applications*	*Difference*
Laurea			
Engineering and architecture	1,425	5,249	3,824
Chemistry, agriculture, natural sciences	577	2,201	1,624
Law and economics	4,107	29,254	25,147
Medicine	64	821	757
General	549	4,137	3,588
Diploma			
Accountant	1,008	4,755	3,747
Technical expert	1,689	10,103	8,414
Nonspecific	10,240	99,082	88,842

SOURCE: See table 8.1.

Table 8.3. Percentage Distribution by Qualification of Candidates in Selected State Concorsi of Groups B and C and for Subordinates Held from 1945 to 1952

Qualification of candidates	*Type of Concorso*		
	Group B	*Group C*	*Subordinates*
Elementary	—	—	74.7
Lower-secondary	—	76.0	19.2
Upper-secondary	97.9	20.9	5.5
University	2.1	3.1	0.6
Total	100.0	100.0	100.0
(Applications)	(18,457)	(2,985)	(672)

SOURCE: See table 8.1. The data in this table are based on a sample of concorsi.

If we consider the 1951 census as having recorded the point of arrival of a long process of arrangement of the intellectual labor force begun three decades before, we can inquire whether the considerable difficulties of employment of which we have spoken so far had brought about a social declassamento of laureati and diplomati. Unfortunately, the type of classification used by ISTAT* gives only a partial answer to this question. As may in fact be seen from table 8.4, the great majority both of diplomati and of laureati were classified in the overly general category of "managers and impiegati" and we do not know how many among these performed clerical functions at a low level of qualification. It is rather significant, however, that about a third of the laureati were entrepre-

*ISTAT: Istituto Centrale di Statistica, the central government office for gathering, analyzing, and publishing statistical data in Italy.

Table 8.4. Distribution of Diplomati and Laureati in 1951 by Sex and Occupation

Occupation	*Diplomati*			*Laureati*		
	M	*F*	*MF*	*M*	*F*	*MF*
Entrepreneurs and liberal professionals	11.15	3.89	8.74	31.84	4.92	28.17
Managers and impiegati	77.64	92.15	82.44	63.74	89.76	67.29
Self-employed laborers	4.19	1.13	3.18	3.27	3.46	3.29
Dependent laborers	4.32	1.50	3.39	0.19	0.20	0.19
Assistants	2.69	1.33	2.25	0.96	1.66	1.06
Total	100.00	100.00	100.00	100.00	100.00	100.00
(N)	(514,664)	(254,857)	(769,521)	(300,330)	(47,555)	(347,885)

SOURCE: Elaboration of data taken from ISTAT, *IX Censimento generale della popolazione* (Rome; 1957), vol. 5: *Istruzione* (hereafter cited as *Istr. '51)*. Discrepancies in the totals are due to rounding.

neurs or liberal professionals. This information, together with the fact that their percentage of "dependent labors" (that is, workers) was extremely low, would make it seem that, despite the difficulties of employment encountered, the laureati had not undergone a very marked process of social declassamento. This process, on the other hand, concerned to a more considerable extent the diplomati, given that 3.3 percent of those employed (but 4.3 percent for males and 5.2 percent for those in the North) were workers. On the whole, therefore, the findings of the census would confirm what was said on the subject of the state concorsi.

The data that we possess would show, on the other hand, a process of premature "tertiarization" of the intellectual labor force, occuring probably both during the fascist period and during the postwar reconstruction, by means of which nearly all the laureati and the great majority of diplomati were able to evade the threat of declassamento despite the great difficulties encountered in employment. The data of tables 8.5 and 8.6 offer at least an idea of this process. To fully assess their significance, we must bear in mind that in 1951, of the *total* population employed almost 44 percent were employed in agriculture, 31 percent in industry and 25 percent in services. What is striking from an examination of the data in tables 8.5 and 8.6 is not so much the very low percentage of laureati and diplomati employed in the primary sector. Most singular and significant is, rather, the low percentage of those employed in industry and the very high one for those in the service sector (indicated by "other activity"), which reached 81 percent for diplomati and 86 percent for laureati. If laureati and diplomati succeeded in evading a processs of declassamento despite the great difficulty of employment, it is, therefore, probably because the pressures they exerted both during the fascist period and in the postwar phase to provoke an increase in demand had a certain success. Because of their efforts, uproductive work positions in the tertiary sector, and in particular in the Public Administration, multiplied, and laureati and diplomati became the recipients of salaries which, as Paolo Sylos-Labini has recently written, "were none other than disguised subsidies for unemployment."[18]

That the demand for intellectual labor did not arise only from the exigencies of the economic system, but was at least in part provoked by the supply, may be seen even better by analyzing closely the data from these two tables. An analysis by geographic area reveals in fact that the phenomenon noted is present to a much greater extent in the South, where the percentage of diplomati and laureati employed in the tertiary sector is much higher than in the North. The

Table 8.5. Distribution of Diplomati in 1951 by Sex, Sector of Economic Activity, and Geographic Area

Sector	North			Center			South			Italy		
	M	*F*	*MF*	*M*	*F*	*MF*	*M*	*F*	*MF*	*M*	*F*	*MF*
Agriculture	3.08	0.58	2.26	4.55	0.75	3.29	3.83	0.38	2.70	3.59	0.57	2.59
Industry	29.04	9.84	22.66	15.34	4.61	11.78	10.64	1.78	7.74	21.38	6.68	16.52
Other Activity	67.88	89.58	75.08	80.11	94.64	84.93	85.53	97.84	89.56	75.03	92.75	80.89
Total	100.00	100.00	100.00	100.00	100.00	100.00	100.00	100.00	100.00	100.00	100.00	100.00
(N)	(271,398)	(135,268)	(406,666)	(113,513)	(56,393)	(169,906)	(129,753)	(63,196)	(192,949)	(514,664)	(254,857)	(769,521)

SOURCE: Elaboration of data taken from *Istr* '51.

Table 8.6. Distribution of Laureati in 1951 by Sex, Sector of Economic Activity, and Geographic Area

Sector	North			Center			South			Italy		
	M	*F*	*MF*	*M*	*F*	*MF*	*M*	*F*	*MF*	*M*	*F*	*MF*
Agriculture	2.20	0.27	1.93	2.90	0.47	2.56	3.72	0.21	3.26	2.85	0.30	2.51
Industry	19.43	4.30	17.32	9.74	2.22	8.70	5.39	0.77	4.79	12.62	2.72	11.26
Other Activity	78.37	95.43	80.75	87.36	97.31	88.74	90.89	99.02	91.95	84.53	96.97	86.23
Total	100.00	100.00	100.00	100.00	100.00	100.00	100.00	100.00	100.00	100.00	100.00	100.00
(N)	(131,417)	(21,372)	(152,789)	(74,588)	(12,002)	(86,590)	(94,325)	(14,181)	(108,506)	(300,330)	(47,555)	(347,885)

SOURCE: Elaboration of data taken from *Istr.* '51.

validity of this interpretation appears even more clearly when we compare the two extreme groups of the intellectual labor force, namely the strongest and the weakest components: northern males and southern females. For the former, the percentage of those employed in the tertiary sector is in fact 68 percent for diplomati and 78 percent for laureati. For the latter, the percentage reaches 97.8 percent for diplomate and 99 percent for laureate.

The enormous expansion of the tertiary sector and the creation of unproductive work positions to confront the surplus of supply was not, however, enough to defeat unemployment. Despite the fact that the census was conducted at the end of 1951, when the situation had noticeably improved over the first years of the postwar period, the difficulties of employment for diplomati and laureati still remained very considerable. Actually, the information furnished by the census concerning unemployment is scanty. In the first place, it shows only the number of persons seeking employment and not the number of those formerly employed. Second, it tells us nothing about the time periods spent waiting for employment. But even with all these drawbacks, which are certainly not inconsiderable, the census data at least give an idea of how serious the imbalance between demand and supply of intellectual labor still was in 1951.

In 1951 there were 23,330 laureati and 112,287 diplomati in search of first employment. It can be useful to calculate the number of those unemployed and in search of first employment as a percentage of total active persons, even though such figures must be utilized with the greatest caution.

As may be seen from table 8.7, in 1951, the unemployment rate was higher for diplomati than for laureati. However, when sex is taken into account, one sees that the differences between laureati and diplomati hold only for males, while for females the unemployment rates show very similar values for these two groups. There were, however, both in the case of diplomati and of laureati, enormous differences according to the geographic area. This may be realized better by comparing, in table 8.7, the unemployment rate of the strongest component (northern males) with that of the weakest (southern females) of the intellectual labor force.

Indirect indications, at least regarding diplomati, can also be obtained on the time periods spent waiting for employment. In table 8.8 the distribution of those awaiting first employment according to age cohorts is compared with the distribution of those newly graduated from the upper-secondary schools. The strong difference between the two percentage distributions provides us with at least an idea of how high must have been the percentage of youth who had to wait several years before finding work.

The Period of Economic Development

The most striking aspect for one who tries to reconstruct the tendencies of intellectual unemployment in that important period of economic and social transformation in Italy from 1951 to 1963 is the very sudden change that occurred toward the end of the 1950s in the definition of the situation on the part of the ruling class and its official experts. The debates over intellectual unemployment, on its causes and consequences, continued for many years during the period of economic development. Then, all of a sudden, in 1959 the terms of the question were simply upended and the thesis of the scarcity of intellectual labor emerged on the Italian scene.

The imbalance between school and labor market was denounced many times during the 1950s by the most authoritative scholars and politicians of every tendency. In 1953 the vice-secretary of the General Confederation of Italian Labor (CGIL),* Vittorio Foa, affirmed that "the weight of intellectual unemployment is acutely felt by the country and by individual families" and argued that the Italian economic system was "resistant to the work of the young" whatever their "preparation, humanistic or technical, intellectual or manual," might be.[19] In 1954, reconsidering Mofetta at a distance of sixty years, Gaetano Salvemini rediscovered among the many unsolved problems of the Mezzogiorno also that of a surplus of qualified personnel. "Unemployment among the intellectuals is frightening...here is the danger zone of southern Italian society. Everything one reads in my writings on the Southern Question from 1897 to 1920 must be multiplied by frightful coefficients by anyone who wants to gain an idea of the explosive materials that are accumulating today in our country."[20]

In the same year the communist Sciorilli Borelli devoted a wide-ranging and highly documented contribution in the Chamber of Deputies to the problem of the relationships betwen school and labor market, in which he reported, among other things, that very many young maestri asked "insistently to be allowed to work in manual jobs in the construction of the hydroelectric stations of Sangro

*CGIL: Confederazione Generale Italiana di Lavoro, the most left-leaning of the three major labor confederations in postwar Italy.

Table 8.7. Diplomati and Laureati in Search of First Employment as a Percentage of Total Active Persons in 1951 by Sex and Geographic Area

Areas	*Diplomati*			*Laureati*		
	M	*F*	*MF*	*M*	*F*	*MF*
North	7.88	13.83	9.95	3.15	12.20	4.53
Center	9.62	16.24	11.93	3.76	12.49	5.07
South	15.61	24.40	18.70	6.95	23.63	9.54
Italy	10.33	17.23	12.74	4.53	16.31	6.28

SOURCE: Elaboration of data taken from *Istr.* '51.

and in other construction firms."[21] Mario Alicata, in the introductory report to the works of an important meeting of the central committee of the PCI in 1955, described Italy as "a country where there are too many maestri and too many illiterates, too many doctors and too few hospitals."[22] And to this theme much space was devoted in the report with which Leopoldo Piccardi opened the conference organized in 1956 by the Friends of the World on the problems of the Italian school.[23]

Suddenly, however, almost as if the phenomenon of intellectual unemployment had never existed and no one had ever spoken of it, there appeared on the Italian scene the thesis of the shortage of highly qualified personnel, and it was an immediate success. One fact more than any other can give us an idea today of how sudden was this change of scene. In 1958, a year before the thesis of a shortage of intellectual labor made its triumphal entrance, a survey was conducted on a large sample of university students. From this was found that a good 39.4 percent of those interviewed thought that once graduated they would remain unemployed. This percentage varied according to the region of residence and the faculty attended, reaching its highest points in Campania (51.5 percent) and in Puglia (50.9 percent) and for students of the faculties of literature and education (50.3 percent) and law (49 percent). On the other hand, 47 percent of those interviewed believed there were much greater chances of employment abroad than in Italy, and 51 percent declared themselves disposed to emigrate to find work.[24]

Evidently, the dominant economic and political groups were not of this view. Availing themselves of the help of the experts from SVIMEZ,* they launched

*SVIMEZ: Cassa per lo Sviluppo Mezzogiorno, or Fund for the Development of the South, is a government funding and reserch agency established in 1950 for the economic development of the South.

Table 8.8. Distribution by Sex and Age of Diplomati Awaiting First Employment in 1951 and of Diplomati in the School Year 1952–53

Age Cohorts	*Diplomati Awaiting First Employment (1951)*			*Diplomati in School Year 1952–53**		
	M	*F*	*MF*	*M*	*F*	*MF*
Up to 21 years	18	29	24	60	78	68
21–25 years	48	41	44	33	19	27
25–35 years	33	28	30	7	3	5
Over 35	2	2	2	—	—	—
Total	100	100	100	100	100	100
(N)	(58,986)	(52,766)	(111,752)	(35,027)	(24,846)	(59,873)

*There is no information on the age distribution of diplomati for the preceding school years.

SOURCE: Elaboration of data taken from *Istr.* '51 and in ISTAT, *Indagini speciali sugli studenti universitari e sui diplomati di scuole medie superiori* (Rome, 1956).

in precisely those years the thesis that Italy was facing an inadequate supply of qualified personnel compared to the demand.[25] It was forecast that, if timely measures were not taken, the scarcity of laureati and diplomati would be very acute in the fifteen years following, enough to become a big obstacle to the process of economic development. But according to the experts at SVIMEZ, the lack of intellectual labor was already serious in those years. "Examination of the daily newspapers," wrote Gino Martinoli, "with the large numbers of conspicuous offers of employment, reveals how acute the search is in Italy today for personnel at all levels of qualification."[26]

The Situation in 1961

That the forecasts of SVIMEZ, which somehow held forth uncontested until 1966,[27] were completely mistaken is too well known to require discussion here. But is it true, we may ask ourselves, that toward the end of the 1950s Italy found itself suddenly facing a shortage of intellectual labor? And more generally: beyond the debates and forecasts, pessimistic at first and then optimistic, what was the actual course of the employment of diplomati and laureati over the period of economic growth?

At least as far as the maestri are concerned, for the entire period of economic growth there was no lack but rather a surplus of labor. For this category of diplomati, in fact, the situation worsened even compared to the period of reconstruction. In truth, it cannot be said that the profession of elementary school teacher offered many privileges in those years, even compared to jobs that required a lower educational qualification. Until 1961 the income of employed teachers was kept at a rather low level, so that a high percentage of males with families to support were forced to find a second job. Moreover, the conviction that their professional prestige was very low and that it threatened to be lowered even further was quite widespread among the elementary teachers.[28] Despite all this, a growing mass of youth, coming mainly from the small bourgeoisie and the proletariat, crammed into the istituti magistrali, and these schools continued to throw onto the market a number of diplomati far greater than was needed.

The professional reviews continued, besides, to discuss over the whole period the problem of the teachers' unemployment, especially on the occasion of concorsi:

> The concorso that is coming to a close [wrote the review *I diritti della scuola* in

> 1951] and which we have termed monstrous because of the enormous number of candidates and because of all the anomalies that are derived from this, brings back first, in all its harshness, the problem of teachers' unemployment – a problem that has dragged on unsolved for many years, and that would require quite other palliatives than those to which the educational authority has limited itself until now, assuaging itself with the blessed illusion that with these measures it has tossed off every responsibility.[29]

Four years later the same review spoke of a "recurrence of the distressing conditions of untenured, unemployed maestri." "Unrest among those affected spreads throughout the country," it observed, "but especially in the areas where unemployment rages more seriously."[30] And indeed the data at our disposal show clearly that the charges brought by the professional press of the maestri were not at all exaggerated. In the four concorsi (table 8.9) held over the decade 1951 – 61, the imblance between positions and candidates not only was very sharp but also far surpassed the points reached in the reconstruction period. While in 1947 the ratio between competitors and positions offered had been three or four to one, in the concorsi of this decade it was about fourteen to one. Even admitting that two candidates of fourteen might have participated only in order to change positions or might already have been employed,[31] at the end of the concorso, the operation of which generally lasted from one to two years, eleven out of fourteen candidates still remained without work. For these began a new period of lengthy waiting for the next announced competition, and in the meantime lay a wearisome pursuit from the "starting point" to surmount the current that pushed the young maestri to accept a job in a *doposcuola** or an evening school. This work was often not only unpaid but also assigned exclusively to those who showed that they shared the political ideas of the majority party.[32]

However, unemployment concerned not only the maestri. At least until 1955 it also struck other categories of diplomati and laureati. The laureati who aspired to teaching continued to encounter serious difficulties in employment.[33] But the situation was not much better for the young coming out of the technical-scientific faculties who sought work in the industrial sector. In 1954, following a directive by the Organization for Economic Cooperation and Development (OECD), ISTAT confronted the problem of the scarcity of qualified personnel by conducting a survey on a sample of industrial firms. From this study it was

**Doposcuola:* literally, "afterschool" instruction, thus a center providing complementary instruction to that of the school.

found that 74.7 percent of the firms had not encountered any difficulty in recruiting laureati, and 48.4 percent had found "an excess of suitably trained candidates compared to the number of available positions." Thus the same ISTAT report was forced to acknowledge, in contrast to its original questions and working hypotheses, that there was in Italy an "excess availability on the labor market" of qualified personnel.[34]

A year later the National Federation of Industrial Technicians argued that their professional position was threatened both from above and from below: from above by the "excess of laureati," who tended to occupy the next lowest positions; from below by the graduates of the scuole tecniche, "no longer workers but still not *tecnici diplomati,*"* and these too, "excessive in number."[35] And, indeed, an inquiry conducted in that year showed a certain weakness in supply compared to demand, given that a sizable percentage of technicians employed in industry found themselves in the position of impiegati of the third category (table 8.10). If we consider that these data were collected in Milan, where the demand was clearly stronger than in other areas, we can then realize that the situation must have been in the rest of the country.[36]

The data we possess show therefore that toward the middle of the 1950s there was still in Italy an excess of qualified labor, not only of elementary school teachers and lawyers but also of those technicians whose shortage would be lamented four years later. Thus the continuation in this period as well of the debate over intellectual unemployment was not a simple ritual act, a tired and monotonous repetition of an old theme by now superseded, but reflected even with the inevitable exaggerations the real situation of the country.

If this is true, it is also undeniable that in the period of economic development there were profound changes in the intellectual labor market, which, however, it must quickly be emphasized, concerned diplomati and laureati in very different measure. If we consider the decade 1951–1961 we see that a change of foremost importance took place on the demand slope, which not only rose in an extraordinary manner but also had some other characteristics that were qualitatively different from those of the preceding periods. While before – and this has been pointed out several times – demand was often produced, so to speak, by supply, and consequently came mainly from the tertiary sector, it now arose from an economy in a phase of strong growth, and therefore demand came from industry. This can be seen by comparing the sectoral composition of

*That is, still not graduates of the *upper*-secondary istituti tecnici.

Table 8.9. Positions and Candidates in Concorsi for Elementary School Teachers Held from 1952 to 1961, by Geographic Area

Areas	1952		1954		1958		1961	
	Positions	*Candidates*	*Positions*	*Candidates*	*Positions*	*Candidates*	*Positions*	*Candidates*
North	2,908	40,292	3,167	42,327	3,709	47,299	3,810	46,817
Center	1,043	17,115	872	16,608	1,892	29,433	1,954	26,620
South	3,620	42,451	3,456	53,534	3,005	46,341	5,240	65,258
Total	7,571	99,854	6,495	112,469	8,606	123,073	11,004	138,695

SOURCE: Elaboration of data taken from *I diritti della scuola,* January 30, 1953; November 15, 1954; January 30, 1959; January 7, 1962.

Table 8.10. Distribution by Occupational Category and Industrial Sector of a Sample of Technicians Employed in Milan in Several Large Industries, 1955

Occupational Categories	*Industries*				
	Chemical	*Electrical*	*Metal-Mechanical*	*Mining*	*Total*
Managers	1	—	2	—	1
Impiegati: 1st cat.	16	11	20	25	16
Impiegati: 2d cat.	83	46	38	30	68
Impiegati: 3d cat.	—	37	38	45	14
Workers	—	6	2	—	1
Total	100	100	100	100	100
(N)	(1,245)	(305)	(248)	(105)	(1,903)

SOURCE: Elaboration of data taken from *Il perito industriale* (December 1955), p. 7.

economic activity of laureati and diplomati employed in 1951 and 1961 (tables 8.5, 6, 11, and 12). For the laureati there was a rise of about 2 points in the percentage of those employed by industry (but 3 points for the males). For the diplomati this rise was 5.5 points on the whole and 7 points considering only males. These data and those which the reader can gather from a more thorough analysis by geographic area of the above tables suffice, therefore, to show that in the period that interests us there was an actual reversal in the trend of intellectual unemployment. A phenomenon of equal importance quantitatively if not qualitatively, was the very sharp increase in the demand for teachers, especially laureati but also diplomati, that occurred beginning in 1955 because of the growth of secondary education.[37]

Then too, a basic change occurred on the supply slope, but this concerned only the laureati. In the decade 1951 – 61 the production of new laureati remained virtually stationary, passing from 20,000 to 23,000 with an average annual rate of increase of 1.7 percent, one of the lowest registered in the history of Italy.[38] Completely different was the course of the supply of diplomati, not only because it grew from 61,000 to 104,000 over the same period (with an average annual rate of increase of 7.10 percent), but also because the composition of supply changed. The percentage of youth provided by the licei, namely those who in any case "had" to enter the university, decreased, while the weight of diplomati from the istituti tecnici and magistrali, or those who had been trained to enter the labor market, increased.

These changes were of such scope that, as far as the laureati are concerned, equilibrium between demand and supply was reached at the start of the 1960s. According to the census of 1961, there were only 14,000 laureati awaiting first employment. In one decade the rate of unemployment was halved. The differences by sex and geographic area, quite pronounced in 1951, had been extraordinarily reduced ten years later (table 8.13). In spite of this, it was probably an exaggeration to speak of a "lack" of laureati. If there were tensions on the labor market because of a shortage of laureati, these concerned geographic areas and sectors of professional specialization covered. "There is the dual and contradictory phenomenon," wrote Alessandro Natta in 1960, "of a persistent unemployment and dequalification of intellectuals of humanistic training on the one hand, and on the other, a distressing deficiency of scientific and technical cadres: both manifestations of an anarchic relationship between school and society, of the inability to face the necessities of the present."[39]

But in reality the demarcation line did not pass simply between humanisti-

Table 8.11. Distribution of Diplomati in 1961 by Sex, Sector of Economic Activity, and Geographic Area

Sector	North			Center			South			Italy		
	M	*F*	*MF*	*M*	*F*	*MF*	*M*	*F*	*MF*	*M*	*F*	*MF*
Agriculture	2.80	0.56	2.08	4.32	0.58	3.07	4.82	0.63	3.32	3.68	0.59	2.63
Industry	37.43	14.33	30.03	22.07	6.97	17.02	15.63	2.37	10.91	28.38	9.25	22.01
Other Activity	59.77	85.11	67.89	73.61	92.45	79.92	79.55	97.00	85.77	67.96	90.16	75.36
Total	100.00	100.00	100.00	100.00	100.00	100.00	100.00	100.00	100.00	100.00	100.00	100.00
(*N*)	(375,575)	(177,336)	(552,911)	(157,971)	(79,357)	(257,328)	(188,240)	(104,245)	(292,485)	(721,786)	(360,938)	(1,082,724)

SOURCE: Elaboration of data taken from ISTAT, *X Censimento generale della popolazione*, vol. 7 (hereafter cited as *Istr.* '61).

Table 8.12. Distribution of Laureati in 1961 by Sex, Sector of Economic Activity, and Geographic Area

Sector	North			Center			South			Italy		
	M	*F*	*MF*	*M*	*F*	*MF*	*M*	*F*	*MF*	*M*	*F*	*MF*
Agriculture	1.76	0.30	1.49	2.28	0.41	1.94	3.19	0.83	2.73	2.33	0.51	1.99
Industry	23.93	5.92	20.65	12.32	3.01	10.61	7.08	1.02	5.92	15.87	3.62	13.59
Other Activity	74.31	93.78	77.86	85.40	96.58	87.45	89.73	98.15	91.35	81.80	95.87	84.42
Total	100.00	100.00	100.00	100.00	100.00	100.00	100.00	100.00	100.00	100.00	100.00	100.00
(*N*)	(177,542)	(39,629)	(217,171)	(97,536)	(21,988)	(119,524)	(123,421)	(29,655)	(153,076)	(398,499)	(91,272)	(489,771)

SOURCE: Elaboration of data taken from *Istr.* '61.

Table 8.13. Diplomati and Laureati in Search of First Employment as a Percentage of Total Active Persons in 1961 by Sex and Geographic Area

Area	Diplomati			Laureati		
	M	*F*	*MF*	*M*	*F*	*MF*
North	4.89	10.27	6.68	1.50	2.94	1.76
Center	8.03	14.43	10.28	2.38	4.61	2.79
South	13.37	19.65	15.72	4.02	6.78	4.57
Italy	7.93	14.09	10.08	2.51	4.62	2.91

SOURCE: Elaboration of data taken from *Istr.* '61.

cally trained intellectuals and technical and scientific cadres. There was, for example, a lack of teachers, especially in literature, so great that in those years it was necessary to resort to university students to cover the large number of positions created by the extraordinary growth of the educational system.[40] But there was also an excess of laureati in law and in economics, and a part of these had to content themselves with being reconverted, at least temporarily, into teachers of literature or languages. For certain technical-scientific faculties, as for example engineering, there was a lack of laureati in some specializations and an excess in others. "The situation of engineers in Italy," wrote the review of their order, "presents remarkably different aspects between the North and South. In fact, while industry complains about a lack of specialized engineers, in southern Italy and the Islands, where nearly all are civil engineers or work in the civil sector, there is a particularly difficult situation of professional placement."[41] The difficulties were, indeed, such that the order saw no other way out than the traditional one of expanding intellectual employment in the tertiary sector: "Many of the engineers available in southern Italy, where industrialization is still only beginning, could be absorbed by the public administrations, where these agencies might by their employment practices serve to compensate for the backward conditions of industry."[42]

It was, however, completely unjustified to speak of a "lack" of diplomati. The data available, however scanty, show us that at the start of the 1960s not only was there no shortage but there was actually a sizable surplus of diplomati. For, if there had been a reversal of the trend in unemployment, it is also true, as has been noted, that the supply curve continued to rise, with a slope indeed much more marked for the diplomati who were to be put onto the labor market. Certainly the situation was considerably improved compared to 1951. Although according to the 1961 census there were 121,000 diplomati in search of first employment, still the rate of unemployment had been reduced (see table 8.13) and the time periods spent waiting had also been shortened. If the 1961 data are compared with those of ten years before (tables 8.8 and 8.14), it can be seen that, while the age distribution of youth coming out of the upper-secondary schools remained substantially unchanged, the distribution of diplomati in search of first employment in the first two age cohorts was higher in 1961.

It seems to me, on the other hand, that these same data, however scanty and not always easily interpretable, indicate that at the beginning of the 1960s the goal of equilibrium between demand and supply of diplomati was still rather far off. This is quite clear for the newly graduated maestri of the istituti magistrali. The data on concorsi show in fact that the imbalance between positions and competitors, after having reached its highest point in 1954, was slightly lessened in the following years, but even so remained quite strong in 1961 (table 8.15). But also as far as the diplomati of the istituti tecnici are concerned there is evidence, as we shall soon see, that leads one to think that here too a certain weakness of supply persisted in face of the demand.

The different situations in which laureati and diplomati found themselves also emerges clearly from an analysis of the changes intervening in this period in the relationship between level of education and occupational status. The fact, according to a survey conducted at the end of the 1950s, that 90 percent of the doctors questioned spoke of a "proletarianization of the profession" cannot be taken too seriously.[43] In reality, in the period that concerns us, there was definitely no loss of status on the part of laureati; if anything the opposite occurred. On the basis of findings of an inquiry conducted in 1960 on laureati employed in ten big industrial firms, Diego De Castro observed that "the phenomenon of declassamento of which much is spoken and which is believed to be very widespread presents, in fact, *very modest proportions*."[44] A comparison of the findings of the two censuses of 1951 and 1961 confirms the validity of this judgment (tables 8.4 and 8.16). It is true, in fact, that an examination of these two tables reveals a reduction of the percentage of laureati who are entrepreneurs or liberal professionals, but if we examine the data broken down by sex we see that this reduction is due in large part to the greater proportion of laureate in 1961 compared to 1951. If it is kept in mind then that in 1961 there were practically no laureati employed as general impiegati[45] and that the category of dependent laborers, already quite small at the beginning of the decade, was further reduced not only in percentage but also in absolute terms, one can say that overall, and at least from 1955 onward, the professional status of laureati did not fall but in fact constantly improved.

A strong process of declassamento took place, on the other hand, for the diplomati over this period. In the decade 1951–61, their presence among the entrepreneurs and liberal professionals decreased, both in percentage and in absolute terms (from 67,000 to 63,000), while their percentage and the number among the workers increased (from 26,000 to 39,000). Perhaps an even more important fact is that in 1961 there was a rather sizable number of diplomati employed as general impiegati.[46]

A more precise idea of the scope of this process of declassamento may be gained by examining the data disaggregated by type of upper-secondary school attended (table 8.17). The group least affected by this process was that of the maestri, for the simple reason that, as was noted earlier, a high percentage of these diplomati – women for the most part – never succeeded in any way in entering the labor market or in finding a professional placement either corresponding to or lower than the level of education they had reached. On the other hand, a considerable number of persons furnished with the diploma from the liceo, made up in part of the educational system's "losers" (that is, those youth who were not able to begin university studies or who had to abandon them early), had a professional status lower than their educational qualification. But the process of declassamento also affected the diplomati of the istituti tecnici (with the exception of the surveyors), in other words, just that category which in those years was considered the privileged component of the supply.

In conclusion, the discussion I have sought to develop in the preceding pages should allow not only a correction of the analysis of the tendencies of intellectual unemployment – especially regarding the diplomati – which was made at the end of the 1950s and which has not until now been questioned, but also an understanding of the reasons (political, naturally) for the sensational forecasting errors of those years. There is no doubt, in the first place, that a new fact was verified in the history of Italy: the period 1951–63 was, in fact, the first, from 1880 onward, in which the unemployment of at least the laureati was reabsorbed. It was, on the other hand, in this period that in many European countries there really was a shortage of intellectual labor, and the insistence by organs of the OECD on this subject ultimately influenced the attitude of the Italian ruling class. If to this is added that particular euphoria with which the "economic miracle" was experienced, it may also be understood how such an

Table 8.14. Distribution by Sex and Age of Diplomati Awaiting First Employment in 1961 and of Diplomati in the School Year 1962–63

Age Cohorts	*Diplomati Awaiting First Employment (1961)*			*Diplomati in School Year 1962–63**		
	M	*F*	*MF*	*M*	*F*	*MF*
Up to 21 years	27	43	35	61	80	69
21–25 years	54	42	48	34	18	27
25–35 years	18	14	16	5	2	4
Over 35	1	1	1	—	—	—
Total	100	100	100	100	100	100
(N)	(62,193)	(59,205)	(121,398)	(57,558)	(36,996)	(94,554)

*There is no information on the distribution by age cohort of diplomati for the two preceding school years.

SOURCE: Source: Elaboration of data taken from *Istr.* '61 and from *Annuario statistico dell'istruzione italiana.*

Table 8.15. Number of Candidates for Each Position in Concorsi for Elementary School Teachers Held from 1952 to 1961 by Geographic Area

Area	*1952*	*1954*	*1958*	*1961*
North	13.86	13.36	12.75	12.29
Center	16.40	19.05	15.55	13.62
South	11.73	15.49	15.42	12.45
Italy	13.19	17.32	14.30	12.60

SOURCE: See table 8.9.

optimistic and partial representation of the relationships between school and labor market might have become so widespread. In fact, it is useful to recall, it was those same men in those same years who believed the Questione Meridionale too would soon be resolved. Finally, the ideology of SVIMEZ, by "demonstrating" that the growth of education was not only politically and socially just but economically necessary, could not help being well received, or actually adopted, by those political groups on the Left which for years had struggled to open the Italian educational system, the discriminatory character of which they denounced, to the youth of the lower social classes.

The Period of the Depressions

Perhaps the most interesting difference between the period which closes and that which opens at the end of 1963 concerns the course of the supply of intellectual labor. A few data suffice to realize this. The laureati produced by the system increased from 24,000 in 1963 to 60,000 in 1971. Diplomati increased from 103,000 to 228,000, and also in this period the percentage of youth "destined" for the labor market increased (namely, those from the istituti tecnici and magistrali).

An important change also took place on the demand slope. Because of the depressions and the stagnation of economic activity in this period, the demand for labor coming from industry decreased. We can gain at least an idea of this phenomenon by comparing the average annual rate of increase of diplomati and laureati employed by sector of economic activity in the two periods 1959–63 and 1963–71 (table 8.18). The reduction of demand from industry was particularly marked for laureati. It is enough to consider that the laureati employed in industry numbered 65,000 in 1963 and still 65,000 in 1970.[47] For many years

Table 8.16. Distribution of Diplomati and Laureati in 1961 by Sex and Occupation

Occupation	*Diplomati*			*Laureati*		
	M	*F*	*MF*	*M*	*F*	*MF*
Entrepreneurs and liberal professionals	7.21	3.14	5.85	31.00	4.88	26.13
Managers and specialized impiegati	70.38	82.36	74.38	64.05	89.64	68.83
General impiegati	8.91	9.62	9.14	0.14	0.10	0.13
Self-employed laborers	6.97	1.46	5.13	4.12	3.55	4.01
Dependent laborers	4.43	2.00	3.63	0.05	0.07	0.06
Assistants	2.10	1.42	1.87	0.64	1.76	0.84
Total	100.00	100.00	100.00	100.00	100.00	100.00
(N)	(721,786)	(360,938)	(1,082,724)	(398,499)	(91,272)	(489,771)

SOURCE: Elaboration of data taken from *Istr.* '61.

Table 8.17. General Impiegati and Dependent Laborers as a Percentage of Diplomati Employed in 1961 by Type of Upper-Secondary School Attended

Type of School	*% General Impiegati (1)*	*% Dependent Laborers (2)*	*Index of Declassamento (1) + (2)*	*Number Employed*
Liceo classico	13.72	3.78	17.50	(123,273)
Liceo scientifico	12.78	5.77	18.55	(38,014)
Istituto magistrale	7.67	1.55	9.22	(363,286)
Liceo artistico	5.11	4.20	9.31	(23,876)
Istituto tecnico agrario	7.93	5.15	13.08	(24,491)
Istituto tecnico commercial	12.65	2.36	15.01	(245,154)
Istituto tecnico geometri	4.43	1.84	6.27	(99,861)
Istituto tecnico industriale	6.78	11.53	18.31	(96,667)
Other schools	6.20	8.27	14.47	(68,102)
Total	9.14	3.63	12.77	(1,082,724)

SOURCE: Elaboration of data taken from *Istr.* '61.

there remained, however, a strong demand for laureati by the school to be employed as teachers.

These few figures suffice to give an understanding of how the imbalance between demand and supply of intellectual labor, which in the period of economic expansion was weakened for diplomati and in large part absorbed for laureati, reproduced itself and was accentuated after 1964.

The quarterly statistics of ISTAT give us a very partial and very optimistic idea of the size of the imbalance between demand and supply of intellectual labor, and it can be affirmed with assurance that they strongly underestimate the effective rate of unemployment of diplomati and laureati. For diplomati they indicate a constant increase, up to 1969, of youth in search of first employment (table 8.19). It could be observed, however, that, in the absence of other information (for example, on the waiting periods for work according to the year of the diploma), these data are not sufficient to show that the difficulties of employment for diplomati were progressively aggravated. That the situation for diplomati really did worsen is shown, however, by information that can be obtained from other sources. An inquiry recently conducted on a sample of diplomati of the istituti tecnici industriali has shown that three to four years after the diploma, only 58 percent were found employed, 28 percent were university students (and the greater part of these had continued their studies because of the impossibility of finding work), and 14 percent were still unemployed.[48] Given that this survey was conducted in several northern areas, there is no risk in assuming that the national percentage of unemployed was much higher.

Even more difficult was the situation in which the diplomati of the istituti magistrali came to find themsleves. As may be seen from the data on concorsi, in 1961 the imbalance between candidates and positions offered was slightly lessened compared to the preceding years, although it was still quite strong. But beginning in that year there was a new reversal of the tendency, and the widening divergence between the curves of demand and supply was accentuated in a truly impressive manner, so that in 1972 for every position offered there were actually 16 competitors (figure 8.1). The results of a survey conducted by the pedagogical institute of Bologna (tables 8.20 and 8.21) on participants in the concorso magistrale of 1970 (still unpublished) give us a more precise picture of the fearful dimensions assumed by the phenomenon of teachers' unemployment.[49] Only 2 out of 10 competitors participated in the concorso in order to be transferred or in any case, already had a job. All the others were

Table 8.18. Average Annual Rates of Increase of Diplomati and Laureati Employed from 1959 to 1971 by Sector of Economic Activity

Period	*Agriculture*	*Industry*	*Other Activities*	*Total*
1959–63				
Diplomati	−1.25	8.08	3.03	3.96
Laureati	−3.57	4.02	1.62	1.84
1963–71				
Diplomati	3.29	6.44	4.19	4.69
Laureati	−6.25	1.15	3.69	3.25

SOURCE: Elaboration of data taken from ISTAT, *Annuario di statistiche del lavoro e dell'emigrazione*, vols. 1–13.

Table 8.19. Diplomati and Laureati: Employed, In Search of First Employment, and Unemployed, 1964 to 1971 (in thousands)

Diplomati	*1964*	*1965*	*1966*	*1967*	*1968*	*1969*	*1970*	*1971*
Employed	1,248	1,229	1,233	1,296	1,317	1,379	1,553	1,580
In search of first employment	68	72	78	97	110	124	124	120
Unemployed (formerly employed)	19	22	31	27	29	30	32	27
Total unemployed	87	95	109	124	139	154	156	147
Laureati								
Employed	509	494	523	542	556	554	565	606
In search of first employment	9	9	12	12	12	15	20	22
Unemployed (formerly employed)	1	1	3	2	2	2	2	3
Total unemployed	10	10	15	14	14	17	22	25

SOURCE: ISTAT, *Annuario di statistiche del lavoro e dell'emigrazione*, vols. 1–13.

Table 8.20. Occupation of Participants in the 1970 Concorso for Elementary School Teachers by Sex

Occupation	*M*	*F*
Steadily employed teachers	10	13
Impiegati	14	11
Intermittent jobs	16	16
University students	33	26
Unemployed	22	25
Housewives	—	9
Workers	3	—
Soldiers	2	—
Total	100	100
(N)	(225)	(1,908)

SOURCE: See the text.

Table 8.21. Number of Concorsi So Far Undergone by Participants in the 1970 Concorso for Elementary School Teachers by Age Cohort

Number of Concorsi	*Age of Participants*					*All Participants*
	18–20	*21–25*	*26–30*	*31–35*	*36–40*	
1st	85	19	4	1	2	41
2nd	15	40	11	13	13	24
3rd	—	38	31	25	15	21
4th	—	3	37	20	20	8
5th or 6th	—	—	17	41	50	6
Total	100	100	100	100	100	100
(N)	(808)	(808)	(320)	(134)	(46)	(2,116)

SOURCE: See the text.

unemployed, manifestly or hidden, or carried out some temporary work. A quarter of them were over twenty-five years of age. If to this is added that one competitor in three was at his third, fourth, fifth, or sixth, consorso, and if one considers that these concorsi took place every two years, one can imagine how long the periods of waiting for employment were for the diplomati of the istituti magistrali.

For the laureati, on the other hand, some years had to pass before the imbalance between demand and supply manifested itself fully. At the beginning of the period, in fact, there was not so much a surplus as a phenomenon of noncorrespondence between the composition of demand and that of supply.

There was, in other words, at least in some areas of the country, still a lack of secondary teachers,[50] but at the same time an excess of laureati from other faculties: from law and economics, but now also from engineering and architecture and from faculties in the midst of expansion, such as political science, not to mention laureati from faculties such as geology, who, having begun their higher studies at a time of great hope, were among the first to receive great disappointment from the new situation of the qualified labor market. Thus it is that in those years the process of reconverting "excess" laureati into teachers already under way at the end of the preceding period, grew stronger and spread; a process that would lead to the description of the school as a self-feeding institution. For laureati of the academic year 1965–66, 31 percent of those in economics and political science turned to teaching, as well as 30 percent of those in agriculture, 16 percent in pharmacy, and 12 percent in engineering and architecture.[51]

The capacity of the school to absorb the excess quota of intellectual labor produced by the university was, nevertheless, not without limits. The findings of a large inquiry conducted on laureati for the academic year 1965–66 show this to us clearly. In fact, it was found that three years after obtaining the *laurea*, 7.8 percent of those interviewed were unemployed (4.8 percent in search of first employment and 3 percent unemployed). This percentage varied according to faculty, reaching the highest points for jurisprudence (21.3 percent), political science (19.1 percent), and pharmacy (10.5 percent), and according to geographic area (12.7 percent in the Mezzogiorno).[52]

In any case, in the following years there was a rapid worsening of the situation due, on the one hand, to the sharp rise in supply from 1968 onward and, on the other hand, to the new economic crisis of the years 1970–72. With the exception of doctors, who even in this period continued to find work easily and to enjoy a high level of income, the difficulties of employment increased for the laureati of all faculties, even for those in the literature group who were so sought after a few years before. Beginning in 1971, a good number of teachers on the lists to be hired in many local education offices remained without a position.

The data at our disposal are still too scanty for us to be able to say safely whether and to what extent the worsening of the imbalance between demand and supply of intellectual labor has influenced the professional status of the youth coming out of the secondary schools and the university. For the diplomati, if we take as an indicator of declassamento (actually a very rough one) the

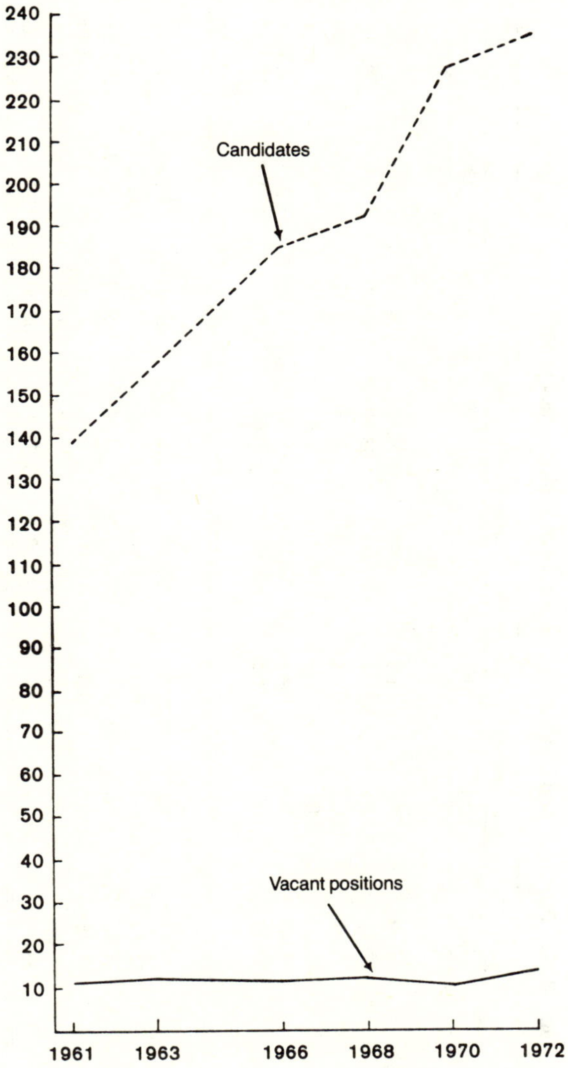

Figure 8.1. Vacant positions for maestri and candidates from 1961 to 1972 (in thousands).

percentage employed as dependent laborers (or workers), we see that this process does not have a linear course. The percentage of dependent laborers declined in fact up to 1966, then began to rise again the year after and reached

Table 8.22. Diplomati and Laureati by Occupational Position, 1964 to 1971

Occupational Position	*1964*	*1965*	*1966*	*1967*	*1968*	*1969*	*1970*	*1971*
				Diplomati				
Entrepreneurs and liberal professionals	4.89	5.29	4.62	4.78	4.52	4.35	3.81	3.29
Managers and impiegati	82.70	82.51	83.94	84.03	83.22	83.18	83.91	84.18
Self-employed laborers	6.01	6.59	6.49	6.10	6.71	6.45	6.44	6.26
Dependent laborers	3.92	3.01	2.52	2.70	2.85	3.19	3.41	3.99
Assistants	2.48	2.60	2.43	2.39	2.70	2.83	2.43	2.28
Total	100.00	100.00	100.00	100.00	100.00	100.00	100.00	100.00
				Laureati				
Entrepreneurs and liberal professionals	25.93	26.92	26.00	25.28	25.00	22.20	22.77	21.95
Managers and impiegati	67.68	66.80	68.83	69.56	69.96	73.11	72.68	72.94
Self-employed laborers	4.32	4.46	3.83	4.24	4.14	3.79	3.37	3.63
Dependent laborers	1.38	0.61	0.38	0.18	—	0.18	0.34	0.33
Assistants	0.59	1.21	0.96	0.74	0.90	0.72	0.84	1.15
Total	100.00	100.00	100.00	100.00	100.00	100.00	100.00	100.00

SOURCE: Elaboration of data taken from ISTAT, *Annuario di statistiche del lavoro e dell'emigrazione,* vols. 1–13.

its highest point in 1971 (table 8.22). I will seek to offer a more precise interpretation of these data in the next two chapters, but it is worth noting here that probably the nonlinear course of this process – and more generally the fact that a sharp declassamento of diplomati does not immediately follow the increased difficulties of employment – is explained by the intervening changes, beginning in 1961, in the educational system, which have allowed a greater number of youth to seek a way of escape into the university.

The process of declassamento is manifested even more slowly for the laureati. At the beginning of this period, it was weakened in fact by the extraordinary possibilities of reabsorption by an educational system in a phase of strong growth. Thus, more frequently there were cases of noncorrespondence between the type of laurea and the type of work performed (laureati in law who taught literature) rather than of actual declassamento (laureati who performed functions for which only a diploma of the upper-secondary school was required). Nevertheless, it is likely that in recent years it has become accentuated even for the laureati.[53]

CHAPTER NINE

Education and Economy, 1945–1970

The situation of Italian education in the last quarter century presents impressive aspects of continuity with the past. In the first place, in this period as well its expansion was distorted and unbalanced, in the sense that the country still had, together with high rates of intellectual unemployment, a considerable percentage of illiterates before and then of truants after the establishment of compulsory schooling. In the second place, as I will try to show in the following pages, in this period also the growth of education was at least in part brought about by the backwardness and underdevelopment of the economy, by the absence of possibilities of employment at the lower- and upper-intermediate levels, and by the scarcity of other channels of social mobility.

"An intense economic life of the country," wrote Adolfo Omodeo in 1945, "often absorbs the youth in their first years of life and provides them with suitably paid careers. On the other hand, the languishing of industrial and commercial life induces even the least endowed to throw themselves into the university adventure in the hope of a better life."[1] The number of university students, observed Antonio Segni some years later, "grows every time periods of economic difficulties are passed through. In every economic crisis the number always increases of those who believe that salvation from the consequences of the crisis lies in obtaining a university degree."[2]

Nevertheless, to draw from these propositions the only keys to interpreting the course of education in the last quarter century would be unjustified and would not allow us to grasp the novelties and the elements of discontinuity that it presents in comparison to the past. It is in fact doubtless that, especially in the second half of this period, there was rapid growth of schooling in Italy, and that for the first time in its history a considerable number of youth from the subordinate social classes entered the secondary and higher schools. Moreover, it is undeniable that this growth was influenced strongly, on the one hand, by the very important changes in the internal structure of the educational system that occurred at the beginning of the 1960s (which we will examine in the next chapter), and on the other, by the rise of per capita income of families and the raising of the level of qualification of the labor force, which were in turn produced by industrialization and by economic development.

If one wished to sum up in a few words the course of secondary and higher education in the last quarter century, it could be said that it was at the same time the singular and contradictory product of expansion and crisis of the economy, of the rise of per capita income and the fall of youth employment, and of the hope of success of the lower social classes and the fear of declassamento on the part of the old and the new ceti medi.

Secondary Education

The Relationship Between Economy and Education by Geographic Area

Analyzing existing differences among geographic areas of Italy in the course of this study, I have had occasion to demonstrate several times a direct relationship between economic development and education at the level of compulsory schooling* and an inverse relationship at the level of secondary schooling. For the period that interests us here, however, the testing of these relationships can be conducted, because of the greater quantity of data at out disposal, by taking the province as the unit of analysis.† At least for one year, 1961,[3] it is possible in fact to consider several variables of a socioeconomic nature and to analyze them in relation to data concerning education at the lower and upper-secondary levels.

By taking as the dependent variable first of all the rate of enrollment at the lower-secondary level, that is, the number of enrollments in the scuola media and the avviamento[4] as a percentage of the age cohort 10–15, we see that it is correlated positively with per capita income (0.58) and with the general index

*Compulsory schooling, set at 8 years of age by the Casati Law, was upped to 9 years in 1877, to 12 years in 1904, and then to 14 years by the Gentile Law of 1923, where it has since remained, although unenforced until well into the postwar period.

†At the intermediate level of subnational government in postwar Italy (that is, between the comune and the region) there is the province, of which there are 92 in all.

of consumption (0.60).* These data as well, therefore, confirm the presence of that well-known direct relationship between level of economic development and enrollment rate at the lower-secondary level.

The surprising feature is once again, however, the course of education in the passage from the lower- to the upper-secondary school. Considering the rate of passage between these two levels we see, in fact, that it correlates positively with the two most significant indices of underdevelopment: illiteracy (0.56) and infant mortality (0.43). These are, naturally, spurious correlations. Nevertheless, no other data can give us a better idea, more forcefully and dramatically, than these two correlation coefficients of how distorted and contradictory the development of secondary education has been in Italy in the last twenty-five years. The rate of passage from the lower to the upper-secondary level is correlated negatively (−0.41) with the percentage of males employed in industry of the total male population employed, and it is correlated positively (0.53) with the number of persons with the licenza (granted after three years in the lower-secondary) who are in search of first employment taken as a percentage of the active (that is, employed or seeking first employment) population with the same educational qualification. Thus according to these data too it is in the less industrialized areas, where there are greater difficulties of employment for the young coming out of the lower-secondary schools, that the strongest pressure to pursue studies by enrolling in the upper-secondary is found.

Not surprisingly, these relationships between economic development and education hold not only for 1961. That in the twenty-five-year period which opens in 1945 the rate of nonattendance of compulsory schooling, of years repeated, and of studies abandoned, is higher in the economically underdeveloped areas is a fact which is too well known to be worth pursuing further here (for the reader interested in a quantification in three different years of this phenomenon, a glance at tables 9.1 and 9.2 will suffice).[5] It is worthwhile, however, to examine the course of the rate of passage between the lower- and the upper-secondary school over the past fifteen years.[6] Figures 9.1, 9.2, and 9.3 report the percentage of students enrolled in the first year of the upper-secondary school (excluding repeaters) as a percentage of licenziati from the scuola media and the avviamento in the preceding academic year. This means, for example, that the value reported for 1954 indicates the percentage of licenziati in June or in September of that year who enrolled in the same month in the

*See the appendix at the end of the chapter.

Table 9.1. Enrollment Rate in the Lower-Secondary (Media + Avviamento) and Upper-Secondary Schools, 1951 and 1961, by Sex and Geographic Area

	Lower-Secondary				*Upper-Secondary*			
Area	*1951*		*1961*		*1951*		*1961*	
	M	*F*	*M*	*F*	*M*	*F*	*M*	*F*
Northwest	44.8	33.5	76.2	64.6	14.9	8.6	26.4	14.4
Center-Northeast	39.4	26.6	77.7	81.1	13.0	8.6	26.9	17.6
South	30.7	17.8	62.7	43.5	11.4	6.6	24.5	17.7
Italy	36.9	24.5	70.7	54.1	12.7	7.8	25.8	16.1

SOURCE: OECD, *Reviews of National Policies for Education: Italy,* p. 83.

Table 9.2. Rate of Enrollment by Age and Geographic Area, 1967

Age	*Northwest*	*Northeast*	*Center*	*South*	*Islands*
11–13	93.5	94.6	93.9	86.5	89.9
14–18	45.2	44.5	55.2	46.6	44.8
19–23	11.0	11.0	21.1	16.1	15.3
24–26	2.8	3.6	7.1	6.0	5.3
Total	34.0	35.4	42.7	38.8	39.3

SOURCE: ISTAT, *Indagine speciale su alcuni aspetti della vita scolastica italiana* (Rome, 1969).

upper-secondary. If we examine figure 9.3 we observe that the rate of passage is subject to fluctuations over the fifteen years in question. One thing nevertheless remains constant over the entire period: that the rate is extraordinarily higher in the Mezzogiorno than in the *Settentrione.**

If we observe figures 9.1 and 9.2, on the other hand, we note that these differences hold not only for males but also for females. In the North and the Center the rate of passage of males is always higher than that of females, while in the South in some years exactly the reverse is true. Moreover, the rate of passage of females in the South is much higher in all years of the period considered than that of their counterparts in the North. Once again, therefore, the data at our disposal show that we cannot explain the course of female instruction by referring to variables of a cultural order, but we must rather begin with structural variables and in particular with the growing difficulties of employment for this component of the labor force.

**Settentrione:* the northern half of Italy, in contrast to the *Mezzogiorno*.

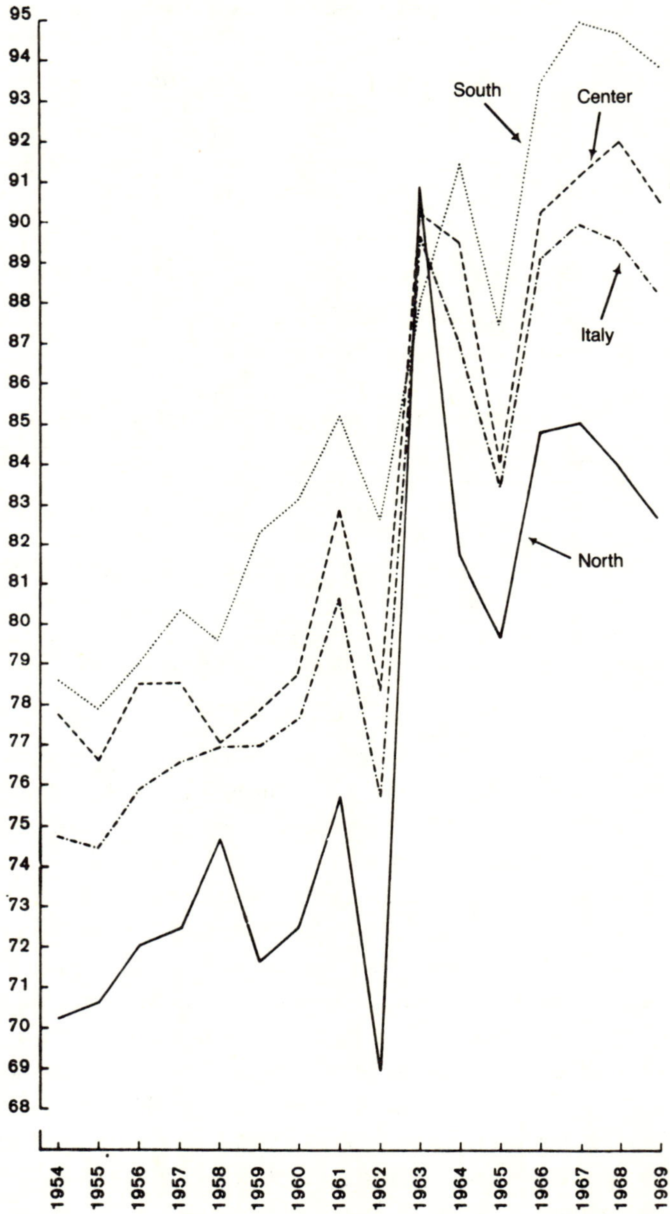

Figure 9.1. Rate of passage (male) to the upper-secondary schools from 1954 to 1969 (percentage enrolled in the first year of upper-secondary school, minus repeaters, of those granted the licenza from the scuola media and the avviamento in the preceding year).

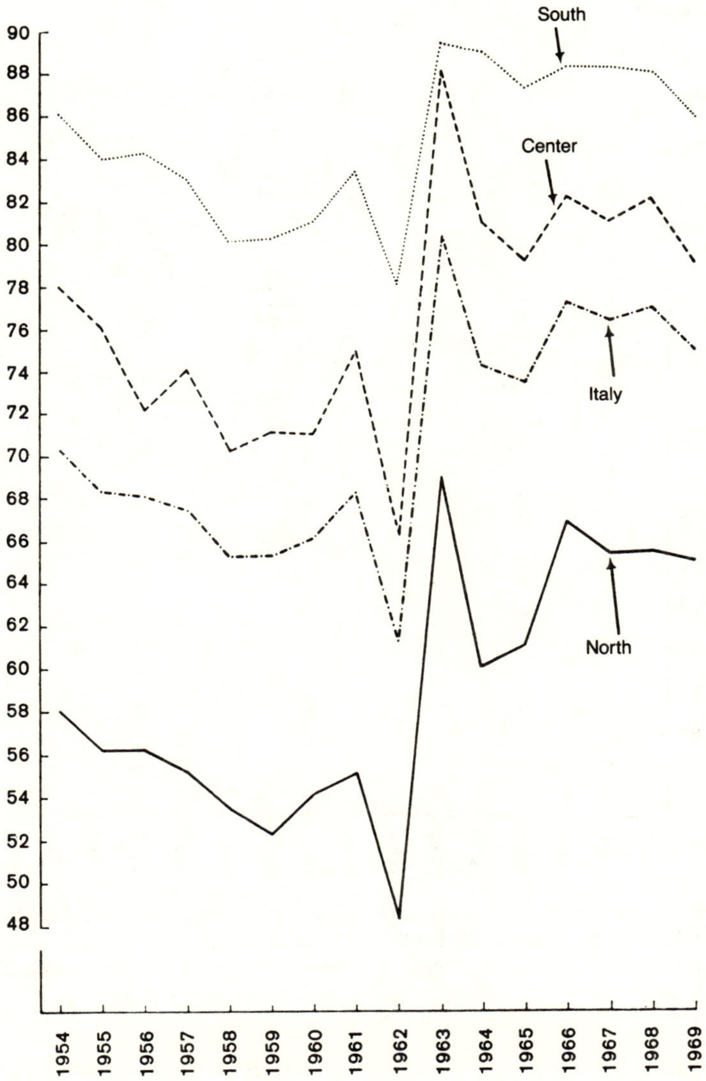

Figure 9.2. Rate of passage (female) to the upper-secondary schools from 1954 to 1969 (percentage enrolled in the first year of the upper-secondary school, minus repeaters, of those granted the licenza from the scuola media and the avviamento in the preceding year).

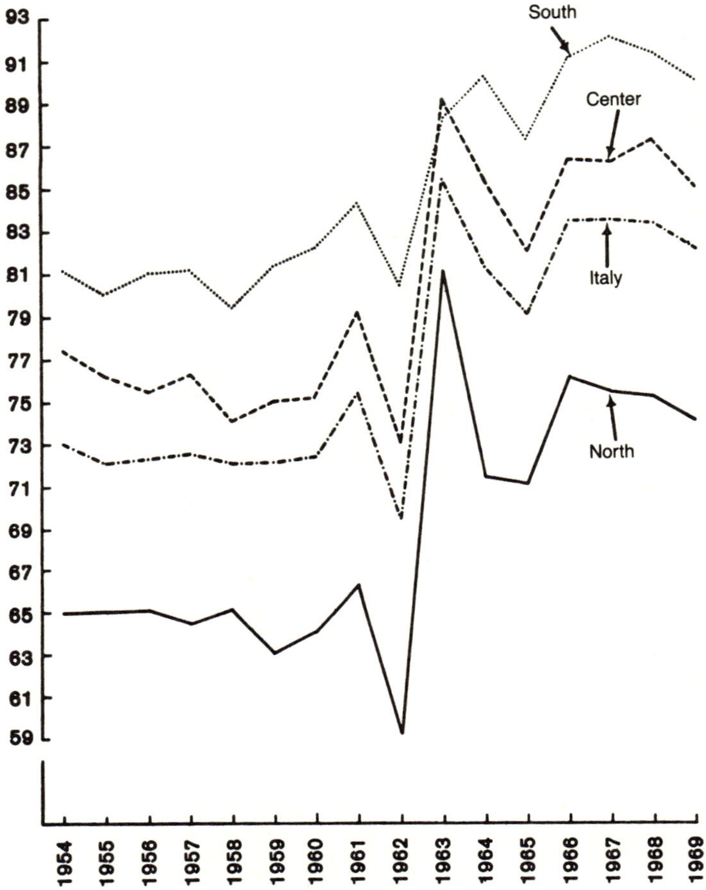

Figure 9.3. Rate of passage (male and female) to the upper-secondary schools from 1954 to 1969 (percentage enrolled in the first year of the upper-secondary school, minus repeaters, of those granted the licenza from the scuole media and the avviamento in the preceding year).

The analysis conducted so far confirms, therefore, the existence of an inverse relationship between economic development and upper-secondary education in the period that opens with the fall of fascism, and it shows that one of the sources of the expansion of upper-secondary education in Italy has been the insufficient labor-market demand for graduates of the lower-secondary school. Nevertheless, the official interpretations of the relationship between economy and secondary education were very different. In one study of Italy conducted in

1969 on behalf of the OECD, several "experts" of the Ministry of Public Education calculated the rates of scholarity according to sex and geographic area at the lower- and upper-secondary school levels (table 9.1). Confronting the fact that "the rate of expansion of the school population" was "higher in the South than in the other regions," they found no other explanation than that:

> [They] reflect a greater demand for education in the Southern regions which used to be particularly underdeveloped in this respect. As we have already emphasized the improvement in living standards and a greater awareness of the need for a higher level of education have led to a general increase in enrollments in the South and in many cases this increase has gradually bridged the gaps between the South and other regions.[7]

ISTAT offered the same interpretation when, commenting on data on rates of enrollment according to geographic area gathered from a large inquiry (table 9.2), it could write nothing other than:

> data from the present report can shed new light and give a new dimension to the constant effort at social elevation of the southern populations. . . . From this it is apparent that the South is passing through a period of transition, from the past depression to a better situation in the future.[8]

In reality, it suffices to examine carefully the data produced by these two studies and to compare them with those we have seen so far to realize that they confirm the interpretive hypothesis that I have advanced. In 1951, 1961, and 1967 alike the South presents a rate of enrollment much lower than that of the North at the lower-secondary level. The greater difficulties of employment of youth who graduate from these schools, however, cause the rate of passage in the South, as we have seen, to be much higher than in the North. The result is that at the upper-secondary level the South recovers a large part of the enormous gap between it and the North at the (compulsory) lower-secondary level. Indeed, in 1961, the enrollment rate for females at the upper-secondary level is already higher in the South than in the Northwest. And as the differences at the compulsory level are weakened, the rate of enrollment of the South at the upper-secondary level surpasses that of the North. This, as can be seen from table 9.2, had already happened by 1967. It is probable that by now, five years later, the differences are even more distinct.[9]

The data that we have seen, therefore, are more than sufficient to safely affirm that the particular course of upper-secondary education in Italy is at least in part the result of its structural imbalances, of the aggravation of territorial differences, of the persistence in large areas (even in times of maximum economic expansion) of considerable contingents of unemployed youth – in a word, of that process of unequal development which has also characterized the last twenty years of Italian history. This naturally does not mean that the increase of per capita income has not had its effect. This variable certainly has had an enormous influence on the course of upper-secondary education, in two different ways. First, indirectly, by bringing about an increase in the rate of enrollment in the primary and lower-secondary schools. To realize this it suffices to recall that enrollments in the latter schools have increased from 795,000 in 1951 to 1,500,000 in 1961, up to and exceeding 2,200,000 in 1971. One can estimate that the enrollment rate for the age cohort 11 – 13 years has increased over the first decade from 31 percent to 62 percent, and that it has reached 90 percent by the end of the second decade.[10] Second, directly, by making it such that, even though the number of licenziati from the lower-secondary has constantly increased, the rate of passage to the upper-secondary has actually occasionally dropped.

The Relationship Between Economy and Education Over Time

It is more difficult to analyze the relationship between the course of the economy and that of secondary education over time. I noted in the preceding chapter that, after the period of reconstruction, the Italian economy experienced a period of strong (although unbalanced) expansion up to 1963 and that from the end of that year to the present it has passed through a crisis, a light recovery, and a new crisis. If, in particular, we use the rate of unemployment provided by ISTAT as an instrument of short-term analysis, we see that it declines steadily up to 1963 and then begins to rise again in the following year, to reach its highest point in 1966. But its course differs according to geographic area. In the South, where it remains in any case always higher than in the North, it decreases until 1963 and then increases again steadily until 1968. In the North, on the other hand, it diminishes until 1963, increases until 1965, and diminishes again until 1968.[11]

Between the period that closes and the one that opens in 1963 there are certainly some important differences concerning labor demand for graduates of the lower-secondary school. In the period up to 1963, the shifting of large masses of the population from the primary to the secondary sector of economic activity brought about an increase in the demand for labor at this level of qualification, even though it is true that this tendency was not very marked. Recent studies have shown in fact that the sharp increase in industrial employment which occurred in the 1950s concerned especially the lowest qualifications (common laborers and apprentices).[12] On the other hand, table 9.3 shows that at the end of that period 59.4 percent of industrial and commercial enterprises required only the elementary school diploma, and 8 percent no qualification at all. However, with the period beginning in 1963, the demand for graduates of the secondary school diminishes. The rate of unemployment increases, but above all the tendency, already present in the preceding years, toward an increasingly greater selectivity of demand directed at the strongest component (males 25 – 40 years of age) to the detriment of the weakest components (women, older workers, and youth) is strengthened.[13]

If we limit ourselves to a division into two periods (before and after 1963), we notice a certain (inverse) correspondence between the course of the rate of passage to the upper-secondary schools and the course of the economy. As may be seen from figure 9.3, the national rate of passage remains constant from 1954 to 1960, rises in 1961, and declines again in 1962, the year in which it reaches its low point. Consistent also with the course of employment is the fact that the decrease in 1962 characterizes much more the curve for the North than that for the South. But especially important is the fact that from 1963 onward the rate of passage reaches levels in all years much higher than those of the preceding years. Therefore, the hypothesis that the vicissitudes of the Italian economy, and particularly the increased difficulties of employment in the second period, have influenced the growth of upper-secondary education would seem at least plausible given the data we have seen.[14]

However, a closer analysis of figures 9.1 – 9.3 highlights the fact that the increase of youth unemployment is not enough in itself to explain the sharp increase in the rate of passage that occurs in the second period. To realize this it is sufficient to concentrate our attention for a moment on 1963. In that year the curve of the rate of passage undergoes a sharp rebound which characterizes both males and females in all areas, even if the slope is greater for northern males. But 1963 means in this case September, since this is the last month that the licenziati of the lower-secondary can enroll in the upper-secondary school. The economic crisis, on the contrary, begins two months later and produces all its consequences on the levels of employment only in the following year.

In effect, to explain the course of upper-secondary education after 1963 it is

Table 9.3. Educational Qualification Required by Industrial and Commercial Enterprises for Various Categories of Workers, 1960

Qualification Required	*Intermediate Categories*	*Specialized Workers*	*Qualified Workers*	*Common and Unskilled Workers*	*Apprentices*
Technical or professional institute	58.7	39.0	16.1	9.4	15.2
Lower-secondary school	34.7	45.5	49.3	23.0	55.7
Elementary school	5.6	14.2	31.8	59.4	26.5
No qualification	1.0	1.3	2.8	8.2	2.6
Total	100.00	100.00	100.00	100.00	100.00
(N)	(3,318)	(3,831)	(3,998)	(3,653)	(3,170)

SOURCE: ISTAT, *Indagine statistica sull'occupazione qualificata* (Rome, 1964).

also necessary to take into account the course of workers' wages, which, after a long period of stasis, undergo a considerable increase just in those years (with the bargaining undertaken and the contract renewals of 1962–63). If, therefore, one limits oneself to considering economic variables, it can be said that the expansion of upper-secondary education that takes place after 1963 is due to the simultaneous occurrence of two conditions: on the one hand, the growing unemployment of youth, which pushes those coming out of the compulsory, lower-secondary school to continue their studies at the upper-secondary level; and on the other, the increases in wages, which make it less difficult for working-class families to support the costs necessary for their children's continuing studies.

The fact is, however, that economic variables are not enough alone to explain the course of education. The profound change of the Italian educational system that occurred at the end of 1962 with the establishment of the unified lower-secondary school (the media unica) had, in fact, a decisive influence on the expansion of secondary education. Because of the very way that the new scuola media was conceived (providing, for example, the possibility of establishing differential classes and leaving Latin instruction still partially in place) and also because of the teaching personnel with which it had to reckon, the media unica was and still is strongly selective. But this does not take away from the fact that it strongly accelerated the process of expansion of upper-secondary education. By abolishing the dumping school of the avviamento, the law of 1962 in fact created that open education system at the lower-secondary level which, as has been observed several times in the course of this study, has always had the effect of raising students' levels of aspiration. One can say, therefore, that the sharp increase in the rate of passage to the upper-secondary school which occurred after 1963 is due as well to the reform of the lower-secondary. On the other hand, the law of 1962, reaffirming and seeking to enforce compulsory schooling up to fourteen years of age, has certainly contributed to the increase in the rate of enrollment for this age group, and also has given no little impetus to the expansion of upper-secondary education.

Higher Education

In his most famous study, Gino Martinoli, having calculated that in the five-year period 1955–59 the rate of passage of diplomati to the university was on the average 57.9 percent, observed:

> The high value of this ratio appears rather serious inasmuch as it means that the secondary school has, and tends to maintain, the original character that it had even a century or so ago as a necessary stage and a springboard toward the laurea or, in any case, toward the university; it appears, that is, that its function of preparing for a multiplicity of intermediate qualifications, intended to maintain the category of technicians, intermediate cadres, lower managers, administrative personnel, etc. has diminished if not completely disappeared.[15]

This passage constitutes, in my opinion, the best proof that by beginning with an analysis such as that conducted by SVIMEZ or Martinoli on the tendencies of intellectual employment, particularly of diplomati, in the years of greatest expansion of the Italian economy, it is definitely not possible to explain adequately the course of higher education in Italy in the 1950s, much less in the following decade. Convinced that he found himself facing a "scarcity of intermediate cadres," Martinoli could explain the "high value" of the rate of passage only by bringing in the incapacity of the Italian educational system to prepare "a multiplicity of intermediate qualifications."

That this type of "explanation" definitely cannot be sustained is readily apparent. If, in fact, the market situation for youth graduating from the secondary schools had been so favorable, as was affirmed, it is evident that the tendency of these students to pursue their studies by enrolling in the university would have been sharply reduced. In reality, if the secondary school did have the character of a "springboard toward the laurea" (although in those years less so than before, as we shall see further on), this was due to the fact that even in 1961, as was mentioned in the preceding chapter, there was no lack but rather an excess of diplomati (despite the situation's having improved considerably compared to 1951).

The Relationship Between Economy and Education by Geographic Area

It is once again, therefore, to the difficulties of employment for diplomati that one must turn in order to understand the course of Italian higher education in the last quarter century. This proposition can be verified, in this case as well, by conducting an analysis according to geographic area. On the basis of data from special inquiries conducted by ISTAT on diplomati and first-year university students, it is possible to calculate the rate of passage to the university by geographic area, at least for some years.[16] Table 9.4 shows that from 1953 to 1967 the rate of passage of diplomati to the university was always higher in the

Table 9.4. Rate of Passage of Diplomati to the University by Geographic Area, 1953 to 1967

Year	*North*	*Center*	*South*	*Italy*
1953	52.56	65.38	65.00	59.70
1954	49.59	72.58	59.01	57.32
1955	49.59	76.86	62.10	59.28
1956	53.47	68.36	60.86	59.19
1957	50.02	70.20	63.43	58.50
1959	52.67	72.06	59.98	59.21
1967	68.76	100.67	79.16	78.68

SOURCE: Elaboration of data taken from ISTAT, *Annuario statistico dell'istruzione italiana.*

South than in the North. Once again, therefore, it is in the areas where the level of economic development is lower[17] and the difficulties of employment for diplomati greater that the rate of passage is higher.[18]

Thus at this level as well, we find an analogous process to the one described in the preceding section. Also in the upper-secondary schools, the rate of years repeated and studies abandoned of students from the underdeveloped areas is higher than that of the other areas. Even so, the greater difficulty of employment encountered after completing the upper-secondary school makes the rate of passage of diplomati to the university higher in these areas than in the others. Hence, at the end of this process, characterized by the contradictory pressures, on the one hand, to terminate studies *during the course of* primary and secondary schooling and, on the other, to continue them *at the point of passage* from one level to the next, we find the highest rate of university enrollment in the underdeveloped zones.

This is not yet very visible in 1953 – 54, even if, as table 9.5 shows, it is certainly significant that the percentage of university students in the 19-year-old population is higher in Campania, Sicily, and even Puglia than in Lombardy. But it is very visible in 1960–61, the year in which the percentage of university students in Piedmont and Lombardy is lower than that of almost all southern regions (six out of seven), including Basilicata and Calabria, which then had and still have today less than half the per capita income of the two northern regions. These differences are accentuated even more over the years, so that by 1967 the rate of enrollment of the Mezziogiorno in the 19- to 23-year-old age cohort is higher by 46 percent than that of the Northwestern regions (see table 9.2).

Table 9.5. First Year University Students as a Percentage of the 19-Year-Old Population Present by Region, 1953–54 and 1960–61

Region	*1953–54*	*1960–61*
Piedmont and Valle d'Aosta	4.42	5.96
Liguria	7.99	7.90
Lombardy	4.01	5.88
Trentino-Alto Adige	2.75	3.69
Veneto	2.67	4.26
Friuli-Venezia Giulia	4.21	7.02
Emilia-Romagna	4.23	7.27
Marche	3.83	7.10
Tuscany	4.26	6.14
Umbria	3.79	7.21
Latium	7.87	10.05
Campania	4.49	5.98
Abruzzi and Molise	3.31	7.68
Puglia	4.08	7.61
Basilicata	2.47	5.96
Calabria	3.31	7.41
Sicily	4.70	7.06
Sardinia	2.92	5.02

Note: The percentages were calculated for the population in 1951 and 1961.

SOURCE: Elaboration of data taken from ISTAT, *Indagini speciali sugli studenti universitari e sui diplomati di scuole medie superiori* (Rome, 1956); ISTAT, *Annuario statistico dell'istruzione italiana 1963–64* (Rome, 1965); ISTAT, *IX Censimento generale della popolazione,* vol. 3, *Sesso, età, stato civile, luogo di nascita* (Rome, 1956); ISTAT, *X Censimento generale della popolazione,* vol. 5, *Sesso, età, stato civile, luogo di nascita* (Rome, 1966).

By introducing another variable into our analysis, we can see even better how distorted and contradictory the development of higher education has been in Italy: the social origin of diplomati and of university students. As may be recalled, we found a higher rate of enrollment at the university level in the underdeveloped areas also in the fascist and prefascist periods. This we understood as indicating that the difficulties of employment encountered upon completing the upper-secondary schools by diplomati from families of the middle and upper social classes (since it was from these social backgrounds that the great majority of those who entered the university then came) pushed them to continue their studies. But what has occurred in the last quarter century, given the increasing admission of youth from the lower social classes into the educational system? To answer this question one must calculate the rate of passage of diplomati to the university according to the father's occupation. That there is a positive relationship between social status of the family of origin

Table 9.6. Rate of Passage to the University of Diplomati Who Are Children of Entrepreneurs and Liberal Professionals, 1953 to 1967, by Geographic Area

Year	*North*	*Center*	*South*	*Italy*
1953	62.76	75.67	74.93	69.27
1954	75.28	109.32	88.54	85.69
1955	66.55	99.77	73.90	74.95
1956	66.81	71.52	70.32	68.99
1957	63.05	76.25	76.13	70.07
1959	62.08	79.65	68.97	67.55
1967	78.87	109.35	77.85	83.47

SOURCE: Elaboration of data taken from ISTAT, *Annuario statistico dell'istruzione italiana.*

Table 9.7. Rate of Passage to the University of Diplomati Who Are Children of Dependent Laborers, 1953 to 1967, by Geographic Area

Year	*North*	*Center*	*South*	*Italy*
1953	34.71	45.43	54.54	42.93
1954	34.02	48.20	47.09	40.76
1955	33.99	44.88	50.98	41.49
1956	36.88	42.89	49.75	42.53
1957	33.20	43.36	53.87	41.88
1959	34.27	53.16	47.57	42.75
1967	51.88	72.43	75.30	64.58

SOURCE: Elaboration of data taken from ISTAT, *Annuario statistico dell'istruzione italiana.*

and rate of passage – that the percentage of diplomati who continue their studies is higher the more elevated the occupational status of the father – is a fact which emerges clearly from the data at our disposal but which certainly is no cause for surprise.

On the other hand, one arrives in some cases at unexpected results by analyzing the rate of passage from 1953 to 1967 according to father's occupation and geographic area. Table 9.6 shows that in the case of diplomati who are children of entrepreneurs and liberal professionals the rate of passage in the South is higher than that in the North. The differences, however, are not very marked up to 1959 and they disappear completely in 1967. The situation of sons of dependent laborers, as may be seen from table 9.7, appears on the other hand to be different. Here the differences are very marked and become increasingly strong in the 1960s (in 1967 they are as much as 23 percentage points).

Let us now look at figures 9.4 and 9.5. From the first one can see that, conforming to our expectations, the percentage of diplomati who are children of dependent laborers remains constantly lower in the South than in the North for the entire period considered. The situation changes radically, on the other hand, in the case of first-year university students. As may be seen from figure 9.5, the percentage of children of dependent laborers is higher in the North than in the other areas up to 1957–58. But after that it is the South, paradoxically, which leads. If one bears in mind the differential composition of the category "dependent laborers" according to geographic area (in the South, agricultural laborers and, among employees in industry, workers with a low level of wage qualification are much more heavily represented), then the significance of the data we have seen is even more understandable.

Therefore, the sharp differences that we have found among different geographic areas in the rate of passage of diplomati from the subordinate classes are due to the difficulties of employment encountered by youth coming out of the upper-secondary schools. These difficulties vary not only according to geographic area but also according to the social status of the family of origin,[19] and are therefore greatest for southern diplomati who are children of dependent laborers, namely for that particular subgroup which at the same time has fewer financial resources than all others for continuing with studies.

The Relationship Between Economy and Education Over Time

In the preceding chapter, examining the trends in intellectual unemployment in the last quarter century, there was occasion to observe that the supply of diplomati proceeds differently from the supply of laureati. While, in fact, the number of diplomati produced by the educational system grows constantly over this entire period, that for laureati remains practically constant up to 1960 and increases over the following decade. If, on the other hand, we examine the rate of passage of diplomati to the university we see that it drops sharply from 1946 to 1952, remains constant or diminishes further in the following eight years, and then begins to rise with a very steep slope beginning in 1961 (figure 9.6).

How can we explain the course of the rate of passage to the university over the last twenty-five years? One could say, first of all, that the drop or the stasis recorded in the first fifteen years is no less than a consequence of the change that occurred in the composition of the flow of diplomati according to the type of upper-secondary school attended. As can be seen in fact from figure 9.6, the number of youth coming from the licei (classico and scientifico) as a percentage

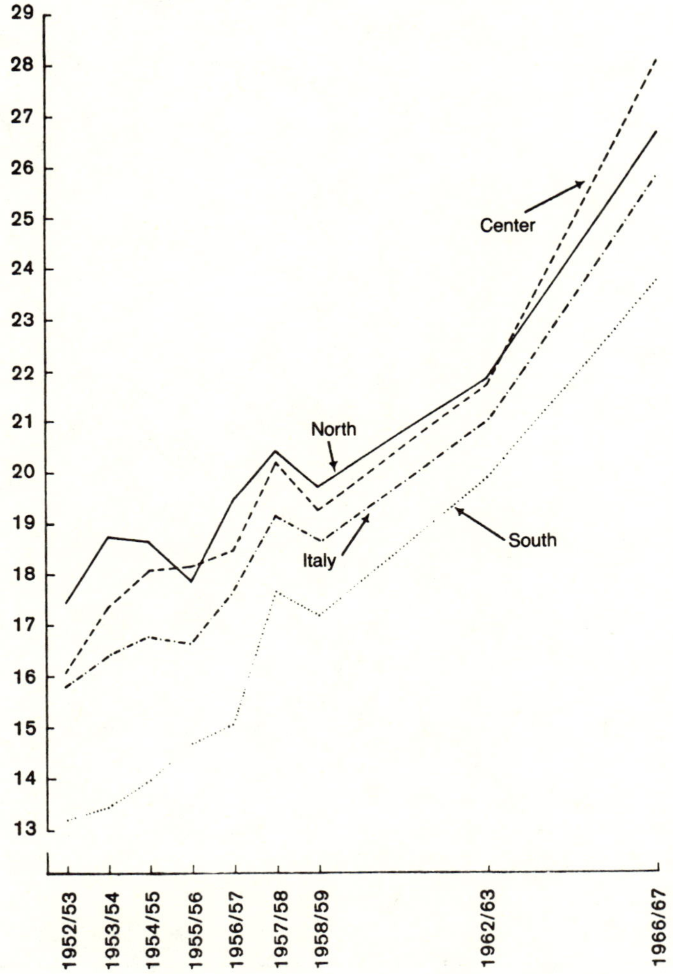

Figure 9.4. Percentage of diplomati (male and female) who are children of dependent laborers, by geographic area, 1952–53 to 1966–67.

of the total number of diplomati diminishes constantly from 1946–47 onward. And since the rate of passage to the university of diplomati from the istituti tecnici and magistrali is obviously much lower than that of those coming out of the licei, it follows, one could say, that the aggregate rate of passage cannot help but diminish or remain constant.

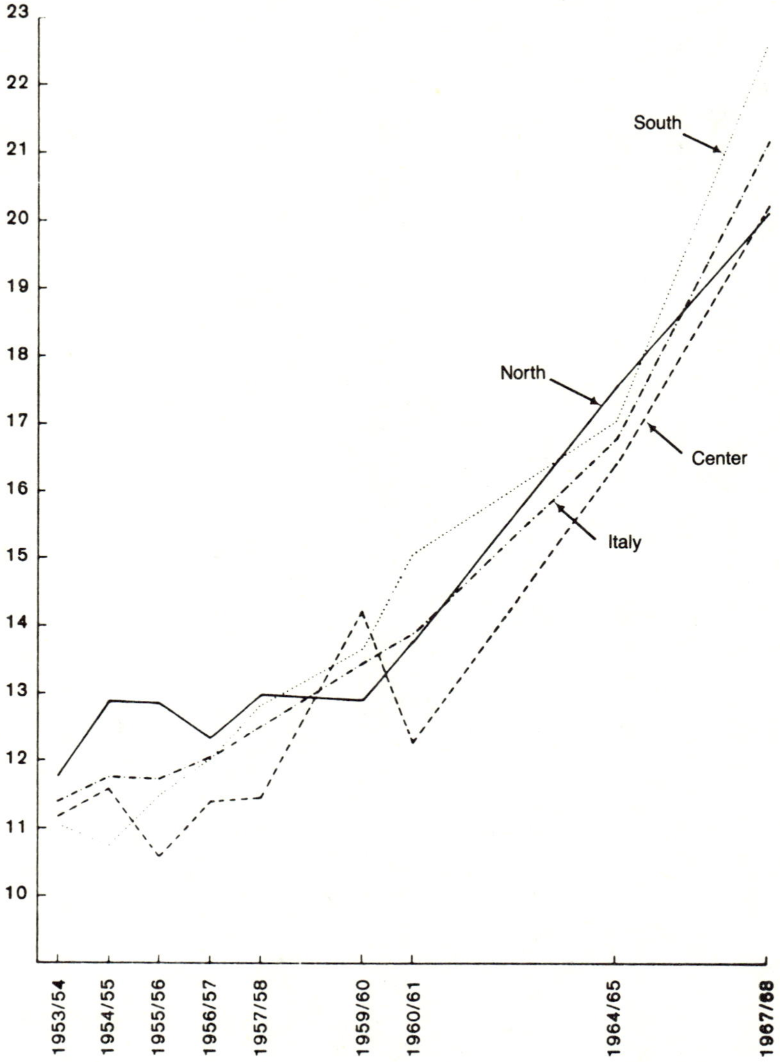

Figure 9.5. Percentage of university students (male and female) enrolled in the first year who are children of dependent laborers, by geographic area, 1953–54 to 1967–68.

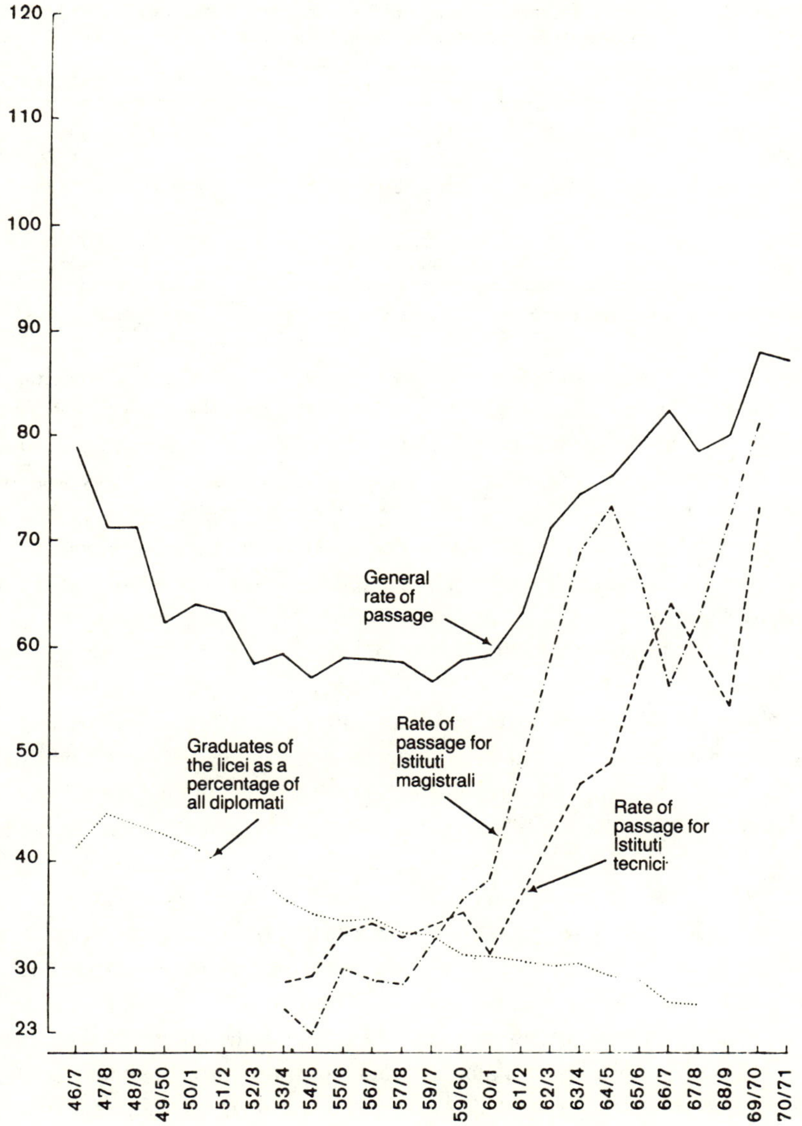

Figure 9.6. Rate of passage of diplomati to the university and graduates of the licei as a percentage of all diplomati, 1946 to 1970.

Table 9.8. University Students Enrolled in First Year and Diplomati Coming out of the Upper-Secondary Schools, 1946–47 to 1970–71

Year	*University Students*	*Diplomati*
1946–47	47,592	60,271
1950–51	39,072	61,078
1955–56	40,536	68,383
1960–61	59,708	100,165
1965–66	105,480	132,257
1970–71	193,974	220,991

SOURCE: Elaboration of data taken from ISTAT, *Annuario statistico dell'istruzione italiana.*

In reality, this type of reasoning does not seem sufficient in itself to account for the phenomena that we wish to explain here. That the rate of passage of diplomati from the istituti tecnici and magistrali is lower than that of those coming from the secondary schools, like the licei, which have always prepared for university studies, is beyond debate. But the fact remains that in the decade 1950 – 1960 the rate of passage of diplomati from the istituti tecnici and magistrali remains at a lower level compared to the immediate postwar period and to the second phase of the fascist period. The differences are very pronounced for the diplomati of the istituti tecnici. If we compare the data reported in figure 9.6 with those of table 6.14 (see chapter 6),[20] we see that the percentage of diplomati and of istituti tecnici who enroll in the university reaches 49 percent in 1930 – 31, rises directly to 75 percent in 1938 – 39, and diminishes considerably in the period of reconstruction, always remaining between 40 and 45 percent. In the decade 1950 to 1960, however, it fluctuates from 28 percent to 35 percent. Less evident, on the other hand, are the differences in the case of the rate of passage for maestri, which does, however, present values in the decade 1950 to 1960 analogous to or lower than those of the second phase of the fascist period, and much lower than those reached during the period of reconstruction.

A variable of foremost importance in explaining the course of the rate of passage to the university of diplomati from the istituti tecnici and magistrali is the course of the labor market. Despite the fact that for the entire period considered there is always a surplus of supply over demand, it can be seen that the unemployment rate of diplomati is steadily reduced in the fifteen years 1946 – 1961, after which it increases again in the following period. If we analyze, therefore, the development over time of the two variables that interest us, unemployment of diplomati and their rate of passage to the university, we can

Table 9.9. Percentage of Diplomati Who Are Children of Dependent Laborers, 1952–53 to 1969–70, by Type of Upper-Secondary School Attended

Year	*Liceo classico*	*Liceo scientifico*	*Istituto tecnico*	*Istituto magistrale*
1952–53	7.57	9.84	24.82	16.97
1953–54	7.61	10.07	25.46	16.97
1954–55	7.70	10.57	25.18	17.63
1955–56	7.36	9.64	24.73	17.99
1956–57	8.63	9.69	25.37	19.64
1957–58	9.13	9.99	26.94	21.12
1958–59	9.01	10.28	26.08	20.08
1962–63	9.98	9.74	28.84	20.98
1966–67	10.54	10.78	33.72	25.47
1969–70	11.03	10.88	33.40	27.56

SOURCE: Elaboration of data taken from ISTAT, *Annuario statistico dell'istruzione italiana* and ISTAT, *Indagini speciali sugli studenti universitari e sui diplomati di scuole medie superiori.*

readily draw the conclusion that there is a direct relationship between them. In fact the rate of passage is much higher when the difficulties of employment are very considerable (the Great Depression and the postwar reconstruction), while it decreases in the decade 1951 to 1961, when there is an improvement of the market situation for diplomati.

A second variable to consider is the social origin of diplomati. While during the fascist period, the great majority of students who succeeded in finishing the secondary schools came from the middle and upper social classes, in the postwar period there is a constant, even if slow, increase of the percentage of diplomati who are children of dependent laborers. This process of upward mobility of students from the lower social classes does not, however, concern the licei but only the istituti tecnici and magistrali (table 9.9). It is precisely the change in the social composition of the diplomati from these two schools that contributes to the lowering of their rate of passage in the fifteen years 1946–61.

Here also, however, as in the case of secondary education, variables at the economic level are not enough alone to explain the course of the phenomena that concerns us. If one wishes to explain adequately the sharp climb in the rate of passage that occurs after 1961 and the very strong expansion of higher education that takes place from that point forward, one must also take into account that important process of transformation of the educational system begun in just those years. The Law of July 21, 1961 (no. 685) opens access for the diplomati of the istituti tecnici to some university faculties: engineering, mathematics and physics, agriculture, languages, statistical and demographic sciences. It provides that for the first three years admission to these faculties take place "following special concorsi established for a number of positions determined annually by decree of the Minister of Public Education in consultation with the respective faculty councils."[21] Beginning with the academic year 1964–65, the admission of diplomati from the istituti tecnici to the faculties mentioned is no longer subject to a concorso, or in other words, to the numero chiuso. This same opening process is concluded with the Law of December 11, 1969 (no. 910) which permits diplomati from all the secondary schools to enter any university faculty. This policy of opening the university was accompanied by provisions aimed at reducing the cost of studies, and particularly by the establishment in February 1963 of the student stipend.[22]

Appendix to Chapter Nine

Following is a list of the variables used in calculating correlation coefficients (some of which were cited in the text), the sources from which these data were taken, and the correlation matrix for these variables (table 9A).

Variables Used

1. Percentage of illiterates in the population 6 years of age or over in 1961.
2. Infant deaths in the first year of life per 1,000 live births in 1961.
3. Net per capita income in 1961.
4. Per capita expenditure for subscription to RAI-TV* in 1961.
5. Per capita expenditure for tobacco in 1961.
6. Per capita expenditure for entertainment in 1961.
7. Consumption per inhabitant of electrical energy for illumination in 1961.
8. Index of motor vehicle acquisition in 1961.
9. General index of consumption in 1961.
10. Male and female enrollments in the lower-secondary school (scuola media + avviamento) in the school year 1961–62 as a percentage of male and female population 10–15 years of age in 1961.
11. Percentage of persons with the upper-secondary diploma in the resident population 6 years of age or over in 1961.
12. Percentage of persons with the laurea in the resident population 6 years of age or over in 1961.

*RAI: Radio Audizioni Italiane, or the Italian Broadcasting Company, which is state owned and operated.

13. Percentage of male entrepreneurs or liberal professionals in the employed male population in 1961.
14. Percentage of male dependent laborers in the employed male population in 1961.
15. Percentage of male dependent laborers in the primary sector in the employed male population in 1961.
16. Percentage of male employees in industry in the employed male population in 1961.
17. Number of males and females with the licenza of the lower-secondary school in search of first employment as a percentage of the active (employed + in search of first employment) population with the licenza of the lower-secondary school.
18. Number of males and females in search of first employment as a percentage of the active population in 1961.
19. Rate of passage: percentage of male and female enrollments in the first year of the upper-secondary schools (classical and scientific, technical, educational, professional, artistic) in 1961 – 62 out of male and female graduates in 1960 – 61 from the lower-secondary school (scuola media + avviamento).
20. Number of male and female enrollments in the first year of the upper-secondary school as a percentage of the population 15 – 20 years of age.
21. Number of male and female enrollments in the first year of the upper-secondary schools that give access to the university (classical and scientific, technical, educational, artistic) as a percentage of the population 15 – 20 years of age.

Sources of Data

For variables 3, 4, 5, 6, 7, 8, 9: G. Tagliacarne, "Calcolo del reddito prodotto dal settore privato e dalla pubblica amministrazione nelle provincie e regioni d'Italia nel 1961 e confronto con gli anni 1960 e 1951. Indici di alcuni consumi e del risparmio bancario," *Moneta e Credito* (September 1962), pp. 339-419.

For variables 1, 10, 11, 12, 19, 20, 21: ISTAT, *Annuario statistico dell'istruzione italiana* (Rome, 1965); ISTAT, *X Censimento generale della popolazione*, vol. 5: *Sesso, età, stato civile, luogo di nascita* (Rome, 1966).

For variables 13, 14, 15, 16, 17, 18: ISTAT, *X Censimento generale della popolazione,* vol. 7: *Istruzione* (Rome, 1968).

For variable 2: ISTAT, *Annuario di statistiche provinciali 1962* (Rome).

Table 9.A. Correlation Coefficient Matrix (on a Provincial Basis) for 21 Variables Taken into Consideration

	1	2	3	4	5	6	7	8	9	10	11	12	13	14	15	16	17	18	19	20	21
1																					
2	0.87																				
3	−0.76	−0.66																			
4	−0.86	−0.76	0.88																		
5	−0.69	−0.65	0.80	0.83																	
6	−0.65	−0.58	0.85	0.80	0.89																
7	−0.73	−0.62	0.92	0.83	0.82	0.85															
8	−0.80	−0.75	0.88	0.89	0.83	0.85	0.83														
9	−0.75	−0.67	0.88	0.88	0.88	0.92	0.91	0.89													
10	−0.45	−0.42	0.58	0.63	0.60	0.60	0.58	0.55	0.60												
11	−0.45	−0.33	0.67	0.62	0.71	0.70	0.75	0.64	0.72	0.72											
12	−0.21	−0.13	0.51	0.38	0.59	0.61	0.62	0.50	0.58	0.49	0.88										
13	−0.36	−0.18	0.60	0.54	0.60	0.61	0.64	0.55	0.62	0.40	0.70	0.72									
14	0.17	0.26	0.04	−0.07	−0.01	0.05	0.18	−0.15	0.04	−0.12	0.06	0.19	0.28								
15	0.71	0.66	−0.50	−0.61	−0.50	−0.42	−0.52	−0.57	−0.55	−0.49	−0.40	−0.12	−0.24	0.47							
16	−0.56	−0.44	0.51	0.51	0.35	0.39	0.59	0.42	0.51	0.21	0.23	0.05	0.41	0.39	−0.56						
17	0.69	0.63	−0.65	−0.64	−0.42	−0.50	−0.56	−0.63	−0.58	−0.26	−0.28	−0.10	−0.31	0.09	0.46	−0.47					
18	0.37	0.33	−0.30	−0.31	−0.01	−0.12	−0.10	−0.33	−0.17	0.01	0.13	0.26	0.02	0.34	0.23	−0.16	0.73				
19	0.56	0.43	−0.47	−0.47	−0.24	−0.23	−0.43	−0.40	−0.36	−0.12	−0.10	0.05	−0.12	0.07	0.39	−0.41	0.53	0.47			
20	−0.01	0.00	0.14	0.21	0.33	0.29	0.15	0.21	0.23	0.61	0.52	0.44	0.31	−0.08	−0.12	−0.13	0.21	0.32	0.55		
21	0.13	0.12	0.09	0.12	0.25	0.21	0.12	0.12	0.15	0.53	0.52	0.49	0.32	−0.02	−0.02	−0.17	0.29	0.42	0.51	0.90	

CHAPTER TEN

The Reforms of the 1960s

There is a reason why we must consider unsatisfactory both of the currently most widespread theses about the course of secondary and higher education over the past fifteen years – the optimistic one which explains the expansion of education with the increase of per capita income, and the pessimistic one, referring to a "parking lot school," which attributes it instead to the scarcity of employment opportunities for youth coming out of the lower- and upper-secondary schools. The reason is that neither of these two theses takes into account the characteristics of the Italian educational system itself and its changes. The analysis conducted in the preceding chapter has led us, in fact, to the conclusion that in order to explain the course of secondary and higher education we cannot rely on economic variables alone, as important as these may be, but must also bear in mind the functioning of the educational system, and particularly the transformations it underwent in the 1960s: the 1962 reform of the scuola media, due to which Italy became, among the countries of the European Economic Community, that with the most open educational system, and the process of de-professionalization of the upper-secondary schools, begun with the partial liberalization of university access in 1961 and brought to conclusion with its total opening in 1969.

Having arrived at this point, however, we must reconstruct and explain the changes undergone by the Italian educational system in the 1960s, to determine which were the most important social and political forces that fought for the transformation or the preservation of the old arrangement inherited from the fascist period, how these forces met and entered into conflict, and how the major social-structural changes that occurred in this period influenced their actions. For convenience of exposition I will examine separately the two principal changes in the educational system, treating the reform of the scuola media in the first and second parts of this chapter and the liberalization of university access in the third part.

The Reform of the Scuola Media: The Forces Arrayed and the First Phase

Even with the imprecision inevitable in every attempt at periodization, I think that three phases can be distinguished in the period preceding the establishment of the scuola media unica. The first is from 1947 to 1951, the second from 1952 to 1958, and the third from 1959 to 1962. The first is the phase of the elaboration of an "inclusive and fundamental"* program of reform of the educational system. Its protagonists are the bourgeoisie and the Christian Democratic Party, encouraged and supported by other actors: the associations of intellectuals in general and that of the elementary school teachers in particular. The proletariat and the political parties that represent it remain totally absent from the scene. The second is the phase of implementation (or rather, of the attempt at implementation) of the program elaborated in the preceding four years. Both the protagonists and the supporting actors are again the same. The former, however, have reshaped their initial ambitious program and aim now – it has been said – at "partial and gradual actualization of a silent reform, made not with laws but with circulars."[1] The proletariat and its political organizations now appear on the scene, and they effectively resist the attempt at "silent reform," finding help from the associations of secondary school teachers. The third is the phase of overthrow of the program elaborated in the four years 1947–51, and of the establishment of the media unica. The protagonists now become the political parties of the working class, which take the initiative, elaborate and present an alternative program for changing the educational system, and receive again, at least initially, important help from the association of secondary school teachers.

Among the many variables that must be taken into consideration, there are three which are most important in explaining the events that led to the reform of the scuola media. In the three phases these variables behave in the following way:

1. The position of the proletariat in class relations. The proletariat is weak in

Globale e organico.

the first phase, is further weakened in the second, and is steadily strengthened in the third.

2. The demand for education and for change in the educational system coming from the subordinate social classes. It is practically nonexistent in the first phase, it is scanty in the second, and it becomes quite strong in the third.

3. The course of the intellectual labor market. In the first phase there is a considerable excess of supply over demand for both laureati and diplomati; although reduced, this excess exists also in the second phase (stronger for diplomati than for laureati); in the third, unemployment of laureati is completely reabsorbed, while for diplomati it persists, especially in certain categories.

The Bourgeoisie and the Christian Democratic Party

The program of educational policy that guided the action of the ruling class for over a decade and that was combated at length and finally defeated at the beginning of the 1960s by the working class and its organizations was elaborated in the four-year period 1947–51 as a fundamental plan for solving the innumerable and serious problems of education. It was conceived at a moment when all the energies of the bourgeoisie were turned to reconstructing the country, reestablishing capitalist relations of production, and readapting the old sources of legitimation for social inequalities to the new situation. But it was not only a conservative program. Strongly influenced both by the fears and anxieties of the bourgeoisie over the situation of the qualified labor market and by demands made by the associations of intellectuals for Malthusian measures, it constituted in its most important part (that concerning the internal structure of the educational system) an attempt to realize what Bottai and his followers had not achieved, namely, to give full implementation to the last and most ambitious reform plan of the ruling fascist group: the Carta della Scuola. In this sense it was, therefore, a reactionary program.

As I had occasion to mention before, both during the period of reconstruction and at the beginning of the 1950s the phenomenon of intellectual unemployment was not denounced solely by the organizations of the working class. As is natural, it aroused quite considerable fear and anxiety in the ruling class which, as had happened in the Giolittian and fascist periods, saw in the imbalance between school and labor market a dangerous source of political instability, a stimulus to the radicalization of the ceti intellettuali and to their alliance with the proletariat. In a speech given over the radio, Minister of Public Education Gonella warned that "the intellectual classes, which once belonged to the small and middle bourgeoisie and which today are more proletarian than the proletariat itself" were no less dangerous than the others. For if it was improbable that the unemployed intellectuals would present themselves "at the barred gates of the Viminale* armed with submachine guns and gnarled clubs," they constituted no less of a threat to the existing order: "The social order can be crushed not only by the revolutionary agitation of the masses, but also by the slow corrosion and the consequent landslide of those forces of moral vitality which are, precisely, the intellectual classes. For a descent into chaos, insurrectional activity by the intellectuals is not necessary – activity moreover that is inconceivable given the education of their character. It is enough that their vitality (which is the vitality of the ruling classes) crumbles for society to plunge into disorder and for every possibility of renewal to vanish."[2]

In actuality there was no lack of attempts, in this period also, to reduce the surplus of intellectual labor through the safety valve of emigration. The question of exporting excess intellectuals was again placed on the agenda of the works undertaken by the Ministry for the Constituent[3] and at the Conference on Problems of Social Assistance held at Tremezzo in 1946. The professional orders, moreover, fought for this solution for many years, particularly that of the doctors, which, in the international arena, supported this line within the World Medical Association, declaring that Italy was in a position to export "some thousands of doctors a year."[4] But the results of these efforts were less than modest. It is true that in the two agreements on emigration contracted between Italy and Argentina in 1947 and 1948, an article was inserted which provided for the departure from Italy of laureati and diplomati, and that in those same years the Italian-American Center for Medical Sciences was created, which undertook to encourage the emigration of young doctors. Nevertheless, the stiffening of legislation of non-European countries on the practice of liberal professions blocked the growth of Italy's migratory flow.[5]

What, then, should be done? In answering this question the professional organizations of intellectuals had no doubts. Reconstituted in the immediate postwar period, they had changed their names but certainly not their political line, and they argued, therefore, that it was necessary to revise the mechanisms that regulated the supply of qualified labor. Already from the inquiry conducted

*Government building in Rome housing ministerial and administrative offices.

by the Ministry of the Constituent it followed clearly that the associations of intellectuals were in complete agreement on the necessity of a Malthusian policy, and they differed among themselves only on the greater or lesser necessity of the measures proposed, which ran from the numero chiuso for access to the university up to the "closing of the faculties of law and of economics for ten years."[6] In the following years as well, they remained substantially faithful to this line. The *Federazione medica,* for example, wrote in its unmistakable style:

> How many colleagues must die prematurely (*quod Deus avertat*) so that in six years' time the enormous excess of doctors – which will be absorbed only in small part by emigration, closed or very limited by now in almost all Western countries – will be able to find normal conditions of professional livelihood?[7]

Within the association of doctors, which was also in those years one of the most active, there were those, in fact, who argued that the evil to combat was not so much "the inflation of doctors" as "the deflation of patients," and who proposed, therefore, to invest all the energies of the association in the struggle to increase demand by halting, first of all, the spread of the medical insurance companies.[8] But for the most part the real solution was sought in reduction of the flow of laureati by introduction of the numero chiuso.[9] The thesis that the only way of escape consisted in revising mechanisms regulating the supply of qualified labor, and therefore in a transformation of the educational system, was immediately embraced by the ruling class. This latter, nevertheless, spent a relatively long time in arriving at the formulation of an articulated plan of fundamental change which confronted all the problems of education from the elementary schools to the university. The process of elaborating the program of educational policy of the bourgeoisie lasted in fact almost four years, from April 17, 1947, the day on which the National Commission of Inquiry for the Reform of the School was established, to July 13, 1951, when Gonella presented to the Chamber of Deputies the bill of law Regulations on Education.

The operation of the National Commission of Inquiry lasted until April 30, 1949. It proceeded in various directions: it became the organizer of several meetings, and it edited sixteen issues of the review *La riforma della scuola;* it prepared a questionnaire with over two hundred questions concerning practically every aspect of Italian education, which was sent to educational personnel at the various levels from maestri to university rectors;[10] it organized the inspection, availing itself of the collaboration of a Special Commission for

Verification, of a large number of schools in order to gather information on their "spiritual and material" conditions. Beginning with the conclusions of the National Commission, Minister of Public Education Gonella laid out a provisional scheme of general reform of the school which in August 1949 became the working document of a new ministerial commission. On the basis of the report presented by this commission in January 1950 and of the judgment expressed subsequently by the Consiglio Superiore della Pubblica Istruzione, Gonella formulated the definitive version of the reform program, which was then presented to Parliament in 1951.[11]

The section of the questionnaire sent by the National Commission of Inquiry that concerned higher education contained three questions on the problem of "university overcrowding" and on measures for combating it. The 154 faculty councils that answered this questionnaire unanimously acknowledged the existence of an excessive number of university students relative to the possiblity of absorption into the market, and maintained that one of the most important causes of this imbalance was the fact that the laurea was required even for "modest functions."[12]

For the "overcrowding of the universities" the questionnaire envisaged six different measures: examinations for admission to the university, the numero chiuso, written exams in addition to orals, periodic obstacles over the course of studies, controls over attendance, and increased fees. The majority of faculty councils and associations of professors and assistants that responded to the questionnaire declared themselves against the admission examination and the numero chiuso (but "above all because of technical difficulties") and in favor of the other four provisions. Even more important, the majority of faculty councils appeared to share the opinion expressed three years earlier by the rector of the University of Florence ("the problem of the universities will be resolved first of all in the secondary schools"),[13] and proposed a "greater selective activity by the secondary schools" as the most effective measure for "uncrowding" the institutions of higher education.

The Italian ruling class took these and other valuable indications into account in the elaboration of the program of educational policy. At the level of higher education, having discarded the solution of the numero chiuso, which appeared impracticable,[14] it aimed at other measures. Two Christian Democratic deputies – Maria Pia dal Canton in 1949, and Ermini in the following year (together with the Communist Concetto Marchesi) – presented two different bills to increase university fees, the second of which was approved.[15] In addition, in order to "uncrowd" the universities, the Gonella bill introduced the distinction between the *diploma dottorale,* obtainable upon finishing any faculty, and the *laurea scientifica* which was instead to be obtained after the laurea in the schools of specialization, hoping thereby to restore to the laurea "its original scientific value, quite distinct from the value of simple professional titles."[16]

It was, however, at the lower-secondary level that the introduction of the biggest changes was sought. At this level, the Gonella bill provided for three different types of school: first, the *secondaria classica,* with Latin instruction, the only one that would allow access to all types of upper-secondary instruction and hence to the university; second, the *secondaria tecnica,* without Latin, which as far as outlets were concerned had a "bivalent" character, "inasmuch as it oriented, by means of different subjects, toward the technical institutes on the one hand and the professional institutes on the other"; third, the *secondaria normale,* which was "normally to complete" the elementary education of that majority of youth who, as Gonella said in a curious expression, had "a prevalent interest in setting off to work rather than to studies." It gave access to no type of upper-secondary instruction, but only to the professional institutes and, moreover, was to be instituted in the sites of elementary schools and to have a teaching body recruited from the maestri.

In order to "uncrowd" the university, overcome the imbalance between school and labor market, and defeat intellectual unemployment, it was sought, therefore, to transform the internal structure of the educational system at the lower-secondary level according to a model quite similar to Bottai's. Certainly, times were much changed, the ruling class had to reckon with strong opposition, and Gonella could not declare explicitly, with the same candor and security of Bottai, what the objectives of the "new" program of change of the educational system were. He had instead to seek to disguise these objectives behind a terminology of the Left, affirming, for example, that he wished to overcome "every class prejudice in the educational arrangement of the young."

This was certainly not enough, however, to obfuscate the substantial continuity between the "new" plan and the fascist Carta della Scuola.[17] In reality the Gonella plan, like Bottai's, was based entirely on the presupposition that to reduce the flow of students entering the universities it was not sufficient to render studies more severe, to increase the number of failings, to exacerbate the selectivity of existing schools, but rather to change the internal structure of the educational system at its most delicate point, in the passage from the elementary to the lower-secondary school. It was for this reason, and not simply to render his bill more acceptable to the opposition, that Gonella affirmed that in order to resolve the problem of "overcrowding" the educational order had "to be predisposed not in a way to make entrance difficult for the young who knocked at the door of the school, but in a way to direct them adequately." "The evil," he observed, "is not in the abundance of the waters that flow through the canal of the school, but, on the contrary, in the unsuitable channeling of these waters."

It is clear enough how it was sought to channel the waters. The fascist regime had left two schools at the lower-secondary level: the scuola media which came to be called "unica," but which precisely was not unified, and the avviamento. According to the Gonella bill, from the scuola media there had to arise two different schools, the secondaria classica and the tecnica, in such a way as to favor a movement into the latter "of those students who currently are directed into the scuola media for the sole purpose of being able to enter the higher schools." Nevertheless, the most important change consisted in the establishment of the secondaria normale, which Gonella himself defined as "one of the principal novelties of the reform." It was undoubtedly a "novelty" of great importance compared to the existing educational arrangement, but certainly not compared to the Carta della Scuola. Because of its close connection with the elementary schools, the type of teaching personnel that it was to employ, and the absolute absence of outlets into other secondary schools, the normale was none other than a faithful copy of the scuola artigiana that Bottai had not succeeded in realizing.[18] From this fascist school and from Gentile's complementare it preserved the basic function: that of serving as a dumping school, of having the large majority of youth 11–14 years of age pass through the political socialization of the new regime without allowing them to continue their studies.

> In society [Gonella had said to the Chamber of Deputies] there must be officials and soldiers: not all officials and not all soldiers. The problem of the ruling class is how to choose the officials. The system of closed castes declares that the officials are only the sons of the officials. The democratic system, on the other hand, affirms that the officials are chosen also from the soldiers and the sons of soldiers.[19]

But in reality, frightened by the excessive number of officials and by the fear that some of these might ally themselves with the soldiers, and unable on the other hand to remove the basic causes of the imbalance between school and labor market, the ruling class once again deluded itself with finding a solution in the revision of mechanisms that regulated the supply of qualified labor, and ended up designing an educational system which, if it had been implemented, would have rendered the barriers that divided the various social classes even more rigid and impenetrable.

The Working Class and the Communist Party

The principal agent of transformation of the Italian educational system was without doubt the workers' movement. However, several years had to pass before it put in motion that process which was to lead to the establishment of the media unica. After having forcefully put forward the objective of the reform of this school in that brief period of collective enthusiasm which went from 1945 to 1947, the workers' movement lost much of its initial interest in the problems of education. Only in 1955 did it begin again to invest its energies in this area, and it was not until 1958–59 that it elaborated and presented a plan of fundamental reform.

Spokesmen of the state of collective effervescence that characterized the first years of the postwar period, carriers of the egalitarian values and orientations widespread among broad sectors of society, enriched by the Gramscian theoretical legacy, the Communist and Socialist parties (PCI and PSIUP) immediately put the structure of the Italian educational system back into question. Criticizing its classist character, its tendency to perpetuate and to crystallize social differences in "oriental forms,"* the workers' parties arrayed themselves against the bifurcation of the educational system, and for the establishment of a scuola media unica.[20] "We do not want right from the start a school of craftsmen," Concetto Marchesi had written, reechoing Gramsci, "we want a school that permits one person to remain a worker and another to rise higher to become the master."[21] And the Socialist Party expressed itself in favor of an elementary school of four years followed by a compulsory one of three years – a "people's school."[22]

This situation lasted only a short time, however. Beginning in 1945, just as the governing political class sought feverishly to disinter and resuscitate a model of the educational system elaborated by Bottai, there was a sudden "dimming of interest" on the part of the Communist Party in problems of education, which would last for as long as seven years. During these years it resurfaced "from time to time, but unsteadily," and above all without ever acquiring "importance as a general political problem." On the other hand, even

**Forme cinese:* that is, tending to perpetuate rigid, caste-like divisions between social classes.

in the brief moments of revival, the problem of the school was confronted only with "uncertainty and timidity."[23] Thus the party press devoted increasingly less care and less space to educational questions. To give only one example, the first article commenting on the Gonella bill was published by the Party's daily, *L'Unità,* two months after it was presented to the Chamber of Deputies, and even then it was not much more than an invitation to confront "the debate with breadth and seriousness, as is our custom."[24] Thus while Communist representatives performed an activity of denunciation, often even quite effective, of the government's educational policy, they took few initiatives, elaborated and presented few bills of law and, of whatever sort, none of them for the reform of the scuola media.

The shift of these years can be explained on the one hand by factors "internal" to the PCI – to its general policy, to the cultural training and to attitudes of its ruling group, and on the other, and especially, by "external" factors, that is, by the structural conditions of Italian society in that period. It is on the former, naturally, that the attention of the Communists was concentrated when they committed themselves to a serious self-critiscism and posed the question of "why this happened." According to Alicata there were three answers to this question. First, there had been "an element of uncertainty derived from that general uncertainty indicated by Togliatti when he said that often we are unable to see how our struggle for unity with the Catholic world can be reconciled itself with the otherwise firm and decisive struggle which we must conduct against the clericalization of the Italian State."[25] Second, the activity of the party had been curbed by its internal conflicts over one of the most important questions for the reform of the scuola media: that of Latin. While, in fact, there were some Communist leaders, such as Antonio Banfi, who favored the abolition of the teaching of this subject in the scuola media, there were others, such as Concetto Marchesi, of a completely different opinion.[26] Third, observed Alicata, the attitude of the PCI toward the problem of education had been no more "than an aspect of that more general phenomenon which occurred from 1947 onward, namely a certain vacillation in the way in which we have posed the problem of structural reforms in our country."[27]

Even more important were two "external" factors , two structural conditions of Italian society at that time. The first was the absence of a demand for change of the educational system on the part of the subordinate social classes, which made it such that, once the collective enthusiasms cooled and the egalitarian aspirations of the immediate postwar period weakened, every push from the base of the party to elaborate a fundamental reform plan vanished. Not that a demand for instruction was absent in these classes; it was probably there, at least to a reduced extent, even in those years. But the objective conditions were such as to prevent its being translated into a demand for change of the educational system. Even the elementary school was still absent in some Italian comuni and, where present, it was strongly selective. As far as the lower-secondary school was concerned, some years had to pass before its dualistic structure objectively became, and was in fact considered by the relevant leaders to be, the principal obstacle to the expansion of education. The few youths from the subordinate social classes who were able to continue their studies entered immediately by the "right" channel and enrolled in the media "unica" (table 10.1). For others, those who attended the avviamento, the much more serious obstacles, of an economic-financial character, to the continuation of studies were far more decisive than the limitations and restraints caused by the educational order itself.

The results of the inquiry conducted by the Gonella Commission confirmed that the situation was not much different from that just described. Almost three-quarters of those who responded to the questionnaire declared themselves in favor a bi- or tripartite educational system, and only the remaining 25 percent supported the scuola media unica.[28] It can be fairly objected that in this survey's sample the intermediate social strata, and particularly the teachers, were over-represented. But another survey conducted in those years on a more representative sample of the Italian population gave rather similar results (table 10.2). The parents who favored the media unica were not only less than a third, but (contrary to what might be expected) the percentage of subjects who demanded this type of school did not increase as one passed from the higher to the lower social classes. Among these latter was, on the contrary, a widespread state of confusion and bewilderment that was both cause and effect of the "uncertainty" and the "timidity" of the educational policy of the workers' parties.

The second "external" factor, on the other hand, probably had to do with the condition of the intellectual labor market. Taking up, at least in part, a hypothesis advanced by Alessandro Natta, it can be said that if the PCI assumed a distrustful and passive attitude concerning the problem of the media unica over the four-year period in which the bourgeoisie sought to draft its program of educational policy; if it was "cautious in considering some general plan of renewal fo the school" even after 1951, that is, "at the moment when a resumption of the idea of a democratic reform became possible and necessary

Table 10.1. Composition of Enrollments in the Media "Unica" and the Avviamento by Father's Occupation in the School Year 1947–48

Father's Occupation	*Media "Unica"*	*Avviamento*	*Total*
Workers, wage earners, day laborers	14.8	39.9	27.6
State workers	12.4	9.3	10.8
Artisans and small shopkeepers	22.8	27.3	25.1
Employees of private firms	13.2	7.5	10.3
Impiegati (categories A and B)	10.2	1.4	5.8
Liberal professionals and teachers	9.2	1.6	5.3
Proprietors, entrepreneurs, and businessmen	7.5	2.2	4.8
Wealthy and those living on interest	0.5	0.1	0.3
Pensioners	9.4	10.7	10.0
Total	100.0	100.0	100.0
(N)	(46,895)	(48,591)	(95,486)

SOURCE: T. Salvemini, "Condizioni sociali e rendimento degli alunni," in National Commission of Inquiry for the Reform of the School, ed., *Le conclusioni dell'inchiesta*, p. 222.

Table 10.2. Attitude of Parents Toward the Scuola Media Unica, According to Social Class Standing, 1949

Attitude Toward the Scuola Media Unica	*Social Class Standing*				*Total*
	Upper Middle	*Middle*	*Lower Middle*	*Lower*	
Favorable	31.1	31.3	25.2	27.4	29.3
Against	56.0	58.6	44.2	33.9	53.0
Indifferent	7.3	4.8	12.4	12.9	7.8
No response	5.6	5.3	18.2	25.8	9.9
Total	100.0	100.0	100.0	100.0	100.0

Note: This survey was conducted on a sample of 2,204 persons.

SOURCE: DOXA, *La scuola media e i genitori* (Milan, 1949).

following the failure of enaction of the Gonella plan";[29] this was also due to the anxieties of the Communist leaders over the growing imbalance between school and labor market. It was, in fact, in the search for a solution to this problem, which appeared then to be the most important and urgent, that a large part of the already scarce energies that the Communists invested in the area of educational policy were directed.

The Communist leaders did not limit themselves, in fact, to analyzing and denouncing the situation, but were among the first to propose concrete measures for at least keeping it under control. "It is necessary to half open, not to throw open, the doors of the university," wrote Concetto Marchesi as early as 1945. And he added: "Immediately and by legislative means it would be fitting to make way for some initial provisions to prevent the university from continuing to be the vestibule of a placement office and to assure that the university diploma may be a document of certain knowledge."[30] To overcome the imbalance between school and labor market was not, therefore, a matter of increasing demand so much as of reducing supply, and thus of limiting the educational population at the secondary and higher levels. Lucio Lombardo Radice pointed this out even more clearly: "The development of the school, of that fomenter of the inept and the misfit, is becoming a national calamity: it is necessary to fight it, to check it, and not to encourage it."[31] Every contrary push, every struggle to defend within the nation those secondary schools that led to the university and to have a growing number of youth enter it, was absurd and dangerous.

> To hear the problem posed seriously, [continued Lombardo Radice] of "how to proceed so that all the classes, even the poorest, can acquire a humanistic education" – as one often does hear, spoken in good faith and with the best intentions – is frightening to one who knows well the evils of the Italian school. Because it means, in substance, *with the school as it is today,* to propose to increase enormously the misfits and parasites, that old plague of Italian life. In Italy it is not only necessary to *open* schools, nor only to open the existing schools to young workers. In Italy many schools must be *closed,* and the way of the school must be closed ruthlessly to many aspirants to qualifications.[32]

Many Communist leaders, and especially the most authoritative, Concetto Marchesi, remained faithful to this line for many years.[33] Indeed, as the number of laureati put onto the labor market increased and intellectual unemployment was aggravated, the attention of the Communists shifted increasingly from the scuola media to the university, and while the reform of the former passed into second place, the reduction of the latter's population became increasingly urgent in their view. In the report on the problems of education presented for his party to the Constituent Assembly, Concetto Marchesi supported the necessity of a "salutary selection" at the close of compulsory schooling. "To select," he observed, "does not mean to build a crowd of outcasts and humiliated, but to disperse the crowd of the misfits, who are becoming increasingly alarming."[34] And the following year, taking a position against the increase of university fees, the Communist students affirmed: "We are in agreement that it is necessary to reduce the number of students, but we shall fight in order that the uncrowding of the university will happen by means of the moralization of studies, in such a way that with greater seriousness and severity the right to accede to the sources of knowledge will be safeguarded for all."[35]

Thus also the legislative provisions that the Communists discussed and the immediate measures that they proposed did not concern the reform of the scuola media, but were directed at reducing the university population. But what, concretely, were these measures? Not the increase of university fees. It is true that, worried about the "growing surge of students destined to end up in the immense plague of unemployment," and convinced that "the meagerness of university fees" was "a pernicious trap for small bourgeois and even proletarian families deceived by the facile illusion of a diploma or a laurea for sons for whom study is a useless torment or a foolish waste of time,"[36] Concetto Marchesi together with the Christian Democrat Ermini presented a bill for increasing fees. But it is also true that the PCI, though tolerating the embarrassing sortie of its prestigious leader,[37] took a position decisively against this bill.[38]

The first measure proposed by the Communists was instead the state examination, "that severe pass-permit which, because it is severe, is humane."[39] They had, naturally, to be "serious exams, very serious, rigorous, very rigorous," said Silipo to the Chamber.[40] And above all they had to take place not only at the end of studies, but also in the passage from one level to another, in such a way as to be really "a timely instrument of selection, because selection at an advanced point is reduced to a summary and cruel execution of human energies."[41] The second measure was to reduce, on the one hand, the number of scuole classiche, which were to be "few and good,"[42] just as the idealists had requested in their day, and to increase, on the other hand, the number of istituti tecnici and professionali, without which, said Marchesi, "primary education will have no outlet and the obesity of the university will have no cure."[43] "The misfits of the universities will find there, in the technical and professional school, their just place."[44]

This does not mean that the educational policy of the Communists, like that of the governing political class, also derived from the program of the idealists.[45] It is true that Concetto Marchesi expressed a positive opinion on the "saving work of selection" of the Gentile Law; [46] it is true that the Communists sought to respond to intellectual unemployment with measures that might reduce supply and therefore the educational population; and it is true that those state exams that they proposed to resume and to make as severe as possible had represented in their day a key point of the idealists' program and in fact had been introduced by them into the Italian Legislature in 1923. Nevertheless, between the educational model that the Communists more or less, in a still uncertain, confused, and contradictory manner, succeeded at least in outlining, and that which had first inspired the idealists and which now guided the action of the governing political class, there was nothing in common.

The model of the educational system elaborated with difficulty in those years by the Communists was relatively open and rigidly meritocratic. In contrast to that conceived by the governing political class, it provided for both a single school for students up to 14 years of age and a certain liberalization of access to university faculties. Selection was to have taken place, only after the common foundation, in the upper-secondary schools, and on the basis of rigorous criteria of "merit." In order to "reinvigorate the intellectual trunk of the ruling class which by now has become so feeble,"[47] it was necessary simultaneously to reduce the number of university students and to increase the percentage of those coming from the subordinate social classes. "It is time that the courtyards of the universities," wrote Marchesi, "without further swarms of idle and clamorous wanderers, feel the steps of those still ignored: of the most deserving children of the working people."[48] "To half open the doors of the universities" meant therefore to render them accessible only to the capable and to the deserving, even if deprived of means – to the "few disposed by nature to the higher studies," whatever their social origin. To the others, to the "misfits," to those who had "nothing any longer to bring to the productivity of the social machine except agitation," it was necessary, on the other hand, to block the way. "We want no citizen to be in the wrong place. If the son of a peasant, of a worker, of a small bourgeois is not able to undertake the great risks to his

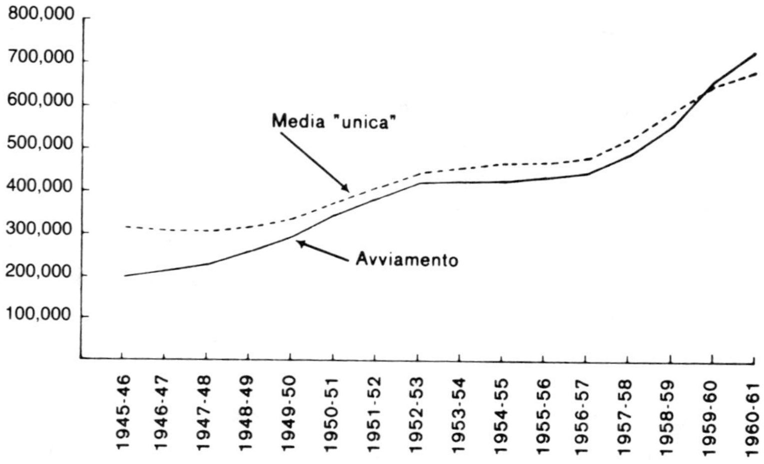

Figure 10.1. Enrollments in the scuola media "unica" and the avviamento, 1945 to 1960.

livelihood, then he can stay at home and give nobly and usefully of those fruits which his natural faculties allow him."[49]

This model and the political line on which it was based were revised in the following years, as soon as the structural conditions of Italian society began to change. The slow improvement of the economic situation, the growth of primary education, and above all the tendency of the avviamento to expand at a pace more rapid than the media "unica" (figure 10.1) produced an initial demand, even if probably modest, for change of the educational system. On the other hand, the reduction of the yield of laureati and the increased demand for qualified personnel made the phenomenon of intellectual unemployment less serious and dramatic. Thus, pushed by these transformations and by certain important events in the school system – a long teachers' strike, the attempt by the governing political class to begin implementation of the program it had formulated – the PCI in 1955 confronted the problems of education in a new and different way. It organized in May a conference of studies at the Gramsci Institute, began publication of an important specialized review, *Riforma della scuola,* and dedicated a part of the central committee meeting of November 28–30 to these problems, opening with a report by Mario Alicata.[50]

At the center of his rich, articulated and courageous report, Mario Alicata placed the Communist Party and the Italian school, analyzed them, sought to reconstruct the history of their past relationships, and made proposals for the future. Alternating challenging observations with quotations from Togliatti, Alicata criticized the scant interest of the Communists in the problems of education, tried to identify the reasons for it and to illuminate the consequences. Speaking of the latter, he noted that the PCI had definitely had no presence among the elementary teachers, and had been very weak as well among the secondary teachers, given that in the latest elections to the Consiglio Superiore della Pubblica Istruzione the lists of the left had obtained only 16 percent of the votes, "with cases that I do not hesitate to call scandalous, such as the case of Genoa where we obtained hardly thirteen votes among the secondary teachers and that of Florence where we received only six of them!" Thus, insisting on these eloquent facts, appealing to the Constitution, patiently disentangling the strands that linked education to the economy, education to politics, education to the class struggle, Alicata relaunched the Party's activity and pledged himself in the name of the ruling group to confront "with greater energy and greater continuity the problem of the Italian school."[51]

The debates at the Gramsci Institute and those of the central committee resulted, however, in more than a realization of the need for a greater commitment to the problems of the school. There also emerged another change of line: the tendency to bring the attention of the party back from the university to the scuola media. Reduction of the university population was no longer spoken of. "The general protest against the excessive 'overcrowding' of the schools and the universities" was, on the contrary, classified among the conservative positions. That there was intellectual unemployment in Italy was not denied, but no longer were the causes of this phenomenon sought in the school, in its functioning, in the lack of severe and rigorous mechanisms of control and selection. "As if in Italy," Alicata observed, "there were too many students and not too few...and as if intellectual unemployment depended on an excessive and mysterious psychological tendency toward study and state employment, rather than being the fruit, just as is the unemployment of workers and peasants, of the backward economic structures of the country!"[52]

At the center of attention was placed the lower-secondary school, considered "the key-point, the link of the chain to be pulled in order to then put all the rest in motion."[53] And, in fact, the first concrete reform program proposed by the Communists concerned precisely this school. "Leaving aside for the moment the question of whether at a later time a definitive unification must be achieved," the Communists aimed meanwhile at "bringing nearer" the media "unica" and the avviamento by means of the following measures: the abolition of Latin instruction and the introduction of work and of the natural sciences into the media "unica," the reduction of professional material in the avviamento, and the realization of a common nucleus of teaching material shared by both schools. It was, therefore, a rather moderate reform program, especially if compared with the ideas and the proposals of 1945. This time, however, it did not arise from a new and ephemeral surge of collective enthusiasm, but was the fruit of profound structural changes scarcely begun in Italian society, and with these pari passu it would grow, becoming more mature and radical.

The Maestri and the AIMC

The most important although not the only actors in the struggle to transform the lower-secondary school were without doubt the bourgeoisie and the proletariat, and the political parties that assembled, articulated, and transmitted the demands coming from these social classes. Along with them, however, worked another social force that played a lesser but not negligible role: the maestri of the elementary schools. In contrast to what might have been expected on the basis of a superficial analysis of the situation, the maestri did not exert the weight of their numerical and organizational strength on behalf of the proletariat. Despite the fact that within that composite and stratified entity that was (and is) the class of intellectuals, the maestri were closer, or perhaps, less distant from the proletariat by way of social origin, difficulty of employment, and level of income and prestige, they fought at length and resolutely against precisely the type of school demanded by the working class and its organizations. Two factors influenced this, at first glance, "inexplicable" behavior of the maestri: the condition of the intellectual labor market on the one hand, and their training and general political orientation on the other.

The most important factor was without doubt the condition of the intellectual labor market. As was seen previously, the maestri had greater difficulty of employment than did all the other categories of diplomati and laureati. Already dramatic during the reconstruction period, their situation was aggravated even in the following period, and it was toward the middle of the 1950s that the imbalance between demand and supply reached its highest points. This being so, it is evident that unemployment became for the elementary teachers' organizations the key problem to be reckoned with and the starting point for every union program and every line of educational policy. Moreover, to give an idea of how dramatic their situation was and how desperate their attempt to find a way out, it suffices to say that in the debate in the professional journals over ways to defeat unemployment there was even a proposal to expel married female teachers.[54]

Nevertheless, in contrast with earlier times, the elementary teachers' organizations did not aim at a Malthusian line of educational policy. In reality, this line, supported by the maestri immediately following the First World War and implemented by the Gentile Reform, was taken up again and recommended in the period of reconstruction by authoritative lay reviews.[55] But its diffusion and affirmation were impeded by two new and important facts: that the great majority of istituti magistrali were Church-affiliated and that the strongest organization of maestri was Catholic.

The maestri and their organizations instead used their strength to pressure more in the direction of an increase in demand than of a reduction of supply. Therefore, in contrast to the other categories of intellectuals, they fought, at least at the level of compulsory schooling, not for reduction but for expansion of the educational population.[56] They demanded the halving of elementary school classes with over thirty students, the establishment of the fourth and fifth years of elementary schooling where these still had not been instituted, and the creation of special schools for combating illiteracy.[57]

Quite soon, however, their efforts on behalf of a sizable increase in demand were extended to a much more promising area of the educational system: the lower-secondary school. At the beginning of the 1950s there were in fact at this level more than a million and a half youngsters not attending, despite the fact that the Constitution had reaffirmed compulsory schooling up to the age of fourteen. It was here, therefore, that the greater prospects for the development of education, and consequently for the expansion of teacher employment, could be opened.

But in order to radically combat the unemployment of maestri it was necessary to enter the "post-elementary" (as the maestri described it) or "secondary" level (as the teachers of the lower-secondary preferred to call it), and to enter this level, the elementary school teachers had to reckon with those of the lower-secondary. This area, in fact, had always been the "preserve" of the latter, and the two existing schools, the media "unica" and the avviamento, had laureati as teachers. The idea of questioning this traditional sectoral division between diplomati and laureati completely, aiming at the appropriation of the entire level of 11- to 14-year-olds, was indulged in for some time by the organizations of the maestri, but was quite soon revealed as less than realistic. Consequently, the only possible solution, the only way to legitimate at least the entry of the maestri at this level seemed to be that of "inventing" a new type of school that was closer in all respects to the elementary than to the secondary schools: first, in terms of the lack of outlets into other secondary schools, but also in terms of calendar, hours, programs, methods of teaching, and even location and teaching apparatus, and therefore the teaching body. But, quite obviously, this type of school did not need to be invented, for it was already provided for in the Carta of Bottai, and was called the scuola artigiana.

The second factor that we must take into account in order to explain the attitude of the maestri concerning reform of the lower-secondary school is their general political orientation. Even if it is difficult, in the absence of specific research, to identify the reasons,[58] it is certain that beginning with the second postwar period the great majority of maestri had a general political orientation that could be described as Catholic-conservative. This certainly influenced their attitude toward the democratization of the school, even if to a lesser extent than did the situation of the labor market. The attitude of the maestri of the "lay Left," which was equally hostile to the establishment of the media unica, and the much more favorable one of the teachers of the Catholic Union of Italian Secondary School Teachers (UCIIM), clearly shows in fact that if the elementary teachers were inspired in their activity by the educational model elaborated by Bottai, it was not only because among them there were many Catholic-conservatives, but above all because there were many who were unemployed. The general political orientation of the maestri was perhaps even more important in another sense, that is, because it made possible the birth and development of the most powerful pressure group that worked in the area of education policy up to 1960: the Italian Association of Catholic Elementary School Teachers (AIMC).

There were three organizations founded by the Catholic elementary teachers in the immediate postwar period: the Movimento Maestri, which performed a primarily religious activity, the Elementary School Union (SINASCEL), which worked exclusively on union problems, and finally the AIMC, the only one that committed itself directly to the area of educational policy, exerting a strong influence over the Christian Democratic Party.

It is not difficult to understand the reasons for this influence. The assertion made several times by the leaders of this association that they were faithful interpreters "of the feelings and the will of the great majority of Italian

Table 10.3. Maestri Enrolled in the AIMC and Maestri Employed, 1946 to 1968

Year	*Maestri Enrolled in AIMC*	*Total Maestri Employed*	*% Enrolled in AIMC*
1946	20,316	144,814	14.03
1948	41,614	165,399	25.16
1950	54,671	169,513	32.25
1953	53,335	176,845	30.16
1954	50,007	178,591	28.01
1956	58,616	183,628	31.92
1957	59,570	189,363	31.46
1958	62,369	191,796	32.52
1959	65,392	197,146	33.17
1960	62,121	199,907	31.07
1961	59,773	201,286	29,70
1962	63,030	204,633	30.80
1963	62,666	205,451	30.50
1964	59,394	205,879	28.85
1965	64,429	207,151	31.10
1968	64,848	213,337	30.00

SOURCE: Elaboration of data taken from: AIMC, *L'Associazione Italiana Maestri Cattolici: 1945–56* (Rome, n.d.); AIMC, *L'Associazione Italiana Maestri Cattolici dal 5° Congresso Nazionale (1956) al 6° Congresso Nazionale (1959)* (Rome, n.d.); AIMC, *L'Associazione Italiana Maestri Cattolici dal 6° al 7° Congresso Nazionale (1959–1962)* (Rome, n.d.); AIMC, *L'Associazione Italiana Maestri Cattolici dal 7° all'8° Congresso Nazionale (1962–1965)* (Rome, n.d.); AIMC, *L'Associazione Italiana Maestri Cattolici dal 1965 al 1968* (Rome, n.d.); ISTAT, *Annuario statistico dell'istruzione italiana.*

maestri''[59] was true, on the whole. After its difficult beginning in the postwar period, the AIMC considerably extended its following, succeeding in assembling among its ranks almost a third of the elementary teachers (table 10.3). In fact, if we consider the votes gathered in elections for the third (elementary school) section of the Consiglio Superiore della Pubblica Istruzione, we see that this association succeeded in representing almost three-quarters of Italian *maestri* (table 10.4). It is therefore no exaggeration to suppose that, directly or indirectly, the AIMC controlled an electoral area of some hundreds of thousands of votes, and that it was in a position to direct them toward the Christian Democratic Party.[60] Indeed, from the elections of 1953 onward, this organization presented its candidates in the lists of the majority party, and thus had a small number of representatives in Parliament.[61] Moreover, the relationship between these two organizations at the local level was quite solid, since in those years thousands of Christian Democratic cadres came from the AIMC.[62]

Of this power to influence the Christian Democrats and the government the

Table 10.4. Votes Obtained by the AIMC-SINASCEL in Elections to Section 3 of the Consiglio Superiore della Pubblica Istruzione, 1948 to 1970

Year	*Total Votes*	*Votes AIMC-SINASCEL*	*% of Votes AIMC-SINASCEL*
1948	86,959	67,013	77.06
1951	104,637	79,672	76.14
1954	136,353	104,905	76.94
1958	159,832	118,062	73.86
1962	164,058	106,729	65.06
1966	178,419	122,928	68.90
1970	200,735	133,719	66.62

SOURCE: Elaboration of data taken from the volumes cited in table 10.3, and from "I candidati per le elezioni di secondo grado della terza sezione del Consiglio Superiore della Pubblica Istruzione," in *Il maestro,* May 27, 1970.

AIMC availed itself above all to produce an increase in the demand for elementary teachers. It obtained a first success in 1947 with the institution in a number of locations of "neighborhood schools," which not only absorbed several thousand unemployed maestri, but were in fact entrusted to the management of the AIMC itself, which took advantage of them to further expand its following.[63] It achieved a second important success in 1953, when Parliament approved an agenda presented by its four deputies which provided for a four-year plan for the establishment of fourth and fifth elementary school classes in all Italian comuni.[64]

Above all, however, the AIMC aimed at a transformation of the educational system at the lower-secondary level. After having argued initially, as a "maximum program," that the entire lower-secondary level should be entrusted to the maestri, it retreated to the thesis of the *post-elementare,* a new "school of the people," which was to be placed beside the media "unica" and the avviamento.[65] According to the ideology elaborated diligently by the AIMC from 1946 to 1951 and widely diffused in debates and meetings,[66] the scuola post-elementare presented many positive aspects. Employing the sites and the resources of existing elementary schools, it could be spread along that network; recruiting maestri as teachers, the true "educators of the people," the only ones prepared "to live even in the small villages,"[67] it would more easily adapt to the needs of the lower social classes and to the various surrounding conditions; finally, by training for work,[68] transmitting not "an education that prepares only for further education, but a spiritual and moral training which is in a certain sense an end in itself,"[69] and rendering it impossible in practice to pursue secondary studies, it would accustom students to accept their future social position with resignation. Combating the thesis of the scuola media unica, which he described as "a misconception and a utopia," the president of the AIMC wrote:

> The equality of human beings and of their rights does not make them a...single set, of a single stamp. To the contrary. Each has a body and soul, similar but not identical, to those of his brothers, differentially endowed: each has his own spiritual physiognomy and his own vocation, namely his place, or rather his task assigned to him by divine will within the marvellous framework of providence which transcends time and space and the individual mind just as the Creator transcends the creature. ...The apologue of Menenio Agrippa has certainly not lost its meaning and so much more the divine Word "many are the duties in the house of the Lord."[70]

As far as the post-elementare was concerned – without doubt the most important part of its program of educational policy – the AIMC also succeeded in profoundly influencing the line of the Christian Democratic Party and the government. Addressing the Catholic maestri in 1949, the Minister of Public Education said clearly: "I have resisted every attempt to create the scuola media unica because I am convinced that the boy of 11 to 14 years of age needs training at the hands of the maestro."[71] In the same year, at the First National Conference on the School organized by the party, a document was approved in which, recognizing the "impossibility of implementing a type of school that satisfies at once the singularity and the multiplicity of directions, especially in rural sites and in the small comuni," pronouncement was made in favor of establishing the post-elementare.[72]

But the influence of the AIMC also made itself felt in the final phase of elaboration of the Gonella bill. The version of this bill which was presented for the examination of the Consiglio Superiore della Pubblica Istruzione also provided, in addition to the three schools mentioned previously (the secondaria classica, tecnica, and normale), for the *secondaria professionale* which, identical to the normale in its lack of access to higher levels, differed from it only in its teaching body, which was to be constituted by secondary rather then elementary teachers. The judgment made on this proposed plan by the various sections of the Consiglio Superiore faithfully reflected the interests of the categories which these represented. While in fact the second section (that of the secondary school teachers) opposed the scuola normale, precisely because it was assigned to the maestri, the third (that of the elementary school teachers) spoke out against the establishment of the scuola professionale. Between the two, Gonella chose the course indicated by the maestri, and the scuola professionale disappeared from the bill that he presented to the Chamber of Deputies.[73]

The Reform of the Scuola Media: The Second and Third Phases

Having analyzed the principal forces arrayed and reconstructed their educational policy in the first phase, it remains now to examine in the next two sections the second and third phases: the one characterized by the struggle over the post-elementare, the other by the passing of initiative from the governing political class to the parties of the working class.

The "Silent Reform" of the Bourgeoisie: The Establishment of the Post-Elementare

The dream of the Italian ruling class of giving a "new" arrangement to the educational system with an "inclusive and fundamental" reform was of brief duration. One can say indeed that it vanished exactly at the moment when the long phase of elaboration of the reform plan formally closed with the presentation to the Chamber of Deputies of the Gonella bill. In fact, not only was it not converted into law, but it was never even discussed in the halls of Parliament. The conditions that had made the birth of this plan possible, however, remained alive for some years: a situation of power relations unfavorable to the proletariat, which in fact was futher weakened in this phase; the lack of a sizable demand for change of the educational system on the part of the lower social classes and the inability of the political organizations of the Left to elaborate and give expression to an alternative reform plan; a serious imbalance between school and labor market and thus the strong pressures exerted by the ceti intellettuali, and particularly the maestri. Thus, although the illusion of an "inclusive and fundamental" reform was fading, the persistence of these conditions kept the education system model elaborated in the four years 1947–51 quite alive in the governing political class.

In the debate over the "troubling phenomenon of educational imbalance" which, as has been mentioned, continued until the mid-1950s, the fear that it might produce a "disturbance of the social equilibrium itself,"[74] as well as the proposal for enacting a Malthusian educational policy, continually reappeared. The idea of introducing the numero chiuso not only continued to circulate, but achieved new and unexpected support. In fact, it was no longer the extreme Right which, making itself the carrier of the demand from the associations of professionals, asked in Parliament for "the limitation of access to the various faculties."[75] Although for totally different reasons, even Gaetano Salvemini in those years acknowledged the necessity of the numero chiuso "at least in southern Italy,"[76] and at the conference of the Friends of the World in 1956, men such as Leopoldo Piccardi, Ernesto Rossi, and Manlio Rossi Doria supported this measure.[77] On the other hand, a survey conducted in 1954 by DOXA* revealed that as many as 69 percent of the non-tenured university teachers interviewed saw no other way out than the numero chiuso.[78]

The governing political class retained the conviction, however, that it was not by such measures that the problem of surplus intellectual labor was to be solved, but rather by intervening in the educational system at the upper-secondary, or even better, the lower-secondary level. Both Antonio Segni and Gaetano Martino, two successors of Gonella at the Ministry of Public Education, declared themselves against the numero chiuso several times. For the former the first way to follow was that of reducing the number of licei and istituti magistrali and expanding simultaneously the schools of technical and professional instruction.[79] For the latter, the "principal remedy" was the "normalization of the secondary school," which consisted in "selecting and reducing the population destined to flow into the university."[80]

In point of fact, the ultimate objective always remained the realization of the Bottai-Gonella educational system model. There reemerged the old dissatisfaction over the inability of the avviamento to function effectively as a dumping school, and therefore the conviction that it was necessary to establish, albeit with a much simpler and quicker procedure than that necessary for approval of the bill of 1951, a truly dead-end school such as the artigiana or the normale. With lines of argument and expressions that seemed to have been taken entirely from the speeches of the Minister of National Education Giuseppe Bottai, a Christian Democratic deputy observed in 1955 that the majority of youth who attended the avviamento,

> rather than finding a stimulus for material labor, rather than understanding the necessity for an agricultural specialization, directly create for themselves a men-

*DOXA: survey research organization similar to the Gallup poll.

> tality of escape from work, of vain search, by means of the licenza taken after three years, for a position as a salaried employee of the municipality or the state. The illusion is indeed pervasive in such classes of being able in such a way to find social redemption, in the belief that office employment may be the way of access to a supposed higher class, and in the very serious misunderstanding (which, unfortunately, is still peculiar to a certain Italian mentality) that the degree of civic dignity is in inverse relation to the level of the materiality of labor."[81]

A few days later, the new president of the Consiglio Superiore, Antonio Segni, echoed him in an interview with the complaint that "the scuole di aviamento al lavoro at times train only for the lower ranks of the state bureaucracy or of local governments, especially because of the absence of subsequent istituti professionali."[82]

Pushing in this direction as well were the maestri and their organizations, whose pressures for "penetrating" the lower-secondary became increasingly strong as the situation of the labor market worsened.[83] The most valuable suggestion for the governing political class for unblocking the situation came, in fact, from the elementary teachers' organizations. If in the short term it was practically impossible to realize that ambitious program which the ruling class had prepared for so long and with such care – argued the AIMC in effect – one could always embark on another course, or rather a short-cut: that of instituting the post-elementare by means of a simple ministerial circular. Gonella had not only bequeathed a bill of law, but had also sought during his long tenure at the Ministry of Public Education to begin the implementation of his program. Taking advantage of the uncertainty of the opposition, and making use of an old fascist regulation,[84] he had authorized by means of a ministerial circular the establishment of the post-elementare in some provinces, a dumping school in all respects equal to the normale and the artigiana.[85] According to the AIMC, therefore, it was a matter of resuming this course with energy and determination, "of authorizing and encouraging, although formally in an experimental capacity, the establishment of other post-elementary schools besides those already in effect, entrusted to the maestri and under the supervision of headmasters in various Italian regions."[86]

It was thus that the Italian ruling class, aware of the impossibility of realizing an inclusive and fundamental reform, embarked upon the way indicated by the maestri and by their organizations, and played the card of a "silent" alteration of the educational system. In 1953 – 54 the Ministry of Public Education put up the first resistance to the opening of new scuole di avviamento.[87] But it was the year after, with the formation of the Scelba-Saragat government (February 1954–July 1955) that the attempt to alter the educational system with a "single blow" took place. In the face of demands from the organizations of maestri, Minister of Public Education Martino sought to win time, still declaring that it was "hoped to be able to offer to the young graduates from the elementary school various types of subsequent schooling."[88] The situation changed, however, when Martino stepped down and Ermini took over his post. In June 1955, on the occasion of the issuing of new plans for the primary school, Ermini also issued plans for the post-elementare, seeking thereby, with a provision taken without the advice of the Consiglio Superiore and without the approval of the two Chambers of Parliament to legitimate this type of school and to put before the opposition an accomplished fact. The text of the plans, moreover, left no doubt about the fact that to the post-elementare was attributed the same function as the dumping school of the "normale." The maestri of this school, one read, were "to encourage in the student the discovery of inclinations and dispositions for employment in the area of manual and practical activities; to help him find his place in the social and economic order."[89]

In September of the same year the new Minister of Public Education Paolo Rossi issued two circulars with which he prohibited "the establishment of any new scuola media or avviamento because of unsurmountable limits of the education budget."[90] With another circular,[91] the ministry's Director General of elementary education established that, beginning with the school year 1955–56, the experiment of the post-elementare – limited until then to a few provinces – was to be extended throughout the national territory in localities that lacked the scuole di avviamento (exactly the schools whose establishment it sought to prevent) and where there was a sufficient number of youth from 11 to 14 years who had finished the scuola elementare.

After so many years of discussion and inquiry, the extension of the post-elementare over the entire national territory undoubtedly constituted the first real step forward in the realization of the educational model elaborated by Gonella. In this sense it represented, therefore, a great success for the ruling class. All the same, this same success, by suddenly putting before the opposition the danger of a rapid and silent counter-reform, pushed them to overcome the remaining uncertainties and to commit themselves with more effort and aggressiveness to the field of educational policy. Thus 1955, although not yet signaling an actual shift in the attitude of the political organizations of the working class, and although not constituting the point of departure for an offensive to establish the scuola media unica, represented nevertheless the initial date of an important defensive battle.

The forces of the lay and socialist Left immediately condemned the government, pointing out the extraordinary continuity between the Christian Democrats' educational policy and the Carta of Bottai. To the Christian Democratic Party was, in fact, attributed the intention of implementing that system of three schools elaborated by the fascist theorist: "one school, the media unica, for the bourgeois class, a second, the avviamento, for the upper part of the proletariat and the small bourgeoisie, and a third, the post-elementare, for the agricultural laborer, for the scattered 'countryfolk,' and for the children of isolated groups of the mountain population."[92]

No less lively was the reaction of the Communists.[93] In September of that year, on occasion of the debate on the budget for the Ministry of Public Education, the Communist deputies accused the government of wanting "to create airtight compartments, veritable closed castes among Italian children."[94] "This old and now new type of school," observed Natta, "will necessarily be allotted a subordinate function for the subordinate classes; it will be or will become the school for the poor, the school of the depressed areas and the mountain zones, and it is because of this that for us it carries the imprint of a class school."[95] Beginning with these considerations, the Communist deputies presented an agenda in Parliament in which they asked for two things: first, that the government review the programs for the primary school and the post-elementare and put them under the examination of the Consiglio Superiore; and second, that in place of the post-elementari, which lacked any "real juridical base," it open new scuole di avviamento al lavoro.[96]

In addition to defending the existing educational order, however, the Communists also counterposed against the post-elementare that still rather moderate reform program that has already been mentioned. *Riforma della scuola* limited itself to asking for an "increasing uniformity in the level of schooling" at the lower-secondary level,[97] and Natta argued that in the short term it was necessary to arrive "at a gradual drawing nearer of the various types of school" "by means of a revision of internal arrangements and of programs" and by introducing "easy passage from one to another by a series of options."[98]

Nevertheless, beyond this program, the Communists realized that in order to avert the danger of a counter-reform and take some steps forward in the direction of a scuola media unica, it was especially necessary to neutralize those intellectual strata, particularly the maestri, which represented the most important allies of the reactionary groups. And to neutralize these strata, the important thing was not so much to conduct battles of ideas and press campaigns but rather to produce a structural change, to alter the conditions of the intellectual labor market. It was because of this that Lozza, in the name of the Communist group, argued the necessity in the Chamber of Deputies of taking several measures, from halving the fullest classes to changing the multiple classes, capable of bringing about a sizable increase in the demand for elementary teachers. "If we succeeded in this," he observed, "we could give work to forty thousand more maestri. A solution to the problem of unemployment of the elementary teachers would be initiated, and the bitter struggles that attend mistaken suggestions and plans for giving the elementary teachers the scuola post-elementare or for maintaining it would be weakened, indeed, extinguished."[99]

A group which, on the other hand, had no need of being neutralized was certainly that of the teachers or of the aspiring teachers of the secondary schools. The same structural causes that led the maestri to fight first for the "normale" and then for the post-elementare pushed the secondary teachers to oppose this type of school, and not only the small minority, as was predictable, of sympathizers of leftist parties but also those of the Catholic Union of Italian Secondary School Teachers, the UCIIM. Established in the immediate postwar period, and soon the strongest association of secondary teachers,[100] the UCIIM committed itself, like the AIMC, to the field of educational policy, but assumed from the start a very different line. For, if their religious matrix as well as their general political orientation and position in relation to the Christian Democratic Party was the same, the interests of the two social groups that these associations represented were different and even in conflict. Thus at the time of the Gonella inquiry the UCIIM sided against the normale and in favor of a "unitary structure articulated into three branches."[101] The possibility of approval of the Gonella bill having been reduced, and facing the threat from the organizations of the maestri, it fought for the defense and the further development of avviamento as a school which cultivated "attitudes toward the manual and clerical professions and towards work in general."[102]

However, in 1955 the UCIIM went beyond this defensive attitude toward the existing educational arrangement. The fear of losing a sizable slice of the lower-secondary school with the establishment of the post-elementare[103] pushed its members toward more radical positions, bringing them closer to those of the parties of the leftist opposition.[104] Thus the UCIIM not only denounced the

Table 10.5. Classes and Students of the Scuola Post-Elementare, 1954 to 1960

Year	*Classes*	*Pupils*
1954–55	1,783	15,890
1955–56	3,121	38,171
1956–57	4,204	40,299
1957–58	6,154	51,876
1958–59	7,266	56,312
1959–60	9,980	92,120
1960–61	10,643	79,996

SOURCE: ISTAT, *Annuario statistico dell'istruzione italiana,* vols. 10 and 14.

danger that "hundreds of thousands of adolescents can be tied to a school that cuts them off from the body of the secondary school and excludes them from the possibility of advancing without constraint into subsequent educational routes for which they show themselves capable" and asked the government to annul the measures taken with a procedure described as illegal; it also asserted the necessity for establishing, for youth 11–14 years old, "a new school, unitary, open to all, socially just and responsive, capable of leading to a personal and pre-professional level of maturity such as *to allow any subsequent educational choice.*"[105]

The battle conducted by the opposition parties and by the organizations of secondary teachers produced immediate effects. Although foreseeing the protests of the maestri and of their powerful organizations,[106] Minister of Public Education Paolo Rossi declared to the Chamber of Deputies that he considered "the remedy" of the post-elementari "neither optimal nor definitive" and, acknowledging the agenda of the leftists, he promised to replace these schools with those of the avviamento.[107] It was, however, a promise that neither Paolo Rossi nor his successors would keep. For a number of years to come – in effect up to 1961 – the opposition continued to denounce the establishment of "clandestinely conceived post-elementary schools."[108] And indeed the data available to us show that in the five-year period 1956–60, the number of post-elementari classes continued to increase (table 10.5). Nevertheless, the firm attitude of the leftists and their growing commitment to the field of educational policy, as well as the pressures by the organizations of the secondary school teachers, were enough at least to block the attempt at making the post-elementare the new dumping school for the majority of Italian children.

In the wake of the first success, the opposition won a second, partial one.

In April 1956, Rossi nominated the Commission for the Study of the Problems of Lower Education, which included representatives of both the lower-secondary school and the elementary school teachers. After a sharp encounter between the supporters of the interests and positions of these two groups, the draft of a final compromise document was arrived at in which the point of view of the secondary school teachers prevailed. This document recommended, in fact, the establishment of a "unitary" scuola media with a group of fundamental subjects in common, and four optional subjects (foreign language, Latin, work, and artistic activity) which allowed access to all types of upper-secondary schools, whatever subject matter had been pre-chosen. It provided also, accepting in part the demands of the AIMC, for the possibility of establishing a scuola complementare (this was the new name assumed by the post-elementare) "wherever it may effectively be necessary" to be assigned to the maestri, but it left its students the possibility "both of passing to the unitary scuola media and of pursuing their studies further."[109]

The Success of the Initiative of the Subordinate Classes: The Establishment of the Media Unica

Toward the end of the 1950s, many of the objective and subjective conditions changed that had made possible the preservation of the existing educational system, or that had actually made the threat of a resumption of the Carta della Scuola appear on the horizon. Or rather, all changed but one. In the first place, power relations changed, becoming more favorable to the working class. Second, the demand from the subordinate social classes for transformation of the educational system became increasingly strong, as did the capacity of the workers' parties to articulate this demand and to translate it into a fundamental plan for reform. Third, the situation of the intellectual labor market changed, and even more so the perception of it by the ruling class: for the first time in Italian history the surplus of laureati was completely reabsorbed, and within the governing political class the conviction gained ground that the period opening would be marked by a serious shortage of qualified personnel. Compared with that of the preceding phase, however, the market situation of the maestri, which was the principal determinant of their hostility in the face of the scuola media, remained virtually unchanged.

As the Italian economy became industrialized, per capita income increased, and the tendency of families to have their children continue studies spread, the demand for education of the lower social classes tended increasingly to translate itself into a demand for change of the educational system. While before the principal obstacle to the continuation of studies had been of an economic nature, now, at least for the families of the upper strata of the urban proletariat, it became the structure of the educational system. Thus, the idea that the separation between the media and the avviamento constituted the most serious impediment to the development of secondary and higher education – an idea that some had sought, with difficulty, to disseminate from books and specialized reviews to newspapers and from these into houses and onto the streets – now became a collective experience and retraced its steps in the reverse direction.

It is in the light of these interesting changes both in the objective conditions and in the orientations and the collective behavior of broad social strata that the turn which occurred at the end of the 1950s in the educational policy of the political parties of the working class, and particularly of the Communist Party, must be viewed. After the battle against the post-elementare, the elaboration of an alternative reform plan advanced at a very rapid pace within the PCI, fed also by the important contribution furnished in those years by scholars quite close to socialist positions, such as Lamberto Borghi, Raffaele Laporta, and Aldo Visalberghi. Already by 1956, at the end of a long debate, *Riforma della scuola* argued the necessity of implementing "a compulsory school of eight years identical for all,"[110] even if at that same time several authoritative Communist leaders seemed disposed, for fear of falling into an "unfruitful maximalism," to support much more moderate proposals for changing the educational system.[111]

A veritable turn in Communist educational policy took place, however, at the end of the second legislature. In the electoral campaign of 1958, the PCI was the only party that put at the center of its educational program the establishment of the "scuola media unica compulsory and free of charge up to 14 years of age,"[112] and at the start of the third legislature the senators of the party presented the bill of law Establishment of State Compulsory Schooling for 6–14-Year Olds (which was then called the Donini-Luporini bill, after the names of the first two sponsors). It was thus a profound turn in a dual sense: first, because the PCI for the first time took legislative initiative for reform of the lower-secondary school and, second, because the reform that it proposed was the most advanced and radical one possible. The report that accompanied the Donini-Luporini bill, which represented probably the most mature fruit of the Communists' theoretical elaboration of these years, was not limited to attacking the recurrent attempt of the bourgeoisie "to safeguard a privileged course after the elementary school by establishing schools of a subordinate type for the popular classes who increasingly pressed toward the conquest of education: the popolare of Orlando, the complementare of Gentile, the avviamento of Bottai, the post-elementare of Ermini." Decisively rejected as well was "the prospect of a single school with options," toward which Communist policy in the preceding phase was from time to time directed. The solution proposed was the radical one of a scuola media unica, compulsory and free for all children from 11 to 14 years of age.[113]

Certainly, as Donini later observed, the PCI proposal was not "a bill presented by a socialist government," and therefore each objective, even the most advanced (as, for example, the introduction of manual labor into the scuola media), retained a strongly ambiguous character. "In present-day society," said Donini, "in which work serves to enrich particular social classes, it is inevitable that the teaching of education for work becomes hypocrisy, an instrument suited for concealing the alienation of man under a regime that forces him to produce not for himself but to promote private interests."[114] All the same, the educational system that the Communists sought to realize through their bill was the most advanced among all those of the European capitalist countries, and certainly represented, as they said, a step forward of extraordinary importance in the direction of "overcoming class barriers" and of establishing "new relations between manual and intellectual labor and between the city and the country."[115]

As for the governing political class, it cannot be said that it was completely insensitive to the demand for education coming from the subordinate social classes. For the first time in the history of Italy, it presented, in September 1958, an explicit planning document, a "Plan for the Development of the School in the Decade 1959 to 1969," which provided for a considerable increase in public expenditure for education.[116] However, toward the demand for altering the internal structure of the educational system, the governing political class still assumed a totally negative attitude. To the Donini-Luporini proposal it counterposed, in August 1959, the Medici bill, which took absolutely no account of the recommendations of the Rossi Commission, and proposed again, in effect, though with a different label, the education system model elaborated in the four-year period 1947–1951.[117]

"One has the impression," wrote Lamberto Borghi of this bill, "that from the Gentile Reform to that of Bottai and to Medici's (in draft) not one single step forward has been taken. Only the language has been changed."[118] And in fact the lower-secondary desired by Medici was divided into as many as four types of school (euphemistically called "sections"): the *umanistica,* with the teaching of Latin and of a foreign language, which gave access to all subsequent schools; the *tecnica,* with the teaching of work and of a foreign language, which allowed entrance into the istituti tecnici and professionali; the *normale,* with work activity, which allowed enrollment only in a dead-end school such as the istituto professionale; and finally the *artistica* which fed into the schools and institutes of art. Therefore, except for the last, which was more or less marginal, these schools were almost identical to those anticipated eight years earlier by Gonella. In particular, the most important, the normale, which remained almost unchanged, was to gather the "students who felt themselves drawn to the fields and to the workshops"[119] and (this was the only innovation) to have a teaching body made up not entirely but 70 percent by maestri.

There is no doubt that the organizations of the maestri also had a strong influence on the direction of the Medici bill. Despite all assertions to the contrary ("it surely will not be the maestri who, in order to resolve the problem of elementary teachers' unemployment, will demand any sort of solution by means of any sort of secondary school whatsoever"),[120] the elementary teachers remained substantially faithful in these years to the political line elaborated in the immediate postwar period,[121] concerning themselves only with perfecting and rendering more credible the ideology that went along it. In defense of the scuola normale, they now brought forward political, pedagogical, and economic-financial arguments. They argued that "social justice, as regards education, and the right of all to equal chances" is not guaranteed by "shutting up all children in a scuola unica, but by realizing the freedom to choose the type of school according to interests, educational ability, and psychological characteristics of each student."[122] They asserted that there were psycho-pedagogical factors that necessitated a "continuity" between the elementary schools and the following three-year period, and that this continuity could be assured only by a school made up of maestri.[123] But, above all, they sought to show that the financial burdens required by the extension of the post-elementare (that is, by the establishment of the normale) were far lighter than those necessary for extending "the school of the traditional secondary type into all populated areas."[124]

This ideology did not remain limited, on the other hand, to the leadership and to the intermediate cadres of the AIMC, but was shared by the large majority of maestri, Catholic or not, because it corresponded fully to their interests or at least presented itself as the only one in a position to offer a convincing escape route from the difficulty of unemployment. We can say this with certainty on the basis of the findings of an impressive survey carried out by an elementary teachers' review in 1961, at a time when the battle conducted by the maestri seemed irrevocably compromised (table 10.6).

This explains at least in part how the governing political class, facing the demand coming from the subordinate social classes and the fundamental reform plan of the Communists, chose an extremely rigid line of defense. It never made a secret of its availability to welcome the demands of the elementary teachers' organizations. Speaking at the Sixth National Congress of the AIMC, Minister of Public Education Medici said: "I would be pleased if the elementary teachers would fully participate in the realization of compulsory schooling," and he guaranteed that about 80 percent of the children would attend the scuola normale.[125] But an even clearer demonstration of the government's "sensitivity" to the demands of the AIMC was given by Medici's changing the text of his bill at the last moment.[126]

The rigid line of defense assumed by the governing political class was quite soon revealed as counterproductive. Against the Medici bill there formed a quite diverse coalition of social forces, which ran from the parties of the Left[127] to the organizations of the secondary school teachers,[128] with a different program of educational policy. It was particularly because of these latter, which influenced the attitude of the Consiglio Superiore, that the governing political class lost the first battle. Although, like the organizations of secondary school teachers, it too referred to the model of the "school articulated on the basis of options" (and not to that of the media unica proposed by the Communists), the Consiglio Superiore expressed a majority judgment strongly opposed to the Medici bill,[129] in effect forcing the government to retreat.

The new bill that the Minister of Education presented to the Senate in January 1960 was in fact certainly more open and advanced than the preceding ones.[130] It provided for a "unitary" scuola media with three different options: Latin gave access to the licei and to the istituti magistrali; scientific and technical subjects to the istituti tecnici; and artistic training to the institutes of artistic instruction. But in order to take into account, although to a lesser extent than before, the demands of the AIMC (whose National President, Maria Badaloni, had in the meantime become Undersecretary of State at the Ministry

Table 10.6. Attitude of Maestri Toward the Problems of the Lower-Secondary School, 1961

	Yes	*No*	*Total**
1. Article 34 of the Constitution, in Clause 2, establishes, "Lower education, imparted for at least eight years, is compulsory and free of charge." Do you consider that such a formulation implies a continuity of educational and didactic activity between the primary school and the following three-year sequence up to 14 years of age?	95	5	100
2. Do you think that current surrounding conditions (position of the locality with respect to means of communication, school buildings, number of 11- to 14-year-olds obliged to attend, etc.) would permit the immediate establishment everywhere of some type of united scuola media?	32	68	100
3. Do you think that the experiment of post-elementary classes has been advisable as a didactic and organizational direction?	73	27	100
4. If so, do you consider that the post-elementary school could usefully augment the activity of the unitary scuola media in Italy?	77	23	100
5. Do you think it is opportune and justified that some of the teaching positions of the united scuola media ought to be reserved for tenured maestri who have the particular requisites?	90	10	100

*12,274 maestri responded to the survey.

SOURCE: "L'inchiesta dei *diritti*," in *I diritti della scuola*, June 20, 1961, pp. 1322–23.

of Public Education), it established that in localities where there was no "unitary" scuola media a "special" scuola media, assigned to the elementary school teachers, could be established for a decade.[131]

Still more important for the fate of the reform of the scuola media was the change that occurred in those years in the attitude of the bourgeoisie toward the problems of education. If this class had earlier shown itself quite worried about the excess of diplomati and laureati and had viewed favorably all interventions in the educational system that tended to make the mechanisms of selection more severe and efficient, now its anxieties and fears had completely changed in nature. Convinced that the sudden economic growth of those years would be prolonged indefinitely and that consequently the demand for qualified labor would increase enormously and, in any case, much more rapidly than supply, the bourgeoisie showed itself more favorable than before to a relative openness of the educational system.

But even apart from the course of the intellectual labor market, there is no doubt that the industrialization of the country and the shifting of enormous masses of the population from the primary to the secondary and tertiary sectors of the economy confronted the Italian entrepreneurs with an increasingly urgent need to socialize the new youthful labor force by means of the school's activity. At least at the lower-secondary level, the type of socialization of the labor force that the bourgeoisie required from the school was not so much technical-professional, as was often claimed, but rather ideological. In the introductory report to the Conference on Compulsory Education organized in April 1959 by Confindustria,* the engineer Renato Lombardi observed: "When we consider children who enter the world of work between 14 and 16 years of age, what industry requires of them on the strictly professional level is very little. Specifically professional knowledge can and often must be acquired later. There are, on the other hand, many, far too many, things which if not acquired in the period of preparation can no longer be acquired." What were these things? "What industry requires of the school," Lombardi observed, "is above all the formation of character and development of the sense of personality, of the spirit of observation, of critical sentiment and the capacity to judge the relative importance of actions and things."

The leading representative of Confindustria made, on the other hand, no mystery of what the entrepreneurs meant by "formation of character": "Ti-

*General Confederation of Italian Industry, the most influential employers' organization in Italy.

diness, order, discipline are indispensable elements in the formation of the character and the personality, and, if one cannot count on prior groundwork, they are made up for only with difficulty in the factory setting." And to be completely clear he added: "Many times I ask myself why it might not be possible to create for professional instruction something similar to that priceless little book that goes by the modest title, *Corporal's Manual*."[132]

Convinced of the need to subject the entire future labor force which was to be used in industry to the bath of educational socialization, and aware that the productivity of this labor force depended, more than on cognitive development or professional knowledge, on those affective personality traits required by the future role of subordinate manual worker, the representatives of Confindustria asked that the compulsory school have "more a formative than an informative function."[133] It was evidently the recognition of the inadequacy of the old scuola di avviamento professionale for the purpose of socializing the labor force that industry needed.

On the other hand, the old educational system was also considered inadequate for another reason. With a lucidity difficult to find in other documents of the time, the Lombardi report confronted, also in regard to the processes of selection, the crucial problem of how to guarantee loyalty to the social system on the part of those excluded from continuing studies, namely of those whom the school would force to occupy for life the position of manual worker. Criticizing the existing mechanisms of selection, he proposed to weaken the division between scuola media and avviamento in order to give at least "the impression of freedom of choice":

> In my opinion [he observed] it is much more important to dispose youth to the impression of having chosen their occupation, of being aware of its essential and differing aspects, and of not being conveyed ineluctably to a certain job, rather than to the impression of having undertaken it without recourse to comparison and judgment and with the conviction that something else would be easier, more pleasant and better paid. . . . At least up to 15 years of age it is necessary to give the impression of freedom of choice: only thus will dispositions emerge that create enthusiasts and therefore good workers.[134]

It was, plainly, a proposal for passing from a system of sponsored mobility to one of contest mobility,[135] of questioning, if not abolishing, the avviamento, namely that dumping school which up to then had had more or less the function of conveying the young "ineluctably to a certain job." Certainly, Lombardi did not call for the scuola media unica, but argued in fact that "a differentiation should be made between the person who will go to the university and the one who at fifteen years of age will have to earn a living." Nevertheless, by affirming the necessity of "allowing children a longer subsequent possibility of choice and of passage, and providing the necessarily differentiated curriculum with a minimum commom denominator constituted primarily by the 'formative' aspect,"[136] he declared himself in favor of a much more open educational system than the existing one.

If to this, and to the changes which were recorded above, one adds the fact that in those years the experiment of the Center-Left coalition began, it can be understood how, in a relatively brief period of time, the political parties of the working class succeeded in having their line approved, at least in two essential points. During the third Fanfani government (July 1960–February 1962), which was elected with the abstention of the Monarchists and the Socialists, Minister of Public Education Bosco elaborated a plan which provided for the establishment of 260 experimental classes of a "united" scuola media which was midway between the second Medici bill and that of Donini-Luporini. The united scuola media, in fact, although providing an option between Latin and technical subjects, established that its degree, the licenza, had identical value whatever preparatory material was chosen.

The reaction of the maestri and their organizations was quite violent. For the first time in its history, the AIMC directly attacked the Minister of Public Education[137] and actually threatened to resort to the most powerful weapon at its disposal, that of no longer conveying the electorate it controlled toward the Christian Democratic lists. Its review expressed all the resentment of the social group it represented by setting diplomati against laureati, and elementary school teachers against those who signed themselves "dott., prof., o avv."* The former, "condemned to lead a wretched life, unsuited to the great responsibilities entrusted to them" yet aware of the "call of duty" and ready to work "ardently" in the local committees on behalf of Christian Democratic propaganda, in the end received no reward or actually saw the post-elementare threatened; the latter, on the other hand, although dwelling blessedly "in slippers" "in one of those villas terrified by the popular uproar" and furnishing in the electoral campaign only "the assistance of prestige," ultimately obtained all the positions and the promotions.[138]

*"*Dottore, professore, o avvocato*": that is, "university graduate, secondary school teacher, or lawyer," titles indicating possession of the laurea.

But neither the threat of the AIMC nor the efforts and the diplomatic activity of its national president, reconfirmed as Undersecretary of State for Public Education also in the third Fanfani government, came to anything. To try to break the worker's movement and to integrate part of it,* the ruling class had to pay a price, and one of these was the reform of the scuola media. Thus, "in order to move against the sizable unemployment of elementary teachers,"[139] the Minister of Public Education succeeded in having Parliament approve, in record time and despite the opposition of the Left, a short law in favor of the neighborhood school excerpted from the more inclusive Plan of Development.[140] But as for the arrangement of the lower-secondary school, the governing political class had to accept in large part the Communist bill, and therefore threw the maestri overboard.

This produced some profound divisions within the Christian Democratic Party. In spite of all the government's efforts and the appeals to discipline from the directive organ of the party, a large number of Christian Democratic deputies and senators who intervened in the debate expressed their reservations and actually their opposition to the new legal text born of the compromise between the Christian Democrats and the Socialists. Lucifredi described it as "a considerable retrogression" and, contrasting it with the Gonella bill of 1951, supported the validity of the principle "schooling for all and to each the proper school," declaring that he preferred "a school with a pluralistic structure to one with a monistic structure."[141] Donati argued that unity of the school was "against nature." "Let us look at our noses," he said; "they are all fine, but they are also all different; let us consider our intellects, our desires, our orientations, those things, in other words, that make each one of us himself and each one of us different from the others."[142] Limoni asserted that the unity of structure would humiliate "those most endowed of intellect and desire, forcing them into an option where they must clip their wings in order to keep themselves in line with those who by nature are required to proceed slowly."[143]

The last trench in which the defenders of the old order moved was that of Latin. Berté denied that Latin was "a subject that discriminates among intellects and family backgrounds."[144] Zannini claimed that the study of Latin, and particularly of grammar, was the "decisive test" for "identifying the aptitudes and the inclinations of the 11- to 14-year-old scholar, the age in which the youngster, not knowing what he wants, is ready to exhaust hours and hours

*That is, by bringing the Socialist Party into the government.

playing football or riding a bike, but is unable to accomplish the little effort of picking up his own shoes."[145] As if the speech itself were not enough, Riccio gave his defense of Latin in Latin and was introduced by the President of the Chamber with the words "dearest and most venerable friends, *sit tibi venia latine loquendi*."*[146]

And in fact, on this point, the defenders of the old order succeeded in extorting some success, obtaining that the new law would leave Latin alive at least as an "optional subject" and that access to the liceo classico would depend on passing an examination in this material.

The De-Professionalization of the Upper-Secondary Schools

The Liberalization of Access in 1961

The protagonists of the struggle to open or to keep shut access to the university to the diplomati of the istituti tecnici are in large part the same ones whom we have seen in speaking of the reform of the scuola media: the working class, the bourgeoisie, the organizations of diplomati (in this case, surveyors and industrial technicians) and of laureati (especially engineers). And the same basic variables are to be taken into consideration. Different, on the other hand, is the weight of these variables, in the sense that the course of the intellectual labor market had much more influence on the liberalization of 1961 than on the reform of 1962.

As was mentioned earlier, the access of diplomati from the techincal institutes to the faculties of mathematics, sciences, engineering, and architecture had been closed by the Gentile Reform in 1923, which had left open only the entrance to economics and commerce. Following that, the considerable unemployment of diplomati which occurred especially after 1930, the increasing tendency of these to enroll in the "authorized" faculties, and the pressures of their associations for a revision of the Gentile Reform, had made it such that Bottai provided in his Carta della Scuola for a certain liberalization of university access. Since, nevertheless, these changes were never approved, in 1945 Italian students found themselves still facing the norms established by Gentile.

The difficult situation of the labor market for diplomati which occurred both in the period of reconstruction and at the beginning of the 1950s provoked new pressures on the part of their professional organizations to gain access to other

*Let there be a little Latin spoken here.

faculties. These pressures did not come from the accountants, who could enroll in economics and commerce, but from the surveyors and the industrial technicians who sought to be admitted to architecture and engineering, and particularly from the latter who, through their national association, organized a student strike in 1948 in all the technical institutes in support of their action.

From the first years of the postwar period, the PCI made itself the spokesman of the demand for liberalization of access. Pursuing the dual objective of reducing the number of university students and of increasing the percentage of those provided by the subordinate social classes, several Communist deputies, including Natta, Lozza, and Marchesi, presented in February 1950 a bill of law that proposed "to extend, with courage and deliberation together, to diplomati of the various sections of the istituto tecnico the right of admission to the university faculties corresponding to the scientific specializations of those sections."[147]

This bill, however, was never even examined by the two chambers. The difficult situation of the labor market for laureati made the counter-pressures of the association of engineers even stronger. The great majority of faculty councils of engineering that responded to the Gonella questionnaire argued that "the only institutions of secondary instruction fit to provide the qualifications for university admission are the licei."[148] Then too, speaking to the Chamber of Deputies, the Minister of Public Education declared that it was "almost anachronistic to speak of new possibilities of access to the universities at a time when the need is felt to uncrowd the universities."[149] And although recognizing that in the case of the industrial technicians things were different, that there was "a question of judgment," Gonella finally entrenched himself behind the strong opposition of the association of engineers, and no longer spoke of liberalization.

Presented again in the second legislature, the Natta bill had no better fortune. The situation was unblocked in fact only in 1957–58, when the profound transformations underway in the Italian economy produced their first effects. At that moment the action of the industrial technicians and the surveyors became more confident, their polemic more lively, and their pressure stronger and more insistent. If formerly an old custom of deference toward engineers had weighed upon their behavior, now they freed themselves of every form of subjection and described as "grotesque" the fact that the engineers' order might consider "dangerous the proposal of opening to diplomati tecnici the greater learning to be acquired at the schools of engineering!" "Danger of what?" they wrote. "Of seeing the qualification and the salary of the engineers who work in industry devalued when more of them come out of the Italian universities? Danger of seeing the engineers provided by the licei devalued in contrast to the few who can be provided by the best among the industrial technicians?"[150]

At the origin of these renewed pressures there was once again the situation of the labor market for diplomati which – as was mentioned before – although having improved considerably, was still characterized by a certain weakness of supply. But to this were added other important factors. In the first place, the greater availability of financial resources for a certain number of diplomati coming from the lower social classes increased the desire to escape from the social destiny imposed by the educational system. Second, the considerable vertical mobility which in those years characterized the qualified labor force employed in industry opened new and unexpected career possibilities, raised the level of aspiration of the diplomati, and made the prohibition against acceding to the faculty of engineering seem to them increasingly painful and unjust:

> The case is not rare of industrial technicians hired in the capacity of workers, not for a reasonable period of apprenticeship, but as a permanent appointment: well, these persons cannot give the required output because they *are not workers*. To this it must be added that, when they are hired for tasks suitable to their studies and give full measure of their capacities with complete satisfaction of the employer, even achieving distinction, they must endure, often for many years, modest payment in unsuitable categories of employment. Above all, they know *a priori* that whatever their preparation, their output, their capacities, they will *never* be able to achieve managerial positions because they are deprived of the "paper" of the laurea.[151]

> Having obtained the diploma [wrote *Il geometra italiano*] and having begun professional activity, in the majority of cases the economic conditions of the young graduate of the istituto tecnico change rapidly for the better, while the ever stronger need emerges to complete his preparation with more advanced studies: with a cycle, that is, of university studies.[152]

To the demands of the diplomati, for whom this time both the Communists and the Socialists (PSI) acted as spokesmen, presenting at the start of the third legislature as many as four bills of law, the engineers were opposed with unremitting firmness. According to them the liberalization of university access would have caused "a serious degeneration of studies and of professional standard."[153] Even recognizing that the industrial technicians had "a truly onerous academic schedule, with a weekly load which is greater by 41 percent than that of the two licei," they argued that the istituti tecnici were not suited to train students of engineering, because they did not teach them those subjects, such as Latin, which constituted "a cultural base necessary to the dignity of the university graduate"[154] and did not accustom them to "reason in a humanistic sense."[155]

The Socialist and Communist bills also ran into strong opposition by several leading representatives of the government. In defense of the existing order, Minister of Justice Gonella, for example, took to the field in 1959. Never, perhaps, had he expounded with so much clarity as then on his model of school and society. Democratic society, he said, is an "organic" society, in the sense that in it "each organ has its own differentiation and its own function: the hands must perform the work of the hands, the feet the work of the feet, the head the work of the head. ...In an organic society each profession has its function, and the question of not confusing organs and functions is a question of the vitality of society." If the society was organic, then so too the school. The school made a fundamental contribution to the survival of the society, providing "the lauree, the diplomi, and the artisans' qualifications" which corresponded, respectively, to the three great divisions of society. Referring in particular to the two higher levels, Gonella observed: "Our schools are organic, our system has this characteristic: there are schools that prepare for the university, and there are schools that instead are conceived as ends in themselves at the secondary level. We cannot lose sight of this distinction, admitting everyone to the university after the attainment of whatever secondary study." To meddle with this arrangement, to revise the delicate mechanisms that regulated the flow of students, to liberalize university access was in fact difficult and, above all, dangerous. "The person who might want to alter these norms would bring chaos into the school, for the very simple reason that the entire educational order is in relation to this organic system."[156]

Nevertheless, this line of educational policy was not long to survive. If the bourgeoisie showed itself disposed even in those years to weaken the division between media and avviamento, it is not surprising that, worried about having to face a serious lack of laureati, and particularly of those with technical qualifications, it assumed a more positive attitude toward the proposals for liberalization of university access. Certainly, the thesis of a "total opening" of outlets seemed still too "drastic" and "the disadvantages and dangers" which it brought too many. In 1960, at the second conference of Confindustria on the problems of education, it was observed, in fact, that this solution not only could produce "a subversion of the founding principle that informs the entire Italian school" and an "abasement of the *tone* both of laureati and of those very diplomati," but also presented another disadvantage: that of increasing the supply of engineers to the detriment of the supply of industrial technicians and surveyors. For "if it is true," as was observed, "that laureati in engineering and physics are lacking, it must be realized that much greater is the scarcity of middle level technicians. It would be irresponsible, therefore, to reduce their number and especially their quality." Confindustria and its experts envisaged instead an intermediate solution between "total opening" and the maintenance of the status quo: that of admitting to the technical-scientific faculties a limited number of specially selected diplomati. In this way, "a glimmer of hope" would be opened "for families which, bound to traditions and customs long established by now, hope to have their sons actually become university graduates," with the "not unimportant benefit of encouraging a greater flow into the schools of a technical nature thereby uncrowding the licei,"[157] and consequently of producing an increase in the supply both of industrial technicians and of engineers.

No different was the attitude assumed that year by the governing political class. Even Medici, in a message sent to the second conference of Confindustria, described as "just" the aspirations of the diplomati of the instituti tecnici.[158] And on June 10, 1960 the Christian Democrat Tirabassi, along with senators of the most differing tendencies, from the Communist Donini to the Neo-Fascist Nencioni, presented a bill of "conditional" liberalization of access which left to each university faculty the freedom "to determine the system and the limits of proof required to assure the applicant's suitability."[159] This bill was precisely the one that, after having undergone some slight modifications, was approved the following year by the two chambers.

The Liberalization of Access in 1969

Too many pages have already been written on the students' contestation in 1968 and on the liberalization of access in 1969 for it to be possible or necessary here to treat these subjects extensively. It will suffice, therefore, to add a few things in order especially to relate the events of 1968 and 1969 to the course of the intellectual labor market.

The liberalization of access in 1961 and the establishment in February 1963 of the student stipend doubtless alleviated somewhat the labor market problem for diplomati and interrupted, or at least slowed down, the process of their social declassamento which, as was seen before, was already rather advanced at the end of the 1950s. But the constant increase of supply on the one hand, and the reduction of demand which occurred after 1964 on the other, again quickly increased the number of unemployed diplomati. On the other hand, their social composition also changed, for by way of the channels of the istituti tecnici and magistrali a new group of diplomati emerged, coming from the lower social classes. Thus the growing difficulties of employment that arose upon departure from the secondary schools, together with the lesser capacity of diplomati from the subordinate social classes to "endure" periods of unemployment, caused the process of declassamento, slowed by the liberalization of 1961, to resume at an even quicker pace.

The student contestation began when this process was already quite advanced. It arose from a plurality of factors widely analyzed at the time and which it would be useless to recall here. But it was also the effect of the growing imbalance between school and labor market. The protagonist of 1968 was, it was said, "the intellectual who now finds himself deprived of his traditional pretences; sees himself, along with millions of others, as a proletarian, but unlike the proletarian, has no secure social base. The mechanism which has led him to the university is closing it in his face. There is no room for an elite of his dimensions."[160] In other words, the "earthquake" of 1968 was provoked also by a situation of partially blocked upward mobility of the ceti intellettuali, a situation which, as was previously noted, has occurred at other times in the history of Italy but which now presented much different characteristics compared to the past: not only because the political regime was different and the social actors and their power relations were different, but also for two other reasons. First, the partially blocked social group was much larger than before. And second, in contrast to the past there was at the same time no corresponding process of partial downward mobility, and therefore the process of radicalization of the young intellectuals quickly assumed a clearly leftist orientation.

It is in the light of these elements that the total liberalization of access in 1969 must be viewed. For in fact, whether aware of it or not, the governing political class found itself having to decide in a hurry, even after years of inconclusive debates on university reform, whether or not to remove the obstacles to the upward mobility of the young diplomati (those that could be removed, naturally), on whether or not to allow their promotion and placement in the ceti medi. The way that it chose was the former, that of checking the process of declassamento, of retarding it as much as possible, of catching its breath by opening all channels of access to higher education. Not by chance, the first barrier to fall was that which protected the education faculty. In December 1968, the government abolished by decree the admission examination to these faculties, accepting in effect the demands of the unemployed maestri who, deprived by now of every other way of escape, sought refuge in the university. On the other hand, in October 1969, Parliament approved a law that extended to five years (formerly three) the duration of a small number of istituti professionali, establishing that the passing of these institutes' qualifying examinations obtained at the end of five years was equivalent to the diploma granted by the istituti tecnici. Finally, in December of the same year, the two chambers approved the law totally liberalizing university access.

Toward which model, after these decisions, the Italian educational system tended was made quite clear by the International Conference at Frascati in 1970, dedicated to the elaboration of a fundamental program of transformation of the secondary schools. Convinced that "the problem of the upper-secondary school" had "by now an obligatory guideline, after such an innovative legislative choice as that of the liberalization of university access,"[161] the leading scholars who participated in this conference proposed an upper-secondary with a unitary structure articulated in five directions (literary-linguistic, social, scientific, technological, and artistic) which would lead to a single final qualification or diploma. And consequently, they declared solemnly:

> Secondary studies do not have, of themselves, a professional character. The school offers the possibility of pre-professional training at various levels and allows lateral exits. Real professional training is subsequent to such lateral movements (and in no case precedes the end of the second year) and is delegated to the regional governments or to initiatives coordinated by them in which the professional associations and unions may also collaborate. Technical and professional training at a higher level shall be carried out in the ambit of the university, or, in any case, at the university level, by means of two- and three-year courses of study always open to continuation toward the laurea.[162]

It was recognition of the fact that the upper-secondary no longer served to produce intermediate cadres, but only university students.

CHAPTER ELEVEN

Education and Internal Migration

Only at this point, after having discussed the trends in intellectual employment and education in the period following the Second World War, is it possible to confront a question not touched upon until now: that of the internal migration of the intellectual labor force. The results of the analysis that I have conducted on the relationship between the process of unequal economic development in Italy and the course of secondary and higher education give rise to some questions. We have seen, in fact, that not only in the period following the Second World War, but also starting at the beginning of the century, the economically underdeveloped areas of Italy have always produced a higher number of diplomati and laureati (relative, of course, to the population present) than the more developed areas. Is there not perhaps an inconsistency, one might ask, between these data and the image we have of Italy as a country split in two, likewise with respect to the distribution of education, with the population of the North at a much higher level of education than the South? Has it not been this image, perhaps, as well as that economic theory which attributes an extraordinary importance to education for initiating or hastening economic development, that has underlain the persistent thesis that in order to overcome the underdevelopment of the Mezzogiorno it was necessary to increase the production of diplomati and laureati in the technical-scientific disciplines?[1]

I believe I have sufficiently demonstrated, in the course of this study, that illiteracy and the overproduction of intellectual labor not only are logically not in conflict, but constitute indeed, in the underdeveloped areas, two sides of the same coin. But how can we explain the fact that after having produced for various years a much greater quantity of intellectual labor than the North, the South might present in 1951 (relative to the population over 6 years of age) 0.9 percent laureati and 2.6 percent diplomati in contrast, respectively, to 1.1

percent and 3.6 percent for the North, and that ten years later these gaps had definitely not been reduced? On the basis of data gathered in 1968 in a sample inquiry on various labor forces in Lombardy, Massimo Paci observed that "contrary to the dominant stereotype which sees in the internal migration of our country a phenomenon that concerns exclusively the least qualified forms of labor, of rural origin, *there exists, rather, a strong current toward Lombardy, mostly of urban origin and of a high level of education and professional qualification.*"[2] In fact, the results of research show that in the decade 1959–68, while immigrants consituted 10 percent of the total work force employed, they reached 17 percent for managers and civil servants, 20 percent for the top two categories of impiegati, and 15 percent for the third category.[3]

Relying therefore on these data, we could easily explain the apparent incongruency between the cultural backwardness of the underdeveloped areas and their overproduction of intellectual labor on the basis of a constant and strong migratory flow of laureati and diplomati from these areas to those more developed. But if we seek to extend the analysis from Lombardy to all of Italy, and beyond the decade 1959–68 studied by Paci, we find ourselves facing no small difficulty owing to the scarcity of available data. The absence of data is absolute regarding the period from 1880 to the outbreak of the First World War (and it is just for this reason that I have waited until now to confront the question). If, however, one considers that this period, as mentioned earlier, was characterized by considerable intellectual migration abroad and that the migratory current came not only from the Mezzogiorno but also from the Settentrione, one can hpothesize that the internal movements of the intellectual labor force might have had a much reduced importance.

On the other hand, the story for the twenty-year fascist period, when, as has been noted, the migratory flow abroad was considerably reduced, is different. The only indirect information on the internal migration of laureati and diplomati during the fascist period comes to us from a study conducted twenty years ago by Isidoro Franco Mariani on a relatively sizable sample of "qualified elements," as the author called them, of the Italian population.[4] Used, however, with the required caution, the findings of this research confirm the presence, during the fascist period, of a strong migratory current of the intellectual labor force from the depressed areas of the country to the developed ones. They show first of all that the qualified labor force presented a much higher territorial mobility than the others. While in fact, according to the census of 1931, only 7.3 percent of the population present were born in regions different from that of their residence, as many as 51.9 percent of the "qualified elements" studied by Mariani found themselves in this condition. However, this territorial mobility did not have a circular nature, but occurred, so to speak, one way, namely from the backward regions to the developed ones of the country. Calculating the percentage in his sample of those born and residing in each region out of the total of those born in the region (resident or not), Mariani found that the percentages were much higher in the central and northern regions than in the southern ones. The calculation of the ratio residents/births in each region showed, on the other hand, that only three regions were areas of attraction for intellectual labor: first, Latium, with a ratio of 3.140 to 1; second, Lombardy, at 1.360; and last, Liguria at 1.124. All the other regions had migratory outflows, with Calabria at the bottom of the classification (0.306), followed by Basilicata (0.250) and by Abruzzi and Molise (0.244). This would explain, therefore, how after decades of overproducing intellectuals, the Mezzogiorno found itself again in 1951 with a percentage of diplomati and laureati lower than that of the Settentrione.

But what happened after the Second World War? For the decade 1951 – 61 one can try to answer this question by examining the data of the two censuses together with those on the number of diplomati and laureati produced in the various areas of the country. This approach does not allow us to estimate how many laureati and diplomati may have moved either from North to South or from South to North in this decade, but only, with a certain approximation, the balance of these movements of intellectual labor (which is, after all, what concerns us).

Table 11.1, which reports the data necessary for this comparison, needs some comment. Rows A and B report the number (in thousands) of diplomati and laureati in the censuses of 1951 and 1961, and row C the increase that occurred over the decade. The data of the three following rows, which indicate the percentages of laureati and diplomati in the population over 6 years of age, allow us to see that in this decade the distance between North and South not only did not diminish but actually increased. The data of row G represent an estimate of the increase of diplomati and laureati (after excluding the effects of internal migration) that occurred over the decade, that is, of the different contributions actually made by the North and the South to the production of diplomati and laureati.[5] Subtracting the values of G from those of C, one obtains the approximate value of the balance of the South-North migratory current over its inverse. From this comparison it follows, therefore, that in the decade 1951–61 the South had a net increase of 211,000 diplomati and 63,000 laureati, but that 33,000 of the former (15.6 percent) and 13,000 of the latter (20.6 percent) emigrated to the North or to the Center. This explains how in this decade too the distances between the levels of instruction of the North and the South were further increased, notwithstanding the greater production of diplomati and laureati by the latter.

Only the findings of the 1971 census will allow us to compare the internal migrations of intellectual labor in the period 1951 – 61 with those of the following decade. But, for the time being, we can attempt to see what has happened in the last decade. This problem was confronted by the Center for Study of Social Investments (CENSIS)* in an inquiry on laureati for the academic year 1965 – 66, which I have already had occasion to mention. Comparing the locality where the laurea was obtained with that of the subsequent employment of the subjects questioned, the CENSIS study pointed out that while the Northwest presents a "considerable positive balance of work positions relative to the number of lauree," the other two areas present a negative balance, with, however, a basic difference: that it is "high" in the case of the Northeast and Center, and "moderate" for the South and for the Islands.

According to CENSIS, these data show, first, "the existence of a 'brain drain' within the country which benefits the area of greater economic development" and, second, that this phenomenon "has a negative impact not so much on the underdeveloped areas, *where the development of education has not yet reached the particular levels necessary for meeting fundamental internal needs,* as on the imbalances among areas that are already developed on the educational level but which differ according to their relative technological, scientific, and economic subordination to areas where the phenomenon of concentration of software is established."[6]

How CENSIS, speaking of the intellectual labor force, could argue that in "the underdeveloped areas, the development of education has not yet reached the particular levels necessary for meeting fundamental internal needs" is certainly difficult to understand. Even ignoring all the data that I have reported in preceding chapters, is it not true, as I have mentioned, that according to the same study the unemployment rate for laureati in 1965–66 was much higher in the South than in the North? Evidently the old conviction that between economy

*CENSIS: Centro Studi Investimenti Sociali, a private social research center in Rome founded in 1964.

Table 11.1. Diplomati and Laureati, 1951 to 1961, and an Estimate of the Migratory Balance Between North and South for the Decade

		Diplomati			*Laureati*		
		*North**	*South*	*Italy*	*North**	*South*	*Italy*
A.	1951 Census†	980	392	1,372	293	136	429
B.	1961 Census	1,361	570	1,931	405	186	591
C.	Census increase 1951–61: (B. − A.)	+381	+178	+559	+112	+50	+162
D.	1951 Census (as a percent of population over 6 years of age)	3.62	2.57	3.24	1.08	0.89	1.01
E.	1961 Census (as a percent of population over 6 years of age)	4.64	3.50	4.24	1.38	1.14	1.30
F.	Percent increase 1951–61 (E. − D.)	+1.02	+0.93	+1.00	+0.30	+0.25	+0.29
G.	Estimated net increase 1951–61	+348	211	+559	+99	+63	+162
H.	Migratory balance (C. − G.)	+33	−33	—	+13	−13	—

* Includes northern and central regions.

† Rows A,B,C,G,H are in thousands.

SOURCE: See the text.

and education there is always and at all levels a positive correlation is so rooted as to hinder an adequate description and explanation of what happened and is happening before our eyes.[7]

In reality, things were rather different. Already in 1967, even though he refered to the conception which sees in the "training of qualified personnel, of intermediate cadres and managers" a "fundamental issue for the development of the Mezzogiorno," Goffredo Zappa observed on the basis of research conducted in Sicily on laureati of the techical faculties that this type of personnel tended to emigrate toward the North. He drew the conclusion that

> this phenomenon negatively affects development policy. . . . first, because it drains that type of personnel needed more by the firms now being established in the Mezzogiorno; and second, because a not insignificant part of the resources allocated for industrial development of the Mezzogiorno flow back in this way to the other areas, and especially to the "triangle."* Thus, although public expenditure continues to be perceived as destined for the growth of the southern regions, in reality these allocations contribute only in part to that purpose.[8]

Thanks to the fact that in recent years ISTAT has begun to publish the distribution of emigrants and immigrants among the various regions according to the level of education, it is now possible, on the basis of data for the six-year period 1964–69, to analyze the phenomena of interest here in a more adequate manner. Comparing the percentage distribution by educational qualification of the Italian population in 1961 with that of those who emigrated in the six years 1964 – 69 (table 11.2), one notes considerable differences. Not knowing the distribution of the Italian population by educational qualification for these six years,† one cannot calculate the ratios of derivation, that is, the tendency to emigrate of the various categories. However, calculating these ratios for the year closest to 1961, namely 1964, we obtain the following values:[9]

Educational Qualification	*Per Thousand Inhabitants*
Literate persons without qualification	60.8
Diplomati	52.7
Laureati	51.3
Licenziati (lower secondary)	39.4
Licenziati (elementary)	28.6
Illiterates	14.9
Total	35.0

*That is, the industrial triangle formed by Turin, Milan, and Genoa.

†Because such information is gathered nationwide only by the ten year census, data from which for the decade of the 1960s were not yet available to the author.

These ratios show clearly that, except for those literate but without educational qualification, who manifest the strongest tendency to emigrate, territorial mobility increases as one passes from the lower educational levels to the higher (the difference between diplomati and laureati is very small). Analyzing table 11.2 we notice, however, that things proceed very differently in the three major areas of the country. In particular, the percentage of laureati and diplomati who changed residence is much higher in the South than in the North.

These data alone, therefore, already indicate a strong tendency of diplomati and laureati from the Mezzogiorno to emigrate. If for a closer analysis we examine the two largest areas of the country – the North (which also includes the Center) and the South – we see that, whatever the level of education considered, the South-North current prevails over the inverse (table 11.3). There are, however, important differences according to educational qualification. The composition of the migratory balance (column d) presents higher values both for the North (column e) and for the South (column f) for the three higher levels of education and for those literate but without qualification, and lower values for persons with the elementary certificate. For the illiterates, on the other hand, these present higher values in the North, but much lower ones in the South. The South, therefore, exports to the Center-North *primarily* intellectual labor (laureati and diplomati) and qualified labor (licenziati from the lower-secondary) or else general manpower (literate but without qualification). As far as intellectual labor in particular is concerned, the South presents a deficit, over the mere six years considered, of as many as 42,000 diplomati and laureati.

An examination of the data at a greater level of disaggregation shows that both for diplomati and for laureati the regions that can be considered areas of attraction number only five, three in the North and two in the Center, while all others have been areas of escape (tables 11.4 and 11.5). Among the former in the North we find Lombardy, Piedmont, and – in contrast to what might have been expected – not Liguria, which has instead a deficit balance, but Veneto. The most important area of attraction, however, just as during the fascist period, is constituted not by the regions of the country's economic centers but by Latium, where the political-administrative center is located (while Tuscany has a very modest positive balance).

The data I have reported give, therefore, a sufficiently precise idea of an aspect of the contradictions of the Italian educational system which is certainly not of secondary importance. The difficulties of employment faced by the young leaving compulsory lower-secondary schooling in the underdeveloped areas of the country have encouraged the expansion of upper-secondary edu-

Table 11.2. Change of Residence by Educational Qualification and Geographic Area, 1964 to 1969, and Distribution of the Italian Population (Over 6 Years of Age) by Educational Qualification, 1961

Educational Qualification	*Residence Changed*				*Italian Population 1961*
	North	*Central*	*South*	*Italy*	
Laureati	1.79	2.78	2.56	2.18	1.30
Diplomati	6.44	8.65	8.86	7.49	4.24
Licenziati (lower-secondary)	13.52	13.74	12.38	13.25	9.58
Licenziati (elementary)	54.46	49.34	46.79	51.48	60.76
Literate persons without qualification	21.82	22.12	24.59	22.62	15.72
Illiterates	1.96	3.34	4.81	2.97	8.41
Total	100.00	100.00	100.00	100.00	100.00
(N)	(4,940,512)	(1,625,190)	(2,404,201)	(8,969,903)	—

SOURCE: Elaboration of data taken from: ISTAT, *Annuario di statistiche demografiche,* vols. 14–18 (for the period 1964–68); ISTAT, *Popolazione e movimento anagrafico dei comuni,* vol. 16 (for 1969).

Table 11.3. North-South and South-North Migratory Currents by Educational Qualification, 1964 to 1969, and Composition of the Population of the North and the South by Educational Qualification, 1961

Educational Qualification	*From North to South (a)*	*From South to North (b)*	*Balance*		*Population 1961*			
			(N) (c)	*% (d)*	*North (e)*	*South (f)*	*(d) − (e)*	*(d) − (f)*
Laureati	13,740	24,383	10,643	1.65	1.38	1.14	0.27	0.51
Diplomati	44,272	76,617	32,345	5.02	4.64	3.50	0.38	1.52
Licenziati (lower-secondary)	72,266	148,750	76,484	11.87	11.08	6.87	0.79	5.00
Licenziati (elementary)	256,347	582,068	325,721	50.54	66.40	50.60	−15.86	− 0.04
Literate persons without qualification	122,178	294,937	172,759	26.81	12.41	21.70	14.40	5.11
Illiterates	20,446	46,957	26,511	4.11	4.09	16.19	0.02	−12.08
Total	529,249	1,173,712	644,463	100.00	100.00	100.00	—	—

SOURCE: See table 11.2

Table 11.4. Migratory Movement Among the Regions of the Population Holding the Upper-Secondary Diploma, 1964 to 1969

Regions	*Enrolled*	*Canceled*	*Net Immigration*	*Net Emigration*	*Balance*
Piedmont	64,367	58,576	6,960	1,169	+ 5,791
Valle D'Aosta	1,626	1,351	278	3	+ 275
Lombardy	107,920	97,359	12,090	1,529	+10,561
Trentino Alto Adige	10,522	11,259	179	916	− 737
Veneto	47,075	45,790	2,183	898	+ 1,285
Friuli Venezia Giulia	18,892	19,306	803	1,217	− 414
Liguria	25,245	25,651	1,283	1,689	− 406
Emilia Romagna	42,414	42,927	1,691	2,204	− 513
Tuscany	41,619	40,178	2,332	1,431	+ 901
Umbria	8,709	9,593	334	1,218	− 884
Marche	16,178	17,785	268	1,875	− 1,607
Latium	74,128	56,035	18,016	13	+18,093
Abruzzi	16,360	18,463	449	2,552	− 2,103
Molise	3,644	4,969	12	1,337	− 1,325
Campania	56,638	64,580	538	8,480	− 7,942
Puglia	35,244	41,208	428	6,392	− 5,964
Basilicata	6,361	7,856	71	1,566	− 1,495
Calabria	22,731	26,982	188	4,439	− 4,251
Sicily	53,454	62,214	—	8,760	− 8,760
Sardinia	18,673	19,178	439	944	− 505

SOURCE: See table 11.2.

Table 11.5. Migratory Movement Among the Regions of the Population Holding the Laurea, 1964 to 1969

Regions	*Enrolled*	*Canceled*	*Net Immigration*	*Net Emigration*	*Balance*
Piedmont	15,264	14,236	1,413	385	+1,028
Valle D'Aosta	412	342	84	14	+ 70
Lombardy	30,939	27,525	3,836	422	+3,414
Trentino Alto Adige	2,741	2,890	189	338	− 149
Veneto	14,013	13,001	1,290	278	+1,012
Friuli Venezia Giulia	4,489	4,432	340	289	+ 51
Liguria	7,816	8,639	251	1,074	− 823
Emilia Romagna	13,016	13,639	758	1,381	− 623
Tuscany	13,299	12,744	1,074	519	+ 555
Umbria	2,966	3,140	167	341	− 174
Marche	5,070	5,537	168	635	− 467
Latium	23,885	17,597	6,292	4	+6,288
Abruzzi	4,081	4,498	107	524	− 417
Molise	1,069	1,343	43	317	− 274
Campania	15,828	18,949	130	3,251	−3,121
Puglia	10,201	11,779	124	1,692	−1,578
Basilicata	1,822	2,125	52	355	− 303
Calabria	5,984	7,167	43	1,226	−1,183
Sicily	17,778	21,010	15	3,247	−3,232
Sardinia	5,247	5,321	244	318	− 74

SOURCE: See table 11.2.

cation in these areas. The employment difficulties faced by diplomati, having finished these schools, have pushed some of them to emigrate to the Center and to the North. Even so, the rate of passage of diplomati to the university has always remained much higher in the South than in the North. At the end of higher studies the same phenomena present themselves again for the laureati: unemployment and escape toward the Center and the North. Underdevelopment therefore produces education, but it produces it for the privileged areas.[10]

APPENDIX 1:

Historical Sketch of the Structure of the Italian Educational System

The law prepared by Count Gabrio Casati and decreed on November 13, 1859 by King Vittorio Emanuele as the new foundation for public education in the regions of Piedmont and Lombardy was soon to become, with the proclamation of the Kingdom of Italy under the House of Savoy on March 17, 1861 and the peninsular consolidation of the new European nation over the following decade, the foundation as well of the national system of public education. It centralized power in the hands of the minister and the central bureaucracy along the lines of the Napoleonic system, from which it drew inspiration, and concentrated state resources on university and secondary classical instruction at the expense of elementary schooling. Technical instruction at the secondary level was soon transfered to the ministry of agriculture and commerce, where it remained until 1876 with passage from the *Destra* to the *Sinistra storica*. The "Casati Law" sought above all to establish, by means of a common humanistic culture, the foundation of a unified, highly educated, and numerically restricted professional and hence political elite. Only secondarily did it seek in practice to address the educational needs – basic literacy, for example – of broad segments of the population.

Secondary-level schooling was divided into two branches, only the first of which merited the title *scuola secondaria*:

1) a branch of humanistic instruction (the *scuola classica*) comprised by the lower-secondary *ginnasio* and the upper-secondary *liceo*, which taught Latin and gave access to all university faculties;

Adapted from the first chapter of Anna Laura Fadiga Zanatta, *Il sistema scolastico italiano* (Bologna: Il Mulino, 1976), pp. 11-24, with additional information taken from Giorgio Canestri and Giuseppe Ricuperati, eds. *La scuola in Italia dalla legge Casati ad oggi* (Turin: Loescher, 1976), pp. 19-30, 136-149.

2) a utilitarian branch comprised by the lower-secondary *scuola tecnica* and, at the upper-secondary level, the *istituto tecnico* and *scuola normale,* which taught no Latin, trained for immediate employment, and offered very limited access to university instruction.

The classical branch recruited primarily the upper classes and was the privileged route to the single university degree called the *laurea* and thence to the liberal professions and upper-level careers in the private sector and in the state apparatus. The technical branch recruited at first among all classes (see table 3.9) and prepared for a limited number of technical jobs (in industry and agriculture, for example) and especially for salaried office employment in the various state administrations and for elementary school teaching. All such positions required no more than the upper-secondary *diploma*.

The division, however, was not airtight. The *istituto tecnico* was equipped with one section, physics-mathematics, which prepared more for further study than for immediate employment and allowed its graduates to enroll in the scientific faculties of the university. (The university in Italy, like its sister institutions throughout Europe, has traditionally been organized by faculties composed of chairs and institutes rather than departments as in the American case.) It was not impossible, therefore, to enter the university via the *scuola tecnica*, just very unlikely. The privileged route remained unquestionably that of the *scuole classiche* even though, as the century wore on, further access was gained to the university by the graduates of other sections of the *istituto tecnico.*

The first attempt to systematically change the arrangement established by the Casati Law was undertaken immediately after takeover by the fascists. The "Gentile Reform," a series of provisions initiated throughout the year 1923 by then Minister of Public Education and idealist philosopher Giovanni Gentile, was founded upon an aristocratic and authoritarian conception of culture and instruction, in contrast to the more classically liberal one of the *Destra storica* and of Casati in particular. Only the most gifted (intellectually, but in practice also materially) were to advance to secondary and higher studies. The humanistic character of the Italian secondary school was reinforced, as was its preparatory function with respect to university studies. Latin was introduced into all lower-secondary schools except for the new and "catch-all" *scuola complementare,* which was designed to give no access to further studies, and into all upper-secondary schools except for the *istituto tecnico.* In further contrast to the Casati Law, entrance exams were required for admission to all secondary schools (except for the *complementare*) and the number of these was restricted (from 153 to 87 in the case of the *scuola normale*, or teachers' school, which was renamed the *istituto magistrale*). In replacing the *scuola tecnica,* the dead-end *scuola complementare,* perhaps the principal novelty of the reform, cut off the major channel of educational and thus social mobility for many middle and lower-class students.

Finally, the distance between humanistic and utilitarian instruction, which had been narrowed following a certain de-professionalization of the curriculum of the *istituto tecnico* in the 1870s, was again widened by Gentile. Graduates of the *liceo classico* continued to enjoy access to all university faculties. Those of the *liceo scientifico* (established in 1923 to replace both the physics-mathematics section of the *istituto tecnico* and the *liceo "moderno,"* itself instituted in 1911), the *istituto tecnico,* and the *istituto magistrale* faced ever greater limits to university admission.

The *scuola complementare* soon proved a failure, however, since it was unable to attract a sufficient number of students (see table 5.7). What was in effect a spontaneous parents' boycott of a school with no prospects was not only a case study in the integral relationship between schooling and social promotion but also one indication of the popular limits to state initiative under an authoritarian regime. The coherence of the Gentile Reform was eroded, by certain "re-touches" in the 1920s and 1930s. In 1929 the *complementare* was replaced, and nominally upgraded, by the *scuola secondaria di avviamento al lavoro* (literally, "secondary school launching into work"), which title was soon further enhanced by replacing *al lavoro* with *professionale.* Substantively, the *avviamento professionale*, which survived until the reform of the entire lower-secondary system in 1962, provided practical instruction for various trades and for low-level office employment. The real difference, however, was that its graduates, although certainly not encouraged to do so, could enroll in the *scuola tecnica* (recreated in 1931) and, by passing the necessary exams, in some sections of the *istituto tecnico.* But even this very modest chance for those attending the *avviamento* (predominantly of lower-class origin) to proceed with studies soon appeared excessive to the fascist ruling group, for whom separation between the classes was a fundamental principle.

Thus the 1939 "Carta della Scuola" (Charter of the School) of Minister of National Education Giuseppe Bottai provided for a partial return to the system of Gentile. In place of the *avviamento,* there were now to be two lower-secondary schools each completely without outlets to further study: the *scuola artigiana* in rural areas and small population centers, and the *scuola professionale* and *tecnica* in the larger centers. Owing to the defeat of fascism, however, Bottai's plans were implemented only in small part: the lower levels of the *ginnasio*, the *istituto tecnico*, and the *istituto magistrale* were unified into one curriculum in 1940, an economy measure which had the effect of postponing students' choice of educational career from 11 to 14 years of age. Since the *avviamento* (and thus the majority of lower-class children) was excluded from the provision, it was only a first, partial step along the path to actual unification of the entire lower-secondary school.

The unification of the *scuola media* and the *avviamento professionale* to create the *scuola media unica* in 1962 may be viewed as a first important departure from the historic separation, in the educational realm no less than in the workplace, between intellectual activity, reserved disproportionately for the middle and upper classes, and manual or practical activity, assigned likewise to the lower classes. At the least, a long-standing institutional barrier fell, and thenceforward at the lower-secondary level channeling of students would have to occur within a single rather than multiple institutional context. Although to date no such step has been taken at the upper-secondary level, despite numerous proposals and efforts to secure the necessary legislation, several less organic contributions to lessening the barrier between the two branches of instruction have been made. The most important of these was the law of 1969, which opened access to all university faculties to graduates of every five-year upper-secondary school, while graduates of four-year schools were allowed a one-year supplementary course in order to gain entry. As a result, total enrollments, including students *fuori corso* (that is, behind the normal schedule of exams; about a third of all students), nearly doubled over the following decade, from 550,000 in 1968 – 69 to 1,022,000 in 1978 – 79, overwhelming the already inadequate university structures. Significant too were the steps taken in 1969 and 1970 to introduce supplementary courses into the *istituti professionali* and *artistici* in order to bring these schools to the same cultural level as the *istituti tecnici* and the *licei*.

Given unification of the lower-secondary school and complete liberalization of university access (modified only slightly by the establishment in 1980 of limits to enrollments in the medical faculties), the surviving division of the upper-secondary into parallel but separate schools will continue to be anomalous until a political solution is reached that will permit the necessary reform legislation to be enacted.

APPENDIX 2:

Notes and Data on the Historical Configuration of the Italian Class Structure

Because of the recurring reference throughout the text to class structure and to the conflictual relations between social class groupings over the arrangement of the educational system in Italy, the following brief remarks may be of some use to the reader. First, I shall comment on the particular conception of social class employed throughout the text, since its logic if not its terminology may be less familiar to some readers, and perhaps particularly to Americans, than other approaches. Second, I shall point to some objective changes in the configuration of class structure in Italy over the historical period in question, employing the figures contained in table A.1.

In referring to such class groupings as the bourgeoisie, the proletariat, and the *ceti medi* or middle strata, Barbagli identifies the major class divisions of industrial society according to the classical economist's notion that to the major *sources* of income in the distribution of national wealth there correspond the major social classes. Class is, accordingly, the social outcome of that economic division of labor in society by which wealth is produced and distributed: to rent for land, profit on capital, and wages for labor, in the eighteenth-century formulation of Adam Smith, there corresponded the class of proprietors, entrepreneurs, and workers (*The Wealth of Nations* [Chicago: University of Chicago Press, 1976], vol. 1, book 1).

Such a formulation is clearly in contrast to the conventional views of social class in the tradition of American sociology, such as that which equates class with social status according to prestige rankings, social-interaction groupings, and common beliefs and values (see, for example, Robin Williams, *American Society: A Sociological Interpretation,* 2d ed. [New York: Knopf, 1960]; and

Table A.1. **Appendix 2**

Italian Population by Social Class, Selected Years 1881–1971 (thousands and percents)

		1881	*1901*	*1921*	*1936*	*1951*	*1961*	*1971*
I	Big and middle bourgeoisie	300 (1.9)	310 (1.7)	350 (1.7)	320 (1.6)	390 (1.9)	400 (2.0)	500 (2.6)
	1 Proprietors, entrepreneurs, and managers	200	180	200	210	245	250	300
	2 Independent or liberal professionals	100	130	150	110	145	150	200
II	Small bourgeoisie (middle strata)	7,470 (45.9)	9,020 (51.2)	10,880 (53.3)	10,760 (54.8)	11,435 (56.9)	10,845 (53.4)	9,720 (49.6)
IIa	Salaried employees ("new" middle class)	350 (2.1)	480 (2.7)	650 (3.2)	990 (5.0)	1,970 (9.8)	2,650 (13.1)	3,330 (17.1)
	1 Impiegati (Private)	100	150	160	340	1,050	1,400	1,750
	2 Impiegati (Public)	173	233	329	436	595	799	980
	3 School teachers	77	97	161	214	325	451	600
IIb	Self-employed ("old" middle class)	6,700 (41.2)	8,100 (45.9)	9,650 (47.3)	9,250 (47.1)	8,930 (44.4)	7,565 (37.2)	5,710 (29.1)
	1 Farmers	1,700	2,820	3,800	3,700			
	2 Tenant farmers,					6,080	4,400	2,380
	leasing peasants	1,950	3,380	3,750	3,300			
	3 Artisans	2,300	1,000	1,000	1,000	1,200	1,215	1,200
	4 Merchants	450	700	900	1,050	1,350	1,550	1,700
	5 Transport and services	300	200	200	200	300	400	430
IIc	Particular categories	420 (2.6)	440 (2.5)	580 (2.8)	520 (2.7)	535 (2.7)	630 (3.1)	680 (3.4)
	1 Military	160	200	360	300	290	325	350
	2 Religious	130	130	120	120	115	120	145
	3 Other	130	110	100	100	130	185	185
III	Proletariat or working class	8,490 (52.2)	8,300 (47.1)	9,190 (45.0)	8,550 (43.6)	8,250 (41.2)	9,060 (44.6)	9,400 (47.8)
	1 Agriculture	5,790	4,270	4,450	3,170	2,370	1,700	1,230
	2 Industry	1,650	2,700	3,300	3,400	3,410	4,190	4,800
	3 Construction	500	600	700	800	1,170	1,700	1,670
	4 Commerce	100	100	100	300	400	500	600
	5 Transport and services	100	150	200	250	520	600	800
	6 Domestic	350	480	440	630	380	370	300
A.	Total	16,260	17,630	20,420	19,630	20,075	20,305	19,620
B.	Population	28,500	32,500	37,930	42,910	47,160	49,900	54,500
C.	Rate of activity	(56.1)	(53.5)	(53.1)	(45.2)	(42.0)	(40.2)	(35.8)

SOURCE: Adapted from tables 1.1 and 1.2 of Paolo Sylos-Labini, *Saggio sulle classi sociali* (Bari: Laterza, 1974), pp. 155, 156.

Talcott Parsons, "Equality and Inequality in Modern Society," in E. O. Lauman, ed. *Social Stratification: Research and Theory for the 1970s* [New York: Bobbs-Merril, 1970]) as well as that which identifies class with income categories, according to which lower, middle, and upper classes have, respectively, low, middle, and high incomes (see, for example, Kurt Mayer and Walter Buckley, *Class and Society,* 3d ed. [New York: Random House, 1970]).

Without entering here even slightly into a discussion of such contrasting typologies and their respective merits, I shall note only the greater suitability and objectivity of an "economic" conception of the Smithian type for the sort of historical research undertaken by Barbagli as well as its origins in the distinctly European formulation of political economy. This formulation, in contrast to the American experience, arose out of the attempt to explain the "great transformation" from feudal to capitalist modes of production and social formations, a transformation, I might add, that has been retarded and at best uneven and is still incomplete in the southern European countries (see Karl Polanyi, *The Great Transformation* [Boston: Beacon Press, 1957]; and for the evolution of class theory in Europe, Anthony Giddens, *The Class Structure of the Advanced Societies* [New York: Harper and Row, 1973]).

The question of the *ceti medi* or middle strata, so-called because in their many components they lack the basic solidarity which for economic and cultural reasons characterizes the modern bourgeoisie and proletariat, provides the transition from the first to the second of my points. No observer of the changes that have occured in the class structure of western societies over the course of industrialization has failed to observe the unprecedented rise of those components of the middle strata which have been called the "new" middle class, of salaried employees who derive their livelihood from the myriad functions attending the growth of large private and public enterprises, state bureaucracies, and public services (see Giddens, chapter 10, for example). In contrast to the working class and to the big and middle bourgeoisie, the income of the "new" middle class derives neither from wages nor profits and rents but rather from salaries that often are even less directly related to any standard of economic productivity or profitability than the earnings of the working or the owning classes. And in contrast to the "old" middle class of small holders – farmers, artisans, merchants, and the like – the "new" middle class is neither self-employed nor relatively autonomous in its work. It is, rather, a mosaic of relatively routinized office employees, "white collar" workers, submanagerial technicians, school teachers and others of the "minor" professions. Together with the "major" independent or liberal professionals (doctors, lawyers, engineers, and the like), those of the lesser "dependent" professions just listed constitute the *ceti intellettuali* of Barbagli's research. As a "class" they share only the fact that their positions depend above all on the training and certification imparted by secondary and post-secondary educational institutions, and as such their fate is often intimately bound up with the educational system. Thus it is, as Barbagli amply demonstrates, that no change in the internal arrangement of that system can be adequately explained without recourse to the organized interests and activities of the "intellectual" strata.

In reviewing table A.1 in conjunction with a reading of the present text, first notice should be taken, therefore, of the dynamics of the *ceti medi* or middle strata, and among these of the *ceti intellettuali*. The impressive continuity in the relative shares of the two major social classes – the big and middle bourgeoisie (in which the independent or liberal professions have grouped) increases from just under 2 to just over 2½ percent of the working population over the ninety-year period considered, while the proletariat decreases from just over to just under half of all employed – is also reflected in the middle strata as a whole. These latter move from 45.9 to 49.6 percent of the total.

Clearly, however, this stability results from significant variation in the internal composition of both the middle strata and the working class. Paralleling the decline of agricultural wage labor and the rise of the industrial proletariat (from 35.6 to 6.2 percent, and from 13.2 to 33 percent of the work force, respectively), there is a comparable drop in the proportion of the self-employed "old" middle class and a rise in that of the salaried "new" middle class (from 41.2 to 29.1 percent, and from 2.1 to 17.1 percent of the work force, respectively). Indeed, the decline of the "old" middle class would have been even more precipitous had it not been for the long-standing governmental policy of protecting the subclass of merchants.

In view of the impressive gains, both absolute and proportional, registered by precisely those components of the work force – private and public salaried employees, school teachers, independent professionals, the "intellectual" strata in short – whose positions depend directly on formal training and certification, it is not difficult to summarily infer a structural tendency characteristic of all industrial societies: the increasing substitution for broad segments of the population of traditional means to acquire occupational roles (intergenerational transmission of skills and property) by educational certificates requisite to particular functions in the work force. What may be tendential in all such societies, however, becomes critical in one such as Italy where, as Barbagli points out at the very outset of his research, the unbalanced and incomplete quality of industrialization has rendered the school and the university virtually the single means by which the aspiration for occupational and social mobility of the large majority of the population might be channeled.

APPENDIX 3:

Geographical Information

As listed in Article 131 of the Italian Constitution, modified by Article 1 of the Constitutional Law no 3. of December 27, 1963 which divided the formerly single region of Abruzzi-Molise into two separate regions, there are twenty (20) regions in Italy: Piedmont, Val d'Aosta, Lombardy, Trentino-Alto Adige, Veneto, Friuli-Venezia Giulia, Liguria, Emilia-Romagna, Tuscany, Umbria, The Marches, Latium, Abruzzi, Molise, Campania, Puglia, Basilicata, Calabria, Sicily, Sardinia.

Reference in the preceding text to the following geographic areas may be read as follows:

North:
Northwest: Piedmont, Val d'Aosta, Lombardy, Liguria.
Northeast: Trento-Alto Adige, Veneto, Friuli-Venezia Giulia.
Center:
Emilia-Romagna, Tuscany, Umbria, The Marches, Latium.

These regions of the North and Center constitute the *Settentrione* or "Northern Italy" in contrast to the remaining regions of the *Mezzogiorno* or "Southern Italy."

South (Mezzogiorno):
Abruzzi, Molise, Campania, Puglia, Basilicata, Calabria, and the Islands of Sicily and Sardinia.

Industrial Triangle:
Piedmont, Val d'Aosta, Liguria, and the Provinces of Milan and Pavia from Lombardy.

At the sub-regional level, Italy is presently composed of 92 provinces and some 8,000 *comuni* or municipalities.

Adapted from P. A. Allum, *Italy: Republic Without Government?* (New York: Norton, 1973), pp. 18-19, 213, 215.

Notes

TRANSLATOR'S INTRODUCTION

1. While such "scholarly" journals as the *European Journal of Sociology* have consistently published the work of leading American sociologists with historical orientations, it may be indicative that the two leading American journals in the field, the *American Sociological Review* and the *American Journal of Sociology*, both highly research oriented, appear to have been admitting more "historical research" in recent years. A further indication of this trend may be the awarding of American sociology's highest prize, the Sorokin award, to Immanuel Wallerstein's *The Modern World-System* (New York: Academic Press, 1974) in 1975 and to Theda Skocpol's *States and Social Revolutions* (Cambridge: Cambridge University Press, 1979) in 1980.

2. In the United States, it was Theodore Schultz's 1960 presidential address to the American Economic Association on the theme of "Investment in Human Capital" that launched more than a decade of research and policy centered on the conviction that education could be viewed and indeed implemented not only as a form of consumption, but as a form of individually and socially productive investment. Schultz went on to win the Nobel Prize in Economic Science in 1979. See the critical summary of "human capital theory" in the editors' introductory essay, "Educational Research: A Review and an Interpretation," to Jerome Karabel and A. H. Halsey, eds., *Power and Ideology in Education* (New York: Oxford University Press, 1977), pp. 12–16. Dissenting somewhat from Karabel and Halsey's judgment is Anthony Heath, in a review essay of *Power and Ideology* which appeared in the *Oxford Review of Education* (1978), vol. 4, no. 1, pp. 95 – 110; see pp. 97 – 99 for a more sanguine view of the contribution of the human capital theorists.

3. See F. H. Harbison and C. Myers, *Education, Manpower, and Economic Growth*.

4. Single expressions taken, respectively, from Ivar Berg, *Education and Jobs: The Great Training Robbery,* Richard B. Freeman, *The Over-Educated American* (New York: Academic Press, 1976); Ronald P. Dore, *The Diploma Disease: Education, Qualification and Development* (London: Allen & Unwin, 1976); International Labor Office (ILO) (Geneva), in cooperation with the European Centre for Higher Education (Bucharest), *Education and Employment Research: Industrialized Countries,* World Employment Programme Research Working Papers (Geneva, 1977); Michael A. Carter, "Contradiction and Correspondence: Analysis of the Relation of Schooling to Work," in Martin Carnoy and Henry M. Levin, eds., *The Limits of Educational Reform* (New York: David McKay, 1976), pp. 52-82; Randall Collins, *The Credential Society: A Historical Sociology of Education and Stratification* (New York: Academic Press, 1979).

5. To cite only two of many indications of mounting concern at high levels for the problem of imbalance in the market for higher qualifications (concern that amply demonstrates the practical and political importance of a correct understanding of its causes): "For some years, Americans have assumed that increasingly higher levels of education are crucial to an individual's chances of 'getting ahead.'. . . The plethora of economic articles that have appeared in recent decades, demonstrating the economic value of ever-higher education, undoubtedly abetted this emphasis on credentials. . . . Yet

the economy itself has not been changing rapidly enough to require or to absorb the spectacular increase in the educational level of the workforce. The expansion of professional, technical, and clerical jobs absorbed only 15% of the new educated workers; the remaining 85% accepted jobs previously performed by individuals with lower credentials. . . . Most employers simply raised educational requirements without changing the nature of the jobs [and] for a large number of jobs, education and job performance appear to be inversely related. . . . If matters continue as they are, the disparity between the supply and demand of educated workers is likely to be exacerbated in the next decade." *Work in America: Report of a Special Task Force to the Secretary of Health, Education, and Welfare* (Cambridge, Mass.: MIT Press, 1973), pp. 134–36. "The 1960s saw a tremendous expansion in higher education throughout the Trilateral Societies [North America, Western Europe, Japan]. . . . The result of this expansion, however, can be the overproduction of people with university education in relation to the jobs available for them, the expenditure of substantial sums of scarce public monies and the imposition on the lower classes of taxes to pay for the free public education of the children of the middle and upper classes. The expansion of higher education can create frustrations and psychological hardships among university graduates who are unable to secure the types of jobs to which they believe their education entitles them, and it can also create frustrations and material hardships for nongraduates who are unable to secure jobs which were previously open to them." Michel Crozier, Samuel Huntington, and Joji Watanuki, *The Crisis of Democracy: Report on the Governability of Democracies to the Trilateral Commission* (New York: New York University Press, 1975), p. 183. The Secretary of HEW at the time was Elliot Richardson and the director of the Trilateral Commission was Zbigniew Brzezinski.

6. For the original coinage of this term, see Angus Campbell, et al., *The American Voter* (New York: Wiley, 1960), pp. 24-32. For pointing it out to me, I thank Professor Gianfranco Poggi of the Department of Sociology, University of Edinburgh.

7. For the distinction between "economic," "economically relevant," and "economically conditioned" phenomena, see Max Weber, *The Methodology of the Social Sciences,* trans. and ed. Edward A. Shils and Henry Finch (New York: Free Press, 1949), pp. 64–66.

8. In this observation, Barbagli is fully consistent with certain of Philip Selznick's conclusions to the important study *TVA and the Grass Roots: A Study in the Sociology of Formal Organization* (1949; reprint, New York: Harper & Row, 1966): "All formal organizations are molded by forces tangential to their rationally ordered structures and stated goals. Every formal organization . . . is imbedded in an institutional matrix and is therefore subject to pressures upon it from its environment, to which some general adjustment is made. As a result, the organization may be significantly viewed as an adaptive social structure. . . . Every such structure has a set of basic needs and develops systematic means of self-defense. . . . The needs in question are organizational, not individual, and include: the security of the organization as a whole in relation to social forces in its environment. . . ." (pp. 251-52).

9. For a wider discussion of Italian class structure, including historical data, see appendix 2.

10. For a wide-ranging analysis of the comparative study of political decision-makers, see Robert D. Putman, *The Comparative Study of Political Elites* (Englewood Cliffs, N.J.: Prentice-Hall, 1976), and on the particular question of integration and interaction among types of elites, see chapter 5, pp. 106-132.

11. Not to mention works of a similar caliber, such as A. Prost, *Histoire de l'Enseignement en France: 1880-1967* (Paris: Colin, 1968) and D.K. Müller, *Sozialstruktur und Schulsystem: Aspekte zum Strukturwandel des Schulwesens im 19. Jahrhundert* (Göttingen: Vandenhoeck & Ruprecht, 1977).

12. Of the type, for example, initiated in the 1960s by the Committee on Comparative Politics of the Social Science Research Council in the field of political development. It is at least interesting to speculate on what the volumes in a comparable series on educational development would contain, given the following partial list of titles, all published by Princeton University Press, in the Committee's "Studies in Political Development": Bureaucracy and Political Development, Political Modernization in Japan and Turkey, Political Culture and Political Development, Political Parties and Political Development, Crises and Sequences in Political Development, The Formation of National States in Western Europe.

13. For a very useful treatment of the methodological issues of present-day comparative research in the social sciences, see Neil Smelser, *Comparative Methods in the Social Sciences* (Englewood Cliffs, N.J.: Prentice-Hall, 1976), chapters 6 and 7. Interesting also are Smelser's earlier chapters on De Toqueville, Durkheim, and Weber in this regard. Patrick Gardiner's *The Nature of Historical Explanation* (1952; reprint, London: Oxford University Press, 1961) offers an excellent introduction to the question of historical explanation. And for a thorough, although now slightly dated, bibliography listing both monographs and articles treating the theoretical, methodological, and technical problems of comparative research as well as comparative studies, see Susan Bettelheim Garfin, "Comparative Studies: A Selective, Annotated Bibliography" in Ivan Vallier, ed. *Comparative Methods in Sociology: Essays on Trends and Applications* (Berkeley: University of California Press, 1971). Interesting on the decline of historicism and its transformation into sociology is Carlo Antoni's study of Dilthey, Troeltsch, Meinecke, Weber, Huizinga, and Wölfflin in *From History to Sociology: The Transition in German Historical Thinking,* trans. Hayden V. White (London: Merlin Press, 1962).

14. From, for example, Max Weber's monumental contributions to the sociologies of economy, law, the family, religion, politics, and the city, and to the elaboration of theory and methodology in such works as *Economy and Society: An Outline of Interpretive Sociology,* Guenther Roth and Claus Wittich, eds. (1922; reprint, Berkeley: University of California Press, 1978) and *The Agrarian Sociology of Ancient Civilizations,* trans. R.I. Frank (1909; reprint, London: New Left Books, 1976) to such contemporary work as Reinhard Bendix, *Work and Authority in Industry* (New York: Wiley, 1956), Seymour Martin Lipset, *Political Man: The Social Bases of Politics* (New York: Doubleday, 1960), Barrington Moore, *The Social Origins of Dictatorship and Democracy* (Boston: Beacon Press, 1966), and Juan J. Linz, *The Breakdown of Democratic Regimes: Crisis, Breakdown, and Reequilibration* (Baltimore: Johns Hopkins University Press, 1978).

15. See, among others, the essay by P. C. Schmitter, "Still the Century of Corporatism?" in F. Pike and T. Stritch, eds., *The New Corporatism: Socio-Political Structures in the Iberian World* (Notre Dame: University of Notre Dame Press, 1974).

ONE. HYPOTHESIS ON ITALIAN EDUCATION

1. See the contribution of P. H. Coombs in E. A. G. Robinson and J. E. Vaizey, eds., *The Economics of Education* (London: Macmillan, 1966), p. 684. The papers in this

volume were delivered at a conference organized in 1963 by the International Economics Association; and Coombs, *The World Educational Crisis,* p. 52.

2. G. Martinoli, *L'università nello sviluppo economico italiano* and "La Conferenza sulle strutture dell'insegnamento post-secondario," *Quindicinale di note e commenti,* September 15, 1973.

3. F. Ciafaloni and C. Donolo, "Contro la falsa coscienza del movimento studentesco," *Quaderni piacentini* (July 1969), p. 40

4. B. R. Clark, "The Study of Educational Systems," pp. 510–11.

5. According to S. Bowles and H. Gintis, "I.Q. and the U.S. Class Structure."

6. By "strategic human capital" is meant highly qualified personnel who perform the "strategic occupations of modern society": entrepreneurs, managers, scientists, engineers, doctors, architects, teachers, etc. See F. H. Harbison and C. Myers, *Education, Manpower and Economic Growth.*

7. For the functionalist theory of social stratification see the essays collected in R. Bendix and S. M. Lipset, eds., *Class, Status and Power.*

8. I have taken these propositions from R. Collins, "Functional and Conflict Theories of Educational Stratification."

9. For the results of these studies and for an exhaustive criticism of the functional theory of education, see Collins, "Functional and Conflict Theories." Among the recent studies on the relationship between education and the labor market in the United States, the most important is certainly that of I. Berg, *Education and Jobs: The Great Training Robbery.* For a criticism of the functionalist model see also Bowles and Gintis, "I.Q. and the U.S. Class Structure," as well as M. Vaughan and M. Scotford Archer, *Social Conflict and Educational Change in England and France, 1789–1848.*

10. It should be pointed out that the expression "open system" does not refer so much to access per se to educational institutions for youth from the lower social classes, as the actual quantitative dimension of these students' presence at the higher levels which this system allows. Because of the presence of other factors (such as more or less meritocratic examinations), these two things do not always coincide. This is shown by the fact that England has always had a lower number of university students (relative to population) than has Italy, but at the same time a higher percentage of university students from the lower social classes.

11. R. Rossanda, M. Cini, and L. Berlinguer, "Tesi sulla scuola," p. 22.

12. The economists of the New Left in America have very much insisted in recent years on the role of the school in ideological formation and on the importance of this formation for the productivity of the labor force in capitalist societies. They have, for example, sought to show that in the United States, "the growth of the modern educational system did not originate with the rising cognitive requirements of the economy. Rather, the birth and early development of universal education was sparked by the critical need of a burgeoning capitalist order for a stable work force and citizenry reconciled, if not inured, to the wage labor system. Order, docility, discipline, sobriety, and humility – attributes required by the new social relations of production – were admitted by all concerned as the social benefits of schooling." Bowles and Gintis, "I.Q. and the U.S. Class Structure," p. 79. But see also H. Gintis, "Education, Technology, and the Characteristics of Worker Productivity"; and S. Bowles, "Contradictions in Higher Education in the United States."

13. L. Stone, "Literacy and Education in England: 1640–1900," p. 85.

14. By "status imbalance" is meant the situation in which persons come to find

themselves when they occupy positions high on a certain social hierarchy and low on another. The "nouveaux riches" who have a high level of income but a low level of education and prestige, or the black professionals in a society such as the American who occupy positions high by education but low by ethnic group, are by now classic examples of status imbalance. For a review of the most important research conducted on status imbalance and some proposals for using this concept in historical-sociological analyses see: A. Pizzorno, "Squilibri (o incongruenze) di status e partecipazione politica."

15. W. H. Riehl, *Die Bürgerliche Gesellschaft* (Stuttgart, 1851), cited by L. O'Boyle, "The Democratic Left in Germany, 1848," *Journal of Modern History* (December 1961), p. 377.

16. As far as other countries are concerned, it is worthwhile to recall that according to L. O'Boyle, unemployed intellectuals "played an important part in 1830 and 1848 in France and Germany. Wherever they did not constitute a serious problem, the danger of a revolution was lessened." L. O'Boyle, "The Problem of an Excess of Educated Men in Western Europe," p. 494. W. M. Kotschnig has maintained that unemployment pushed many intellectuals to support the Nazi movement; see *Unemployment in the Learned Professions*. For its importance for the diffusion of communism in Asia, see M. Watnick, "The Appeal of Communism to the Peoples of the Underdeveloped Areas," in Bendix and Lipset, *Class, Status, and Power*. For other bibliographical information on the subject, see W. Kornhauser, *The Politics of Mass Society*, pp. 183-94.

17. For this distinction, see G. Germani, *Sociologia della modernizzazione: L'esperienza dell'America Latina*, especially pp. 130-35.

18. J. Ben-David, "The Growth of the Professions and the Class System," in Bendix and Lipset, *Class, Status, and Power*, pp. 470-71. The second hypothesis advanced by Ben-David is not as valid: that intellectual unemployment is due to the rigidity of the higher education system, to its incapacity to adapt itself rapidly to changes that occur in the economic system. According to Ben-David, in the period between the two World Wars, intellectual unemployment obtained in countries with rigid systems such as the European ones, which even in the 1920s and 1930s continued to produce the same types of qualified personnel that they furnished in the preceding century (especially lawyers and doctors), while countries with flexible systems, such as those of the United States and the Soviet Union, which adjusted quickly to economic changes and gave greater importance to the training of teachers and engineers, did not experience this phenomenon. This hypothesis, however, does not hold up under examination of the facts, since in European countries of the 1920s and 1930s unemployment hit not only physicians and lawyers but also teachers, engineers, and graduates in the sciences.

TWO. INTELLECTUAL UNEMPLOYMENT AND ILLITERACY

1. E. Nathan, *Vent'anni di vita italiana attraverso all' "Annuario"* (Rome, Turin: Roux e Viarengo, 1906), p. 130.

2. A. Gabelli, *Relazione statistica sull'istruzione pubblica e privata* (Rome: Eredi Botta, 1878), p. 156.

3. A. Gabelli, *L'istruzione in Italia*, p. 237, which reprints his essay entitled "L'istruzione classica," first published in 1888.

4. E. Ciccotti, *Cause ed effetti. Note sulle presenti condizioni dell'avvocatura e su di un nuovo ordinamento di essa* (Turin: Bocca, 1889), p. 6.

5. B. King and T. Okey, *Italy Today*, p. 249-50

6. Gabelli, *L'istruzione,* p. 235.

7. "La tassa di esami a scala progressiva," *La riforma universitaria* (1890), no. 21–23, p. 7.

8. King and Okey, *Italy Today,* p. 250.

9. AP [Atti Parlementari: Parliamentary Papers], Camera [Chamber of Deputies], *Discussioni* [Debates], 21st Legislature, 2d Session of May 29, 1901.

10. R. Michels, *Proletariato e borghesia nel movimento socialista italiano,* p. 117. Antonio Gramsci, as well, considered intellectual unemployment a phenomenon typical of capitalist society, born at the moment the dominant classes needed to move to large-scale production, employing the clerks necessary to maintain their hegemony: "this necessity of creating the widest possible base for the selection and development of the highest intellectual qualifications – to give, that is, to high culture and higher technical study a democratic structure – is not without inconveniences. There is created thereby the possibility of extensive crises of unemployment of the intellectual middle strata, as has happened, in fact, in all the modern societies." *Gli intellettuali e l'organizzazione della cultura,* p. 8. Gramsci, however, pointed out that the phenomenon of intellectual unemployment presented some characteristics that were peculiar to Italy. See *Il Risorgimento,* p. 197, and also *La questione meridionale,* pp. 150–52.

11. N. Colajanni *Manuale di Demografia* (Naples: M. Pierro, 1909), p. 152 spoke of the existence of an intellectual proletariat in France and in Germany. For Germany, see also P. Ernst, "Les prolétaires intellectuels en Allemagne," *Revue des Revues* (1896), pp. 24-31, and the forecasts on the relation between demand and supply of laureati made by G. Lexis, reported in part in F. Martini and C. F. Ferraris, *Ordinamento generale degli istituti d'istruzione superiore,* pp. 172–74. Concerning England, on the other hand, to find significant intellectual unemployment it is necessary to go back to the seventeenth century. See M. H. Curtis, "The Alienated Intellectual of Early Stuart England." It is doubtful that there was intellectual unemployment in England in the first half of the nineteenth century or, if there was, its dimensions were very modest. See L. O'Boyle, "The Problem of an Excess of Educated Men." Concerning the second half of the nineteenth century, see F. Musgrove, "Middle Class Education and Employment in the Nineteenth Century,"*Economic History Review* (August 1958), pp. 99 – 111; H. J. Perkin, "Middle Class Education and Employment in the Nineteenth Century: A Critical Note," *Economic History Review* (August 1961), pp. 122–30; F. Musgrove, "Middle Class Education and Employment in the Nineteenth Century: A Rejoinder," *Economic History Review* (December 1961), pp. 320–29.

12. Michels, *Proletariato e borghesia,* pp. 120, 122, and 123.

13. For these data, see Ministry of Agriculture, Industry and Commerce, *Censimento della Popolazione del Regno d'Italia al 10 febbraio 1901. Relazione sul metodo di esecuzione e sui risultati del censimento raffrontati con quelli dei censimenti italiani precedenti e dei censimenti esteri* (Rome, 1904), 5:102.

14. Michels describes the population of northern Italy as a "more affluent population, able to provide a living to doctors, less inclined to superstition and to witchcraft, and thus more inclined to avail itself of medicine." *Proletariato e borghesia,* p. 127.

15. Moreover, in returning to the question twenty years later, Michels recognized the existence of a surplus of university students and of laureati in Italy (and not only in the South) at the beginning of the century. See his *Italien von heute: Politische und wirtschaftliche Kultursgeschichte von 1860 bis 1930,* p. 280.

16. Ciccotti, *Cause ed effetti,* p. 5.

17. See Martini and Ferraris, *Ordinamento generale,* p. 174.

18. C. F. Ferraris, "Gli iscritti nelle Università e negli Istituti superiori d'Italia negli ultimi quattro anni," *La riforma sociale* (1897), p. 1067.

19. For Luigi Bodio's study see "Il proletariato accademico" in F. S. Nitti, *La ricchezza dell'Italia,* pp. 92-103.

20. Bodio's forecasts were taken up again by the statistician Gaetano Ferroglio, who sought to show (unfortunately without presenting any evidence) that "for present-day Italy, the condition of intellectual labor is really miserable." He considered the conditions imposed upon magistrates not "suitable to the delicate mission they exercise," and the salaries of teachers, completely inadequate. Concerning the independent professions he argued that "surrounding a minority that makes handsome profits, there is a rabble of professionals who in their practice obtain scarcely enough for a very modest existence." See G. Ferroglio, "Sul proletariato accademico," *La riforma sociale* (1896), vol. 3, no. 8.

21. AP, Camera, *Discussioni,* 21st Legislature, 2d Session of May 29, 1901.

22. AP, Camera, *Documenti,* 17th Legislature, Bill of Law presented on December 6, 1894 by the Minister of Public Education (Baccelli): *Sull'autonomia delle Università, Istituti e Scuole superiori del Regno,* Doc. no. 1.

23. AP, Camera, *Documenti,* 20th Legislature, Session of January 28, 1899. Report of the Hon. Fusinato on the Bill of Law presented by the Minister of Public Education (Baccelli), Doc. no. 20-A (emphasis in the text).

24. AP, Senato, *Documenti,* 17th Legislature, Bill of Law presented on November 30, 1891 by the Minister of Public Education (Villari): *Organici, stipendi e tasse per gl'istituti d'istruzione secondaria classica,* Doc. no. 114.

25. AP, Senato, *Documenti,* 17th Legislature, Report of the Central Office on the Bill of Law *Organici, stipendi e tasse per gl'istituti d'istruzione secondaria classica,* Doc. no. 114-A. With Law no. 259 of July 12, 1900, fees for classical secondary schools and for the technical schools were further increased, while with the Law of July 12, 1896, fees for enrollees at those which trained primary school teachers were instituted for the first time.

26. AP, Camera, *Documenti,* 17th Legislature, Bill of Law presented on December 6, 1894, by the Minister of Public Education (Baccelli): *Sull'autonomia delle Università, Istituti e Scuole superiori del Regno,* Doc. no. 1.

27. AP, Camera, *Documenti,* 20th Legislature, Bill of Law presented on May 4, 1897 by the Minister of Public Education (Gianturco): *Modificazioni alle legge vigenti sull'istruzione superiore,* Doc. no. 79, and Bill of Law presented on April 18, 1898 by the Minister of Public Education (Gallo): *Provvedimenti sulla Pubblica Istruzione,* Doc. no. 283.

28. AP, Camera, *Documenti,* 21st Legislature, Bill of Law presented on May 17, 1902, by Morelli Gualtierotti and other deputies, Doc. no. 145, and Bill of Law presented on May 17, 1902, by the Minister of Public Education (Nasi), Doc. no 146; Law no. 224, May, 28, 1903.

29. Minister Gianturco had few illusions about the efficacy of the provisions: "If the increase of fees," he observed, "could contribute to the reduction of our educational population, which is, evidently, higher than what is socially necessary; if, that is, one could little by little thin out the line of the intellectual proletariat which is truly a threat to the future of our country, then perhaps one might agree without hesitation to the decision to double these fees. But the opposite is demonstrated by many experiences,

two of the most recent and conclusive being: first, that the increase of fees imposed by the Villari Law did not decrease the population of our secondary schools; and second, that the population of our technical and teacher training schools did not decrease at all, even though last year's law imposed a brand new fee." From *Modificazioni alle leggi*.

30. AP, Camera, *Discussioni*, 21st Legislature, Session of June 20, 1902.

31. For these data see Alexander Gerschenkron, *Economic Backwardness in Historical Perspective*, p. 76.

32. There were some who argued that a part of Germany's intellectual emigration was due to unemployment. See A. Landra, *L'educazione dei Nord-Americani e l'emigrazione del nostro proletariato intellettuale*, p. 15 for France as well as Germany. For England see the data reported by F. Musgrove, *The Migratory Elite*, pp. 19–20.

33. F. S. Nitti, *Il partito radicale e la nuova democrazia industriale* (Turin-Rome: Società Tipografica Editrice Nazionale, 1907), p. 68.

34. Musgrove, *Migratory Elite*, p. 3.

35. R. F. Foerster, *The Italian Emigration of Our Times*, p. 130.

36. *IX Congresso degli Ingegneri e degli Architetti Italiani in Bologna* (Bologna: Regia Tipografia, 1901), pp. 209–10.

37. See Foerster, *Italian Emigration*, pp. 330–31.

38. "Bolletino dell'emigrazione" (1907), no. 2, p. 116.

39. Minister of Agriculture, Industry, and Commerce, *Censimento della Popolazione del Regno d'Italia al 10 febbraio 1901*, p. xlix.

40. Nitti, *Il partito radicale*, p. 68.

41. Landra, *L'educazione dei Nord-Americani*, pp. 15 and 19. According to Nitti, in fact, it was from the surplus of laureati and from their consequent loss of professional and social status ("whereby individuals who have followed higher studies need content themselves with the poorest employment; often with remuneration that the lowliest worker would not accept") that there arose "in Italy the greatest danger of revolution." "The most truly subversive part of the population," he observed, "is made up of laureati and diplomati in search of employment, and above all by lawyers." F. S. Nitti, *L'Italia all'alba del secolo XX. Discorsi ai giovani d'Italia* (Turin-Rome: Roux e Viarengo, 1901), p. 193. See also E. Cocchia, "Il proletariato intellettuale e il problema dell'emigrazione," *Nuova Antologia* (May–June 1904), pp. 89–99.

42. Fortunately, the General Commission of Emigration kept to the distinction between the group "in liberal professions" and two other groups of intellectuals: a) theater artists and musicians; b) painters, sculptors, designers, engravers, and photographers.

43. As F. Coletti argues in his book *Dell'emigrazione italiana* (Milan: Hoepli, 1912), p. 56.

44. This expedient has an advantage. It is likely, in fact, that among the teachers the General Commission of Emigration had also included the elementary teachers who were diplomati and not laureati. It is true that this would probably not affect the number of emigrants in the liberal professions because, at least throughout the nineteenth century, there was not a surplus of elementary teachers but rather a shortage, and it is thus improbable that these would have emigrated. Still, if we consider only the male emigrants in the liberal professions, it is even easier to avoid the risk that their number might be inflated by the presence of these teachers, for the simple reason that by the last two decades of the past century the majority of them were women.

45. Strictly speaking, the comparison would have to be made not with the distribution

of the population as a whole but with the distribution of laureati in various years by *area of residence.* Unfortunately we do not possess these data.

46. In 1927 (the only year for which there are data on the number and whereabouts of Italians abroad "in liberal professions") after the flow of emigrants had diminished (as we shall see further on), there were 20,092 Italians who carried out these occupations in the United States, at least as many in Argentina, 165 in Mexico, 234 in the one district of Brazil (Belo Horizonte) for which there are data, and 209 in other Latin American countries. For Europe the data are even spottier: for France there are data only for the districts of Bastia on the island of Corsica (200) and Marseilles (1,500); for Switzerland only for those of Lausanne (668) and Lugano (224). See Ministry of Foreign Affairs, *Censimento degli Italiani all'estero alla metà dell'anno 1927* (Rome: Provveditorato Generale dello Stato, 1928).

47. Nathan, *Vent'anni di vita italiana,* p. 130.

48. C. F. Ferraris, "Gli inscritti nelle Università e negli Istituti superiori italiani nel decennio scolastico dal 1893–94 al 1902–03," *La riforma sociale* (1903), pp. 877-903 and 965-73.

49. Nathan, *Vent'anni de vita italiana,* p. 130.

50. C. F. Ferraris, "Statistiche delle Università e degli Istituti superiori," *Annali di statistica,* 5th ser. (1913), vol. 5.

51. P. Calamandrei, *Troppi avvocati!,* p. 53.

52. *Ibid.,* p. 45.

53. Michels, *Italien von heute,* p. 283.

54. Ferraris, "Gli inscritti," p. 894.

55. Ferraris, "Statistiche delle Università," p. xiv.

56. Ferraris, "Gli inscritti," "Statistiche delle Università," and "Gli inscritti nelle Università e negli Istituti superiori del Regno nel quinquennio scolastico dal 1893–94 al 1897–98," *La riforma sociale* (1898), pp. 1097–1109; "Gli inscritti nelle Università e negli Istituti superiori del Regno nel settennio scolastico 1893–94/1899–1900," *ibid.* (1901), pp. 131-42; "Gli inscritti nelle Università e negli Istituti superiori italiani nel dodicennio scolastico dal 1893 – 94 al 1904 – 05," *ibid.* (1906), pp. 333-39. For the academic years 1896–97 to 1904–5, precise information on the number of laureati in various faculites is missing. As for laureati in engineering, there is no precise data on their specializations (building construction or industrial) before 1909 – 10. For this reason I have depended mainly on data regarding enrollments.

57. G. Abignente, *La riforma dell'amministrazione pubblica in Italia* (Bari, 1916).

58. A. Puviani, *Teoria dell'illusione finanziaria* (Palermo: Sandron, 1903), p. 258.

59. Abignente, *La riforma dell'amministrazione,* pp. 5, 55, and 99.

60. E. Lolini, *La riforma della burocrazia* (Rome: Edizioni *La voce,* 1919), p. 41.

61. Nitti, *Il partito radicale,* pp. 70-72.

62. G. Salvemini, "La piccola borghesia intellettuale nel Mezzogiorno d'Italia," in B. Caizzi, ed., *Nuova Antologia della questione meridionale,* p. 379. Earlier Salvemini had addressed the same problem in the amusing essay, "Cocò all'Università di Napoli," *La voce,* December 31, 1908, reprinted in G. Salvemini, *Scritti sulla scuola,* pp. 974-77.

THREE. FORMATION OF THE NATIONAL SYSTEM OF EDUCATION

1. C. Correnti, *Dei provvedimenti finanziari* (Report presented to the Chamber of Deputies in the Session of April 2, 1866), in *Scritti scelti,* 3:129.

2. This debate, which lasted almost uninterruptedly from the promulgation of the Casati Law until the Gentile Reform of 1923, was taken up again, although in more subdued tones, during the fascist period.

3. S. De Luca Carnazza, *La questione universitaria, Studi e proposte* (Catania: Galati, 1891), p. 35.

4. I say interests because the abolitionists were represented especially among the professors of the larger universities, while the preservationists were widespread among the professors of the smaller universities threatened by closure. "The problem that incites us has acquired the aspect of a sort of class conflict between the professors of the larger universities and those of the smaller ones." L. Rossi, *La riduzione delle Università in Italia,* p. 7.

5. "Riduzione delle Università," *La riforma Universitaria* (April 5, 1891), p. 4.

6. T. Mozzani, *Questione universitaria. Richerche statistiche,* p. 16.

7. Domenico Zanichelli argued that "the common accusation against the universities and the other higher institutions that they manufacture misfits, cannot be considered correct." He denied that there was a surplus of laureati in medicine and in literature and philosophy while for laureati in engineering he argued that "even if there were an overflow. . .this would not be deplorable because it would help Italy's industrial development"; for laureati in law he observed that "it would be useless to deny that the only real misfits in modern society among the youth who possess a laurea come from the law faculties." D. Zanichelli, *La questione universitaria in Italia,* pp. 11–13.

8. Mozzani, *Questione,* pp. 23–24.

9. C. F. Ferraris, "Osservazioni sul precedente articolo," *La riforma sociale* (1895), pp. 768–74.

10. F. Martini and C. F. Ferraris, *Ordiamento generale degli istituti d'istruzione superiore,* p. 121.

11. Even lower was the ratio of teachers to students in the four free universities, the most extreme case being that of the faculty of mathematical and natural sciences at Urbino, in which there were five professors and four students (two enrolled in the first and two in the second year). See G. S., "Professori e studenti nelle quattro università libere," *La riforma universitaria,* March 15, 1891, pp. 6–7.

12. C. Matteucci, "Discussione in Senato sul bilancio della pubblica istruzione," in *Raccolta di scritti vari intorno all'istruzione pubblica,* 2:397–419.

13. Ministry of the Treasury, State Accountant General, *Statistica comparata dei bilanci dei principali Stati di Europa per gli esercizi dal 1882–83 al 1887–88* (Rome: Eredi Botta, 1889), p. 165.

14. Martini and Ferraris, *Ordinamento generale,* p. 111; and for the expenses incurred by local institutions for universities, see document cited in note 13, pp. 108–9 for a summary.

15. Matteucci, *Raccolta,* 1:139.

16. Matteucci, "Relazione e progetto di legge per il riordinamento dell'istruzione superiore," in *Raccolta,* p. 54.

17. Matteucci, "Agli studiosi del migliore ordinamento delle scuole in Italia," in *Raccolta,* p. 10.

18. Matteucci, "Relazione e progetto," in *Raccolta,* p. 55.

19. See in this regard, and for other information on the debate over autonomy versus centralization of the organization of higher education, A. Caracciolo, "Autonomia o centralizzazione degli studi superiori nell'età della Destra."

20. Correnti, *Le economie* (Report presented by Minister Correnti to the Chamber of Deputies in the Session of March 10, 1870), in *Scritti scelti,* 3:183.

21. It is from this bill of law, which was to be presented to the Chamber in the 1892–93 session but was then not introduced, that the volume by Martini and Ferraris cited earlier, *Ordinamento generale,* arose.

22. Correnti, *Le economie,* p. 185.

23. The educational system discussed herein will be referred to as that of Casati, even though one of its most important characteristics, the access granted to some university faculties for diplomati of the istituti tecnici, was introduced not by the Casati Law of November 13, 1859 but by the Mamiani By-law of September 19, 1860.

24. See the collection of writings by A. Gramsci, *La formazione dell'uomo,* pp. 84–86 and pp. 394–403 and the interesting observations of the editor of the collection, Giovanni Urbani, on pp. 151–52.

25. See K. Roberts, "The Organization of Education and the Ambitions of School-Leavers: A Comparative Review."

26. G. Salvemini and A. Galletti, *La riforma della scuola media* (Palermo: Sandron, 1908); reprinted in G. Salvemini, *Scritti sulla scuola,* pp. 320–21.

27. A. Gabelli, "Le riforme urgenti dell'istruzione," reprinted in *L'istruzione in Italia,* p. 174. Amerigo Namias also lamented that in Italy there were no schools like the German *Bürgerschulen*. See A. Namias, *Trattato di legislazione comparata* (Turin: UTET, 1904), pp. 135–38.

28. The establishment of an educational system for the working class, characterized especially by the expansion of elementary and technical education, was often demanded by the workers' trade unions. To give only one example, at the Second Congress of the Unions of State Workers, held in Alessandria in September 1854, a petition was approved to be presented to Parliament which, among other things, declared: "Sir, we present ourselves to You, with the highest trust and in good conscience, and we ask of you something that no one can impugn: that which is not only our *right,* but is a duty, that which is not only the means by which so many miseries may be ended, but a necessity for the happiness and tranquillity of every social class: education. As soon as the worker is educated and instructed, he will live comfortably; that is, he will have a way to make a living; and he will not look with covetousness on the pleasures of men of property. Educate the worker, and you will have dispelled all the bogies of the socialist school. The instruction, good Sirs, which we ask you to institute, is the technical, agricultural, industrial, and commercial elementary school." Quoted in G. Limiti, "L'istruzione tecnica nella legge Casati in rapporto allo sviluppo del tempo e alla situazione politica," *I problemi della pedagogia* (January–June, 1959), p. 177. But documents such as these serve only to indicate how moderate was the political orientation of the trade unions, considering that their capacity to pressure was virtually nil.

29. From the periodical *Il vero amico del popolo* (1843), no. 49, quoted in E. Formiggini Santamaria, *L'istruzione popolare nello Stato Pontifico (1842-1870)* (Bologna: Formiggini, 1909), p. 115.

30. From a memorandum on elementary education sent to the Grand Duke of Tuscany in 1838, kept at the Historical Archive of Florence, and reprinted in its entirely in the appendix to A. Angeli, *Storia delle Scuole elementari e popolari d'Italia* (Florence: Lastrucci, 1908), p. 378.

31. Minister of Public Education Carlo Matteucci, citing Napoleon, said: "As long as one does not learn from childhood whether he must be a republican or a monarchist,

religious or irreligious, the State will form no nation; to place it on such uncertain and vague foundations means that it will be exposed to disorder and to change." C. Matteucci, "Discussione in Senato," in *Raccolta,* p. 418.

32. D. Bertoni Jovine, *Storia dell'educazione popolare in Italia,* p. 139.

33. V. Masi, "Istruzione pubblica e privata," in R. Accademia dei Lincei, ed., *Cinquanta anni di storia italiana* (Milan: Hoepli, 1911), pp. 6–7.

34. See Namias, *Trattato,* pp. 84–85. Namias mentions that only the law of 1903 weakened the diffuse character of the teacher's role by acknowledging that "the person who carries on his own work outside the school and far away from his students, such as that of agitator or apostle of new or old ideas, has to answer, like all other citizens, to the magistrates." Some examples of dismissals of teachers for political reasons in the second half of the nineteenth century are reported by G. Vigo, *Istruzione e sviluppo economico in Italia nel secolo XIX,* p. 31.

35. D. Berti, "Esame del progetto di legge per l'istruzione secondaria presentato alla Camera dei Deputati nella tornata del 18 aprile 1850 dal Cav. Boncompagni," *Rivista italiana* (May-June 1850), pp. 446–68.

36. See, on this point, Ministry of Public Education, Royal Commission for the Ordering of Italian Secondary Studies, *Relazione* (Rome: Cecchini, 1909), 1:25.

37. G. Vigo, "Il contributo della spesa pubblica all'investimento in capitale umano in Italia, 1870–1914."

38. Berti, "Esame del progetto," p. 446.

39. G. M. Bertini, "Dell'Istruzione Pubblica in Piemonte. Considerazioni e proposte" (March 1857), reprinted in *Per la riforma delle scuole medie* (selected writings collected by C. L. Bertini) (Turin: G. Scioldo, 1889), p. 15.

40. For a review of these studies, see H. I. Safa, "Education, Modernization, and the Process of National Integration."

41. Quoted in Ministry of Public Education, *Relazione,* p. 12. The importance of the middle class and of secondary education was affirmed many times in the following decades. For example, in 1885 Minister of Public Education Coppino declared to the Senate: "Between the working people and the people of independent professional practice is a very large number of persons who attend to various businesses, who have their own or public positions of various sorts, such that discord would reign and spread if the work of literature and of science at the middle level of instruction did not form almost a chain of moral and intellectual concord or if a common atmosphere, so to speak, were not cultivated in which all the minds of the Nation could breathe." The *Relazione* of Coppino is reported by C. Saredo, *Vicende legislative della Pubblica Istruzione in Italia dall'anno 1859 al 1899* (Turin: Unione Tipografica Editrice, 1901), pp. 253–77.

42. Matteucci, *Raccolta,* p. 415.

43. Still in 1867–68, 28 percent of the maestri in service were priests. In Calabria it reached 49 percent and in Liguria 40 percent. See E. Maestri, *L'Italia economica nel 1868* (Florence: Civitelli, 1870), p. 161.

44. P. Villari, "La scuola e la questione sociale in Italia," *Nuova antologia* (1872), p. 493.

45. Analyses of data on illiteracy show that rates of illiteracy were higher in those regions, such as Basilicata, Calabria, Puglia, and Sardinia, where children were forced "by urgent necessity to follow their fathers into the fields and to contribute their labor from the earliest years to the father's business." G. Vita, *Il fattore economico*

nell'educazione del popolo (Turin: Bocca, 1921), p. 90, to which reference is made, also, for its data.

46. Cited by Bertoni Jovine, *Storia dell'educazione,* p. 58.

47. G. Tarozzi, *Il problema della scuola media*, p. 11.

48. Bertini, *Per la riforma,* p. 107.

49. Ministry of Agriculture, Industry, and Commerce, *Gli istituti tecnici in Italia* (Florence: Barbera, 1869), p. 96. Emphasis added.

50. Namias, *Trattato,* p. 141.

51. Ministry of Agriculture, Industry, and Commerce, *Gli istituti,* p. 259.

52. *Ibid.,* p. xvii.

53. F. Carli, *L'altra guerra* (Milan: Treves, 1916), p. 85.

54. In particular we do not possess disaggregated data for successive years. To make temporal comparisons, we must therefore keep in mind the changes that occurred in the educational system during this period, in order not to mistake a lengthening of the course of studies for an increase in the rate of enrollment. It has already been noted that, for example, in 1871 the course of technical studies was brought from three to four years. It must now be added that in 1870 a two-year course of preparation for the scuola normale was instituted, which in 1889 became a three-year course.

55. A. Gabelli, "L'istruzione classica in Italia," *Nuova antologia* (October 1888); reprinted in *L'istruzione in Italia,* p. 226.

56. "There are a great many families," wrote Tarozzi, "who if asked, during the elementary school course of their children, whether they will have them go on to the scuole medie, answer: 'We would like that. We shall see if it is possible.' But when the time comes, the effort is made and the boy enters the scuola tecnica. Why not the ginnasio? The answer plain and simple is this: 'If the liceo-ginnasio is not completed, it is time lost. If the child must give up either because we cannot afford it or he doesn't succeed, what is to be made of what he's learned in the ginnasio? The scuola tecnica at least, if he doesn't continue, prepares him for some job or trade.'" Tarozzi, *Il problema,* p. 101.

57. Gabelli, "Le riforme urgenti," p. 167.

58. *Ibid.,* p. 237.

59. *Ibid.,* p. 167.

FOUR. EDUCATION, INDUSTRIALIZATION, AND ECONOMIC DUALISM

1. AP, Camera, *Documenti*, 21st Legislature, Bill of Law presented by the Minister of Public Education (Gallo): *Sull'insegnamento secondario e professionale* (Session of January 25, 1901).

2. It is to this hypothesis that reference is made by V. Zamagni, "Istruzione e sviluppo economico in Italia 1861–1913," to date the only systematically conducted study on the relationship between economy and education in this historical period.

3. AP, Camera, *Documenti,* cited in note 1.

4. AP, Camera, *Documenti,* 18th Legislature, Bill of Law: *Sull'autonomia delle Università, Istituti, e Scuole superiori del Regno,* presented December 6, 1894 (emphasis added).

5. See in this regard A. Gerschenkron, *Economic Backwardness in Historical Perspective,* chapter 4, and the essays in A. Caracciolo, ed., *La formazione dell'Italia industriale.*

6. G. Vigo, *Istruzione e sviluppo economico in Italia nel secolo XIX,* especially pp. 101-11.

7. L. Stone, "Literacy and Education in England 1640–1900."

8. M. Sanderson, "Literacy and Social Mobility in the Industrial Revolution in England." By the same author, one may usefully read as well: "Education and the Factory in Industrial Lancashire 1780–1840," *Economic History Review* (1967), pp. 266-79 and "Social Change and Elementary Education in Industrial Lancashire 1780-1840," *Northern History,* (1968), pp. 131–54. Carlo Maria Cipolla, in his book *Literacy and Development in the West,* reports that as much as a hundred years ago Sargant, in a study conducted on a sample of English parishes, had found that in 1754–62 about 51 percent of those who had been married knew how to write their own names and that in 1800 this percentage had risen only to 54. Stone's data and those of Sanderson (especially those in "Literacy and Social Mobility") considerably enrich the picture of the relationship between education and employment during the industrial revolution.

9. Sanderson, "Literacy and Social Mobility," p. 89 (emphasis in the text).

10. L. Cafagna, "La formazione di una 'base industriale' fra il 1896 e il 1914," in Caracciolo, ed., *La formazione,* p. 160.

11. Much detailed information on child and female labor in Italy in the period of the first industrialization may be found in S. Merli, *Proletariato di fabbrica e capitalismo industriale. Il caso italiano, 1880–1900,* pp. 212–76.

12. R. Morandi, *Storia della grande industria in Italia,* p. 129.

13. Thus wrote the physician Bonomi in 1872 in *Intorno alle condizioni igieniche degli operai e in particolare delle operaie in seta nella provincia di Como* (Milan, 1873), quoted in L. Osnaghi Dodi, "Sfruttamento del lavoro nell'industria tessile comasca e prime esperienze di organizzazione operaia," *Classe* (February 1972), p. 99. In this essay may also be found much information on female and child labor in this period.

14. G. Procacci, "La classe operaia italiana agli inizi del secolo XX," in *La lotta di classe in Italia agli inizi del secolo XX* (Rome: Editori Riuniti, 1970), pp. 3–74.

15. On the low level of qualification required in the machine and metalworking industry, see L. Davite, "I lavoratori meccanici e metallurgici in Lombardia dall'Unità alla prima guerra mondiale," *Classe* (February 1972), pp. 333–434. For the employment of child labor in the cotton and wool industry, see V. Castronovo, *L'industria laniera in Piemonte nel secolo XIX,* pp. 553–66, and idem, *L'industria cotoniera in Piemonte nel secolo XIX,* pp. 345–62.

16. The schools of professional instruction, which in Italy arose and spread especially by private initiative, must not be confused with the scuole techniche or the istituti tecnici of which I have spoken. It is not possible to examine here the great variety of professional schools existing in Italy in that period. Reference is made to the two following works: R. Castelli, *L'istruzione professionale in Italia* (Milan: Vallardi, 1915), and E. Congedo, *Le scuole industriali all'estero e in Italia* (Teramo: "La Fiorita," 1915).

17. "Relazione a S. E. il Ministro dell'Istruzione Pubblica sull'istruzione elementare nell'anno scolastico 1895–96," *Bolletino Ufficiale del Ministero dell'Istruzione Pubblica* (November 29, 1897), no. 47, Supplement, p. 65.

18. Between 1901 and 1921, the only year for which data are available on elementary school enrollments by sex and region is 1907.

19. Quoted in Osnaghi Dodi, "Sfruttamento," p. 141.

20. G. Arangio-Ruiz, "Sull'aumento delle tasse universitarie," *L'università italiana* (August 10, 1902), pp. 91 and 92. This phenomenon was described also by many novelists. See, for example, *Nétty* by V. Brocchi (Milan: Mondadori, 1925), in which it is said: "Of his sons the older, who was named Francesco, did not need to study, precisely because he was the oldest and would be the inheritor of the father's considerable estate. Virgilio and Valerio studied law" (p. 77).

21. G. Tarozzi, *Il problema della scuola media,* pp. 12–13.

22. The changes undergone by the scuole normali in 1889 (already noted in chapter 3) make a comparison of enrollments at these schools impossible over the period that interests us. The analysis here concerns, therefore, the four other secondary schools: ginnasi, licei, scuole tecniche, and istituti tecnici.

23. Moreover, referring to England, Michael Sanderson has written: "the clerical and administrative superstructure of even a large concern was often amazingly small. At McConnel and Kennedy's in 1833 there were only two counting-house employees compared with 1,600 other employees. Indeed in the 1820's it was noted that there was an overproduction of the clerk class in Lancashire. It is somewhat an illusion to think that this great advance of industrialization created a commensurate increase in demand for clerical labour and hence for the literate man." Sanderson, "Literacy and Social Mobility," pp. 92–93.

24. It does not seem to me that the significance of the rate IT/ST can be put in doubt by the fact that degree-holders from the scuole tecniche could enroll also in the scuole normali. In fact after 1870, as noted earlier, the girls who wanted to enroll in the scuole normali had to enter by way of a "preparatory course." As for boys, it is known that the percentage of them that enrolled in the scuole normali was always extremely low.

25. "Relazione a S. M. e R. Decreto No. 488 col quale alcune scuole tecniche vengono indirizzate ai bisogni dell'agricoltura, dell'industria, del commercio e dei pubblici servizi d'indole tecnica," *Bolletino Ufficiale del Ministero dell'Istruzione Pubblica* (December 15, 1898), pp. 2322–23.

26. A. Galletti and G. Salvemini, *La riforma della scuola media* (Palermo: Sandron, 1908), reprinted in G. Salvemini, *Scritti sulla scuola,* p. 319.

27. This means, in other words, that if we were able to calculate the rate of passage from the secondary schools to the university, the proof of the hypothesis of an inverse relationship between economy and education would be much easier.

28. C. F. Ferraris, "Statistiche dell'Università e degli Istituti superiori," *Annali di statistica,* 5th ser. (1913), 6:xxvi.

29. See for this information A. Tonelli, *L'istruzione tecnica e professionale di Stato nelle strutture e nei programmi da Casati ai nostri giorni,* pp. 36–38.

30. See L. O'Boyle, "The Democratic Left in Germany: 1848," *Journal of Modern History* (December 1961), pp. 374–83, and "The Problem of an Excess of Educated Men in Western Europe."

31. This was due also to the expansion of higher education that occurred in Germany at the end of the eighteenth century and that produced considerable intellectual unemployment. Speaking of this period, Henry Brunschwig has written that those who go to the university "are pulled by the prestige of the learning and at the same time pushed by the shortage of professional outlets. Then, as today, the sharp increase in the number of students is a form of unemployment; they instruct themselves there to gain time and to increase, with the appropriate skills, their own chances of finding employment." H. Brunschwig, *La crise de l'État prussien à la fin du XXVIIIe siècle et la genèse de la*

mentalité romantique (Paris: PUF, 1947), p. 146. Similarly, the phenomenon of higher educational "inflation," which has come about in the last twenty years in such underdeveloped countries as India, may be attributed to the unemployment of graduates of the secondary schools, who "join colleges and tend to mark time in the hope that 'something may turn up' in due course." M. Blaug, P. R. Layard, and M. Woodhall, *The Causes of Graduate Unemployment in India,* p. 56.

32. O'Boyle, "The Democratic Left," p. 383. This interpretation has been proposed also by Stone, "Literacy and Education," pp. 74–76.

33. G. Salvemini, "La piccola borghesia intellettuale nel Mezzogiorno d'Italia," reprinted in B. Caizzi, ed., *Nuova antologia della questione meridionale,* p. 380. This same thesis had already been argued by Salvemini, then twenty-three, in the essay "Un comune dell'Italia meridionale: Molfetta," *Critica sociale,* March 1, March 16, and April 1, 1897, reprinted in G. Salvemini, *Movimento socialista e questione meridionale,* pp. 9–26.

34. The number of students recorded by the census is probably greater than the actual number. This fact, however, is of no importance for the kind of analysis that I will undertake using these data.

35. In the thirty years 1881–1911 the percentage of the *male* population employed in industry increases strongly in the North, remains almost constant in the South, and diminishes in the Islands. See for some relevant data: O. Vitali, *Aspetti dello sviluppo economico italiano alla luce della ricostruzione della popolazione attiva.*

36. E. Ciccotti, *Sulla questione meridionale* (Milan: Moderna, 1904), p. 57. "In the Mezzogiorno," wrote Ciccotti, "the scuole classiche and those inaccurately called tecniche absorb the payments if not the attentions of the state and local governments, and, constituting the single outlet for those who do not want or are not able to give themselves to the manual arts, become disastrously busy factories of misfits" (p. 119).

37. P. Sylos-Labini, *Problemi dello sviluppo economico.*

38. Ferraris, *Statistiche,* p. xlv.

39. It is, in fact, impossible to examine the course of higher education over time and by geographic area because, having data only on enrollees by university site and not by family residence, and the geographic mobility of university students being rather high, the significance of the resulting variations would be ambiguous. As I will have occasion to say further on, the only specific inquiry on the residence of families of enrollees was conducted by ISTAT in 1931.

40. For the sources of the data utilized to calculate the rate IT/ST by region (that is, the percentage of enrollments in istituti tecnici over enrollments *in the same year* in scuole tecniche), see the note at the end of this chapter. The percentage of males employed in industry over the total of active males by region was calculated for various years using data published by Vitali in *Aspetti*. These are data gathered on the occasion of the censuses of 1881, 1901, 1911, and 1921. In 1891 the census was not taken, and therefore we do not have comparable information by region. This is why for 1888–89 I have not calculated the correlation coefficient.

FIVE. CHANGING THE EDUCATIONAL SYSTEM: THE GENTILE REFORM

1. L. Borghi, *Educazione e autorità nell'Italia moderna;* D. Bertoni Jovine, *La scuola italiana dal 1870 ai giorni nostri;* T. Tomasi, *Idealismo e fascismo nella scuola italiana.*

2. G. Gentile, *La riforma della scuola. Discorso tenuto il 15 novembre 1923 al Consiglio Superiore della Pubblica Istruzione,* p. 17.

3. U. Gobbi, "Gli spostati," *Idea liberale* (June 1893); reprinted in *Scritti vari di economia* (Milan: Guiffrè, 1934), pp. 347-48. C. Gide arrived at the same conclusions in the article, "Professioni liberali e lavoro manuale," *Riforma sociale* (1895).

4. G. Tarozzi, *La coltura intellettuale contemporanea e il suo avviamento morale,* pp. 231-32.

5. G. Arcoleo, "Gli Spostati," p. 89.

6. A. Galletti and G. Salvemini, *La riforma delle scuola media* (Palermo: Sandron, 1908), reprinted in G. Salvemini, *Scritti sulla scuola,* p. 284.

7. Quoted in Ministry of Public Education, Royal Commission for the Reordering of the Higher Studies, *Relazione e proposte,* Part 4: *Relazione generale* (Rome: Tipografia Operaia Romana Cooperativa, 1914), p. 6.

8. A. Monti, "La crisi della scuola media in Italia," *La voce* (1913), no. 14.

9. P. Gobetti, "Il problema della scuola media. Il liceo," *Energie nuove* (March 1–15, 1919), pp. 121-22.

10. G. Arcoleo, "La scienza nella vita sociale," *Nuova antologia* (1906); reprinted in G. Arcoleo *Forme vecchie idee nuove,* p. 54.

11. Ministry of Public Education, Royal Commission for the Ordering of Italian Secondary Studies, *Relazione* (Rome: Cecchini, 1909), p. 14.

12. Ibid.

13. On the debates and the positions expressed in the FNISM see L. Ambrosoli, *La Federazione Nazionale Insegnanti Scuola Media dalle origini al 1925* (Florence: La Nuova Italia, 1967); and also chapter 9 of Borghi, *Educazione e autorità,* pp. 104–18.

14. G. Salvemini, "Il metodo sperimentale nella scuola media," reprinted in *Scritti sulla scuola,* p. 234.

15. G. Gentile, *La nuova scuola media,* p. 106, which reprints the text of the speech given by Gentile in November 1905 to the Naples section of the Secondary School Teachers Federation.

16. Cited by L. Borghi in the preface to Salvemini, *Scritti sulla scuola,* p. xxiv.

17. For data on employed maestri see ISTAT, *Sommario di statistiche storiche, 1861–1955.*

18. F. C. Fabbrini, "La pletora dei concorrenti e la disoccupazione magistrale," *I diritti della scuola* (November 8, 1922), p. 58.

19. F. Mastrigli, "Impiegomania e Universitarismo," *Studium* (January 1922), pp. 6-8 (an article first published in *Tempo,* September 24, 1921).

20. P. Calamandrei, *Troppi Avvocati!,* p. 38.

21. Editorial, "Revisione totale," *La federazione medica,* October 15, 1921, p. 9.

22. G. Perrando, "Sulla eccedenza dei professionisti," *La federazione medica,* May 15, 1923.

23. L. Verney, "Pletora professionale," *Policlinico,* August 8, 1921, p. 1090.

24. "La legge per la disoccupazione e gli ingegneri," *L'ingegnere italiano,* September 20, 1922.

25. "I giovani ingegneri e l'ANII," *Giornale dell'Associazione Nazionale degli Ingegneri Italiani,* July 23, 1921.

26. "Consiglio Generale," *Giornale dell'Associazione Nazionale degli Ingegneri Italiani* (June 1921).

27. "Assemblee generali delle Sezioni. Sezione di Roma. Assemblea collegiale del

30 gennaio 1922," *Giornale dell'Associazione Nazionale degli Ingegneri Italiani* (1922), no. 4, p. 3.

28. R. Zinnari, "L'esportazione degli Ingegneri," *Giornale dell'Associazione Nazionale degli Ingegneri Italiani* (1920), pp. 113-14, and "Per l'emigrazione dei lavoratori intellettuali," *Giornale dell'Associazione Nazionale degli Ingegneri Italiani* (1922), no. 2, p. 4.

29. "Per l'emigrazione dei giovani ingegneri negli Stati Uniti," *L'ingegnere italiano*, June 30, 1923.

30. "L'on. Caetani parla dell'emigrazione dei giovani ingegneri negli Stati Uniti," *L'ingegnere italiano*, July 25, 1923.

31. "Per l'emigrazione degli ingegneri negli Stati Uniti," *L'ingegnere italiano*, August 25, 1923.

32 . The observations of Daniel Guérin, though, are worth recording: "The characteristic elements of this student youth have always been impatience and envy. The young doctor, the young lawyer, the young artist must wait long years before establishing themselves in the career they have chosen. Against the elders who block their way, they form an association of malcontents. Thus about 1910 in Italy the intellectual and student youth was, with Marinetti, futurist. These youths succeeded in defining themselves only by affirming their youth and by writing the word *youth* on their banner. They knew only one thing: yearning for the future. Their enemy was the adult, the bald man, the *passatista*. 'The oldest of us is not yet thirty. We must make haste to remake everything. It is necessary to go against the current,' was their *leitmotiv*." *Fascismo e gran capitale*, pp. 58-59. [*Passatista:* word coined by the futurists surrounding Marinetti, meaning "one superseded, standing in the way of progress." TR.]

33. A. Gramsci, "Voluntarismo e masse sociali," in *Il Risorgimento*, pp. 197-98.

34. R. Michels, *Proletariato e borghesia nel movimento socialista italiano*, p. 129. The same thesis was taken up again by Michels in an essay written twenty years later: "La psicologia sociale della Bohème e il proletariato intellettuale."

35. The best analysis in this regard is that of G. Germani, "Fascismo e classe sociale." Already in 1922, Zibordi had written: "Now, Fascism is also a movement of social geology, the vulcanism of a few strata which after the war found themselves compressed between the weight of the big bourgeoisie and the newly rich which weighs heavily from above, and the shove of the working class which pushes from below. ...Here, in sum, was the great strength of Fascism: that it combined in itself, against the socialist proletariat, the conscious and cool hostility of the authentic bourgeoisie and the fanaticism and aberrant hatred of those middle strata which, crushed in the crisis of the postwar period, turn and pour out on the proletariat all the agitation and the rancor of their hardship rather than on the dominant class, that is, on the dominant regime." G. Zibordi, *Critica socialista del fascismo, p. 20.*

36. I think that the best way to give an empirical basis to this analysis would be to reconstruct the composition by occupation of the *candidates* of the parties at elections, especially the administrative elections of 1920. In any case, Luigi Salvatorelli's analysis of the "humanistic" small bourgeoisie must be recalled, of its rhetorical training completely comprised of "general culture," of its "tendency to dogmatic affirmation, to credulousness of the *ipse dixit,* to the exaltation of the deed and the work usurping the place of facts and ideas, to fanaticism for the indisputable and unquestionable formula," of its difficulty of inserting itself into the modern world, toward which "it feels a mixture of moralistic and unintelligent repulsion and of covetous envy." L.

Salvatorelli, *Nazional-fascismo* (Turin: Gobetti, 1923); partially reprinted in R. De Felice, *Il fascismo: Le interpretazioni degli storici e dei contemporanei,* pp. 54–63.

37. In 1901 the UMN had 30,180 members and in 1904 it had 34,228.

38. Cited by L. Cremaschi, *Cinquant'anni di battaglie scolastiche* (Rome: Edizioni de *I dirritti della scuola,* 1951), p. 35.

39. *Ibid.,* p. 135.

40. These same engineers were aware of the "extraordinary" character of this process: "It is symptomatic that the mentality of *class* has undergone in a few years such a profound modification and that the engineer, the cultivator of the most independent and most individualistic of the professions, has convinced himself of the necessity of a solid system of class organization to guarantee his own conditions of existence..." C. Chiodi, "Ciò che si pensa all'estero in fatto di organizzazione professionale di classe degli ingegneri: A proposito dell'ANII," *Il monitore tecnico* (1919), p. 121.

41. "Per la costituzione de una Associazione Nazionale degli Ingegneri Italiani," *Il monitore tecnico* (1919), p. 38.

42. C. Chiodi, "Per una Confederazione del lavoro intellettuale," *Giornale dell'Associazione Nazionale degli Ingegneri Italiani,* February 10, 1920, p. 26.

43. "Relazione della Commissione della Sezione di Torino sulla Confederazione del Lavoro Intellettuale," *Giornale dell'Associazione Nazionale degli Ingegneri Italiani,* August 20, 1920, p. 177. The March 20, 1921 issue of *Avanti!* noted: "Our intellectuals are not of the Party or the Parish of Menenio Agrippa, and consider themselves so above it all that they cannot agree – for the sake of dignity – to join the manual workers. Of this division it is capitalism that laughs, rejoices, and takes advantage. ... But so it is: the intellectuals, in homage to the saying that 'in union there is strength,' have established the Chamber of Labor – indeed of 'intellectual' Labor! May it prosper!"

44. R. Mondolfo, "Il problema delle classi medie," *Critica sociale* (1925), p. 135.

45. See W. G. Runciman, *Relative Deprivation and Social Justice,* especially chap. 2.

46. "Il Sindacato magistrale a congresso," *I diritti della scuola* (January 15, 1922), p. 193.

47. G. Measso, "Lavoratori dell'intelletto, uniamoci!" *La scuola* (January 20–30, 1920), p. 3.

48. "Questione di pane," *La scuola* (February 10, 1920),

49. Untitled article in *L'ingegneria italiana* (February 12, 1920), no. 109, p. 105.

50. Untitled article in *L'ingegneria italiana* (February 19, 1920), no. 110, p. 121. The May 20, 1919 issue of *Avanti!* described these contrasts as "idiotic and antediluvian" and wrote: "the mason, the plumber, the metal worker have no duty to live worse off than an office employee, than a young elementary school teacher or a professor of the liceo. The work of plumbing, metallurgy, or masonry is infinitely more tiring than what the office employee, teacher, or professor does, and they don't even, like the mason, run the risk of sacrificing their life to their work. Besides, if they have an academic qualification, it is usually only because they have have had the money to procure it."

51. Already at the Milan conference of 1906, the engineers said: "Between such imposing organizations – the capitalists' on the one hand and the workers' on the other – the engineer remains isolated, lost in the midst of conflict, attacked, and confused, first by the one, then by the other of the two contenders. This is another of the causes that have contributed to the slight esteem in which the engineer is held in present-day

society, since it is clear that he lacks the power necessary to influence, with hope of success, the various economic questions that presently are tossed about." L. Caracciolo, "La professione dell'ingegnere in rapporto alla società moderna," in *Atti dell'XI Congresso degli Ingegneri e Architetti Italiani in Milano* (Milan: Capriolo e Massimino, 1907).

52. E. C., "L'affermazione degli ingegneri nella crisi dell'industria metallurgica e meccanica," *Giornale dell'Associazione Nazionale degli Ingegneri Italiani* (September 1920), p. 188.

53. *L'ingegneria italiana* (February 19, 1920), no. 110, p. 120.

54. "Il primo Congresso del Sindacato Magistrale Italiano a Bologna," *Avanguardia magistrale* (January 1920).

55. Cremaschi, *Cinquant'anni*, p. 127.

56. "A raccolta!," *Avanguardia magistrale,* December 16, 1919.

57. "Il Sindacato Magistrale a congresso," *I diritti della scuola,* January 15, 1922, p. 193.

58. Untitled article in *Ingegneria italiana,* June 3, 1920, pp. 316 – 17; P. Lanino, "Tutela o lotta di classe?," *Ingegneria italiana,* June 17, 1920, pp. 329-31.

59. "L'agitazione dei giovani ingegneri," *Ingegneria italiana,* June 10, 1921, p. 92.

60. "Consiglio Generale (Roma: 27, 28, and 29 June 1921)," *Giornale dell'Associazione Nazionale Ingegneri Italiani* (1921), p. 7.

61. "La vivacità fattiva dei giovani," *L'ingegnere italiano,* November 30, 1922.

62. "Sindacato Ingegneri Italiani," *Giornale del Sindacato Ingegneri Italiani,* May 1, 1922. For an understanding of this schism and the political behavior of the young engineers, more useful than the programmatic declarations are pieces such as the following, in which the creation of an employment office for newly qualified, unemployed engineers in Turin is commented upon: "And at via Chiaia #216 what deeds the commendables who mismanage the Naples section of the ANII accomplish! They continuously compile agendas that the relevant authorities do well to reject. These are the objects of their *exhausting* pursuits: the bell tower of S. Giacomo della Piazza, the agreement for the aquaduct to assist that *shark* Fizzarotti. All the while the young struggling engineers suffer the crisis of unemployment which overspreads all of industry and pay bi-weekly rent for a spacious office that would better be transformed into some civic entertainment hall." *Giornale del Sindacato Ingegneri Italiani,* July 15–30, 1922.

63. "Al Consiglio Nazionale dell'Unione. Gli argomenti trattati e le deliberazioni," *La scuola*, February 29, 1920, pp. 1-2.

64. F. C. Fabbrini, "La pletora dei concorrenti e la disoccupazione magistrale," *I diritti della scuola,* November 8, 1922, p. 58.

65. G. Minucci, "Della disoccupazione," *L'ingegnere italiano,* March 20–31, 1923.

66. A. Manfredini, "Le proposte della Commissione ministeriale per la Riforma delle Scuole per gli Ingegneri," *Il monitore tecnico* (1919), p. 365.

67. "Relazione della Commissione nominata da S. E. il Ministro della Pubblica Istruzione per lo studio del nuovo ordinamento delle Scuole d'Ingegneria," *Il monitore tecnico* (1920), p. 42. Naturally, the other groups of laureati were also demanding a change of the educational system. *Il policlinico,* for example, inveighed against "those enriched by the war, the workers and peasants who've become gentlemen [who] long for all their offspring to complete higher studies" and demanded that the state intervene by "disciplining studies, reforming programs, preventing crowding into a few liberal

careers which leads to creating veritable hordes of misfits." L. Verney, "Pletora professionale," *Il policlinico,* August 8, 1921, p. 1091.

68. B. Mussolini, *My Autobiography,* translated with a foreword by Richard Washburn Child (New York: Scribner's, 1928), quoted by F. E. Boffi, *La scuola media fascista,* p. 14.

69. B. Giuliano, *La politica scolastica del governo nazionale,* p. 72.

70. *Ibid.*, p. 60. The director general for higher education during the Gentile ministry, Ugo Frascherelli, wrote: "The universities poured out every year onto the market for professionals and salaried employees a huge number of laureati, greater by far than the needs of that market, widening thus and exacerbating the wound of intellectual unemployment, one of the most dangerous of the social body. " U. Frascherelli, "Per l'istruzione superiore," in D. Lupi, ed,. *La riforma Gentile e la nuova anima della scuola,* p. 109.

71. E. Agostinone, *La piú fascista della riforme fasciste. Il pensiero socialista su la riforma regalataci dal Filosofo del managanello,* p. 21. That this was Gentile's intent was argued by many. See among others the contribution of the Hon. Bruschi in the Chamber of Deputies in AP, Camera, *Discussioni,* Session of May 16, 1931.

72. The text of this interview is reprinted in G. Gentile, *La riforma della scuola in Italia,* p. 182. In another interview granted on January 17, 1924 to the *Corriere Italiano,* Gentile observed that the limitation on enrollments depended above all on the necessity of "recommending to the Italians a different direction for their activity. We have far too many professionals who, when they are not talented, are also useless; and on the other hand, we have much need for industrialists, businessmen, artisans, lesser professionals. . . ." The text of this second interview is reprinted under the title: "Il riordinamento della scuola," in G. Gentile, *Il fascismo al governo della scuola. Discorsi e interviste,* p. 250.

73. Gentile, *La riforma della scuola: Discorso,* p. 22 In this same speech, Gentile observed: "The scuola normale each year produced an exceptionally large number of maestri, far greater than the need of public and private education. . . . Of these, despite the system of concorsi (the greater number of which required only the certificate of study rather than a further proof of suitability and were therefore insufficient for a sure selection of only the best), many thousands remained unemployed to trouble the education administrators with their persistent demands and to threaten the people's public educational system with their continual pressure" (p. 19).

74. AP, Senato, *Discussioni,* 27th Legislature, Session of February 2, 1925.

75. AP, Camera, *Discussioni,* 27th Legislature, Session of May 14, 1926.

76. Gentile, *La riforma della scuola. Discorso,* p. 21.

77. G. Gentile, *La riforma scolastica. Discorso pronunciato in Senato il 5 febbraio 1925* (Florence: Vallecchi, 1925), p. 12.

78. Gobetti, "Il problema," p. 122.

79. Interesting information on the reactions to the Gentile Reform may be found in F. E. Boffi, *La riforma scolastica e l'Ufficio Stampa del Gabinetto Gentile* (Palermo: Sandron, 1925).

80. "Le riforme della scuola," *Ingegneria tecnica,* August 1, 1923.

81. G. Sangiorgio, "La scuola complementare e il corso integrativo di avviamento professionale," *Annali dell'istruzione media* (1928), p. 357.

82. F. Turati, Introduction to Agostinone, *La piú fascista,* p. 111.

83. Boffi, *La scuola media fascista,* p. 20.

SIX. EDUCATION AND LABOR MARKET IN THE FASCIST PERIOD

1. W. M. Kotschnig, *Unemployment in the Learned Professions.*

2. AP, Camera, *Discussioni,* 27th Legislature, Session of February 2, 1925.

3. Gentile, who defined himself as "one who had been guilty of offending so many interests," said on the subject: "Having gained the threshold of the scuola complementare, the student body doesn't necessarily have only one option. First of all, agreements between the systems of instruction run by the Ministry of Public Education and those run by the Ministry of National Economy make it possible for the students of these scuole complementari to pursue studies in those industrial and commercial schools by which one can reach a higher social position. But why should all schools prepare for other schools? And do we not have a great mass of citizens, the humblest and most numerous class of the proletariat, which must at a certain point leave the school and enter into life, into the lesser functions, into jobs for which a solid but still elementary learning is necessary, a civic education worthy of a people aware of its national duties?" G. Gentile, *La riforma scolastica. Discorso pronunciato in Senato il 5 febbraio 1925* (Florence: Vallechi, 1925), p. 21.

4. G. Sangiorgio, "La scuola complementare e il corso integrativo di avviamento professionale," *Annali dell'istruzione media* (1928), p. 358.

5. For further information on this subject see A. Tonelli, *L'istruzione tecnica e professionale di Stato nelle strutture e nei programmi da Casati ai giorni nostri,* especially pp. 131–40.

6. Even the limitations placed by the Gentile Reform on the number of students who could enroll in the secondary schools were progressively abolished.

7. "L'impiego dei lavoratori intellettuali all'estero," *Informazioni sociali* (1935) 14:542.

8. Kotschnig, *Unemployment in the Learned Professions.* Unless otherwise indicated, the information in this section is drawn from Kotschnig's book.

9. The data regarding Bulgaria and Finland are taken from M. Dubois, *Que deviendront les étudiants? Étude sur le Chomage des jeunes diplomés,* p. 30.

10. "Come attenuare la disoccupazione dei lavoratori intellettuali," *Informazioni sociali* (1936) 15:387.

11. *Ibid.,* p. 395.

12. G. di Giacomo, "Verso una cultura fascista," *Echi e commenti* March 15, 1927; reprinted in G. di Giacomo, *Intellettuali e fascismo,* p. 92.

13. G. di Giacomo, "Il problema dell'emigrazione intellettuale e le corporazioni," *La stirpe,* March 25, 1925; reprinted in *Intellettuali e fascismo,* p. 76.

14. ISTAT, *Nomenclatura professionale,* 3d ed. (Rome; 1937).

15. *Atti del I Congresso della Corporazione Provinciale di Milano dei Sindacati Fascisti delle Professioni Intellettuali* (Milan: A. Cordani, 1925), p. 158. Speaking to the Chamber of Deputies in 1935, Bernocco observed: "Unfortunately, practically insurmountable barriers have risen also against intellectual exportation. Many Italian engineers, architects, and doctors, who after the war found the opportunity to work outside the borders of the Country, today are forced to join the unemployed crowd who await some placement." AP, Camera, *Discussioni,* 29th Legislature, Session of March 5, 1935.

16. Of significance on this subject are the data on rates of activity by sex and age

cohort for the period 1901–1961 calculated by M. Livi Bacci, "Fattori demografici dello sviluppo economico," p. 67. Concerning males in particular, the rate of activity in the age cohort 15–24 years rose from 1901 to 1931 and fell in the following period.

17. See ISTAT, *Statistica dell'istruzione elementare nell'anno scolastico 1926-27* (Rome, 1931), p. 53.

18. See the contribution of Balbino Giuliano in AP, Camera, *Discussioni,* 28th Legislature, Session of April 15, 1932.

19. The population in the age cohort 15–25 years increases, in fact, from 1921 to 1931, but it decreases again in the following fifteen years. It must also be dismissed that the expansion of secondary education that happened after 1929 may be a simple consequence of the expansion of elementary education. As may be seen (table 6.6) the number of students enrolled in the elementary schools decreases up to 1926 and even in the two following years remains below the level achieved in 1921.

20. This is the interpretation although using different terms, that ISTAT gives to the very strong expansion of the istituti magistrali in *Statistica dell'istruzione media nell'anno scolastico1945-46* (Rome 1950), p. 125.

21. There are no data, unfortunately, for the preceding period.

22. Against "the female invasion of the secondary schools," Vittorio Cian observed, for example: "It is necessary immediately to get rid of that conception inspired by the foolish ideologies of democratic egalitarianism according to which women are endowed not only with equal rights but also with aptitudes perfectly equal to those of men." AP, Camera, *Discussioni,* 17th Legislature, Session of May 15, 1926. In an article entitled "Le donne nelle professioni" published in *La Stampa,* September 16, 1930, Giacomo di Giacomo sought to convince girls not to undertake secondary and higher studies in order not to further increase the existing "plethora" in many professions. "In all the professions, studies are long, exhausting, costly, the first steps discouraging and very difficult: it is necessary therefore for the young candidate for the professional *via crucis* to have a substantial and uncommon intelligence and an unusual physical endurance."

23. For these data, see O. Vitali, *Aspetti dello sviluppo economico italiano alla luce della ricostruzione della popolazione attiva,* p. 145.

24. See Livi Bacci, "Fattori demografici," pp. 17–95.

25. See the data of N. Federici, "Le caratteristiche e i problemi dell'occupazione e della disoccupazione femminile," in Parliamentary Commission of Inquiry on Unemployment. *La disoccupazione in Italia* (Rome, 1953), vol. 4, part 5, pp. 93-94. Federici attributes the lack of absorption of the female labor force expelled from agriculture to the "rigidity of the economic structure" in Italy.

26. For this interpretation see Bacci, "Fattori demografici," pp. 72–73.

27. Refers to data from reports made in December of each year.

28. "La relazione del Segretario Nazionale sull'attività svolta nel biennio 1935-36," *Il geometra italiano* (May–June 1937), no. 37.

29. F. S., "I ragionieri professionisti. . . sono anch'essi troppi?," *Il ragioniere professionista* (July–August 1937), p. 214. Emphasis in the text.

30. F. S., "La disoccupazione dei professionisti quarantenni (e di maggiore età. . .)," *Il ragioniere professionista* (January 1938), p. 154. Emphasis in the text.

31. *Ibid.*

32. A. Tempis, "La disoccupazione dei tecnici," *Il Perito Industriale* (October 1936), p. 17. Emphasis in the text.

33. L. Vivarelli, "Osservazioni e rilievi sulle attività professionali del Perito agrario," *L'avanguardia rurale,* July 1, 1931, pp. 3-5.

34. N. Federici, "Aspetti della disoccupazione intellettuale in Italia," in Italian Statistical Society, ed., *Atti della terza riunione scientifica* (Rome, 1941), pp. 156-71.

35. AP, Camera, *Discussioni,* 27th Legislature, Session of May 14, 1926.

36. G. Bottai, *La Carta della Scuola,* p. 31.

37. I have taken the hypothesis of a mortality rate of 0.7 percent per year given by Libero Lenti with regard to laureati in "Ingegneri, Architetti e Chimici in Italia alla fine del 1940," *L'ingegnere* (February 1942), pp. 141-46; as regards retirement from work for reasons of age, I have used the distribution of employed maestri by age cohort in 1936–37 reported in ISTAT, *Statistica dell'insegnamento elementare per l'anno scolastico 1936-37* (Rome, 1941). This is the only inquiry of the type conducted in this period.

38. E. Fanti, "Le arti minori," *Il geometra italiano* (November 1931), p. 155. Of the same sort are the arguments in an article by the same author published six years later: "La rivalutazione della scuola media quale fattore risolutivo della disoccupazione dei giovani," *Il geometra italiano* (March–April 1937), pp. 15-16.

39. E. Bodrero, "Grandezza e decadenza della laurea," *Il geometra italiano* (March–April 1936), p. 6. Emilio Bodrero was Undersecretary of State for National Education and President of the Fascist Confederation of Professionals and Artists. This article was published originally in the review *Pan.*

40. These data concern only maestri and not school administrators. For these latter there are no data for the year 1926–27, while for 1936 the ISTAT report cited above (note 37) informs us that of 2,008 subjects, 49 percent were laureati.

41. According to an inquiry conducted by the National Fascist Union of Professional Accountants for the academic year 1933-34, only 4 percent of enrollments in the first course of economics and commerce came from the liceo classico or scientifico; see M. Mazzantini, "Studio sul riordinamento delle Università commerciali," *Il ragioniere professionista* (December 1935), p. 331.

42. G. Del Vecchio and P. M. Arcari, *L'affollamento delle Università e la disoccupazione dei lavoratori intellettuali,* p. 8. The crisis of 1929 produced a strong expansion of secondary and higher education in other countries as well. Concerning the United States, see, for example, S. E. Harris, *The Market for College Graduates,* p. 156. In addition, in 1931 the International Labor Office proposed the prolongation of compulsory schooling "because of the need to take off the labor market many young men by keeping them occupied in school." See T. Salvemini, "La popolazione scolastica ed il suo incremento in rapporto allo sviluppo demografico ed economico del Paese," in Parliamentary Commission of Inquiry on Unemployment, ed., *La disoccupazione in Italia,* vol. 4, part 2, p. 205.

43. E. Comini, "Riforma degli studi," *Il geometra italiano* (August 1934), p. 111.

44. F. Berio, "I periti industriali e le Università," *Il perito industriale* (July 1933), p. 1.

45. G. B., "I periti industriali e le Università," *Il perito industriale* (July 1933), p. 4.

46. G. di Giacomo, "La disoccupazione degli intellettuali," *Il lavoro d'Italia,* August 24, 1928.

47. According to F. Coscera, *Professioni ed arti nello Stato fascista,* p. 41, engineers enrolled in the union numbered 10,510 in 1928 and 10,500 in the following year. According to *L'ingegnere,* the organ of the National Fascist Union of Engineers, in 1926

there were 6,312 engineers (35 percent) enrolled in the union, in 1927 10,271 (55 percent) and in 1928 11,561 (64 percent). According to these same data, the percentage of members who were laureati in engineering increased from the North (58 percent), to the Center (64 percent), to the South (78 percent).

48. F. B., "La disoccupazione fra gli ingegneri e le sue conseguenze," *Il lavoro d'Italia,* August 20, 1928.

49. G. Bigi, "La disoccupazione degli ingegneri," *L'Ingegnere* (April 1929), p. 234.

50. *Ibid.*

51. See among others: L. Ruffo, "Analisi dei prezzi, industria edilizia e disoccupazione degl'ingegneri," *L'ingegnere* (June 1929), pp. 360–61; M. Spremolla, "A propositio di disoccupazione degli ingegneri," (July 1929), p. 431; G. Maccagni, "Sulla crisi economica degli ingegneri," (August 1929), p. 513; G. Stellingwerff, "Uffici tecnici e disoccupazione degli ingegneri" (November 1929), p. 725, and "Il piano quinquennale sovietico e gli ingegneri" (June 1931), pp. 419–20.

52. E. Del Bufalo, "La disoccupazione. Gli Enti pubblici ed i Professionisti," *L'ingegnere* (1932), p. 374.

53. "Relazione letta dal Commissario Ministeriale nella riunione del Consiglio Nazionale del Sindacato Fascista Ingegneri," *L'ingegnere,* May 1, 1938, p. 4.

54. See the contribution in the Chamber of Deputies of the Hon. Bernocco, in AP, Camera, *Discussioni,* 29th Legislature, Session of March 5, 1935.

55. M. Pompei, "Integralità della bonifica e disoccupazione intellettuale," *Il geometra italiano* (January 1935), p. 4.

56. Federici, "Aspetti della disoccupazione," p. 170.

57. di Giacomo, *Intellettuali e fascismo,* p. 179.

58. R. Covone, "La pletora...dei Medici," *La federazione medica,* March 15, 1924, p. 172.

59. O. R., "La pletora medica," *La federazione medica* (1927), p. 811.

60. U. Gobbi, "Pletore professionali," *La federazione medica,* March 1, 1931, p. 2.

61. P. Colli, "Albo chiuso," *La federazione medica,* October 1, 1924, p. 616.

62. "Gli studenti e la pletora dei medici," *Le professioni e le arti,* (November 1932), p. 37.

63. See among others the following articles that appeared in the review *Rassegna del sindacalismo forense:* N. Sansanelli, "Del disagio economico delle professioni forensi," May 1, 1935, pp. 29–32; M. Aureli, "I giovani e l'avvocatura" (December 1935), pp. 91–93; G. Secreti, "Crisi dell'avvocatura?" (December 1935), pp. 94–97; A. Tedeschi, "Disoccupazione professionale: Cause e possibili rimedi" (January 1936), pp. 121–27; M. C. M., "Il problema dei giovani nella professione forense" (February 1938), pp. 212–13; M. Ravatini, "Crisi della professione forense" (December 1938), pp. 70–101; G. Podaliri, "Crisi degli avvocati" (July 1939), pp. 433–35.

64. G. Checchia, *Il collocamento degli intellettuali,* p. 39. During the fascist period as well the phenomenon of the surplus of lawyers was even more widespread in the *Mezzogiorno.* "In Naples," observed Limoncelli to the Chamber, "the densest judicial center, you will find a staggering number of lawyers: nearly three thousand. But meanwhile those who really practice profitably reach more or less five hundred. Here is the bloody selection of reality. Five hundred, and the others? It is a mass which must still do something—retreat, learn what compromise means, live in discomfort.... Do not believe that things go differently in other places, in other regions." AP, Camera, *Discussioni,* 28th Legislature, Session of May 13, 1931.

65. R. Romeo, *Breve storia della grande industria in Italia,* pp. 145, 157, and 186.
66. O. Forte, "Per la creazione della Facoltà di Chimica," *Il chimico italiano* (March 1935), pp. 68-69.
67. N. Curcio, "Cause della disoccupazione dei chimici," *Il chimico italiano* (February 1935), p. 43.
68. L. Sarcoli, "Disoccupazione tra chimici e tecnici affini," *Il chimico italiano* (September 1936), p. 167.
69. Il Segretario Nazionale, "Diminuire. . . ," *Il chimico italiano* (June 1935), p. 147.
70. Il Segretario Nazionale, "Invasioni professionali," *Il chimico italiano* (March 1935), p. 66.

SEVEN. THE CORPORATE ASSOCIATIONS OF INTELLECTUALS AND THE CARTA DELLA SCUOLA

1. G. D'Onofrio and D. G. Pellegrini, *Le funzioni dei sindacati intellettuali,* p. 29.
2. M. De Rosa, "La pletora dei medici e l'albo chiuso," *La federazione medica,* November 1, 1924, p. 653.
3. F. Gazzetti, "Professionisti, Artisti, e Sindacati," *Le professioni e le arti* (May–June 1936), p. 2.
4. G. Stellingwerff, "Uffici tecnici e disoccupazione degli ingegneri," *L'ingegnere* (November 1929), p. 724.
5. D. Ortensi, "Tecnici condotti?," *L'ingegnere (November 1929),* p. 725.
6. Stellingwerff, "Uffici tecnici."
7. A. Pariani, "Gli ingegneri e l'industria meccanica italiana," *L'ingegnere* (May 1930), p. 324.
8. A. Schiavon, "La riforma degli studi nelle scuole di ingegneria e il prestigio dell'ingegnere," *L'ingegnere* (July 1931), p. 475.
9. F. B., "La disoccupazione fra gli ingegneri e le sue conseguenze," *Il lavoro d'Italia,* August 20, 1928.
10. Schiavon, "La riforma degli studi." Comparable attacks against the industrialists were carried out by the National Fascist Union of Chemists. See the National Secretary "Troppi laureati?," *Il chimico italiano* (April 1935), pp. 91-92.
11. G. di Giacomo, "La disoccupazione degli intellettuali," *Il lavoro d'Italia,* August 24, 1928; G. di Giacomo, "Provvidenze e rimedi per la disoccupazione degli intellettuali," *L'ingegnere* (June 1930), pp. 427-28.
12. P. Calamandrei, *Troppi avvocati!*, p. 68.
13. M. Ravatini, "Crisi della professione forense. Cause e rimedi. Abbozzo di un sistema professionale corporativo," *Rassegna del sindacalismo forense* (December 1938), p. 88.
14. Calamandrei, *Troppi avvocati!,* p. 61.
15. Ravatini, "Crisi della professione forense," p. 79.
16. "L'attività sindacale nelle controversie del lavoro," in Fascist Confederation of Industrial Workers, *I 10 anni della Carta del Lavoro* (Rocca S. Casciano: Cappelli, 1937), pp. 171-79.
17. Ravatini, "Crisi della professione forense," pp. 82, 83, and 91.
18. N. Sansanelli, "Del disagio economico delle professioni forensi," *Rassegna del sindacalismo forense* (May 1935), pp. 29-32.

19. J. A. Jackson, ed., *Professions and Professionalisation,* p. 7.

20. "Il III Congresso ed il I Consiglio del Sindacato Nazionale Fascista dei Medici," *La federazione medica,* December 10, 1931, p. 4. Emphasis added.

21. U. Contento, "L'uso del latino nelle questione mediche," *La federazione medica,* June 20, 1931, p. 7.

22. Fraschetti, "Disoccupazione o... quasi," *La federazione medica,* December 15, 1927, p. 808.

23. Fraschetti, "Le tasse e i medici," *La federazione medica,* December 15, 1928, p. 742.

24. *Ibid.,* p. 743.

25. "Il III Congresso," p. 22.

26. *Ibid.,* p. 23. The Confederation of Professionals and Artists presented at the beginning of 1933 an agenda to the National Council of Corporative Associations in which among other things it was asked that "the establishment of medical insurance companies... be held within the strictest possible limits." See "I professionisti e gli incarichi professionali," *Le professioni e le arti* (April 1933), p. 4. On the struggle against the medical insurance companies as well as the legal offices of union organizations see the report by the President of the Confederation, Alessandro Pavolini, "Problemi all'ordine del giorno," *Le professioni e le arti* (February–March 1935), pp. 1-3.

27. Fraschetti, "Le tasse e i medici," p. 743.

28. "Il III Congresso," p. 8.

29. A Tedeschi, "Disoccupazione professionale. Cause e possibili rimedi," *Rassegna del sindacalismo forense* (January 1936), p. 125.

30. G. Bonavera, "Dell'albo chiuso," *La federazione medica,* September 1, 1924, p. 527.

31. A. Dal Prato, "Terapia della pletora," *La federazione medica,* August 15, 1924, p. 488.

32. A. Martinelli, "L'Albo chiuso," *La federazione medica,* November 1, 1924, p. 656.

33. G. Cajozzo, "Pletora medica," *La federazione medica,* August 15, 1924, p. 487.

34. For these data see ISTAT, *Statistica dell'istruzione superiore nell'anno accademico 1926–27* (Rome, 1933), p. 144; and ISTAT, *Statistica dell'istruzione superiore per l'anno accademico 1931–32 e notizie storiche per gli anni accademici dal 1927–28 al 1930–31* (Rome, 1936), p. 43.

35. B. Erba, "Rivendicazione ideale e necessità practica," *La federazione medica,* April 1, 1929, p. 3.

36. A. Fiori, "Medici stranieri in Italia. Escercizio professionale. Chiarimenti," *La federazione medica,* March 1, 1929.

37. Foreign students were exempted from payment of educational fees.

38. "Il III Congresso," p. 18.

39. Ravatini, "Crisi della professione forense," p. 72.

40. Martinelli, "L'albo chiuso," p. 659.

41. O. R., "Anomalie del dopoguerra. La pletora medica," *La federazione medica* (1927), p. 822.

42. *L'ingegnere,* February 30, 1930, p. 148.

43. Ravatini, "Crisi della professione forense," p. 76.

44. *Ibid.,* p. 74.

45. "Many thousands of diplomati and laureati in Italy come out of the secondary schools, the universities and the higher institutes each year and, thrown on the market, are unsuccessful in finding employment. Many of these youth could find employment in the new colonial possessions which the bravery of our soldiers is conquering for the Mother Country, thus resolving one of our greatest problems which is not only demographic and economic but also social." E. Lolini, "Guerra impresa rivoluzionaria. Necessità demografiche ed economiche dell'espansione italiana," *Critica fascista,* October 15, 1935, p. 470.

46. P. Cogliolo, *Malinconie universitarie,* p. 283.

47. The organ of the Confederation of Professionals and Artists showed much admiration for the Nazi government in taking this step. It affirmed that "such uncrowding does not harm the diffusion of higher learning. A badly trained and deficient professional does harm to higher learning after having lowered the value of the qualification," and recalled that "just this defense of culture and of the prestige of university qualifications has pushed many unions to call for restrictive measures in our higher schools as well. The uncrowding called for tends in practice to reduce the production of laureati and the formation of the so-called intellectual proletariat. . . . The uncrowding of the universities and the other centers of learning would be highly satisfactory in Italy also. Such uncrowding can be achieved even short of numero chiuso by a very severe prior selection of pupils, which is already in operation in the secondary schools." "Lo sfollamento delle università tedesche," *Le professioni e le arti* (July 1953), p. 4.

48. Such was, according to Mario Govi, the "general consideration" on the universities in 1930. "La funzione delle università," *Critica fascista,* May 15, 1930, p. 188.

49. See De Vecchi's contribution in AP, Camera, *Discussioni,* 29th Legislature, 1:886, Session of March 7, 1935.

50. G. Bottai, *La Carta della Scuola,* p. 106.

51. M. A. Levi, "Pletora e contingentamento di laureati," *Il lavoro fascista,* April 27, 1935.

52. *Ibid.*

53. The educational review *I diritti della scuola* commented on the provision thus: "So, after thirty-two years, the maestri may enter the University, no longer to wait in the antechamber or to end up in the servants' quarters, but to enter the halls of the faculties; no longer to obtain a simple diploma, but to earn a laurea." F. Bascone, "Dalla scuola pedagogica alla Facoltà di magistero," *I diritti della scuola,* November 29, 1936, p. 120.

54. A. Gemelli, "Pletora e selezione di studenti," *Vita universitaria,* April 5, 1937, p. 7.

55. P. P. Luzzatto Fegiz, "Orientamento universitario e disoccupazione intellettuale," *Vita universitaria,* June 20, 1938.

56. Punctator, "Orientamento universitario e disoccupazione intellettuale," *Vita universitaria,* April 20, 1938. This problem was also confronted by F. Banissoni, "Orientamento universitario e disoccupazione intellettuale. Gli universitari e la scelta della professione," *Vita universitaria,* June 5, 1938; and L. Volpicelli, "Orientamento universitario e disoccupazione intellettuale. Orientamento sull'orientamento," *Vita universitaria,* July 5, 1938. "Each year throngs of students (and the greater the unemployment, the higher, logically, is their number) crowd together to take the concorso in order to enter the education faculty. . . . How many of these, after having received the

laurea, may be employed is not known; but from our numerous questions we have learned that they knew of no other outlet than the university, to which they went not for the love of the higher studies, but only because they were unaware of the possibility of any other even modest occupation." So wrote "Punctator" to demonstrate the importance of educational and vocational guidance, without realizing that precisely this analysis showed that much more was needed in order to "regulate" the growth of higher education.

57. G. Lombardo Radice, "Propaganda a noi medesimi," *Vita universitaria,* May 20, 1938.

58. G. Bottai, "Sul bilancio dell'educazione nazionale: Discorso pronunciato alla Camera fascista nella seduta del 17 marzo 1937," in *La Carta della Scuola,* p. 99 and "Relazione al Duce e ai Camerati del Gran Consiglio sulla Carta della Scuola," in *La Carta della Scuola,* p. 28 and 34.

59. G. Bottai, "Sul bilancio dell'educazione nazionale: Discorso pronunciato al Senato del Regno nella seduta del 26 marzo 1938," in *La Carta della Scuola,* p. 139.

60. See *Il lavoro produttivo nella Carta della Scuola* (Messina: G. D'Anna, 1940), which assembles writings of De Ruggiero, Calò, Volpicelli, and others.

61. See *Bibliografia della Carta della Scuola.*

62. "Non piú signorini," *Calabria fascista,* March 4, 1939.

63. See F. Sissini, *La Scuola media dalla legge Casati ad oggi,* especially pp. 71-80.

64. G. Bottai, "Lavoro e lavoratori nella *Carta della Scuola,*" in *La Carta della Scuola,* p. 399.

65. *Ibid.,* p. 105.

66. G. Germani, "La socializzazione politica dei giovani nei regimi fascisti: Italia e Spagna."

67. The most noted contribution on this subject is that of R. Zangrandi, *Il lungo viaggio attraverso il fascismo.* See also P. Spriano, *Storia del Partito comunista italiano,* vol. 2: *Gli anni della clandestinità* (Turin: Einaudi, 1969); especially chapter 18, "I giovani tra corporativismo e comunismo."

68. Germani, "La socializzazione politica dei giovani nei regimi fascisti"; C. Giglio, "I giovani e l'impiego," *Critica fascista,* December 1, 1931, p. 454. According to Giglio, the contrast between occupational aspirations and real possibilities of employment was made more acute also by the fact that the promises of finding new positions for diplomati and laureati in the colonies were shown to be purely propagandistic, such that at a concorso held by the Minister of Colonies for nine posts in colonial occupations many hundreds of competitors presented themselves. Thus, after having chosen specializations in colonial studies just to find a job, "suddenly the door shuts in front of them, illusions fall, and harsh reality lies ahead, as they face the tormenting problem of how to make do, how to obtain employment, muttering and cursing among themselves" (p. 453).

69. Bottai, "Sul bilancio... del 17 marzo 1937," p. 95.

70. *Ibid.,* p. 96.

71. In 1937 70 percent of the youth 6 – 13 years old were enrolled in the *Balilla* organizations and 60 percent of those 14–17 in the *Avanguardisti* organizations. Germani, "La socializzazione politica," p. 26.

72. Bottai, "Sul bilancio... del 17 marzo 1937," p. 95.

73. *Ibid.,* p. 79.

EIGHT. INTELLECTUAL EMPLOYMENT AND UNEMPLOYMENT, 1945 – 1973

1. A. Omodeo, "Politica universitaria," *Il corriere d'informazione,* December 20, 1945, reprinted in *Libertà e storia. Scritti e discorsi politici,* p. 384, and "Vita universitaria," also in *Libertà e storia,* p. 163.

2. L. Lombardo Radice, "Studenti nuovi per una nuova scuola," p. 60. Emphasis in the text.

3. C. Marchesi, "Motivi di politica scolastica," p. 246.

4. AP, Camera, *Discussioni,* 1st Legislature, Session of September 27, 1950. Addressing the Chamber the year before, Silipo had observed: "The function of an agricultural school would be to assemble the sons of peasants, to give them an adequate technical preparation and to restore them to the fields: our agricultural school, on the contrary, removes them from the fields and has them scurrying in search of a 'position' in the offices." AP, Camera, *Discussioni,* 1st Legislature, Session of October 10, 1949.

5. AP, Camera, *Discussioni,* 1st Legislature, Session of October 13, 1948.

6. AP, Camera, *Discussioni,* 1st Legislature, Session of September 27, 1950.

7. AP, Camera, *Discussioni,* 1st Legislature, Session of October 2, 1951.

8. G. Gonella, *Una campagna contro la disoccupazione degli intellettuali.*

9. AP, Camera, *Disegni di legge-relazioni-documenti,* 1st Legislature, Bill of Law presented by the Minister of Public Education (Gonella): *Norme generali sull'istruzione,* July 13, 1951, Doc. no. 2100.

10. AP, Camera, *Discussioni,* 1st Legislature, Session of October 4, 1951.

11. D. Verzili, "Disoccupazione intellettuale," *Realtà,* October 17, 1952.

12. So B. Grazia-Resi observed in his study "Elementi qualitativi delle forze intellettuali di lavoro," in Parliamentary Commission of Inquiry on Unemployment, ed., *La disoccupazione in Italia,* vol. 4, part 2, pp. 179-200. See also the study by the same author, "Primi dati sulle forze di lavoro non manuali," *ibid.,* vol. 4, part 5, pp. 237-52.

13. C. Ramaccioti, "Il lavoro degli intellettuali," *Orientamenti sociali* (1950), nos. 7 – 8.

14. A. Tona, "Al di là del concorso magistrale," *I diritti della scuola,* November 30, 1947.

15. "Popolazione universitaria e situazione economica."

16. The data of the Ministry of Public Education contained in table 8.1 do not concern the concorsi for elementary school teachers. Of the other concorsi held by this ministry the most important quantitatively were those for teachers in the secondary schools, and it can be assumed that a rather high percentage of participants were already employed, even if often in a very temporary way. Useful data on these concorsi may be found in T. Salvemini, "Inchiesta sui partecipanti ai concorsi per cattedre di scuole secondarie nel 1949," *Riforma della scuola,* final issue of the year 1949, pp. 234-44.

17. "The opinion that intellectual unemployment exists," observed, for example, an ISTAT study commenting on the data for 1951, "has reference to some sectors, as for example that of the laureati in the humanistic disciplines and that of medicine." ISTAT, *Indagine statistica sulla disponibilità di personale scientifico e tecnico,* p. 20.

18. P. Sylos-Labini, "Sviluppo economico e classi sociali in Italia," p. 393. Naturally, this phenomenon was particularly marked in the South. And in fact the research conducted in this period identified a strong tendency to the "southernization" of cadres

of the Public Administration. See A. M. Morgantini, "Caratteri demografici e sociali di un gruppo di dipendenti dello Stato," *Rassegna di statistiche del lavoro* (May – June 1954), pp. 231 – 63. But also: L. Cappelletti, *Burocrazia e società*, p. 80.

19. V. Foa, "Studio or lavoro?," *Educazione democratica* (June 1953), pp. 39-40.

20. G. Salvemini, "Molfetta 1954," in *Scritti sulla questione meridionale* (Turin: Einaudi, 1955); reprinted in *Movimento socialista e questione meridionale,* p. 662. This book also contains Salvemini's original article, "Un comune dell'Italia meridionale: Molfetta."

21. AP, Camera, *Discussioni,* 2d Legislature, Session of July 9, 1954.

22. M. Alicata, *La riforma della scuola,* p. 14.

23. L. Piccardi et al., *Dibattito sulla scuola,* pp. 3-27.

24. Center for Public Opinion and Market Analyses, ed., *Laurea e occupazione* (Milan: Angeli, 1959).

25. See the *Proceedings* of the Conference of Ischia organized by the General Confederation of Italian Industry in June 1960: *Secondo Convegno: l'istruzione e l'industria: l'università e l'industria* (Rome, n.d.), and National Committee for Productivity, ed., *L'economia italiana ha bisogno di laureati* (Rome: SPEI, 1961); and particularly the piece by Minister Giacinto Bosco, "Le esigenze di domani e la funzione dello Stato," pp. 15-17. For the ideology of SVIMEZ, see the following volumes: SVIMEZ, *Mutamenti della struttura professionale e ruolo della scuola. Previsioni per il prossimo quindicennio* (Rome: Guiffrè, 1961); SVIMEZ, *Transformazioni sociali e culturali in Italia e loro riflessi sulla scuola* (Rome: Guiffrè, 1962).

26. G. Martinoli, *L'università nello sviluppo economico italiano,* p. 59.

27. The last important publication to be based on the SVIMEZ forecasts was published in 1966: European Center for Education, ed., *Le strutture formative al 1975* (Rome: Palombi, 1966). Two years later, however, the study of N. Cacace and M. d'Ambrosio arrived at totally opposite findings, "Domanda e offerta di laureati in Italia," *Futuribili,* no. 2, supplement, which for the fifteen years 1965 – 1980 forecast a surplus of supply over demand of 177,000 laureati.

28. Some interesting data on the professional situation of the maestri, which justify my assertions, may be found in "La scuola vista da chi la fa," *I diritti della scuola,* (April 30, 1955) no. 15, supplement, pp. 1-31. It reports the results of a survey conducted by this review on a sample of about 500 subjects.

29. "Il dramma dei giovani maestri," *I diritti della scuola,* June 30, 1951.

30. "La tragedia dei disoccupati," *I diritti della scuola,* November 15, 1955. For the concorso of 1958, see V. Masselli, "Pane per 1 su 12 abilitati," *I diritti della scuola,* December 5, 1958.

31. There are no data on the jobs performed by concorso participants in these years. See, however, for the elementary teachers' concorso of 1970, table 8.20. For further data and information on the unemployment of elementary teachers at the beginning of the 1950s, see the following articles by T. Salvemini in the review *Il Maestro:* "Ritmo di assorbimento dei licenziati degli istituti magistrali e prospettive per il futuro," May 15, 1954; "Il numero dei candidati nei concorsi magistrali del 1950 – 51 e 1952 – 53: riflessioni e considerazioni," June 1, 1954; "La selezione dei concorsi magistrali," July 1, 1954; "Possibilità di occupazione per i giovani maestri," September 15, 1954.

32. See S. Zaccara, "Condizione dei neo-maestri in Basilicata," *Riforma della scuola* (April 1958).

33. On the unemployment of secondary teachers in these years, see the following

articles published in the review *La voce della scuola democratica:* A. De Lauro Matera, "Disoccupazione degli insegnati," January 16, 1954; A. Agnelli, "Disoccupazione e pensioni," February 16, 1954; "L'istruzione nel Mezzogiorno," November 16, 1954.

34. ISTAT, *Indagine statistica sulla disponibilità di personale scientifico e tecnico,* p. 21. This inquiry had a peculiar fate: it was the only one cited by the Minister of Public Education Aldo Moro in a report in which he said that "it cannot seriously be asserted that there is in Italy an excess of laureati"; see A. Moro, "Gli studi universitari e l'avvenire dei laureati," in National Committee for Productivity, ed., *I laureati nell'industria* (Milan: Angeli, 1959), p. 39. The data at our disposal would demonstrate, on the contrary, that at the beginning of the 1950s the process of declassamento of laureati, still quite contained during the period of reconstruction, was becoming progressively worse. It is enough to consider that in 1954, 18 percent of the specialized impiegati of the Public Administration possessed a university degree. "Even in the career of general impiegato there was a non-negligible number of laureati: 1,230, or 2 percent of the total." L. Cappelletti, *Burocrazia e società*, p. 61.

35. "Il discorso di apertura del presidente della Fe. Na. P. I.," *Il perito industriale* (December 1955), pp. 4-6.

36. Even more eloquent are the data of a recent inquiry conducted on a sample of northern Italian industrial technicians. According to this inquiry, of the diplomati tecnici who graduated in 1958–59 and who entered the labor market in the period of economic boom, about 15 percent were forced to become employed as workers. See P. G. Corbetta, "Istruzione tecnica e mercato del lavoro."

37. On this point, see the accurate study of U. Paniccia and A. Ruberto, "I laureati nell'insegnamento."

38. I will return to this point in the next chapter.

39. AP, Camera, *Disegni e proposte di legge. Relazioni: Relazione di minoranza (Natta) al Disegno di legge: Stato di previsione della spesa del Ministero della P. I. per l'esercizio finanziario dal 1 luglio 1959 al 30 giungo 1960,* Doc. no. 829-A-bis.

40. For data on this subject, see Paniccia and Ruberto, "I laureati."

41. "Vita dell'ANIAI. Assemblea federale e Consiglio federale di S. Vincent," *L'ingegnere* (February 1961), pp. 119–24.

42. *Ibid.* Other categories of laureati as well found considerable difficulties of employment in the South. This explains how the phenomenon of the "southernization" of cadres of the Public Administration worsened in the decade 1951–1961. Consider that in 1961, per 100,000 persons residing in the respective area, there were 15 managerial functionaries in the Northwest, 48 in the Northeast and in the Center, 103 in the South and 127 in the Islands. See, for these and other data, Cappelletti, *Burocrazia*, pp. 75–78.

43. See C. Mannucci, S. Pozzani, E. Spaltro, and G. Trentini, *La crisi della medicina. Inchiesta sulla professione medica* (Milan: Nuova Mercurio, 1959). This work reports research conducted with a mailed questionnaire to which 641 doctors replied (20 percent of those to which it was sent). The question asked was: "Does there exist a proletarianization of the medical profession–that is, are doctors generally seeing their incomes diminish while hard work increases and new constraints arise?" Commenting on the results obtained the authors observed: "Certainly more important than the concern over current economic conditions seems here to be fear of what could happen in the future. This interpretation would be supported, moreover, by the results of the preceding

questions, which could be interpreted to indicate a substantial state of well-being of the medical class." (p. 103)

44. D. De Castro, "Le strade dell'economia dentro e fuori l'azienda," *L'ingegnere* (February 1960), p. 138; emphasis in text.

45. Bear in mind that in the 1961 census the distinction was introduced between specialized impiegati and general impiegati, which is of considerable importance for the analysis of the relationship between level of education and occupational status. This, as I mentioned, was not possible with the data of the 1951 census.

46. As was said, a comparison for this category between 1961 and 1951 is not possible.

47. The inquiry conducted in 1965 by Gianfranco Bettin on the provinces of Genoa, La Spezia, Alessandria, Imperia, and Savona documents quite well that the number of laureati (of all faculties) hired, after having sharply increased in the period 1958–1962, undergoes an abrupt drop in 1963–1964. Moreover, comparing the forecasts for hiring made by firms and by public entities of the province of Genoa for the five years 1965 –1969 with the number of laureati produced by the local university, Bettin arrived at the conclusion that "there exists a problem of 'underemployment' for the laureato." G. Bettin, *L'inserimento professionale dei laureati in economia e commercio nel sistema economico ligure* (Genoa: ILRES, 1966).

48. Corbetta, "Istruzione tecnica." For other data on the subject, see M. Miegge, "Sviluppo capitalistico e scuola lunga"; S. Cardinali, N. Fanelli, and M. Miegge, "Istruzione tecnica, sbocchi professionali e stabilizzazione sociale"; Naples Chamber of Commerce, *Periti e industria chimica nel Mezzogiorno* (Naples, 1970), which reports the findings of an inquiry conducted on a sample of chemical technicians in Campania.

49. The survey was conducted by a group directed by Vittorio Capecchi on a sample of participants at concorsi in Bologna and Rovigo, which amounts to saying that the situation for the entire national territory is even more serious than what appears from tables 8.20 and 8.21.

50. For data on this subject for 1965, see Paniccia and Ruberto, "I laureati."

51. National Economics and Labor Council–Center for Study of Social Investments (CNEL-CENSIS), *Rapporto sugli aspetti sociali ed economici della situazione universitaria italiana*.

52. *Ibid.*, p. 64.

53. While this volume was in proof, the first (unofficial) data of the quarterly ISTAT statistics on the labor force for 1972 were made available. These indicated that in that year the number of laureati in search of first employment had risen to 26,000 and that of diplomati to 139,000. These data show among other things that the liberalization of access to the university in 1969, which produced an easing of the labor market for diplomati (as may be seen from table 8.19, the number of diplomati in search of first employment was slightly reduced in the two years 1970 and 1971), is no longer sufficient to contain the rate of unemployment of youth coming out of the secondary schools.

NINE. EDUCATION AND ECONOMY, 1945–1970

1. A. Omodeo, "Vita universitaria," in *Libertà e storia. Scritti e discorsi politici*, p. 163.

2. AP, Camera, *Discussioni,* 1st Legislature, session of October 4, 1951.

3. For 1951 we do not possess data which would allow us to subtract repeaters from enrollments in the first year of the upper-secondary school; therefore it is not possible to calculate exactly the rate of passage from the lower to the upper-secondary school.

4. For 1961 the data published by the *Annuario statistico dell'istruzione italiana* do not distinguish between the enrollments of the scuola media and the avviamento.

5. For the distribution of years repeated and studies abandoned according to geographic area, see the following studies: M. Cecchini, "Il disadattamento scolastico nella scuola dell'obbligo," *Formazione e lavoro* (September – October 1970), pp. 56-66, and CNEL-CENSIS, *VI Rapporto sulla situazione sociale del paese* (Rome, 1972).

6. In order to calculate the rate of passage, one must eliminate the number of repeaters from the number of enrollments in the upper-secondary schools. Since before 1954, ISTAT did not report the number of repeaters by region, I have begun with that year, in order to make the data comparable.

7. OECD, *Reviews of National Policies for Education: Italy,* p. 82.

8. ISTAT, *Indagine speciale su alcuni aspetti della vita scolastica italiana,* p. 22.

9. Adina Ciorli and Rodolfo Jannaccone Pazzi have tested the hypothesis that "there exist sharp differences from region to region in the costs-benefits of education." Taking the region as the unit of analysis, they have verified that in 1967: 1) there is a positive but very low correlation (0.12 for males and 0.25 for females) between level of education of the adult population present and the rate of enrollment in the age cohort 14–20 years; 2) there is a rather strong negative correlation both for males (–0.556) and for females (–0.565) between the enrollment for this same cohort and the average level of net income per inhabitant. See A. Ciorli and R. Jannaccone Pazzi, *I tassi di attività della popolazione italiana. Reattivitá ciclica e modificazioni di struttura* (Milan: ILSES, 1971), especially pp. 181-84.

10. CNEL-CENSIS, *V Rapporto sulla situazione sociale del paese* (Rome, 1971).

11. See on this subject L. Meldolesi, *Disoccupazione ed esercito industriale di riserva in Italia,* especially pp. 10-14.

12. G. Bianchi and M. D'Ambrosio, "L'evoluzione della qualificazione del lavoro in Italia dal 1951 al 1968," and M. Paci, "Le contraddizioni del mercato del lavoro."

13. See on this subject, besides the book already cited by Luca Meldolesi, also M. De Cecco, "Una interpretazione ricardiana della dinamica della forza-lavoro in Italia nel decennio 1959–69."

14. That the unemployment of youth, especially after 1963, influenced the expansion of upper-secondary education has been argued also by L. Frey, *Occupazione e disoccupazione giovanile in Italia.* According to others, the expansion of upper-secondary education would be due exclusively to the increase of family income. See P. Napoli, L. Ricolfi, and U. Colombino, "Sistema produttivo e strutture formative," *Monthly Review* Italian ed. (October 1972), pp. 11-34. The drawback of these studies is that they only consider variables of an economic order and neglect the influence exerted on growth of education (both secondary and higher) by the profound changes in the educational system that occurred at the beginning of the 1960s.

15. G. Martinoli, *L'università nello sviluppo economico italiano,* p. 56. Scholars who gave a different interpretation of this phenomenon were not absent, however, even in the 1950s. On the basis of the findings of a survey conducted in July 1956 on a sample of students soon to graduate from the liceo classico, researchers from DOXA wrote: "The hypothesis that many young people enroll in the university only because they

have little possibility of finding a job soon after having finished the liceo is confirmed." And they added: "There is no doubt that among those who obtain the diploma from the istituti magistrali or istituti tecnici the propensity toward immediate employment would be even stronger." "I progetti dei maturandi dei licei classici," in P. Luzzatto Fegiz, *Il volto sconosciuto dell' Italia,* 2d ser., 1956–1965 (Milan: Giuffrè, 1966), pp. 1228-29. [DOXA is a survey research organization similar to the Gallup poll. TR.]

16. The rate of passage has been calculated on the basis of data gathered by ISTAT (and published in the *Annuario statistico dell'istruzione italiana*) on the occasion of the special inquiries conducted on diplomati and on students enrolled in the first year of the university. Naturally this calculation has been possible only each time ISTAT conducted the inquiry on diplomati (which has happened seven times so far, as indicated by figures 9.4, 9.5, and 9.6 for the years 1953, 1954, 1955, 1956, 1957, 1959, and 1967). Since the ISTAT investigations never concern the whole universe of subjects, but only a (very large) sample, the results obtained (concerning, for example, composition according to family residence or to father's occupation) are meant to represent all diplomati or university students. This means that the results obtained must be considered approximations.

17. The nature of the data available does not allow us to disaggregate further. It would be mistaken, however, to read the data reported in the text only in North-South terms. To be convinced of this it suffices to look as well at table 9.5, which shows how, among the regions of the industrial triangle, it is the least developed, namely Liguria, that has by far the highest percentage of university students in relation to the corresponding age cohort.

18. The high rate of passage to the university in the central regions is probably due to the migratory flow of diplomati from the South to the Center that has taken place over the last twenty years (see, on this subject, the last chapter of this study). In other words, the rate of passage of Southern diplomati would be even higher than that indicated by table 9.4, since some of them, once having finished secondary schooling, emigrate in search of a position to the central and northern areas, and it is in these areas that they enroll in the university. That the percentage of diplomati who enroll in the university is higher in the South than in the Center (not to mention the North) is indicated also by other inquiries. See ISTAT, "Indagine speciale sui diplomati di scuole medie superiori," *Bollettino mensile di statistica* (August 1969), special supplement, which reports data for 1963 and for 1967.

19. An inquiry conducted by CENSIS on a sample of university students enrolled in 1967–68 shows, for example, that the percentage of those who declared themselves enrolled in the university "because they did not find work" was 14 percent for those whose fathers had obtained the laurea and 28.4 percent for those whose fathers had an elementary school diploma. See CNEL-CENSIS, *Rapporto sugli aspetti sociali ed economici della situazione universitaria italiana,* p. 204.

20. The rates of passage in table 6.14 and those of figure 9.6 were calculated according to different procedures. This does not, however, weaken the validity of the comparisons made in the text.

21. AP, Senato, *Disegni di legge e relazioni,* 3d Legislature, Doc. no. 1076. In the year 1961–62 there were 3,309 positions offered by concorso, 4,416 applications for admission, and 2,162 winners. For these data see T. Salvemini, "Riflessi finanziari e sociali dell'assegno di studio agli universitari," *Realtà del Mezzogiorno* (February–March 1963), pp. 245-46.

22. The Law of April 21, 1969 (no. 162) revised and corrected the arrangements provided by the 1963 law. According to recent data, in 1970–71 nearly 170,000 student stipends were granted.

TEN. THE REFORMS OF THE 1960s

1. "Riforma della scuola," *Riforma della scuola* (November 1955).

2. G. Gonella, *Una campagna contro la disoccupazione degli intellettuali*.

3. See U. Giusti, "Disoccupazione e sovrapopolamento: Emigrazione." Adolfo Omodeo also supported in those years the necessity of "a plan of emigration for a considerable contingent of degree holders to countries which have need of them." *Libertà e storia. Scritti e discorsi politici,* p. 163..

4. A. Spinelli, "Pletora medica," *Federazione medica,* September 30, 1952. Concerning the engineers, see "Lo sviluppo della carriera dell'ingegnere," *L'ingegnere* (August 1952), pp. 927-30.

5. See M. Gianturco, "Emigrazione intellettuale e titoli universitari," and idem, "La scuola e la disoccupazione dei lavoratori intellettuali," *Notiziario della scuola e della cultura* (1951), p. 12.

6. "Popolazione universitaria e situazione economica," in Ministry for the Constituent, *Atti della Commissione per lo studio dei problemi del lavoro* (Roma: UESISA, 1946): 1:391.

7. M. Gioia, "Dove arriveremo?" *La federazione medica,* August 15, 1948, p. 11.

8. D. Cancelmo, "Inflazione di medici o deflazione di pazienti?" *La federazione medica,* December 31, 1951, pp. 27-28.

9. G. Sbrana, "Ancora della pletora medica," *La federazione medica,* February 15, 1950. Among others, the Liberal deputy Antonio Capua, secretary of the parliamentary medical group, became the bearer of the medical order's demands. To the Chamber of Deputies he argued that "to continue distributing lauree in medicine without limitation is, if I may be pardoned the phrase, a fraud. Very many young doctors consider it so who, while in the past when professional fortune was adverse to them were able to make do on their own, have for some time now been accustomed to blaming the Government. And they are not completely wrong." "La pletora medica allo studio del governo," *La federazione medica,* October 15, 1949, pp. 6-7.

10. This delimitation of the sampling universe naturally rendered the findings of the inquiry all but representative. Giovanni Gozzer, who was secretary of the central office of the commission, has recently acknowledged as much. G. Gozzer, *Rapporto sulla secondaria,* pp. 23-24. For the present discussion, however, the findings of the Gonella Commission retain great value.

11. For more details on the various phases of the process of elaborating the Gonella bill, see "La riforma della scuola," *Scuola e città,* March 31, 1950, pp. 33-41 and 78-85, and also G. Gozzer, *Scuola per tutti*, pp. 15-22.

12. National Commission of Inquiry for the Reform of the School, ed., *Le conclusioni dell'inchiesta nazionale per la riforma della scuola,* final issue of *La riforma della scuola,* (1949), pp. 125-78. According to many of the rectors and presidents of faculties questioned by the Commission for Verification, this phenomenon constituted "a serious disturbance and a serious danger." *Ibid.,* p. 286.

13. "Popolazione universitaria," p. 385.

14. See, for example, Gonella's contribution in AP, Camera, *Discussioni,* 1st Leg-

islature, Session of October 15, 1948. As mentioned, in the period of reconstruction even nonreactionary scholars declared themselves in favor of the numero chiuso. See for example what G. Ferretti wrote in those years, in *Scuola e democrazia* (Turin: Einaudi, 1956), pp. 108-11 (in which an article from 1944 is reprinted) and also A. C. Jemolo, *Italia tormentata* (Bari: Laterza, 1951), Pp. 151-53.

15. Law no. 1551, December 18, 1951.

16. This and the following citations are taken from AP, Camera, *Disegni di legge-relazioni-documenti,* 1st Legislature, Bill of Law presented by the Minister of Public Education (Gonella): *Norme generali sull'istruzione,* Session of July 13, 1951, Doc. no. 2100.

17. The continuity between the old and the new regime was assured also by the group of high fascist functionaries with which Minister of Public Education Gonella surrounded himself. This was denounced several times by the Communists. See, for example, L. Lombardo Radice, "Due scandali nella scuola," *Unità,* January 3, 1950, and idem, "Citazioni dai testi del signor Padellaro," *Unità,* January 7, 1950.

18. Gonella was reproached in those years by the most acute observers for this similarity. See L. Borghi, "Il probelma della riforma scolastica in Italia,"*Scuola e città* (December 1951), pp. 387-98.

19. AP, Camera, *Discussioni,* 1st Legislature, Session of October 24, 1949.

20. For the attitude of the parties toward the problem of the lower-secondary school in this period see A. Basso, "Il problema della scuola media inferiore," *La riforma della scuola* (March 1948), pp. 46-47, and idem, "Scuola media inferiore," *La riforma della scuola* (August – September 1948), pp. 11-14.

21. C. Marchesi, "Motivi di politica scolastica," p. 244.

22. F. Lombardi, *La riforma della scuola* (Milan-Rome: Società editrice *Avanti!,* 1946), which is the text of a report presented to the central committee of the PSIUP in the meeting of October 17-23, 1945.

23. Quotations are taken from the speech given by Mario Alicata to the central committee of the PCI on November 28-30, 1955, published in M. Alicata, *La riforma della scuola,* pp. 7-55.

24. L. Lombardo Radice, "Libertà della scuola," *l'Unità,* October 9, 1951. The Gonella bill was criticized in an article by Banfi published some days later ("In difesa della scuola," *l'Unità,* October 16, 1951). The Communist senator made, however, only brief mention of the question of the lower-secondary school ("the radically democratic principle of the scuola unica is avoided"), while he concentrated his criticisms on the lack of a financial commitment on the part of the government for realizing the Gonella reform and on the danger that it might cause "the liquidation of the state school."

25. Alicata, *La riforma,* p. 49.

26. "It should be asked," wrote Marchesi in polemic with Banfi, "whether in the learning of languages, as in other aspects of life, the dead might not help the living to grow and to nourish themselves." C. Marchesi, "Risposta al compagno Banfi," *l'Unità,* January 22, 1946. Many Communist leaders remained attached to Latin even in 1955, by which time Marchesi's position had been repudiated. Probably reacting to an assertion in the document prepared by the Commission for the Reform of the School of the Gramsci Institute ("our Commission would not hesitate to eliminate Latin from upper-secondary studies, except, it is agreed, for the *liceo classico*"), both Donini and Terracini declared themselves completely opposed to this eventuality. Quite weak as well was the motivation of Togliatti, who limited himself to saying only that Latin

"because of the way it was taught cannot be considered the basis for a serious educational preparation." Thus in the end, in his response, Alicata had to specify that the abolition of Latin from the lower-secondary was "simply a proposal that the Party and the Nation must discuss." "Proposte dei communisti per la riforma della scuola e per un largo movimento unitario che la realizzi," *l'Unità*, December 1, 1955.

27. Alicata, *La riforma*, p. 50.

28. National Commission of Inquiry, ed., *Le conclusioni dell'inchiesta*, p. 67.

29. A. Natta, "Concetto Marchesi: la sua opera al Parlamento," *Riforma della scuola* (March 1957), pp. 15–17.

30. Marchesi, "Motivi di politica scolastica," p. 246.

31. L. Lombardo Radice, "Studenti nuovi per una nuova scuola," p. 60. Emphasis in text.

32. *Ibid.*

33. Not all, however. Antonio Banfi, for example, was opposed throughout to the idea that it was necessary to reduce the university population. "It is necessary to take heed," he said, "that reducing the student population not mean misfortune and discouragement rather than a setting in order." "How should this reduction take place? Have the young in fact found other paths, or have difficulties forced those who had struggled valiantly to keep at their studies to give up every hope and to fall into the ranks of the indifferent seekers of work?" AP, Senato, *Discussioni*, 1st Legislature, Session of October 24, 1949. Two years later he observed that the "overpopulation of the university" was decreasing, and he added: "The problem is not that of decreasing the number of university students by artificial means, but of opening new outlets for their activity." AP, Senato, *Discussioni*, 1st Legislature, Session of October 3, 1951.

34. C. Marchesi, "La cultura e la scuola," *Rinascita* (September 1946), p. 220, which reprints the text of a speech given to the Constituent. Again to the Constituent, for the purpose of "restoring dignity to doctoral qualification," [the laurea, that is] Marchesi proposed to insert into the Constitution the following article: "The doctoral qualification constitutes the first level of academic rank and is not required for the practice of the liberal professions." Togliatti declared himself in agreement with the amendment proposed by Mastrojanni, which appeared as follows: "The doctoral qualification is not required for the practice of the liberal professions, nor can it be required for public employment." Lucifero also declared himself in agreement with this position, because "to establish that one can accede to state employment without the doctoral qualification would mean not only to resolve a problem in the exalted area of science but also to take a step toward the less advantaged classes which seek their advancement by means of such salaried office employment and of the liberal professions, and which today are forced to ruin themselves to maintain their children at the university." *Atti dell'Assemblea Costituente*, 1st Subcommission, Session of October 23, 1946.

35. P. De Benedetti, "Gli studenti comunisti per una maggiore severità degli studi universitari," *Rinascita* (November–December 1947), p. 332.

36. C. Marchesi, "Tasse universitarie," *l'Unità*, August 19, 1950.

37. "This is an old sin," said Marchesi to the Chamber of Deputies, speaking of his proposal, "which my comrades have forgiven me and which I believe even my other colleagues will forgive me." AP, Camera, *Discussioni*, 1st Legislature, Session of October 10, 1949. Replying to the party organ of the Christian Democrats, Marchesi denied having been under pressure from his own party, and spoke of having always

expressed his opinion "very freely, by Togliatti's own request." C. Marchesi, "Replica al *Popolo,*" *l'Unità,* August 19, 1950.

38. See the contribution of Natta in AP, Camera, *Discussioni,* 1st Legislature, Session of January 18, 1951, and that of Banfi in AP, Senato, *Discussioni,* 1st Legislature, Session of October 3, 1951. Even the Secretary of the Italian Communist Youth Federation took a position against the increase of university fees and supported "a full severity of studies" as "the only means for the necessary selection." E. Berlinguer, "Il problema delle tasse universitarie," *l'Unità,* September 9, 1950.

39. AP, Camera, *Discussioni,* 1st Legislature, Session of October 13, 1948.

40. AP, Camera, *Discussioni,* 1st Legislature, Session of January 16, 1951.

41. AP, Camera, *Discussioni,* 1st Legislature, Session of October 10, 1949.

42. C. Marchesi, "Crisi di scuola e di cultura," *Rinascita* (July 1948), p. 262.

43. C. Marchesi, "L'istruzione superiore," *Rinascita* (August – September 1949), p. 380.

44. AP, Camera, *Discussioni,* 1st Legislature, Session of October 3, 1951.

45. It is curious that it was Gonella who addressed this accusation to the Communists. Note this passage, taken from AP, Camera, *Discussioni,* 1st Legislature, Session of October 15, 1948: GONELLA: "As for the Hon. Marchesi, I must say that the pure and simple return to what was considered (I don't know with what foundation) 'the most fascist of reforms' because of the essential bearing of the reform –" (interruption by MARCHESI): "The word 'fascist' doesn't frighten me." GONELLA: "The word fascist is not meant to frighten, but it is certain that Gentile was also described as 'the philosopher of the cudgel.' I don't know if the Communist Party wants to return to this philosophy."

46. Natta, "Concetto Marchesi."

47. Contribution of Marchesi in AP, Camera, *Discussioni,* 1st Legislature, Session of October 13, 1948.

48. Marchesi, "Crisi di scuola," p. 262.

49. Contribution of Marchesi in AP, Camera, *Discussioni,* 1st Legislature, Session of October 13, 1948.

50. This report has already been cited (note 23) and is reprinted in Alicata, *La riforma della scuola*. This volume also contains the *Proposte per una riforma della scuola dell'obbligo* elaborated by the Commission for the Reform of the School established at the Gramsci Institute (pp. 65-100). With the exception of Concetto Marchesi, all the qualified Communist students of the problems of education were part of this commission.

51. *Ibid.,* pp. 35, 50-51.

52. *Ibid.,* p. 13.

53. *Ibid.,* p. 36.

54. With an arduous attempt at reconceptualization, it was affirmed that "No woman, living together with an employed husband, can consider herself unemployed, as long as there is a man who has the same capacities and who is without work." "Disoccupazione maschile e femminile," *I diritti della scuola,* November 15, 1951, p. 57. It was further argued that it was not fair that a woman teacher could bring "a second salary" into the family, "when young male teachers, because of the lack of a salary, either cannot start their own family, or cannot support what has already been started." "Disoccupazione magistrale maschile e femminile," *I diritti della scuola*, August 30,

1951, p. 471. But see also "Disoccupazione magistrale: la parola alle maestre," *I diritti della scuola,* September 20, 1951, pp. 498-99.

55. The editor of the review *I diritti della scuola,* Annibale Tona, demanded a "reduction in the number of istituti magistrali." A. Tona, "Al di là del concorso magistrale," *I diritti della scuola,* November 30, 1947. "We formally demand the numero chiuso for teachers' certificates," wrote G. Gabrielli. "La fabbrica dei disoccupati," *I diritti della scuola,* July 20, 1951. To those who considered this proposal less than democratic, the author replied in "Ancora la fabbrica dei spostati," *I diritti della scuola,* August 10, 1951, pp. 444-45, asking if it was "democratic to grant with such ease a piece of paper of no practical value to thousands of people who will not be able to use it and who will combine to feed the socially dangerous procession of unemployed intellectuals who naturally gravitate toward antidemocratic activity."

56. "Perhaps because we were worried about intellectual unemployment," wrote the President of the AIMC some years later, "and in trying (legitimately, it may be granted) to resolve the problem for teachers at every level, we concealed the primary ends of the school. We let it be thought that we considered it a means of employment to be extended without limit and to be fought over, elementary against secondary teachers, to the detriment of its seriousness and its functioning." M. Badaloni, "Politica scolastica," *Il maestro* (February 1953).

57. "Contro la disoccupazione magistrale," *I dirittri della scuola,* December 15-30, 1946, pp. 81-82.

58. Perhaps these reasons can be found, on the one hand, in the type of training received in the istituti magistrali, for the most part church-related, and on the other, in the fact that over the fascist period, with the disbanding of professional organizations, *Azione Cattolica* progressively increased its influence over the elementary teachers. [Azione Cattolica: Catholic lay organization founded in 1898 which has served ever since to defend the interests of the church in secular affairs. Tr.]

59. Thus the leaders of the AIMC expressed themselves in a letter directed to all deputies at a crucial moment in the struggle for the scuola media unica. See "Lettera ai Parliamentari (February 19, 1960)," in AIMC, *L'Associazione Italian Maestri Cattolici dal 6° al 7° Congresso Nazionale (1959–1962)* (Rome, n.d.), p. 67.

60. A considerable expert on the Catholic world has written that "before the stability and the strength, electoral as well, of the AIMC, the Christian Democratic Party was without defense." V. Sinistrero, *La politica scolastica 1945-65 e la scuola cattolica,* p. 66.

61. There were four candidates of the AIMC elected on the DC list in 1953, five in 1958, and seven in 1963. See A. Manoukian, ed., *La presenza sociale del PCI e della DC,* p. 428.

62. See AIMC, *L'Associazione Italiana Maestri Cattolici: 1945-1956* (Rome, n.d.), p. 29.

63. Law Decree December 17, 1947, no. 1599. According to the AIMC, these schools afforded the possibility of work "to over ten thousand teachers." See *L'Associazione,* p. 105. The leftists attacked this initiative very harshly. The Socialist Deputy Cessi said, for example, that Gonella had succeeded neither in "giving firm life and sound bearing to the system of neighborhood schools" nor in "weakening let alone resolving the crisis of intellectual unemployment." AP, Camera, *Discussioni*, 1st Legislature, Session of October 14, 1948. Lucio Lombardo Radice, "Problemi seri e politica allegra," *Rinascita*

(February 1948), pp. 81-82 observed that behind the "beautiful facade" of the new schools there was "nothing but a subsidy for some unemployed maestri."

64. Agenda of Badolini, Da Villa, Buzzi, Titomanlio, approved in the session of October 21, 1953. In the five-year period 1946 – 1951, the AIMC obtained the halving of 34,507 classes. See *L'Associazione,* p. 107.

65. Indeed, the final motion of the first national conference of the AIMC demanded the establishment of "a three-year school entrusted to suitably chosen maestri, of a practical nature and providing professional training." "Il I Congresso Nazionale dell'AIMC," *Il maestro* (October 1946). The establishment of the post-elementare was calculated to give work to 40–50,000 maestri, according to M. Frano, "La scuola post-elementare," *Il maestro* (1949), no. 4.

66. See among others: *La scuola primaria secondo l'inchiesta*. Reports given to the First National Conference of Officials in Charge of Cultural Activities of the AIMC (July 1949) (Rome: Editrice *Il Maestro,* n.d. [1950]).

67. P. Bertea, "I maestri e la riforma," *Il maestro* (1950) no. 6.

68. "The person who does not begin work at 11 – 12 years of age is afterwards ill-adapted to work and is even less likely to become a good and skillful worker," wrote M. Frano, "La scuola post-elementare." Without the post-elementare, which was to be the school of the people and of work, one ran "the grave danger of furthering the formation of a mass of misfits, ex-students, who at fifteen years of age would hardly resign themselves to learn a manual trade," wrote G. M. Grossi, "Obbligo scolastico e scuola poste-elementare," *Il maestro* (June 1946).

69. "Scuola di popolo o scuola di elite?," *Il maestro* (1949) no. 10.

70. M. Baldolini, "Scuola di poveri?," *Il maestro* (1949), no. 11.

71. "Il Ministero della P. I. Guido Gonella al Convegno Nazionale dell'AIMC per gli incaricati di attività culturale," in *L'Associazione,* p. 184.

72. "Il I Convegno della scuola indetto dalla Democrazia cristiana," *Il maestro* (1949), no. 10.

73. "La riforma davanti al Consiglio Superiore," *Scuola e città* (April 1950), pp. 86-90.

74. In the words of Christian Democratic deputy Pedini, AP, Camera, *Discussioni,* 2d Legislature, Session of September 24, 1955.

75. Contribution of the monarchist Rubino in AP, Camera, *Discussioni,* 2d Legislature, Session of September 24, 1955.

76. G. Salvemini, "Una scuola 'sciagurata,' " *Il ponte* (May 1956), reprinted in *Scritti sulla scuola,* pp. 794-95.

77. L. Piccardi *et al., Dibattito sulla scuola* (Bari: Laterza, 1956). On the other hand, Aldo Visalberghi and Lamberto Borghi opposed the numero chiuso on that occasion. Even Compagna argued that year that the reduction of the university population was "to be hoped for." Nevertheless he proposed as a means of selection not the numero chiuso but "severe exams" which could facilitate university access for "persons foreign to the traditional classes" and to make it more difficult for the "misfits who belong to families with three or four generations of laureati." F. Compagna, "Le classi dirigenti nel Mezzogiorno," *Occidente* (January-February 1956).

78. See the *Bolletino Doxa,* (October 1954), no. 17-18. Some data from this survey are reported also by L. Caiani, *Problemi dell'università italiana* (Milan: Comunità, 1955).

79. AP, Camera, *Discussioni,* 1st Legislature, Session of October 4, 1951.

80. AP, Camera, *Discussioni,* 2d Legislature, Session of July 13, 1954. See also the text of the speech given by Martino to the Association of the Foreign Press: "L'università nella vita italiana d'oggi," in G. Martino, *La scuola nella vita nazionale,* pp. 81 – 88. Minister Martino succeeded in having a law approved (August 9, 1954, no. 645) that provided for an increase of fees for the secondary schools. See on this subject his article, "L'aumento delle tasse scolastiche" in *La scuola nella vita nazionale,* pp. 165-68.

81. Contribution of the Christian Democrat Pedini in AP, Camera, *Discussioni,* 2d Legislature, Session of September 24, 1955.

82. "Si aprono le scuole: parla un vecchio professore," *L'espresso* October 2, 1955.

83. That the unemployment of elementary teachers could be overcome only by "penetrating" the lower-secondary school was, for example, argued explicitly in those years by S. Sarchioto, "Disoccupazione magistrale?" *Il maestro* (November – December 1952).

84. See R. Moro, "Il corso post-elementare nella nostra legislazione scolastica," *Scuola di base* (April – June 1954), pp. 31-38.

85. On the experiments with the scuola post-elementare authorized by Gonella see, in the above issue of *Scuola di base,* the following articles: B. Credaro, "Esperimenti di scuola post-elementare in Valtellina," pp. 50-55; G. Ranieri, "Esperienze di scuola post-elementare nel Trentino," pp. 56-60; C. Raffa, "La scuola post-elementare in Sicilia," pp. 60-63.

86. So said Buzzi to the Fourth National Congress of the AIMC. See C. Buzzi, "Problemi della scuola d'oggi," *Il maestro,* October 1-15, 1953.

87. A. Banfi, "A proposito della post-elementare," *Riforma della scuola* (November 1955).

88. "Precisazioni del Ministro Martino su importanti problemi della scuola e della categoria," *Il maestro,* April 15, 1954.

89. "I nuovi programmi didattici per la scuola primaria," *Scuola e città* (August 1955), p. 347.

90. Quoted in Banfi, "A proposito."

91. See, for the text of this cirucular, "Esperimenti di scuola post-elementare," *Scuola di base* (July – December 1955), pp. 149-50.

92. L. Borghi, "Il dibattito sulla post-elementare," *Scuola e città* (November 1955), p. 435. In March of the following year the Movement of Educational Cooperation organized, with the collaboration of other associations, an important conference on the schooling of 11- to 14-year-olds. For the reports given at this conference by Borghi, De Bartolomeis, Laporta, Masucco Costa, Visalberghi, see the special issue of *Scuola e città* (May 1956). At the Conference of "Friends of the World" of 1956, the problem of the post-elementare was confronted in the Borghi report. See L. Piccardi *et al. Dibattito,* pp. 185-267.

93. The reaction of *l'Unità* was, however, rather slow. It announced, in fact, on September 17 the decision of Paolo Rossi to extend the experiment of the post-elementare over the entire national territory, with the following words: "A certain interest has been aroused by a decision of the Ministry which concerns an old provision relative to compulsory education." And only ten days later it published an article by Dina Bertoni Jovine, "Scoperte 'episodiche e svagate' in luogo di una concreta conscenza," in which

it was claimed that "the character they want to give" the post-elementare "is the rough and pitiless one of an inferior school."

94. Contribution of Sciorilli Borelli in AP, Camera, *Discussioni,* 2d Legislature, Session of September 29, 1955.

95. AP, Camera, *Discussioni,* 2d Legislature, Session of September 24, 1955.

96. The Communist agenda was presented in the Session of September 28, 1955 by Lozza, Jotti, Marchesi, Natta, Alicata, and others.

97. "Riforma della scuola," *Riforma della scuola* (November 1955).

98. AP, Camera, *Discussioni,* 2d Legislature, Session of September 24, 1955.

99. AP, Camera, *Discussioni,* 2d Legislature, Session of September 28, 1955. Speaking in the session of the following day, the Hon. Maria Badaloni, Christian Democrat and President of the AIMC, polemicized with Lozza, denying that the maestri aimed at "positions." However, she added: "This I can say with certainty, even knowing that I will be believed by no one."

100. At the Congress of the National Secondary School Union held in June 1947, when it was still part of the General Confederation of Labor, the Christian current of the union obtained 67 percent of the vote. A. Granella and M. Pagella, *Sindacalismo e scuola media* (Rome: UCIIM, 11955), p. 49. The votes won by this current at the Congress of 1950 dropped to 53 percent, *Il rinnovamento della scuola,* January 10, 1951, and it rose again in the following years to reach 63 percent in 1957, "L'UCIIM nel 1957," *Cattedra. Prontuario del professore italiano* (Rome: n.d. [1958]), pp. 157-64.

101. "Ordine del giorno del Convegno di Castelnuovo Fogliani (24 – 29 August 1948)," in President's Office, UCIIM, *Contributi di studio per una dottrina della professione e della scuola* (Rome: UCIIM, 1956), pp. 133-34.

102. "Dichiarazione conclusiva del XXV Convegno Nazionale (1 – 3 November 1953)," in President's Office, UCIIM, *Contributi di studio,* p. 147.

103. According to an observer very close to the positions of the maestri, the secondary school teachers were "motivated by their interest in assuring as many positions as possible in their hunger for jobs." See "I buoni propositi del Ministro Rossi," *Scuola e città* (October 1955), p. 420.

104. This was recognized by the Communists themselves. Alicata said that the leaders of the UCIIM "posed the problems of reform of the compulsory school almost in the same terms in which we pose them." Alicata, *La riforma,* p. 47.

105. "Ordine del giorno approvato dal Consiglio Nazionale il 16 ottobre 1955," in President's Office, UCIIM, *Contributi di studio,* pp. 154 – 55. Emphasis added. The most elaborated contribution of UCIIM in this period to solving the problem of the school for 11- to 14-year-olds was, however, published the following year: G. Gozzer, *Scuola per tutti.*

106. In fact, SINASCEL announced the state of agitation of the maestri. See the reasons for it in "L'Ordine del giorno del Sindacato magistrale CISL," *I diritti della scuola,* October 15, 1955.

107. AP, Camera, *Discussioni,* 2d Legislature, Session of September 30, 1955.

108. See, for example, the contribution of the Communist Alicata in AP, Camera, *Discussioni,* 2d Legislature, Session of July 16, 1956. Exactly five years after Paolo Rossi's "promise," the Socialist Codignola denounced the establishment of two thousand "clandestinely conceived post-elementary schools" "more for the purpose of avoiding this way the unemployment of elementary teachers than that of offering our

children a new and useful possibility of educational placement." AP, Camera, *Discussioni,* 3d Legislature, Session of September 30, 1960.

109. The *Proceedings* of the Rossi Commission have been published in *La scuola dagli 11 ai 14 anni* (Florence: Centro Didattico Nazionale, 1957). On the importance of the Rossi Commission, see also the comments of a scholar who took part in it: V. Sinistrero, *La politica scolastica,* pp. 67–69.

110. "Non utopia ma necessità," *Riforma della scuola* (March 1956).

111. At the beginning of 1956, Minister of Public Education Paolo Rossi had announced his intention of proceeding with a small reform by instituting some classes of the scuola media without Latin. Lucio Lombardo Radice, commenting on this announcement, argued privately for a "realistic line": "revision of the programs of the scuola di avviamento; their 'drawing-nearer' to those of the classes without Latin of the scuola media; the possibility of moving from the scuola di avviamento to the liceo scientifico without examination or with a short and simple qualifying exam." From a short, untitled lead piece introducing an article by G. DiVittorio, "Orientamenti ideali e riforme immediate," *Riforma della scuola* (April 1956).

112. On the educational program of the parties at the elections in 1958, see G. Gozzer, "I programmi scolastici dei partiti politici," *Cattedra 1960* (Rome: UCIIM, n.d. [1961]), pp. 81-93.

113. AP, Senato, *Disegni di legge e relazioni-Discussioni,* Bill of Law: "Istituzione della scuola obbligatoria statale dai 6. ai 14 anni," sponsored by Senators Donini, Luporini, and others, issued January 21, 1959.

114. Contribution of Donini, AP, Senato, *Discussioni,* 3d Legislature, Session of September 25, 1962.

115. AP, Senato, cited in note 113.

116. For the most important documents on the subject, see Ministry of Public Education, *Il piano della scuola: documenti parlamentari.*

117. The text of this bill is also reported in "Il disegno di legge della scuola secondaria (11 – 14 anni)," *Scuola e città* (September 1959), pp. 317-23 and "La Relazione del Ministro sul disegno di legge sulla scuola secondaria," *Scuola e città* (October 1959), pp. 345-52.

118. L. Borghi, "Il governo e la scuola dell'obbligo," *Scuola e città* (September 1959), p. 292.

119. "La relazione del Ministro," p. 347.

120. L. Rampa, "Il completamento dell'istruzione inferiore nel piano della scuola," *Il maestro,* September 25, 1959.

121. At the Fifth Congress of the AIMC (September 1-5, 1956), a motion was approved that asked for "the establishment in every elementary school site of a subsequent three-year school, entrusted to the maestri, of a training and professional character." See AIMC, *Sviluppo della scuola italiana: prospettive di politica scolastica. Atti del V Congresso Nazionale* (Rome, n.d.), p. 167. The motion approved by the Sixth Congress (September 2-6, 1959) reaffirmed "the irreplaceable function" in the 11- to 14-year-olds' school "of the elementary teachers." See AIMC, *L'istruzione inferiore nel piano della scuola. Atti del VI Congresso Nazionale* (Rome, n.d.), p. 209.

122. S. Sarchioto, "La scuola dagli 11 ai 14 anni. Progetti e proposte," *Il maestro,* July 25, 1959.

123. For the defense of the second Medici bill, see among others, L. Laeng, "Tanto

peggio per la realtà," *Il maestro,* February 25, 1960, and idem, "Delenda Carthago," *Il Maestro*, March 25, 1960.

124. "Cronaca dei convegni organizzati dall'AIMC: a Catanzaro," *Il maestro,* May 10, 1959.

125. G. Medici, "L'istruzione inferiore nella politica scolastica italiana," in AIMC, *L'istruzione inferiore,* p. 147.

126. The Minister of Public Education presented the outline of his bill to the Consiglio Superiore in August 1959. Before it met again, however, Medici produced several corrections to the original text. The percentage of maestri who were to teach in the scuola normale was brought from 50 percent to 70 percent. Also very important was the change brought about in Article 4. The first text read: "A secondary school can be established if it is found that there are in the same site or in bordering sites at least sixty persons obliged to attend." In the second text, instead, one read: "[A secondary school can be established] if it is found that there are in the same site or in bordering sites at least eighty persons obliged. Exception is made when there are, within a radius of four kilometers, at least twenty-five persons obliged, in which case a secondary school provided only with a section of the normale may be established." See B. Nosengo, "I disegni di legge e la nostra posizione," *La scuola e l'uomo* (August – September 1959.

127. See L. Lombardo Radice, "Cultura una e quadrupla," *Riforma della scuola* (August – September 1959).

128. UCIIM, for example, in unusual language, described the Medici bill as "conservative and reactionary." Nosengo, "I disegni."

129. The third section of the Consiglio Superiore (that of the maestri) asked that not 70 percent but "the entire section of the normale" be assigned to the maestri. See "Parere della Terza Sezione del Consiglio Superiore sullo schema di disegno di legge per l'istituzione della scuola secondaria," *Il maestro* (October 25 – November 10, 1959). The negative opinion came from the first (university) and especially from the second (secondary) section. See "Il parere della Seconda Sezione del Consiglio Superiore sul progetto Medici," *Scuola e città* (October 1959), pp. 353-60.

130. The text of the second Medici bill is reprinted in "Il nuovo disegno di Medici sulla instituzione della scuola media," *Scuola e città* (May 1960), pp. 183-91.

131. Naturally this latest version of the scuola normale was criticized harshly by the secondary school teachers and defended by the maestri. See G. B., "Di chi l'abilità manovriera?," *Il maestro,* January 25, 1960. The maestri asked, anyhow, that "the special scuola media be established wherever there was need for it and without time limits." "I tre ordini del giorno del Sindacato Nazionale della Scuola Elementare," *Il maestro,* February 10, 1960.

132. R. Lombardi, "L'industria e l'istruzione e l'addestramento professionale," in General Confederation of Italian Industry, *Primo Convegno "L'istruzione e l'industria": Istruzione d'obbligo, istruzione tecnica e professionale, addestramento professionale (Gardone, 23 – 25 April 1959)* (Rome, n.d.), pp. 57-70.

133. "Le conclusioni di R. Lombardi," in General Confederation, *Primo Convegno,* p. 372.

134. *Ibid.*, p. 65.

135. For the distinction between systems of sponsored and contest mobility, see R. Turner, "Modes of Social Ascent through Education: Sponsored and Contest Mobility."

136. "Le conclusioni di R. Lombardi," p. 372.

137. C. Buzzi, "La posizione dei maestri di fronte alla tesi di una scuola media unica," *Il maestro,* September 25, 1960.

138. Citations taken from the following articles from *Il maestro* with the signature of A. T. Stirelli: "Il maestri prima e dopo le elezioni: Signor sindaco, sono il maestro Bianchi! Ma il sindaco non lo riconosce," April 10, 1961; "I maestri prima e dopo le elezioni: la grande delusione della maestra Rossi," April 25, 1961; "I maestri prima e dopo le elezioni: Tre poveri maestri e un avvocato in pantofole," May 10, 1961; "I maestri prima e dopo le elezioni: Nell'Italia dei dottori l'ultimo posto al 'signor maestro,' " July 10, 1961.

139. As Minister of Public Education Bosco put it during the work of the Chamber of Deputies' Eighth (Education) Commission. See G. C. Boccardi, "Scuole popolari e 'disoccupazione magistrale,' " *Il maestro,* September 25, 1960.

140. Law no. 53, February 15, 1961. The Socialist Codignola argued that the neighborhood school was nothing more than "a form of 'electoral' insurance against elementary teachers' unemployment." And citing Valitutti he observed: "The invention of worksites as instruments for combatting the unemployment of unskilled workers is a practice that is not transferable to the schools." "La relazione Codignola," in Ministry of Public Education, *Il piano della scuola,* p. 365.

141. AP, Camera, *Discussioni,* 3d Legislature, Session of December 19, 1962.

142. AP, Senato, *Discussioni,* 3d Legislature, Session of September 20, 1962.

143. AP, Camera, *Discussioni,* 3d Legislature, Session of December 13, 1962.

144. AP, Camera, *Discussioni,* 3d Legislature, Session of December 19, 1962.

145. AP, Camera, *Discussioni,* 3d Legislature, Session of September 19, 1962.

146. AP, Camera, *Discussioni,* 3d Legislature, Session of December 14, 1962.

147. See, for the text of this bill, "Ammissione dei diplomati degli istituti tecnici alle facoltà universitarie," *Il perito industriale* (March–April 1950), pp. 13-14. Along with it, this review published another article entitled: "Accordo sindacale per lenire la disoccupazione."

148. National Commission of Inquiry for the Reform of the School, *Le conclusioni dell'inchiesta,* p. 173.

149. Contribution of Gonella in AP, Camera, *Discussioni,* 1st Legislature, Session of October 15, 1948.

150. G. Castellani, "L'ammissione dei periti industriali alle facoltà techniche universitarie," *Il perito industriale* (June 1957), p. 39.

151. G. Perone, "La voce dei periti industriali sui quotidiani d'informazione," *Il perito industriale* (April 1959), p. 46.

152. P. Giani, "I tecnici e l'università," *Il geometra italiano,* (February 1957), p. 21.

153. "Secondo Convegno dei Presidenti degli Ordini provinciali degli Ingegneri," *L'ingegnere* (September 1959), p. 835.

154. R. Foresti, "Accesso ai Politecnici dei Periti Industriali e dei Geometri," *Bolletino ingegeneri di Firenze* (January 1960), reprinted in *Il perito industriale* (June 1960), pp. 33-34.

155. A. Bonomo, "Ingegneri, Tecnica e Umanesimo," *L'ingegnere* (May 1961), p. 441.

156. This speech of Gonella's, given August 10, 1959, is reprinted in "Il Convegno sul tema: Ammissione indiscriminata dei Geometri e dei Periti alle Facoltà di Ingegneria e di Architettura," *L'ingegnere* (September 1960), pp. 866-67.

157. This and the preceding quotations are taken from A. A. Capocaccia, "Problemi

delle facoltà tecniche e scientifiche," in General Confederation of Industry, *Secondo Convegno "L'istruzione e l'industria": L'Università e l'industria (Ischia 26–28 June 1960)* (Rome, n.d.), pp. 61–98.

158. General Confederation, *Secondo Convegno,* p. 38.

159. AP, Senato, *Disegni di legge e relazioni-Documenti,* Bill of Law sponsored by Senators Tirabassi, Marchisio, Bellisario, Macaggi, Baldini, Parri, Zaccari, Donini, Luporini, Nencioni, Granata: *Ammissione dei diplomati degli Istituti tecnici alle Facoltà universitarie,* issued June 10, 1960.

160. R. Rossanda, *L'anno degli studenti,* p. 168.

161. Thus observed Minister of Public Education Misasi in the opening speech of the Frascati Conference. R. Misasi, *Questa scuola impossibile* (Rome: Edizioni EBE, 1972), p. 65.

162. "Conclusioni dell'incontro di lavoro sui 'nuovi indirizzi dell'istruzione superiore,' " *Formazione e lavoro* (May–June 1970), p. 134.

ELEVEN. EDUCATION AND INTERNAL MIGRATION

1. Among the many writings on the subject, see those contained in "Gli studi universitari nel Mezzogiorno." In his contribution, the president of the National Institute for Industrial Reconstruction (IRI), Giuseppe Petrilli, observed: "Note is taken of the forecasts of requirements for highly qualified personnel which in the coming years would have to be made available for suitable progress of productive activities, and it is therefore clear that a dearth of supply on the part of the university can represent a strangling of the economic future of the country. If this is the situation that Italy faces in general, and even more so in the Mezzogiorno—given the industrial undertakings they have realized on their own and also those assisted by the State (it suffices to consider the Steel Plant at Taranto)—then the yearly output of only 1,700–1,800 laureati in the technical and scientific faculties cannot be considered sufficient." *Ibid.,* p. 46. Marcello Rodinò noted: "The prediction can be advanced that the number of laureati needed in the South within 10–15 years will be three times the present number. Will the Mezzogiorno be in a position to cope with the instruction of such a number of laureati in order to keep in step with the current tendencies?" *Ibid.,* p. 51. [IRI was founded as a temporary public body to reorganize industrial holdings of Italy's leading banks during the economic crisis of the early 1930s. It has been a permanent state holding institution since 1937. TR.]

2. M. Paci, "Migrazioni interne e mercato capitalistico del lavoro," p. 769. (Emphasis in text.)

3. G. Barile and M. Paci, *La qualificazione del lavoro nell'industria lombarda.*

4. See I. F. Mariani, "Una ricerca sulla regione di nascita e di residenza di elementi delle classi dirigenti italiane," in Società italiana di Statistica, *Atti della XIII e XIV riunione scientifica (gennaio 1953–giugno 1954)* (Rome, 1955), pp. 251–70. The inquiry was conducted on a sample of 7,680 persons taken from two biographical dictionaries. Since these two dictionaries are from 1947, even with all their limitations, it can be assumed that this research provides us with information on the internal migration of the preceding twenty years. On the value and the limits of these data, see the author's observations.

5. To estimate the number of laureati produced by the South, I used the findings of special ISTAT reports on laureati, reports which have the advantage of giving the

distribution of laureati not only by university site but also by family residence. Using data from five completed reports (years: 1953-54, 1954-55, 1955-56, 1956-57, 1958-59), I calculated the number of laureati from families residing in the South as a percentage of the total (38.7 percent). For these data, see ISTAT, *Annuario statistico dell'istruzione italiana*.

6. CNEL-CENSIS, *Rapporto sugli aspetti sociali ed economici della situazione universitaria italiana,* pp. 103-14 (emphasis added).

7. It is less difficult, on the other hand, to understand how CENSIS, on the basis of the data collected, arrived at the conclusion that internal migration of the intellectual labor force concerned only the Northwest (the area of attraction) and the Center-Northeast (area of escape). In the study mentioned these conclusions are drawn by comparing the *site of the laurea* with the *work site* of the subjects questioned. But it is clear that a comparison of this type makes absolutely no sense for measuring the migratory flows of intellectuals for the simple reason that a relatively high number of university students who are residents of the South enroll in northern universities and especially in those of the Center. According to the data of special inquiries conducted by ISTAT, in the academic year 1964–65, only 85.6 percent of university students who were residents of the South were actually enrolled in southern universities. The tendency of northern residents to enroll in universities of their own regions was very high (95.8 percent). These figures are calculated from data taken from ISTAT, *Annuario statistico dell'istruzione italiana 1966.* This tendency is also confirmed by data concerning other academic years.

8. See the contribution of Goffredo Zappa in *Nord e Sud nella società e nell'economia italiana di oggi,* pp. 132-35.

9. See for these data, M. De Vergottini, "Le migrazioni interne in Italia secondo il grado d'istruzione dei migranti." In this study the author has analyzed ISTAT data for 1964.

10. For a wider analysis of the consequences of internal labor force migration for the maintenance of North-South differences, see chapter 14 of L. Gallino, *Indagini di sociologia economica e industriale,* pp. 487-519.

Selected Bibliography

The following entries, all of which occur in the author's text, have been compiled with the English reader in mind. Where the source listed is Italian in the original and has been found to be translated into English, both versions are cited with the English following. Where the source is in English in the original and has subsequently been translated into Italian and cited as such by the author, the English is cited first with the Italian following.

Agostinone, E. *La più fascista delle riforme fasciste: Il pensiero socialista su la riforma regalataci dal Filosofo del manganello.* Rome: Ufficio Stampa del Partito Socialista Unitario Italiano, 1925.

Alicata, M. *La riforma della scuola*. Rome: Editori Riuniti, 1956.

Arcoleo, G. "Gli Spostati." Speech given to the Press Association, March 23, 1906. Published in G. Arcoleo, *Forme vecchie idee nuove,* pp. 77-120. Bari: Laterza, 1909.

Barile, G. and M. Paci. *La qualificazione del lavoro nell'industria lombarda*. Milan: ILSES, 1969.

Ben-David, J. "The Growth of the Professions and the Class System." In R. Bendix and S. M. Lipset, eds. *Class, Status, and Power: Social Stratification in Comparative Perspective,* pp. 459-72. New York: Free Press, 1966.

Bendix, R. and S. M. Lipset, eds. *Class, Status, and Power: Social Stratification in Comparative Perspective.* New York: Free Press, 1966. *Classe, potere, status: teorie sulla struttura di classe.* Padua: Marsilio, 1969.

Berg, I. *Education and Jobs: The Great Training Robbery.* New York: Praeger, 1970.

Bertoni Jovine, D. *La scuola italiana dal 1870 ai giorni nostri*. Rome: Editori Riuniti, 1967.

—— *Storia dell'educazione popolare in Italia*. Bari: Laterza, 1965.

Bianchi, G. and M. D'Ambrosio. "L'evoluzione della qualificazione del lavoro in Italia dal 1951 al 1968." *Quaderni ISRIL* (July–September 1970), pp. 55-61.

Bibliografia della Carta della Scuola. Rome: Palombi, 1940.

Blaug, M., P. R. Layard, and M. Woodhall. *The Causes of Graduate Unemployment in India*. London: Allen Lane, 1969.

Boffi, F. E. *La scuola media fascista*. Rome: Libreria del Littorio, 1929.

Borghi, L. *Educazione e authorità nell'Italia moderna*. Florence: La Nuova Italia, 1959.

Bottai, G. *La Carta della Scuola*. 2d ed. Milan: Mondadori, 1941.

Bowles, S. "Contradictions in Higher Education in the United States." In Richard C. Edwards et al., eds., *The Capitalist System,* pp. 491-502. Englewood Cliffs, N.J.: Prentice-Hall, 1972. "Contradictions de l'enseignement supérieur." *Les Temps Modernes* (August–September 1971), pp. 198-240.

Bowles, S. and H. Gintis. "I.Q. and the U.S. Class Structure." *Social Policy* (November–December 1972/January–February 1973), pp. 65-96.

Brunschwig, H. *La crise de l'Etat prussien à la fin du XVIIIe siècle et la genèse de la mentalité romantique*. Paris, PUF, 1947.

Caizzi, B., ed. *Nuova Antologia della questione meridionale.* Milan: Comunità, 1970.

Calamandrei, P. *Troppi Avvocati!* Florence: Quaderni de *La voce,* 1921.

Cappelleti, L. *Burocrazia e società*. Milan: Guiffrè, 1968.

Caracciolo, A. "Autonomia o centralizzazione degli studi superiori nell'età della Destra." *Rassegna storica del Risorgimento* (1958), 14:573–603.

Caracciolo, A., ed. *La formazione dell'Italia industriale.* Bari: Laterza, 1969.

Cardinali, S., N. Fanelli, and M. Miegge. "Istruzione tecnica, sbocchi professionali e stabilizzazione sociale." *Inchiesta* (1972), no. 6, pp. 39-48.

Castronovo, V. *L'industria laniera in Piemonte nel secolo XIX*. Turin: ILTE, 1964.

——*L'industria cotoniera in Piemonte nel secolo XIX*. Turin: ILTE, 1965.

Checchia, G. *Il collocamento degli intellettuali*. Naples: Amodio, 1938.

Cipolla, Carlo Maria. *Literacy and Development in the West*. Baltimore: Penguin, 1969. *Istruzione e sviluppo.* Turin: UTET, 1971.

Clark, B. R. "The Study of Educational Systems." In *International Encyclopedia of the Social Sciences,* 4:509-17. New York: Macmillan and Free Press, 1968.

CNEL–CENSIS (National Economic and Labor Council-Center for Study of Social Investments). *Rapporto sugli aspetti sociali ed economici della situazione universtaria italiana*. Milan: Angeli, 1971.

Cogliolo, P. *Malinconie universitarie*. Florence: Barbera, 1936.

Collins, R. "Functional and Conflict Theories of Educational Stratification." *American Sociological Review* (1971), 36:1002–19.

Coombs, H. B. *The World Educational Crisis: A Systems Analysis.* New York: Oxford University Press, 1968. *La crisi dell'educazione nel mondo.* Rome: Collana di *Formazione e lavoro,* 1968.

Corbetta, P. G. "Istruzione tecnica e mercato del lavoro." *Inchiesta* (1973), no. 3, pp. 23-35.

Correnti, C. *Scritti scelti*. Vol. 3. Rome: Forzani, 1893.

Coscera, F. *Professioni ed arti nello Stato fascista*. Rome, 1941.

Curtis, M. H. "The Alienated Intellectual of Early Stuart England." *Past and Present* (November 1962), pp. 25-43.

De Cecco, M. "Una interpretazione ricardiana dalla dinamica della forza-lavoro in Italia nel decennio 1959-69." *Note economiche* (January–February 1972), pp. 76-120.

De Felice, R. *Il Fascismo: Le interpretazioni degli storici e dei contemporanei*. Bari: Laterza, 1970.

De Luca Carnazza, S. *La questione universitaria: Studi e proposte.* Catania: Galati, 1891.

Del Vecchio, G. and P. M. Arcari. *L'affollamento delle Università e la disoccupazione dei lavoratori intellettuali*. Rome: L'Economia Italiana, 1934.

De Vergottini, M. "Le migrazioni interne in Italia secondo il grado d'istruzione dei migranti." *Stato sociale* (January 1969), pp. 2-13.

di Giacomo, G. *Intellettuali e fascismo.* Rome: Libreria del Littorio, 1931.

D'Onofrio, G. and D. G. Pellegrini. *Le funzioni dei sindacati intellettuali*. Naples: Razzi, 1927.

Dubois, M. *Que deviendront les étudiants? Etude sur le Chomage des jeunes diplomés.* Paris: Librarie du Recueil Sirey, 1937.

Foerster, R. F. *The Italian Emigration of Our Times.* New York: Russell & Russell, 1919.

Frey, L. *Occupazione e disoccupazione giovanile in Italia*. Rome: Documenti ISVET no. 37, 1972.

Gabelli, A. *L'istruzione in Italia*. Bologna: Zanichelli, 1903.

Gallino, L. *Indagini di sociologia economica e industriale.* Milan: Comunità, 1972.

Gentile, G. *La nuova scuola media*. Florence: Vallecchi, 1925.

—— *La riforma della scuola: Discorso tenuto il 15 novembre 1923 al Consiglio Superiore della Pubblica Istruzione.* Bari: Laterza, 1924.

—— *La riforma della scuola in Italia*. Vol. 3 of the *Opere Complete.* Milan: Treves, 1932.

——*Il fascismo al governo della scuola: Discorsi e interviste.* Palermo: Sandron, 1924.

Germani, G. "Fascismo e classe sociale." *Critica sociologica* (1967), nos. 1 and 2; reprinted in G. Sivini, ed. *Partiti e partecipazione politica in Italia,* pp. 43-73. Milan: Giuffrè, 1969. "Fascism and Class." In S. J. Woolf, ed., *The Nature of Fascism,* pp. 65-96. London: Weidenfeld and Nicholson, 1968.

—— "La socializzazione politica dei giovani nei regimi fascisti: Italia e Spagna." *Quaderni di sociologia* (January–June 1969), pp. 11-58. "Political Socialization of Youth in Fascist Regimes: Italy and Spain." In S. P. Huntington and C. H. Moore, eds., *Authoritarian Politics in Modern Society: The Dynamics of One-Party Systems*. New York: Basic Books, 1968.

—— *Sociologia della modernizzazione: L'esperienza dell'America Latina*. Bari: Laterza, 1971.

Gerschenkron, A. *Economic Backwardness in Historical Perspective.* Cambridge, Mass.: Belknap Press, 1962. *Il problema storico dell'arretratezza economica*. Turin: Einaudi, 1965.

Gianturco, M. "Emigrazione intellettuale e titoli universitari." *Italiani nel mondo* (March 25, 1949), pp. 8-9.

Gintis, H. "Education, Technology, and the Characteristics of Worker Productivity." *American Economic Review* (May 1971), pp. 266-79. "Istruzione, tecnologia e caratteristiche della produttività del lavoro." *Rassegna Italiana di Sociologia* (July–September 1972), pp. 535-58.

Giuliano, B. *La politica scolastica del governo nazionale.* Milan: Biblioteca di Coltura Politica, 1924.

Giusti, U. "Disoccupazione e sovrapopolamento: Emigrazione." In Ministry for the Constituent, *Atti della Commissione per lo studio dei problemi del lavoro,* 3:251-69. Rome: UESISA, 1946.

"Gli studi universitari nel Mezzogiorno." *Quaderni di Nuovo Mezzogiorno* (1962), no. 7.

Gonella, G. *Una compagna contro la disoccupazione degli intellettuali*. Rome: Istituto Poligrafico dello Stato, 1946.

Gozzer, G. *Rapporto sulla secondaria*. Rome: Coines, 1973.

—— *Scuola per tutti*. Rome: UCIIM, 1956.

Gramsci, A. *La formazione dell'uomo.* Rome: Editori Riuniti, 1967.

—— *Gli intellettuali e l'organizzazione della cultura*. Turin: Einaudi, 1949. [Selections from *Gli intellettuali* are to be found in Q. Hoare and G. N. Smith, eds. and trans., *Selections from the Prison Notebooks of Antonio Gramsci,* pp. 5-43. New York: International Publishers, 1971.]

——*Il Risorgimento.* Turin: Einaudi, 1955. [Selections from *Il Risorgimento* are to be found in Hoare and Smith, *Selections,* pp. 52-120.]

—— *La questione meridionale.* Rome: Editori Riuniti, 1966. [First compiled in 1951, this work is made up of selections from *Il Risorgimento* and by the essay "Alcuni temi della questione meridionale," which was written in 1926 and first published in *Stato operaio* (January 1930), vol. 4, no. 1; it may be found in A. Gramsci, *The Modern Prince and Other Writings,* pp. 28-51. Translated with an Introduction by L. Marks. New York: International Publishers, 1968.]

Guerin, D. *Fascismo e gran capitale.* Milan: Schwarz, 1956.

Harbison, F. H. and C. Myers. *Education, Manpower, and Economic Growth.* New York: McGraw-Hill, 1964.

Harris, S. E. *The Market for College Graduates.* Cambridge: Harvard University Press, 1948; reprinted with a new introduction by the author. Westport, Conn.: Greenwood Press, 1970.

ISTAT (Central Institute of Statistics). *Indagine speciale su alcuni aspetti della vita scolastica italiana.* Rome, 1969.

—— *Indagine statistica sulla disponibilità di personale scientifico e tecnico.* Rome, 1958.

—— *Sommario di statistiche storiche italiane, 1861–1955.* Rome, 1958.

Jackson, J. A., ed. *Professions and Professionalization.* London: Cambridge University Press, 1970.

Kaser, M. C. "Education and Economic Progress: Experience in Industrialized Market Economies." In E. A. G. Robinson and J. E. Vaizey, eds., *The Economics of Education,* pp. 89-173. London: Macmillan, 1966.

King, R. and T. Okey. *Italy Today.* New York: Scribner's, 1901. *L'Italia d'oggi.* 3d ed. Bari: Laterza, 1910 (1st ed., 1902).

Kornhauser, W. *The Politics of Mass Society.* Glencoe: Free Press, 1959.

Kotschnig, W. M. *Unemployment in the Learned Professions: An International Study of Occupational and Educational Planning.* London: Oxford University Press, 1937.

Landra, A. *L'educazione dei Nord-Americani e l'emigrazione del nostro proletariato intellettuale.* Rome: Unione Coopertiva Editrice, 1907.

Livi Bacci, M. "Fattori demografici dello sviluppo economico." In G. Fuà, ed., *Lo sviluppo economico in Italia.* Vol. 2. Milan: Angeli, 1969.

Lombardo Radice, L. "Studenti nuovi per una nuova scuola." *Rinascita* (February 1945).

Lupi, D., ed. *La riforma Gentile e la nuova anima della scuola.* Milan: Mondadori, 1924.

Manoukian, A., ed. *La presenza sociale del PCI and della DC.* Bologna: Il Mulino, 1968.

Marchesi, C. "Motivi di politica scolastica." *Rinascita* (November 1945).

Martini, F. and C. F. Ferraris. *Ordinamento generale degli instituti d'istruzione superiore.* Milan: Hoepli, 1895.

Martino, G. *La scuola nella vita nazionale.* Florence: Le Monnier, 1956.

Martinoli, G. *L'università nello sviluppo economico italiano.* Milan: Giuffrè, 1962.

Matteucci, C. *Raccolta di scritti vari intorno all'istruzione pubblica.* Prato: Alberghetti, 1867.

Meldolesi, L. *Disoccupazione ed esercito industriale di riserva in Italia.* Bari: Laterza, 1972.

Merli, S. *Proletariato di fabbrica e capitalismo industriale: Il caso italiano, 1880-1900.* Florence: La Nuova Italia, 1972.

Michels, R. *Italian von heute: Politische und wirtschaftliche Kulturgeschichte von 1860 bis 1930.* Zürich-Leipzig: Orell Füssli, 1930.

—— *Proletariato e borghesia nel movimento socialista italiano.* Turin: Bocca, 1908.

—— "La psicologia sociale della Bohème e il proletariato intellettuale." In Royal Society of Naples, ed., *Atti della Reale Accademia di Scienze Morali e Politiche,* 54:181-99. Naples: Sangiovanni, 1931.

Miegge, M. "Sviluppo capitalistico e scuola lunga." *Inchiesta* (1971), no. 1, pp. 23-35.

Ministry of Public Education. *Il piano della scuola: Documenti parlamentari.* Rome: Palombi, 1963.

Morandi, R. *Storia della grande industria in Italia.* Turin: Einaudi, 1959.

Mozzani, T. *Questione universitaria. Richerche statistiche.* Siena: Lazzeri, 1895.

Musgrove, F. *The Migratory Elite.* London: Heinemann, 1963.

National Commission of Inquiry for the Reform of the School, ed. "Le conclusioni dell'inchiesta nazionale per la riforma della scuola." Final Issue of *La riforma della scuola* (1949), pp. 125-78.

Nitti, F. S. *La richezza dell'Italia.* Bari: Laterza, 1966.

O'Boyle, L. "The Problem of an Excess of Educated Men in Western Europe, 1800–1850." *Journal of Modern History* (1970), pp. 471–95.

OECD. *Reviews of National Policies for Education: Italy.* Paris, 1969.

Omodeo, A. *Libertà e storia: Scritti e discorsi politici.* Turin: Einaudi, 1960.

Paci, M. "Le contraddizioni del mercato del lavoro." *Inchiesta* (Spring 1972), pp. 3–19.

—— "Migrazioni interne e mercato capitalistico del lavoro." *Problemi del Socialismo* (September–October 1970).

Paniccia, U. and A. Ruberto. "I laureati nell'insegnamento." In Study Committee for the Problems of the Italian School and University, ed., *I laureati in Italia,* pp. 295–359. Bologna.

Piccardi, L. et al. *Dibattito sulla scuola*. Bari: Laterza, 1956.

Pizzorno, A. "Squilibri (o incongruenze) di status e participazione politica." *Quaderni di sociologia* (July–December 1966), pp. 372-86.

"Popolazione universitaria e situazione economica." In Ministry for the Constituent, *Atti della Commissione per lo studio dei problemi del lavoro,* 1:381-91. Rome: UESISA, 1946.

Roberts, K. "The Organization of Education and the Ambitions of School-Leavers: A Comparative Review." *Comparative Education* (March 1968), 4:87-96.

Romeo, R. *Breve storia della grande industria in Italia*. Bologna: Cappelli, 1967.

Rossanda, R. *L'anno degli studenti*. Bari: De Donato, 1969.

Rossanda, R., M. Cini, and L. Berlinguer. "Tesi sulla scuola," *Il Manifesto* (February 1970). "Theses on Education: A Marxist View." In J. Karabel and A. H. Halsey, eds., *Power and Ideology in Education,* pp. 647-58. New York: Oxford University Press, 1977.

Rossi, L. *La riduzione delle Università in Italia*. Bologna: Zanichelli, 1892.

Runciman, W. G. *Relative Deprivation and Social Justice: A Study of Attitudes to Social Inequality in Twentieth-Century England.* London: Routledge and Kegan Paul, 1966. *Ineguaglianza e conscienza sociale.* Turin: Einaudi, 1972.

Safa, H. I. "Education, Modernization, and the Process of National Integration." In M. L. Wax, S. Diamond, and F. O. Gearing, eds., *Anthropological Perspectives in Education,* pp. 208-29. New York: Basic Books, 1971.

Salvemini, G. *Movimento socialista e questione meridionale.* Milan: Feltrinelli, 1968.

—— *Scritti sulla scuola*. Milan: Feltrinelli, 1966.

Sanderson, M. "Literacy and Social Mobility in the Industrial Revolution in England." *Past and Present* (1972), no. 56, pp. 75-104.

Sinistrero, V. *La politica scolastica 1945–65 e la scuola cattolica*. Rome: Fidae, 1967.

Sissini, F. *La Scuola media dalla legge Casati ad oggi*. Rome: Armando, 1969.

Stone, L. "Literacy and Education in England, 1640-1900." *Past and Present* (1969), no. 42, pp. 69-139.

SVIMEZ (Fund for the Development of the South). *Un secolo di statistiche italiane: Nord e Sud (1861–1961).* Rome, 1961.

Sylos-Labini, P. *Problemi dello sviluppo economico.* Bari: Laterza, 1972.

—— "Sviluppo economico e classi sociali in Italia." *Quaderni di sociologia* (October–December 1972), pp. 371–443.

Tarozzi, G. *La coltura intellettuale contemporanea e il suo avviamento morale.* Civitanova: Natalucci, 1897.

——*Il problema della scuola media*. Milan: Albrighi e Segati, 1922.

Tomasi, T. *Idealismo e fascismo nelle scuola italiana*. Florence: La Nuova Italia, 1969.

Tonelli, A. *L'istruzione tecnica e professionale di Stato nelle strutture e nei programmi da Casati ai nostri giorni*. Milan: Giuffrè, 1964.

Turner, R. "Modes of Social Ascent through Education: Sponsored and Contest Mobility." In R. Bendix and S. M. Lipset, eds., *Class, Status, and Power: Social Stratification in Comparative Perspective,* pp. 449-58. New York: Free Press, 1966. "Mobilità cooptativa e competitiva e sistemi scolastici." In M. Barbagli, ed. *Scuola, potere, e ideologia,* pp. 37-58. Bologna: Il Mulino, 1972.

Vaughan, M. and M. Scotford Archer. *Social Conflict and Educational Change in England and France, 1789–1848.* Cambridge: Cambridge University Press, 1971.

Vigo, G. *Istruzione e sviluppo economico in Italia nel secolo XIX*. Turin: ILTE, 1971.

—— "Il contributo della spesa pubblica all'investimento in capitale umano in Italia, 1870–1914." *Annales cisalpines d'histoire sociale* (1971), no. 2, pp. 139–91.

Vitali, O. *Aspetti dello sviluppo economico italiano alla luce della ricostruzione della popolazione attiva*. Rome: Istituto di Demografia, 1970.

Watnick, M. "The Appeal of Communism to the Peoples of the Underdeveloped Areas." In R. Bendix and S. M. Lipset, eds., *Class, Status, and Power: Social Stratification in Comparative Perspective,* pp. 428-36. New York: Free Press, 1966.

Zamagni, V. "Istruzione e sviluppo economico in Italia, 1861–1913." In G. Toniolo, ed., *Lo sviluppo economico italiano 1860-1940,* pp. 187-240. Bari: Laterza, 1973.

Zangrandi, R. *Il lungo viaggo attraverso il fascismo.* Milan: Feltrinelli, 1962.

Zanichelli, D. *La questione universitaria in Italia*. Bologna: Zanichelli, 1890.

Zappa, G. *Nord e Sud nella società e nell'economia italiana di oggi*. Turin: Einaudi, 1968.

Zibordi, G. *Critica socialista del fascismo.* Bologna: Cappelli, 1922.

Glossary

Note: The plural in Italian is formed by changing the final *-o* or *-e* of the masculine singular to *-i*, and the final *-a* of the feminine singular to *-e*. Examples, used often in the present text, include:

diplomato: diplomati	scuola tecnica: scuole tecniche
laureato: laureati	scuola normale: scuole normali
istituto tecnico: istituti tecnici	scuola classica: scuole classiche

A P: Atti Parlamentari or Parliamentary Proceedings.

Avviamento (al lavoro or *professionale):* see *Scuola secondaria di avviamento professionale.*

Carta del Lavoro: corporatist statute regulating labor relations during the fascist period. From 1926 the regime occupied itself with the question of collective labor relations, and the term "corporation" (which has been translated "corporative association" in the present text) appeared officially for the first time in a decree of July 1, 1926. On April 21, 1927, the Carta del Lavoro was issued. Among its 30 articles, one read, "Work... is a social duty. By virtue of this, and only by virtue of this, it is protected by the State. The whole of production is unitary from the point of view of the nation. Its objectives are unitary and reside in the well-being of the individual and the increasing might of the nation." (Art. 2). Thus, according to Federico Chabod, "Economic life was to depend on the State and would no longer be abandoned to a liberal individualism nor remain the outcome solely of individual efforts.... On February 5, 1934, the law on corporations was promulgated.... [And] within the ambit of the 22 corporations created by Mussolini, the entire national economy in its various sectors was to be assembled. The National Council of Corporations was the supreme regulator of the Italian economy.... The law of January 19, 1939 abolished the Chamber of Deputies. The new Chamber was called the 'Camera dei Fasci e delle Corporazioni' [Chamber of Fascist Groups and Corporations] and, together with the Senate which was appointed by royal decree, collaborated with the government in the elaboration of laws.... No opposition was permitted." *L'Italia Contemporanea (1918–1948),* Turin: Einaudi, 1961, pp. 84–87. 84–87.

Ceti intellettuali: see *Ceti sociali.*

Ceti medi: see *Ceti sociali.*

Ceti sociali: social strata or classes, generally with reference to the middle strata or those situated between the two major social classes, bourgeoisie and proletariat; hence synonymous with the *ceti medi* as both are used in the present text. *Ceti intellettuali:* those of the middle strata or classes whose livelihoods depend primarily upon the possession of post-compulsory educational qualifications; hence synonymous with the salaried or office employed *impiegati* or "new" middle class as well as the liberal professions (see appendix 2).

Complementare: see *Scuola complementare.*

Comune: municipality, of which there are about 8,000 in Italy.

Concorso: competitive state examination held to fill all civil service positions, including teaching and administrative posts at each level of the educational system. For example, *concorso magistrale:* state exam to fill teaching positions in the elementary school.

Consiglio superiore della pubblica istruzione: academic body advising the minister of public education, established by the Casati Law of 1859; since divided into three sections corresponding to the university, secondary, and primary levels. Members were appointed during the fascist period and subsequently elected by their respective constituents.

Declassamento: downward social mobility, loss of social and professional standing. *Declassati:* persons who have dropped to a lower social standing, e.g., one who has earned a *laurea* in engineering and yet is employed as a technician, schoolteacher, or manual worker.

Destra storica: the "historical Right" of the Risorgimento and of National Unification (1815–1870), in contrast to the "new" or "nationalist Right" of the late nineteenth and early twentieth centuries. Best exemplified by the political and economic liberalism and social conservatism of Count Camillo Cavour (see *Sinistra storica).*

Diplomato: upper-secondary graduate, or one who holds the *diploma,* the generic title given to degrees granted at this level. For example, *diplomato tecnico* is a graduate of the *istituto tecnico; diplomato magistrale* is a graduate of the *istituto magistrale.*

Fuori corso: "Off course." A student *fuori corso* is one not *in corso,* not making normal progress toward the *laurea*.

Ginnasio: lower-secondary school that prepared for entrance into the *liceo.* Together the *ginnasio* and the *liceo* constituted the classical studies that opened access to all university faculties (thus they are referred to as the *scuole classiche).* In 1962 all lower-secondary schools were unified into the *scuola media unica*.

Impiegato: salaried employee, usually involving office work at varying levels of responsibility. The *impiegato di concetto,* or specialized office employee, has a certain specialized knowledge testified to by an upper-secondary diploma, while the *impiegato esecutivo,* or general office employee, has only a general competence and usually only a lower-secondary diploma. Thus, while the former exercises a degree of initiative and decision-making at the submanagerial level, the latter "executes" others' decisions.

ISTAT: Istituto centrale di statistica, the central governmental office for gathering, analyzing, and publishing statistical data in Italy.

Istituto magistrale: upper-secondary school for training elementary school teachers which replaced the *scuola normale* in 1923.

Istituto professionale: upper-secondary school of purely practical instruction primarily for training skilled workers. Until their curricular upgrading and de-professionalization in 1969, the various *istituti professionali* were segregated from both technical and classical branches of upper-secondary instruction and had no, even restricted, direct access to the university. Prior to 1928, when they were transferred to the Ministry of Public Education, they were administered (e.g., in the recruitment of teachers) by the Ministry of Agriculture, Industry, and Commerce.

Istituto tecnico: upper-secondary school with sections, for example, of agricultural, industrial and commercial instruction, established by the Casati Law of 1859. The *istituto tecnico* has always been bivalent with respect to preparation for immediate employment or for university study, but in the latter case access has always been restricted to a few university faculties until the 1960s.

Laureato: university graduate, or one who holds the *laurea,* the single national degree granted by the Italian university (until 1980, when a higher degree, the *dottorato di ricerca,* was instituted experimentally).

Liceo: upper-secondary school preparing for university studies, equivalent to the French lycée. Equipped with a single national curriculum of classical studies, therefore called the *liceo classico,* by the Casati Law of 1859, a new section, the *liceo moderno,* was added in 1911 which itself was merged in 1923 with the physics-mathematics section of the *istituto tecnico* to form the *liceo scientifico.* The *liceo* has never ceased to be the privileged route to university studies, since it opened access to all university faculties, above all those of medicine, law, and literature and philosophy, which until 1969 were closed to all other *diplomati.*

Liceo femminile: upper-secondary school established by the Gentile Reform of 1923, which gave no outlet to further studies and was intended to complete the education of the majority of girls who reached the upper-secondary.

Maestro: elementary school teacher.

Media unica: see *Scuola media unica.*

Mezzogiorno: southern Italy.

Numero chiuso: fixed number, or system of limiting enrollments according to quotas.

Scuola classica: "classical" school. See *Ginnasio.*

Scuola complementare: lower-secondary school established in 1923 by the Gentile Reform to replace the *scuola tecnica.* It gave no access to further study and was meant to channel the majority of students out of the educational system. Replaced by the *scuola secondaria di avviamento al lavoro* in 1929.

Scuola media: literally, "middle school." While the term is commonly used to refer to the entire secondary (thus the *media inferiore* and *superiore* refer, respectively, to the lower- and upper-secondary), its use has been restricted in the present translation to refer to the lower-secondary (as with the American or English "grammar" school) to avoid confusion. As such, however, it may be used generically to mean the entire lower-secondary or specifically to mean only that branch which gives direct access to upper-secondary studies that lead to the university (thus excluding, for example, the *scuola complementare* of Gentile and, until 1962, the *avviamento).*

Scuola media unica: the unified or comprehensive lower-secondary school created in 1962 by the merger of the *scuola media* and the *avviamento.*

Scuola normale: upper-secondary school for the training of elementary school teachers, replaced by the *istituto magistrale* by the Gentile Reform in 1923. Also, name given to one of the lower-secondary schools proposed by various ministers of public education in the 1950s.

Scuola secondaria di avviamento professionale: replacing the *scuola complementare* in 1929 and called the *avviamento al lavoro* ("introductory to work") until 1932, the *avviamento professionale* was designed to furnish terminal and practical instruction at the lower-secondary level. Unlike the *complementare,* however, it did allow access to the *scuola tecnica* and thence to the *istituto tecnico.*

Scuola tecnica: lower-secondary school with sections, for example, of agricultural, industrial, and commercial instruction coinciding with those of the *istituto tecnico;* established by the Casati Law of 1859, replaced in 1923 by the *scuola complementare,* reestablished in 1931 with the reform of technical education, and merged into the reformed *istituti professionali* after 1969. *Scuole tecniche* is a term used generically to refer to the technical (until 1962 *scuola tecnica–istituto tecnico*) branch of secondary instruction in contrast to the classical branch or *scuole classiche.*

Settentrione: northern Italy.

Sinistra storica: the "historical Left" of the Risorgimento and of National Unification (1815–1870), in contrast to the socialist Left of the late nineteenth and early twentieth century. Represented by the opposition to Cavour's Right (see *Destra storica*), first in the pre-unification Piedmontese parliament and subsequently in the Italian parliament, and particularly by Giuseppe Mazzini, Giuseppe Garibaldi, and their followers.

Spostato: derogatory term indicating a person who doesn't fit in, hence a "misfit," one who has no employment or prospects, a drifter.

Index